P9-EEB-523

THE PSYCHOLOGY OF VISUAL ILLUSION

Psychology

Editor

GEORGE WESTBY

Professor of Psychology, University College Cardiff
University of Wales

WITHDRAWN

'Waterfall' by M. C. Escher

THE PSYCHOLOGY OF VISUAL ILLUSION

J. O. Robinson
Senior Lecturer in Psychology, University College Cardiff
University of Wales

HUTCHINSON UNIVERSITY LIBRARY
LONDON

HUTCHINSON & CO (*Publishers*) LTD
3 Fitzroy Square, London W1

London Melbourne Sydney Auckland
Wellington Johannesburg Cape Town
and agencies throughout the world

First published 1972

The paperback edition of this book is sold subject to the condition that it shall not, by way of trade or otherwise, be lent, re-sold, hired out or otherwise circulated without the publisher's prior consent in any form of binding or cover other than that in which it is published and without a similar condition including this condition being imposed on the subsequent purchaser

The picture on the jacket and cover is
'Relativity' by M. C. Escher

© J. O. Robinson 1972

This book has been set in Times type, printed in Great Britain on antique wove paper by Anchor Press, and bound by Wm. Brendon, both of Tiptree, Essex

ISBN 0 09 112280 5 (cased)
0 09 112281 3 (paper)

To

The gentle swineherd

753975

CONTENTS

PREFACE

The aim of this book has been to present the current state of knowledge and theory on phenomena that would generally be called visual illusions. It seemed useful in doing this also to gather together a very large collection of published figures and demonstrations so that, as well as being an assessment of the current state of the field, the book might have some use as a reference book. But the making of such a collection has had another use. It has shown clearly the restricted nature of most of the theories of visual illusions, even those which seem to be regarded by their authors as general theories.

The origin of each figure, where there seems to be some agreement that it was indeed the origin, appears with the figure and often does not have further mention in the text. This is an unusual step, taken in the interest of brevity, and justified by the claim that, for the present purpose, all that is of interest is the original reference and not detail of the original presentation. Where the figure has a fairly widely used name this is also included.

The depth of treatment of the different topics in the book varies. The geometrical–optical illusions, because they seem to form the core of the subject, are treated fully and the modern literature on the subject is fairly well covered. In other topics, for example apparent movement and after-effects of movement, I have had to leave out much more. To avoid making just a limp review of this material I have selected themes which seem to me to be central and interesting, and have not gone into the wealth of detail that the literature affords. Other topics, which might have been included in a fuller treatment, have been omitted. Visual masking, particularly backward masking, is one of these. The perception of causality is another. Both are on the edge of the subject and the planned size of the book excluded them. Almost all the work dealing with subject variables has been omitted for the same reason. Visual illusions have been shown to vary in abnormal states such as mental disorder, brain damage, and during recovery from sensory deprivation. Personality variables have been shown to be effective too, for example the field dependence/independence variable, but there has not been space to include such work.

The level of treatment of the material ought to be suitable for the middle range of undergraduate in psychology. It assumes in the reader an elementary knowledge of visual anatomy, physiology and perception, but I hope that the arguments and descriptions will usually stand by themselves.

It is with the greatest pleasure that I acknowledge the help that many people have given me in writing this book. The encouragement and interest of Professor George Westby has constantly maintained my spirits and his practical advice and judgment have been of enormous value. Dr Norman Dixon, Ian Reece and Patrick Wesley did me the very great service of reading and criticising the manuscript and some of the points they made have been absorbed into it. Professor R. L. Gregory also made extremely valuable comments. Jan Adam discovered in my interests the difficulties of translating his native German tongue when the passages in question were written before 1900. I am very grateful to him and to Drs John Wilson and Hugh Wagner for many interesting and relevant discussions. Many of my colleagues have most kindly brought to my notice material which they thought relevant. My students too have contributed in this way as well as kindly humouring me in my esoteric preoccupation. My wife endured it all and did a draft typescript. To them and to her I owe a great deal.

A book of this kind depends heavily on its illustrations and I believe that the work of Mr A. S. Kennard, who did the drawings, should clearly be acknowledged. With astonishing calm he has dealt with the formidable difficulties of condensation and of sometimes elusive illusory effects. If the book is readable he must share the credit.

Penarth **J.O.R.**
September 1971

ACKNOWLEDGMENTS

The author and publishers are grateful to the following for permission to use illustration material: *Acta Physiologica Scandinavica*; American Institute of Physics for *Journal of the Optical Society of America*; American Philosophical Society; American Psychological Association for *Journal of Experimental Psychology, Psychological Monographs* and *Psychological Review*; *Archives de Psychologie*; *Archives Italiennes de Biologie*; J. A. Barth Verlag for *Poggendorffs Annalen der Physik und Chemie,* and *Raumaesthetik und geometrisch-optische Täuschungen* by T. Lipps; C. H. Beck'sche Verlag for *Neuen Psychologischen Studien*; British Psychological Society for *British Journal of Psychology*; Professor L. B. Brown; *Bulletin de l'Académie Royale de Belgique*; Dr C. F. Cochran; Dover Publications Inc. for *Treatise on Physiological Optics* by H. von Helmholtz and *Visual Illusions* by M. Luckiesh; Professor E. S. Eriksson; Escher Foundation, Haags Geenemtemuseum, The Hague; Dr G. H. Fisher; Professor L. Ganz; Professor J. C. Hay; D. C. Heath & Co. for *A course in experimental psychology* by E. C. Sanford; Dr W. H. N. Hotopf; *Jahresbericht Physikalischer Verein*; Japanese Psychological Association for the *Japanese Journal of Psychology*; H. J. Jeffrey, Esq.; *Journal of Physiology*; The Journal Press for the *Journal of General Psychology*; Dr T. Künnapas; Professor D. M. MacKay; Macmillan Co. New York for *Experimental Psychology: a Manual of Laboratory Practice* by E. B. Titchener; Massachusetts Institute of Technology Press; *Nature*; North-Holland Publishing Co. for *Acta Psychologica*; Professor C. E. Osgood; *Perception and Psychophysics*; *Perceptual and Motor Skills*; Pergamon Press Ltd. for *The Spiral After-Effect* by H. C. Holland and *Optical Illusions* by S. Tolanski; *Psychonomic Science*; *Quarterly Journal of Experimental Psychology*;

Dr W. Richards; *Scandinavian Journal of Psychology*; *Scientific American*; Professor B. F. Skinner; Springer-Verlag for *Pflüger's Archiv für gesampt Physiologie*; University of Illinois Press for *American Journal of Psychology*; Weidenfeld & Nicolson for *The Intelligent Eye* by R. L. Gregory; Dr M. Zanforlin; *Zeitschrift für Psychologie.*

Every effort has been made to trace copyright owners. The author and publishers would be grateful to know of any omissions, so that acknowledgment may be made in future editions.

I

INTRODUCTION

The study of visual illusions dates further back than the recognition of psychology as a separate discipline and a large proportion of all that is in this book was described by Helmholtz (1856) in his *Handbuch der Physiologischen Optik*. Boring (1942) and Titchener (1901) have both reviewed the early literature. The volume of writing on the subject, particularly the geometrical optical illusions, in the late nineteenth century can give the impression that interest faded after the turn of the century. This impression is expressed by Tolanski (1964), but Zusne (1968) did a count of all such publications over the years. This clearly shows that the number of papers published on the geometrical optical illusions has increased steadily, quite closely in step with the total number of papers published in psychology.

The steadily increasing number of papers has not, however, found an echo in an increase in the publication of books. I have found in the English language only two, Tolanski (1964) and Luckiesh (1922), published since the First World War. Although Tolanski's book is the more recent it is the lighter of the two and is neither extensive nor detailed in its treatment. There seems to be a need for a work drawing together the very large literature on illusions and attempting to assess the various theoretical positions which have more recently been described.

The act of perception may be characterised as a decision which is based largely (though not solely) on information, picked from a display, about the 'real' nature of the display (Gregory, 1970, talks of the perceptual system 'making a bet'). The information consists of cues about, for example, whether the display contains objects, how many objects, whether they are large or small, near or distant. There is also movement information, cues about whether parts of the objects are moving with reference to other parts, whether the objects as wholes are moving, whether the observer's eyes, head, or whole body is moving.

The perceptual decision is biased by states of the organism such as hunger, emotion, expectancy and so on. There is a large literature on such bias, but it is beyond the scope of this book. More important for my argument is ambiguity in the visual display. More than one perceptual decision is possible for most displays. Displays can vary from complete ambiguity to partial ambiguity. The latter are ones in which a particular interpretation is by far the most likely one, but other interpretations are probable and still others, although bizarre, are possible. Paucity of cues, brought about, for example, by the brevity of the period of sampling or by reduced illumination, can increase ambiguity.

One potent source of illusions is misinterpretation of cues in a situation in which there is at least a small amount of ambiguity. It is easy to invent displays in which the ambiguity is permanent and unresolvable (several are mentioned in Chapter 7) and which make the perceptual system continue indefinitely and mysteriously to vacillate between the possible perceptual conclusions about the 'real' nature of the display. But most of the illusions of this sort which one meets in everyday life involve situations which are ambiguous mainly because of brevity of sampling or paucity of cues. In these circumstances the perceptual decision is more difficult and cues arriving after the first perceptual decision often cause a revocation of it. Most of us must have accosted a stranger believing him to be a friend because in the first flash of seeing him we have 'recognised' a friend. Here the first sample of cues was brief. We resolved any ambiguity it contained and made a decision, but subsequent cues showed the decision to be wrong.

Cues in the illusion displays described in this book are generally rather sparse. Line drawings have nothing of the richness we are used to in visual scenes, nor have small lights and luminous lines in the dark. Ambiguity is therefore both more likely to be present and more likely to be resolved in a way which, by other evidence, is erroneous.

Another way in which illusions are thought to occur is by the inappropriate operation of some mechanism which generally works in favour of veridicality (truthfulness). This probably accounts for most of the illusions involving simple line-figures, though the precise nature of the process is unknown. Gregory, for example, supposes that constancy, a mechanism which generally helps us to judge size and distance, is accidentally set off by the line illusions and leads to distortions (see Chapter 6). Other writers maintain that a process which helps us to see edges, lateral inhibition in the visual system, also misleads us when lines run close together in the visual field.

A third way in which illusions occur is by the failure of the visual system to cope with input. Dixon's spinning chequered disc (Chapter 10) comes first to mind. When this disc is spun at more than about 20 rev/min the checks are no longer seen and a slowly rotating grey cross takes their place. The most common everyday example of this is probably ordinary visual blurring of fast-moving objects, but I would hesitate, perhaps unreasonably, to call this an illusion.

That psychologists have taken such a steady and enduring interest in visual illusions might be taken as an indication of long-standing intellectual perversity, but there are arguments against such a view. A very important strategy in finding out how correct perception operates is to observe situations in which misperceptions occur; to test, that is, the limits of the satisfactory function of perception whilst carefully altering the conditions under which it is working. It is fairly easy to formulate a theory which is consistent with the facts of correct perception, but it is a much more demanding task to produce a theory which is capable of predicting the failures as well as the successes of the perceptual system. People have long been aware of this and probably the chief cause of the continued interest in illusions is that they have been used as test instruments for theory, particularly by the Gestalt school. They have also in themselves furnished important ideas. Thus Mach, having observed the bright and dark bands which now bear his name (Chapter 8), advanced the idea of lateral inhibition in the visual system which has since been demonstrated physiologically and has become accepted as an important factor in seeing.

There are many practical perceptual situations where illusions, stemming from misleading cues or misleading interactions of stimuli, are likely to lead to serious error. This happens particularly when there is a shortage of visual information. A man flying an aircraft or driving at night or in fog is relatively error prone because cues about the correct situation are relatively scarce. However, the practical importance of illusions should not be overestimated; most perceptual environments are too rich in information to give rise to illusions.

Illusions might also have potential as a means of preventing error. One example of this, reported by Denton (1971), is a method of road marking which causes drivers to overestimate their speed. This is proposed as a way of counteracting the underestimation of speed to which drivers leaving a motorway are prone. Such 'correction' of perception by the use of the principles of illusion is, of course, not new. In the ancient world stone columns were shaped in such a way as to affect perception of their height.

This book begins with an extensive treatment of the so-called geometrical optical illusions. In Chapters 2 and 3 I review studies of these illusions and try to pick out important themes. In Chapter 2 the themes are the Müller-Lyer effect, a framing effect and a contrast effect. These three among them seem capable of accounting for the illusions described in that chapter. No suggestion is made of how the effects are wrought. This is left to the theorists in Chapter 5. In Chapter 3, which deals with illusions involving angles and direction, again I pick out themes that seem to me to be important. These are the effect of the apex of an angle on the lines comprising the angle, and the effect of the orientation of those lines. In this chapter too I make clear the sort of explanation of this type of illusion which I favour; it is an explanation in terms of specifically tuned orientation analysers which extract from the display information about the orientation of lines contained in it and are misled by certain configurations. This is only a general *type* of explanation and could not at this stage be advanced as a theory of illusions.

Some subject variables are treated in Chapter 4, but there was room for only a selection of those that might have been included. The treatment of figural after-effects in Chapter 5 is a prelude to Chapter 6 in which some of the theories of geometrical optical illusions described regard figural after-effects and illusions as the results of the same processes. It is often (though not invariably) the case that theories have a characteristic career; an author discovers that one particular illusion figure or small set of figures can be accounted for by a simple principle or a simple mathematical expression. He finds it difficult to apply this successfully to other figures and so introduces another, generally more vague, principle, auxilliary to the first. The nature of this second principle makes experimental test of the theory very difficult and contributions to the literature cease.

The remaining chapters deal with illusions arising in displays other than line displays. Illusions stem from misperceptions of depth, contrast and movement as well as from fast-moving or intermittently lit displays. These have tempted authors into theory a little less often and in some cases, for example in illusions involving cues of depth, it is fairly clear how the perceptual system is being misled.

2

THE GEOMETRICAL OPTICAL ILLUSIONS (I)

The term 'geometrical optical illusion', a translation of the German 'geometrisch-optische Täuschung', seems to have been coined by Oppel (1855) in a paper about the overestimation of an interrupted as compared with an uninterrupted spatial extent, later called the Oppel–Kundt illusion because Kundt also studied it (Kundt, 1863). The term has been used for any illusion seen in line drawings. Interest in such illusions was intense during the second half of the nineteenth century, particularly in Germany, and the literature on the subject has increased steadily ever since.

From the beginning, and particularly in recent years, a great deal of interest has been directed towards theories of illusions. It has clearly been the hope of some to find a general theory which would account for all the geometrical optical illusions. There is no better indicator of the forlornness of this hope than a thorough review of the illusions themselves. Such a review follows. It avoids theory as far as it is reasonable to do so, and gives some idea of the breadth of the field and the diversity of both phenomena and research results. (The reader hungry for a systematic treatment of theory may wish to turn forthwith to Chapter 6. Some reference back would then be necessary, but for a quick reading this course is probably a good one.)

I shall present a large collection of this type of illusion. It does not pretend to be comprehensive because that would probably be impossible. It would not be too bold to claim that stimuli in the visual field almost always interact, especially if they are close together or concurrent. Thus, judgments of the degree of separation and the orientation of lines or areas is influenced by the degree of separation and the orientation of other lines or areas in the visual field, especially if they are close by. This makes it easy to invent variations of illusion figures once one has appreciated the essential configuration that gives rise to the illusion. To do this there is no need to understand in any deeper way why the illusion occurs. This collection does however contain most of the published line illusions, with the exception of those which seem to be trivial variations and have not had special attention in the literature.

THE CLASSIFICATION OF ILLUSIONS

Classification is a taxonomic exercise and does not itself provide explanations. It may help in the process of finding them by ordering the material in a way that makes thinking easier, but it could also obscure important similarities or differences.

Boring (1942) summarises early work, and those interested in the history of the subject will find his contribution worth reading. It is sufficient here to accept his claim that all classifications up to that time boil down to two groups: illusions of extent (where size or length is misjudged) and illusions of direction (where orientation of a line or figure is misjudged), 'to which may be added some special complicated cases' (p. 243). The argument here is broadly in agreement with this classification though it is difficult fully and clearly to justify it.

Neither Luckiesh (1922) nor Tolanski (1964) justifies the classifications he uses. Luckiesh classifies his rather small collection into (1) the effect of the location in the visual field, which includes the vertical–horizontal illusion; (2) illusions of interrupted extent, which includes both Ebbinghaus's figure (Fig. 2.70) and also Fig. 2.12; (3) illusions of contour, which includes several of Müller-Lyer's figures (Figs. 3.87 and 3.92); (4) illusions of contrast which includes both Fig. 2.14 and the Ponzo illusion (Fig. 2.31); and (5) illusions of perspective, which includes the Sander parallelogram (Fig. 2.23) and two figures (Figs. 3.9 and 3.10) which are clear relatives of the Zöllner figure (Fig. 3.1).

Some of these classifications seem illogical. The vertical–horizontal illusion is a result of orientation of lines, not of their position in the visual field. In Ebbinghaus's figure the filled space is overestimated, whereas in Fig. 2.12 it is underestimated. This latter figure is much better classified as a variant of the Müller-Lyer illusion. To classify

---

2.1 Müller-Lyer (1889) 2.2 Müller-Lyer, composite version
2.3 Delbœuf (1892) 2.4 Brentano (1892); Delbœuf (1892) 2.5 Delbœuf (1892) 2.6 Delbœuf (1892) 2.7 Brentano (1892); Delbœuf (1892)
2.8 Brentano (1892); Delbœuf (1892) 2.9 Brentano (1892); Delbœuf (1892)
2.10 Coren (1970)

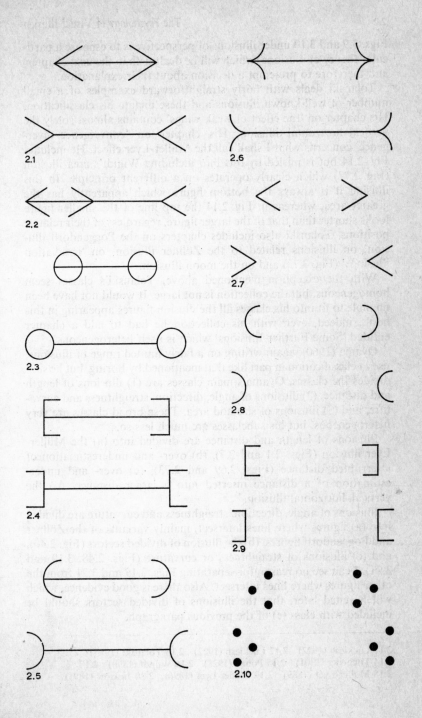

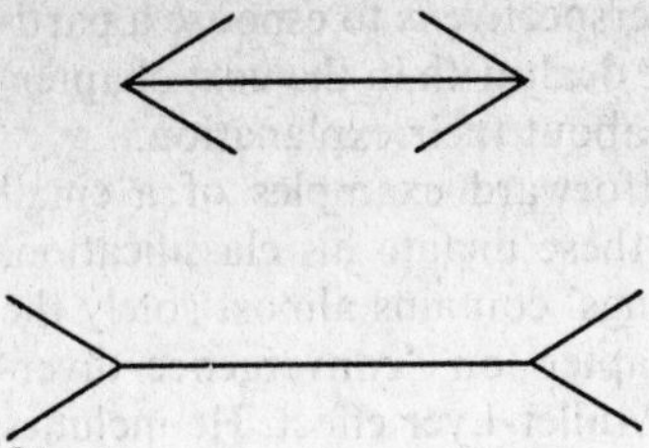

2.1

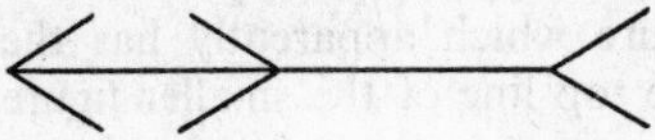

2.2

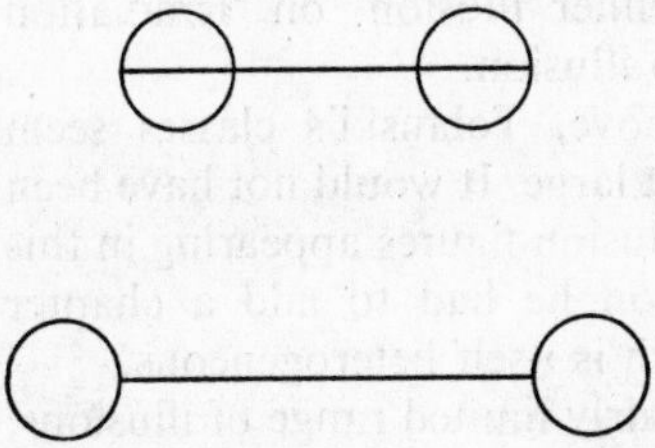

2.3

2.4

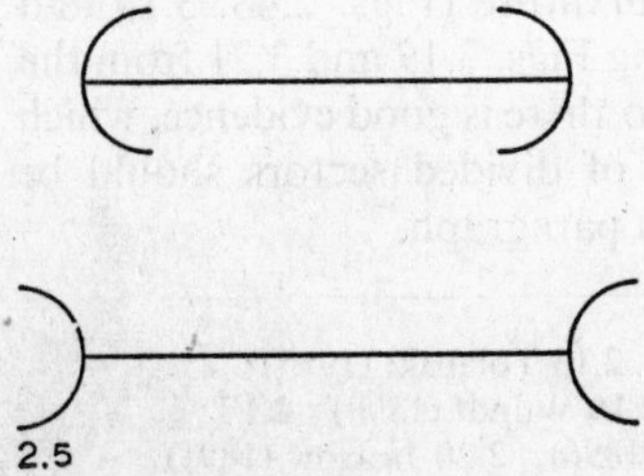

2.5

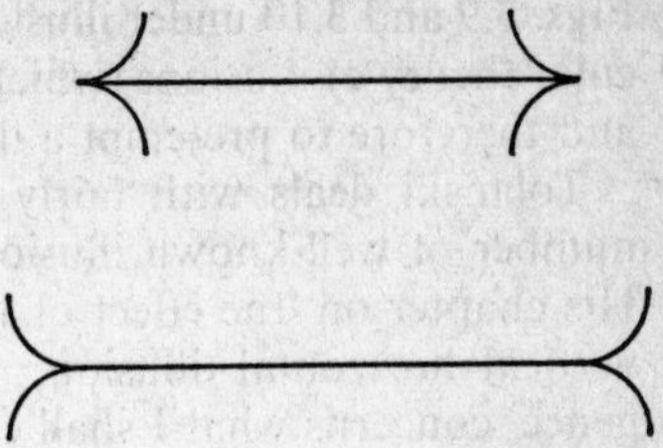

2.6

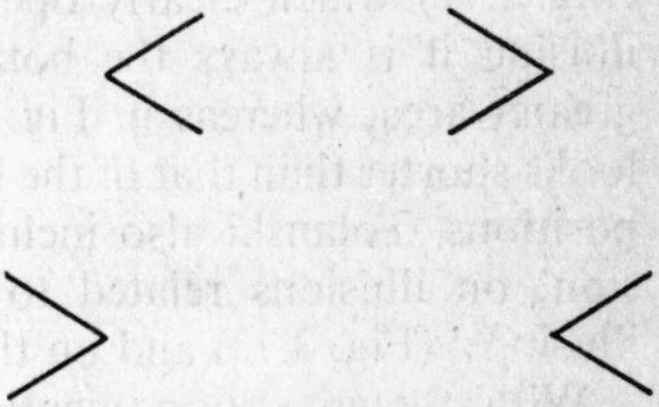

2.7

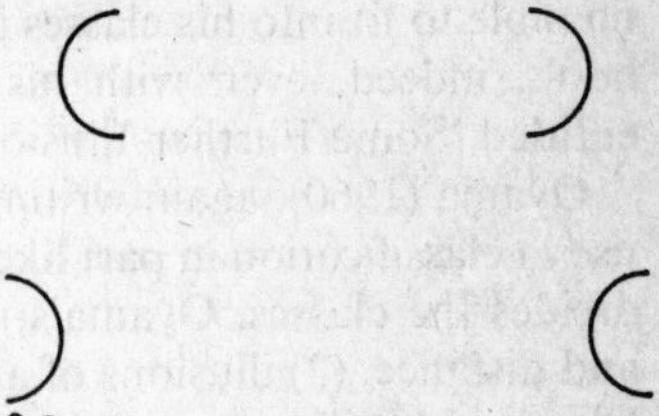

2.8

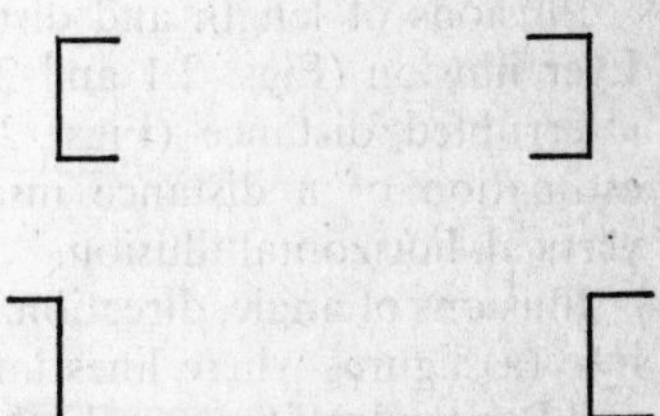

2.9

2.10

Figs. 3.9 and 3.10 under illusions of perspective is to espouse a particular theory of illusions (which will be dealt with in the next chapter) and therefore to pre-empt a decision about their explanation.

Tolanski deals with fairly straightforward examples of a small number of well-known illusions and these dictate his classification. His chapter on 'the effect of weak wings' contains almost solely the vertical–horizontal illusion. His chapter on 'convergence–divergence' concerns what I shall call the Müller-Lyer effect. He includes Fig. 2.14 but is misled by this into including Wundt's area illusion (Fig. 2.77) which clearly operates on a different principle. In this illusion it is always the bottom figure which apparently has the greater area, whereas in Fig. 2.14 the top line of the smaller figure looks shorter than that of the larger figure, regardless of their relative positions. Tolanski also includes chapters on the Poggendorff illusion, on illusions related to the Zöllner illusion, on 'irradiation illusions' (Fig. 3.72) and on the moon illusion.

With the exception mentioned above, Tolanski's classes seem homogeneous, but the collection is not large. It would not have been possible to fit into his classes all the illusion figures appearing in this book, indeed, even with his collection he had to add a chapter entitled 'Some Further Illusions' which is itself heterogeneous.

Oyama (1960), again writing on a fairly limited range of illusions, uses a classification in part like that mentioned by Boring, but he subdivides the classes. Oyama's main classes are (1) illusions of length and distance, (2) illusions of angle, direction, straightness and curvature, and (3) illusions of size and area. These broad classes are very heterogeneous, but his subclasses are much less so.

Illusions of length and distance are divided into (a) the Müller-Lyer illusion (Figs. 2.1 and 2.7), (b) over- and underestimation of interrupted distance (Figs. 2.69 and 2.73), (c) over- and underestimation of a distance inserted into a larger distance, (d) the vertical–horizontal illusion.

Illusions of angle, direction, straightness and curvature are divided into (a) figures where lines intersect, mainly variants of the Zöllner and Poggendorff figures, (b) the illusion of divided sectors (Fig. 2.40), and (c) illusions of straightness or curvature (Figs. 2.48, 3.19 and 3.21). I can see no reason for separating Figs. 3.19 and 3.21 from the other figures where lines intersect. Also there is good evidence, which will be cited later, that the illusions of divided sectors should be included with class (c) of the previous paragraph.

2.11 Luckiesh (1922) 2.12 Luckiesh (1922) 2.13 Tolanski (1964)
2.14 Titchener (1901) 2.15 Ponzo (1928) 2.16 Wundt (1898) 2.17
2.18 Müller-Lyer (1889) 2.19 Müller-Lyer (1896) 2.20 Jastrow (1891)

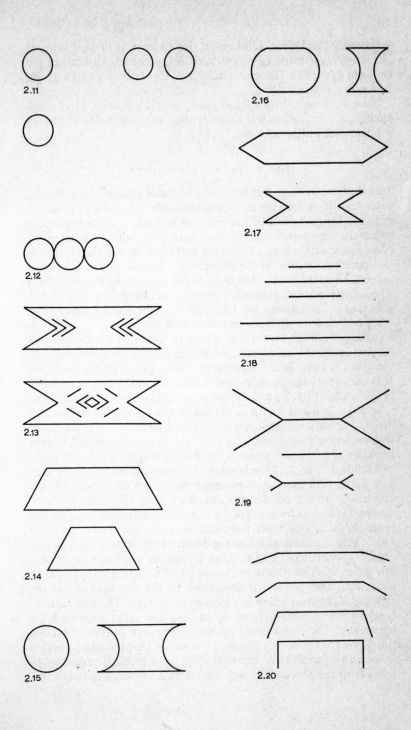

2.11

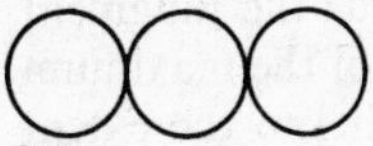

2.12

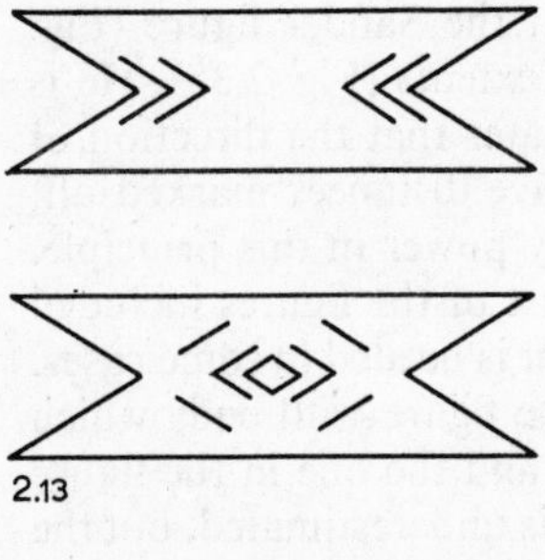

2.13

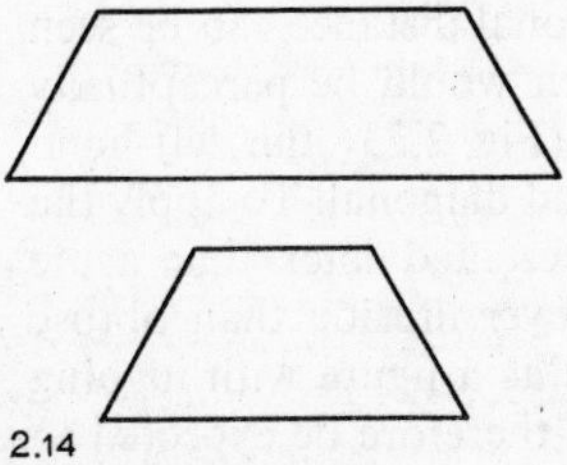

2.14

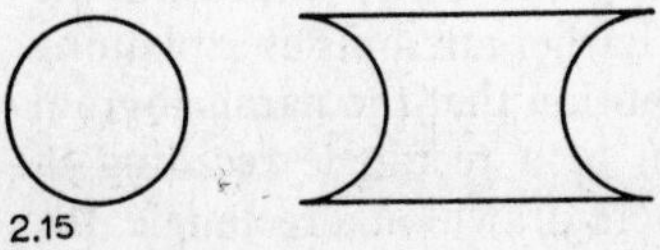

2.15

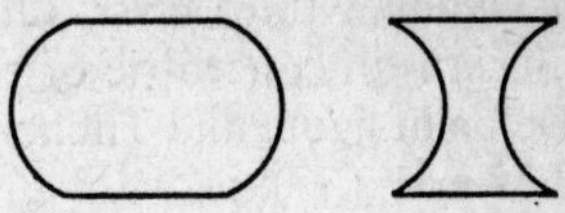

2.16

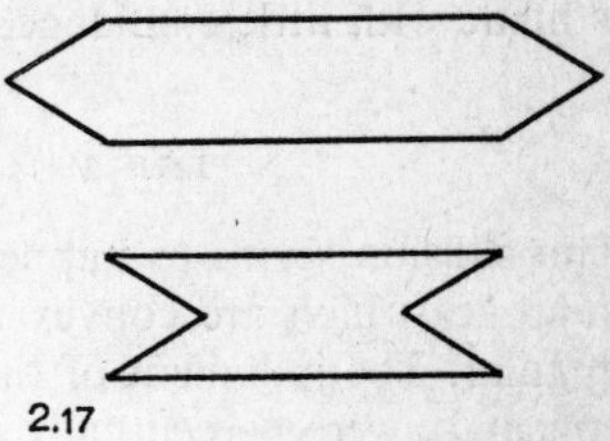

2.17

2.18

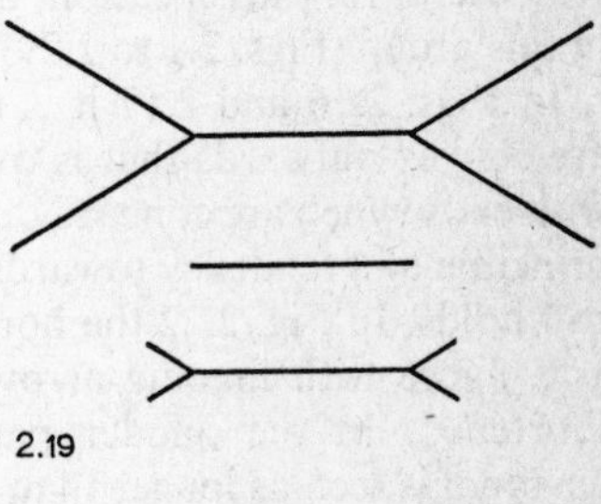

2.19

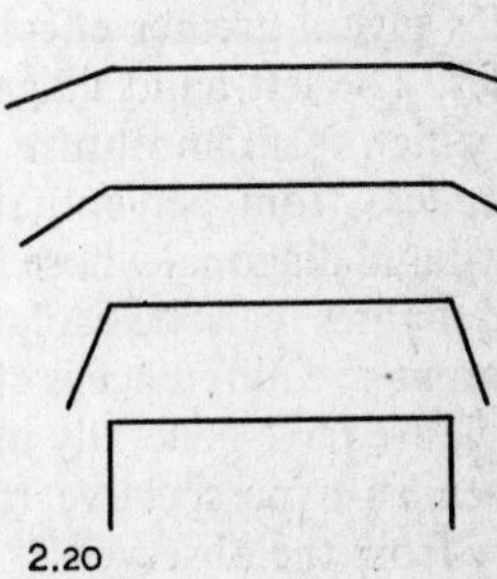

2.20

Oyama's third class, illusions of size or area, is divided into (a) illusions in concentric or eccentric circles, which are variants of the Delbœuf figure and Titchener circles, and (b) 'Jastrow's figure' (Figs. 2.75 and 2.77).

None of these writers tries to justify his classification. Here some attempt at justification will be made, but some allocation to classes is made with little confidence.

THE MÜLLER-LYER EFFECT

This illusion seems to happen when a spatial extent is bounded by contours which are convex or concave outwards, either curved or angular. The judgment of the extent is made as if the convexity or concavity were perceptually flattened. In other words the judgment of an extent within such a figure is a sort of average of the maximum and minimum extents in the figure which run parallel to the extent judged. This idea is very like the one put forward by Pressey (1967) who called it a 'central tendency explanation'. He points out that this principal could account for the illusion in the Sander figure (Fig. 2.23) and also for illusions of interrupted extents (Fig. 2.38). He is mistaken about the latter; it will be seen later that the direction of illusion in this figure depends on the relative distances marked off. No claim is made here for any explanatory power in this principle. It is useful for classification, and it fits most of the figures included in this group (Figs. 2.1 to 2.29) but comment is needed in some cases.

In Figs. 2.16 and 2.17 it is the line in the figure with ends which are convex outwards that is overestimated and the one in the figure with ends which are concave outwards that is underestimated, but the principle of a tendency towards the average length within each figure still holds. In Fig. 2.22 the horizontal–diagonal distance can be seen as a figure with ingoing arrow-heads which would be perceptually shortened. In the Sander parallelogram (Fig. 2.23) the left-hand diagonal is seen as longer than the right-hand diagonal. To apply the principle here, one must use evidence presented later that acute angles give a greater effect in the Müller-Lyer illusion than obtuse angles. The left-hand diagonal can be seen as a figure with ingoing fins which form an obtuse angle and could therefore be expected to suffer less from perceptual shortening by the fins than would the right-hand diagonal whose fins form an acute angle. These two arrow-head figures can be isolated by erasing the other lines and the apparent size difference is clearly there. Earlier attempts at explaining this figure have generally involved the notion that the parallelogram is seen as a perspective representation of a rectangle receding in space from the observer. If such lines were drawn on a rectangle, the

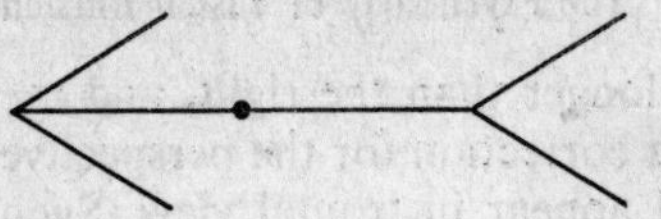

2.21

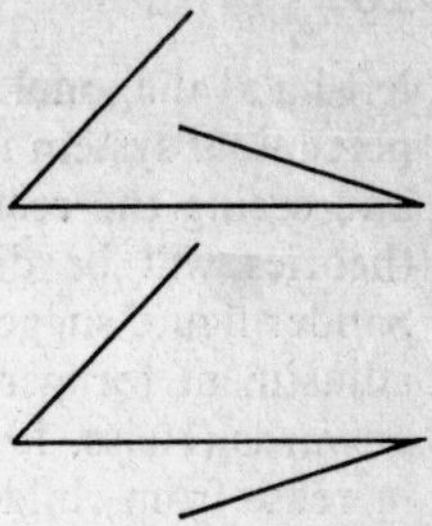

2.26

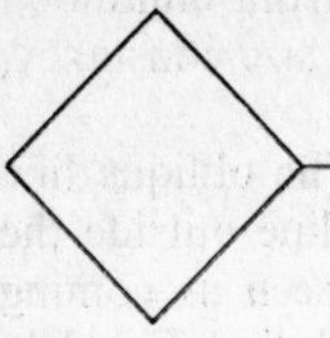

2.22

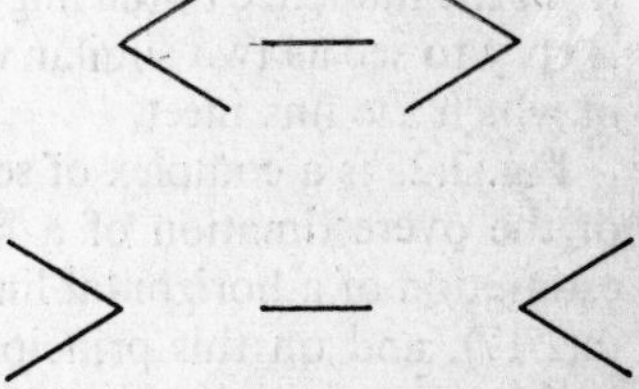

2.27

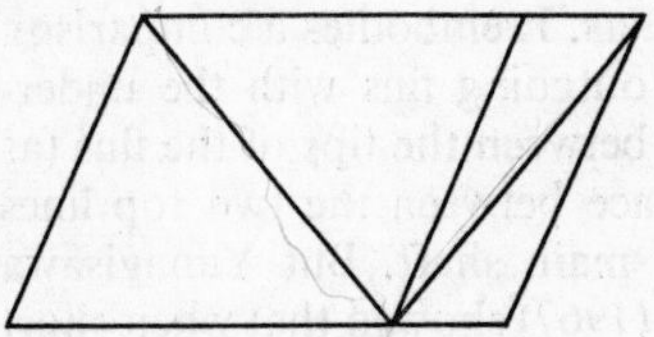

2.23

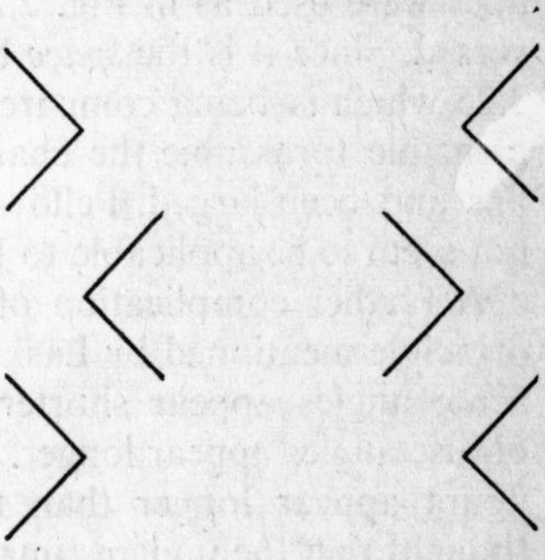

2.28

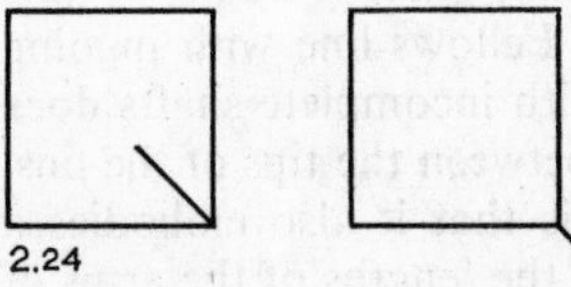

2.24

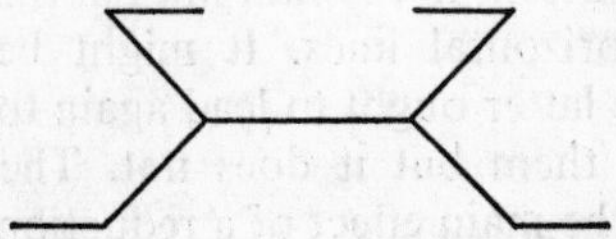

2.25

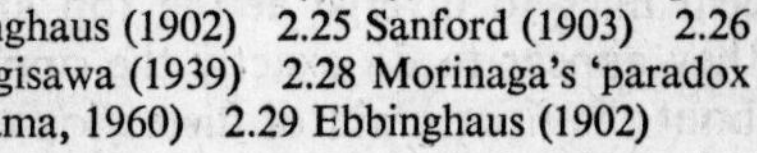

2.29

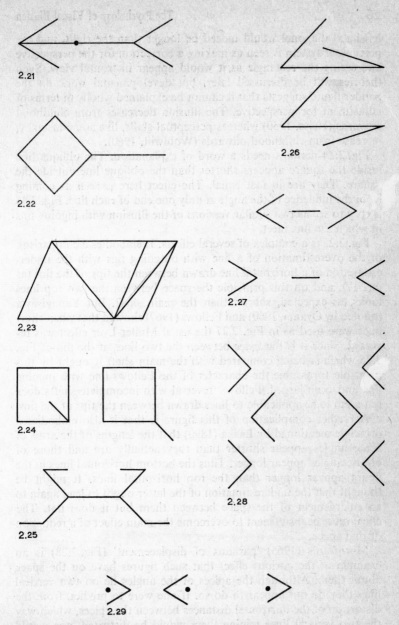

2.21 Judd (1899) 2.22 Schumann (1900) 2.23 Sander parallelogram (1926) 2.24 Ebbinghaus (1902) 2.25 Sanford (1903) 2.26 Láska (1890) 2.27 Yanagisawa (1939) 2.28 Morinaga's 'paradox of displacement' (Oyama, 1960) 2.29 Ebbinghaus (1902)

left-hand diagonal would indeed be longer than the right, and the perceptual system is seen as making a correction for the perspective and seeing the rectangle as it would appear in frontal view. Such theories will be discussed later, but developmental work on the Sander figure suggests that it cannot be explained wholly in terms of adjustment for perspective. The illusion decreases from childhood onwards (Heiss, 1930) whereas perceptual skills, like size constancy, increase from childhood onwards (Wohlwill, 1960).

Fig. 2.24 perhaps needs a word of explanation. The oblique line inside the square appears shorter than the oblique line outside the square. They are in fact equal. The effect here is seen as coming from the influence of the angle at only one end of each line. Fig. 2.43 is easy to see as two similar versions of the illusion with ingoing fins in which the fins meet.

Fig. 2.25 is a complex of several effects. It embodies a comparison of the overestimation of a line with outgoing fins with the underestimation of a horizontal line drawn between the tips of the fins (as in 2.17), and on this principle the space between the two top lines looks, as expected, shorter than the main shaft. But Yanagisawa (quoted by Oyama, 1960) and Fellows (1967) showed that when short lines were used as in Fig. 2.27 the usual Müller-Lyer effect was reversed. Since it is the *space* between the two lines at the top of Fig. 2.25 which is being compared with the main shaft it ought by this principle to assume the character of the Fellows line with ingoing fins and been larged. Fellows' reversal with incomplete shafts does not seem to be applicable to lines drawn between the tips of the fins.

A further complication of this figure is that it also embodies a principle mentioned by Láska (1890) that the lengths of the arms of acute angles appear shorter than they actually are and those of obtuse angles appear longer. Thus the bottom horizontal lines in the figure appear longer than the top horizontal lines. It might be thought that the underestimation of the latter ought to lead again to an enlargement of the space between them but it does not. The effect must be insufficient to overcome the main effect of a reduction of that space.

Morinaga's (1965) 'paradox of displacement' (Fig. 2.28) is an example of the curious effect that such figures have on the space about them. Although the apices of the angles lie on two vertical lines they do not appear to do so. If one were to predict, from the distortion of the horizontal distances between the apices, which way the two vertical lines joining them would be distorted, one would expect such vertical lines to diverge at the top and bottom. The paradox is that they appear to do exactly the opposite. Relatively little is known about the finer grain of distortion effects near configurations of lines and a great deal of interesting research waits to be done. Fig. 2.29 is another example. It is as if the dots were perceptually pulled towards the apices of the angles so that the space between the left-hand dot and the middle one seems smaller than that between the right-hand dot and the middle one.

Returning to Láska's point, Fig. 2.26 was used by him to point out that the arm of the more acute angle appears longer than the arm of the less acute angle. This he claimed was the reverse of the usual effect. But the usual effect presumably involved a comparison of the arms of acute and obtuse angles, not comparisons *within* either class. A detailed study of the error of estimation of the lengths of the arms of various angles remains to be done. Judd (1899) also mentions the over- and underestimation of the arms of angles and notes that if, on a figure where an oblique line ends on a horizontal line of unlimited length, one tries to mark off equal intervals on the horizontal line on either side of the junction, the interval on the side of the acute angle will be larger than the one on the side of the obtuse angle. He goes on to use this principle to explain all illusions involving angles and for the Müller-Lyer figure this explanation is particularly convincing. If the arms of the angles in the figure with ingoing fins are perceptually shortened then the shaft will appear shorter, and if the arms of the obtuse angles in the figure with outgoing fins are perceptually lengthened then the shaft will appear longer. The fins will be perceptually lengthened too, but no comparison line is usually present to make this obvious to the viewer. The only difficulty about such an explanation is that there is an acute angle between the fins of the outgoing figure even though there are obtuse angles between each fin and the shaft. One would have to say that the effect of the two obtuse angles overcomes the effect of the single acute angle, and this does not sound convincing.

The effects of alteration of the angle of the fins

To avoid confusion I shall refer to the angle between the two fins, not to the angle each fin makes with the shaft. Lewis (1909), using the standard figures (Fig. 2.1) and comparing each with a plain line, found a maximum illusion with an angle of 20°, the smallest angle he used. The illusion decreased as the angle was increased to 180°. These results agree with those of two of the earlier studies quoted by Lewis, namely those by Heymans and Wundt, but disagree with those of the other two, Auerbach and Brentano. Auerbach found a maximum illusion with an angle of 60° and Brentano with one of 120°. Since Lewis's work several studies have appeared more or less confirming his findings. Dewar (1967a), for example, confirmed these findings over the more limited range of 30° to 120°, using the composite version (Fig. 2.2). Nakagawa (1953) agreed more with Auerbach. Using the figure with outgoing fins he found a maximum at 40°. Gregory (1968) demonstrated differences between the figure with ingoing and the figure with outgoing fins. For the former the maximum illusion occurred at angles between 60° and 140° and for the latter it lay at 60°. Clearly opinion on the influence on the illusion of the angle of the fins is far from being unanimous.

An interesting finding reported by Erlebacher and Sekuler (1969) is that, for the figure with ingoing fins, the horizontal distance between the tips of the fins is the critical dimension. When the angle was changed but this horizontal distance was kept constant by alteration of the shaft length there was no change in the extent of illusion. With constant angle, increase of the horizontal distance between the tips of the fins decreased the illusion. The idea is easy to fit in with the statement made earlier of the principle of this sort of illusion. The smaller this horizontal distance the smaller the minimum horizontal dimension of the figure and therefore the smaller the average value arrived at by the perceptual system. Also something of this sort might be responsible for the disagreement on the effects of varying the angle of the fins, since different shaft lengths were used by the various writers. Unfortunately, however, the finding of Erlebacher and Sekuler does not fit in with reports of the effect of varying the length of the fins reviewed in the next section.

Piaget and Albertini (1950) studied the parallel-lines figure (Fig. 2.18). It is not difficult to see this as a version of the Müller-Lyer figure complementary to the one including only the fins (Fig. 2.7). The result is very similar; when the outer lines are longer the centre line is overestimated and when the outer lines are shorter the centre line is underestimated. Altering the relative lengths of the outer and centre lines is very like altering both the angle and length of the fins of a Müller-Lyer figure simultaneously. Whether the illusion behaves like the Müller-Lyer illusion when such variations are made has apparently not been studied.

The effects of alteration of the length of the fins

The findings of Erlebacher and Sekuler (1959), mentioned in the last section, lead to the prediction that the maximum illusion should be found when the ends of the fins meet; that is, when the horizontal distance between the ends of the fins is minimal. Most work dealing with variation of fin length does not fulfil this prediction however. Lewis (1909) claimed an increase to a maximum and thereafter a decrease as fin length increased. Later estimates of this maximum are in broad agreement. Nakagawa (1958) places it where the length of each fin is equal to $\frac{1}{3}$ of the length of the shaft, for both sorts of figure. Hayami and Miya (reported by Oyama 1960) agree only for the figure with ingoing fins. For the other figure they give a ratio of 1:2. Dewar's (1967b) results, as far as they go, support these findings. He showed, again using the composite figure, that increasing the ratio of fin to shaft length from 1:20 to 1:5 caused an increase in illusion. Since in the composite figure the shaft length is doubled, these ratios are equivalent to about 1:10 and 2:5 in the single figure versions. Thus Dewar's maximum of 2:5 is near those of the 1:3 to 1:2 reported by other workers.

The figure with ingoing fins has a limit to its fin length, that is, when the fins meet. The figure with outgoing fins has no such limit and appears to reverse when the fins are long (Fig. 2.19). At least this is so for the original figure of Müller-Lyer which did not include a plain line for comparison. I have included such a line in Fig. 2.19 and it will be seen that with fins of the length of those of the upper figure, there is still overestimation of the shaft. I have found no indication in the literature of exactly how long the fins must be before the shaft is underestimated when compared with a plain line, but my figure does not reach the point of inflexion.

The effects of an incomplete shaft

When the shaft does not reach the apices of the arrow-heads (Fig. 2.27) the illusion can be reversed. Oyama (1960) reports work by Yanagisawa in which the shaft was kept constant and the arrow-heads moved away from its ends. For the figure with ingoing fins, the illusion decreased with increasing distance from the ends of the shaft to the apices. It reversed when the distance between each end and apex was $\frac{1}{5}$ of the length of the fins. For the figure with outgoing fins, the illusion is reduced as the fins are pulled away, but it does not reverse. This has been confirmed recently by Pollack and Chaplin (1964) and by Fellows (1968) and is not the only instance of differences between the two figures. As early as 1895 Binet claimed that the extent of the illusion in the figure with outgoing fins was five times that of the other figure. This emphasises the inadequacy, as an explanation, of the principle used in making the classification used here. If indeed the percept is an average of the longest and shortest dimensions of the figure, why does the average for the outgoing figure lead to greater error than that for the ingoing figure when the shaft length, fin length and fin angle are all identical?

Differences in illusion for figures with complete and incomplete shafts clearly suggest that the parts of the shaft near the apices are affected differently from those away from the apices. Oyama (1960) quotes two relevant studies. The first, by Morinaga, divided the shaft in the two figures into seven segments and had subjects compare the various segments with plain lines. Only the segments next to the apices were misjudged. The second study, by Koboyashi, got similar results using the composite figure.

In a study by Yokose and Kawamura (1952) only single angles were used. A dot of light was superimposed on an angular figure and an estimation was made of the perceptual displacement of the dot from the apex for various positions along a line bisecting the angle. These authors found that, within the angle, the dot was displaced away from the apex when placed near it and towards the apex when placed further away from it. The latter effect reached a maximum when the dot was placed on a line joining the tips of the arms of the angle. When the dot was placed outside the angle, again on the line bisecting it (that is, in the obtuse angle), displacement was always away from the apex.

It has already been noted that there are differences between the ingoing and outgoing figures. The overall extent of illusion is larger in the latter and the reversal of the illusion with incomplete shaft occurs only in the former. The different effects of the acute and obtuse angle formed by a pair of lines, reported by these authors, is interesting in this connection but it is very difficult to say how such patterns of distortion could bring about the Müller-Lyer effect.

In his work on the reversal of the illusion in this figure Fellows (1967, 1968) introduced an extra concept, that of 'framing'. He compared lines of various lengths enclosed in rectangles with ingoing Müller-Lyer figures, having various lengths of shaft, with gaps between their ends and the apices of the fins. He found very similar effects both in degree of distortion (expansion as compared with an unenclosed line) and in the length of line (as a proportion of the total width of the figure) at which maximum distortion occurred. This length was one-half of the total width of the figure, so the spaces at the ends of the line were equal to one-quarter of the width of the figure. As the line was shortened, the illusion (of expansion of the line) diminished in much the same way for the two figures. As the line was lengthened however, the two functions diverged to give reversal to contraction of the line at a value of $\frac{7}{8}$ for the rectangle and $\frac{3}{4}$ for the fins. Fellows sees the fins as responsible for the Müller-Lyer figure reversing sooner. As the shaft is extended, the lines of the fins approach nearer to it sooner than do the ends of the rectangle.

This important point of inflexion in the Müller-Lyer has received remarkably little attention. Fellows' discovery of the similar behaviour of lines enclosed in rectangles emphasises its interest. Künnapas (1955a), in a study of the effect of square frames on horizontal lines, stopped short of the critical ratio where reversal takes place. His longest line was $\frac{5}{7}$ of the width of the square. Restle and Merryman

(1969) were concerned with the judgment of lines with squares placed at various distances from their ends. This is much more like the Müller-Lyer figure with outgoing fins shown in Fig. 2.4. One does not expect reversal with incomplete shafts in the outgoing figure, and indeed they found no reversal even with a ratio of 19:22·2.

The complexity of the effects on the illusion of relationships among the various dimensions of the figure are further shown in Fig. 2.32 (Fisher, 1967a, 1968a). It is a composite figure with 90° angles and incomplete shafts. Horizontal lines, the same length as the incomplete shafts, lie between the tips of the fins. The distance between the apices of the fins is only twice the length of the fins, and the incomplete shafts are equal to $\frac{1}{3}$ of the distance between the apices of the fins. Now the length of the shafts is such that one would expect the one between the ingoing fins to appear longer than the one between the outgoing fins (the usual reversal of the Müller-Lyer effect with incomplete shafts). It appears the same length. This may be due to the presence of the other horizontal lines or it may be a result of the dimensions of this particular figure. The expansion of the shaft of the ingoing figure must nicely balance the expansion of the shaft of the outgoing figure which does not reverse.

The effects of repeated judgments

Work on the decrement of the Müller-Lyer illusion has been fairly extensive, seemingly because such decrement has been claimed by Köhler and Fishback (1950a,b) as evidence in favour of the Gestalt idea of 'satiation' of neural tissue. Decrement was observed as early as 1902 by Judd. Using the composite figure he found that after many trials the illusion was reduced to zero, and even in some cases reversed. Such decrement has been demonstrated many times since then, both in the Müller-Lyer illusion and others, for example the Zöllner illusion (Judd and Courten, 1905). Subjects have had no knowledge of results, and have been unable to see any difference in the figure at the beginning and end of the trials. Thus the decrement is not due to any conscious correction on the part of the subject.

The essence of the satiation explanation of perceptual phenomena is that where a contour is fed into the visual system it causes a 'figure current' which has its maximal flow at the contour. This flow builds up 'electrotonus' which is 'satiation'. The presence of satiation at a particular location in the system causes any contour subsequently fed into that location to be perceptually displaced. It will be displaced towards an area of less satiation. Köhler and Fishback (1950a,b) considered that the decrement in the Müller-Lyer illusion over repeated trials supported the theory. Satiation was seen as building up within the acute angles defined by the fins. On continued inspection these would therefore be more and more displaced towards a less satiated area, that is the figure with ingoing fins would be perceptually elongated and the figure with outgoing fins would be perceptually shortened, thus reducing the illusion.

These authors were concerned to show first that the decrement was not a practice effect. They demonstrated that it occurred without knowledge of results and even with mere inspection without adjustment of the figure. They also demonstrated the importance of the location of the contours by achieving decrement with the figure in one orientation and then demonstrating its absence when the orientation was changed. They also showed that with tachistoscopic presentation where, they assume, there is no time for satiation to occur, decrement does not occur either. It is interesting that some of their subjects showed complete absence of illusion after only twenty-four trials. The subjects of other workers often took hundreds.

If there is no decrement with tachistoscopic presentation there should be maximum decrement with deliberate fixation of a point on the display, because this should cause maximum satiation. Unfortunately for the theory Day (1962a) failed to demonstrate decrement with fixation, even though it appeared with free inspection. Festinger, White and Allyn (1968) also found no decrement when the display was fixated. They also measured eye movements and found that saccades (rapid, relatively large eye movements which perform the function of centralising a target on the fovea) across the figure with ingoing fins, the perceptually shorter one, were shorter than saccades across the figure with outgoing fins. During repeated trials this asymmetry evens out. The authors suggest that during these trials the system adjusts its eye movements as a result of the experienced inaccuracies of fixation. This is part of Festinger's idea of 'efferent readiness' and is the 'recalibration of efferent processes'. Thus they assume that the original illusion is caused by inaccurate eye movements. Eye-movement theories will be considered later, but a point made by Yarbus (1967) is relevant. He made a similar observation of eye-movements over the Müller-Lyer figure and concluded that the figure affects eye movements. In other words it is just as likely that the illusion gives rise to this particular eye-movement pattern as that the eye-movement pattern gives rise to the illusion.

In fact a study by McLaughlin, DeSisto and Kelly (1969) suggests that the eye movements result from, rather than cause, the illusion. They developed a technique of moving the target after a saccade seeking that target had begun. Subjects' perceptual systems learned to accommodate this and to make only a 5° saccade instead of the 10° saccade that the starting position of the target (10° from the centre of the fovea) ought to have triggered. At the same time subjects adjusted a pointer, which they could not see, to place it under the apparent position of the target. During the learning process the apparent position of the target did not alter. Thus it seems that eye movements can be successfully discounted in the judgment of the position (and therefore, in this argument, the size) of the percept.

Moed (1959) obtained some support for Köhler and Fishback by exposing the Müller-Lyer figure to subjects for many short periods and for few long periods, the total time of exposure being the same. If satiation is simply additive then the amount of satiation in the two conditions ought to be the same. He found similar decrement. In another experiment he showed the composite figure and its mirror image alternately for various proportions of the total time. The decrement was the same for all conditions. This does not fit the theory. In the condition, for example, where one figure was exposed all the time the amount of satiation *for that version* ought to be double the amount occurring when the figure alternated with its mirror image for half the time.

Also difficult for Köhler and Fishback are studies where higher processes have been shown to effect decrement. Thus Parker and Newbigging (1960) trained subjects with a dumb-bell figure (Fig. 2.3) and showed that this training speeded up decrement in illusion using the standard figure. Mountjoy (1965) gave his subjects incorrect information about results and found no decrement.

An alternative explanation for decrement is put forward by Pollack (1970) in terms of diminishing sensitivity to contrast. He draws on previous work of his own in which contrast sensitivity was shown to decline during childhood, and that of Wickelgren (1965) who showed that black fins on a white ground and white fins on a black ground both gave a greater illusion than combinations involving grey fins or grey ground. Pollack tested the decline in contrast sensitivity by measuring the thresholds in children aged 8–12 years for seeing an edge between two areas differently illuminated. The threshold rose with age and the Müller-Lyer illusion decreased with age. Pollack's claim rests on the assumption that decrement with age is the same process as decrement with repeated trials. In this latter situation he considers that adaption to brightness reduces contrast and therefore reduces the extent of the illusion. He produces evidence of the role of contrast by presenting to children Müller-Lyer figures in which the lines and background were the same hue but different in saturation. He used coloured displays because he was interested in the effect of colour too, but the brightness contrast of the coloured display was less than that of the usual black and white version. He found no high readings in the younger ages with these coloured displays; the extent of the illusion remained the same through the ages tested. With black and white displays, on the other hand, young children showed a larger illusion. Pollack's case is interesting especially since other illusions also seem to vary with brightness contrast.

A final puzzle about decrement with repeated trials is posed by Mountjoy (1966). He asked subjects to equate the distance, not between the ends of the shafts, but between the tips of the fins. The illusion was reversed, of course, as in Fig. 2.17, but repeated trials resulted in an *increase* of this effect, not a decrease.

The effects of variation of attitude

Like so many illusions the Müller-Lyer illusion is influenced by the subjects' attitude. Bates (1923), for example, showed that an instruction to subjects to adopt a wholistic view resulted in the usual illusion, but an instruction to abstract the shaft and ignore the fins eliminated the illusion and sometimes even reversed it. Even without the instruction to ignore the fins, concentration on the shaft reduces the illusion (Gardner and Long, 1961).

Considering the large amount that has been written on the Müller-Lyer illusion, remarkably little is yet known about it. The few studies on the effect of change of angle show disagreement. The interaction between shaft length and fin length has hardly been studied at all. We have little knowledge of what distortion takes place in the area around an angle. A disproportionate amount of the work done has concentrated on decrement over repeated trials, trying to confirm or refute a particular theory which, as is plainly shown by Köhler (1964) in his replies to criticism of the theory, is so flexible as to run the risk of becoming irrefutable.

Two interesting themes which are beginning to emerge, and which will be developed later, are the 'frame' effect mentioned by Fellows and the distorting effect of an angle on the area about it. An interesting and little-mentioned additional factor is the apparent lengthening and shortening of the arms of obtuse and acute angles respectively.

THE PONZO ILLUSION

This illusion occurs when two equal figures are enclosed between converging lines (Figs. 2.30 and 2.31). The figure nearer the 'vanishing point' of the lines is perceptually enlarged. Fisher (1967a,

---

2.30 Ponzo (1928) 2.31 Ponzo (1912) 2.32 Fisher (1968a)
2.33 Morinaga and Ikeda (1965) 2.34 Fisher (1968) 2.35 Fisher (1968)
2.36 Fisher (1969a)

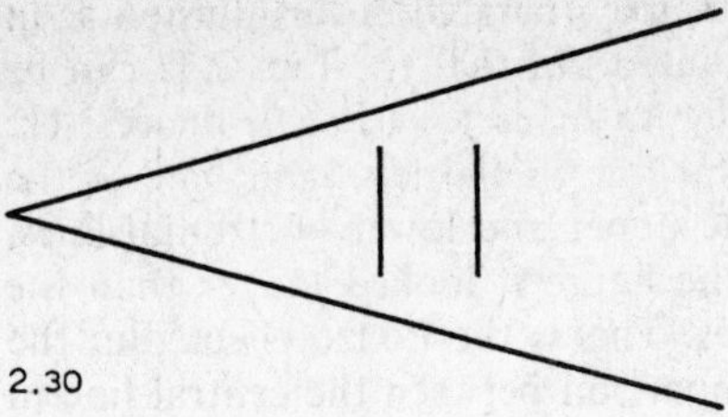

2.30

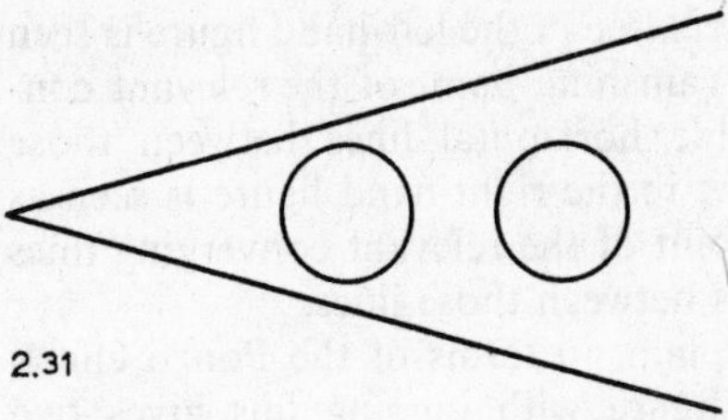

2.31

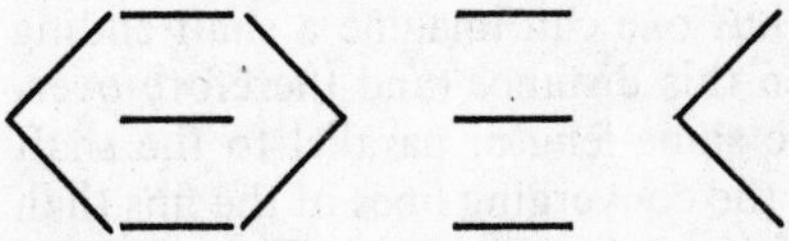

2.32

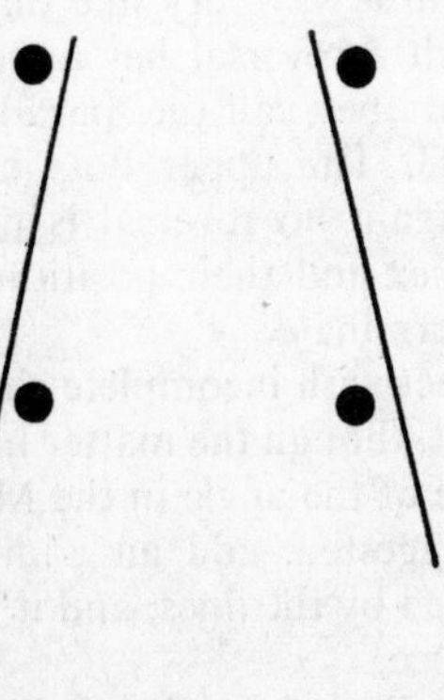

2.33

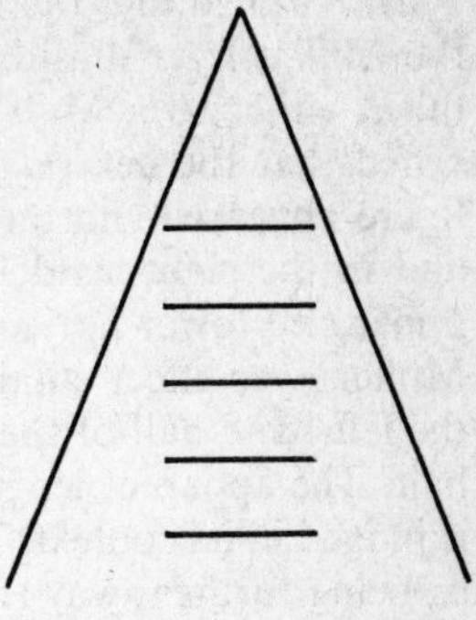

2.34

2.35

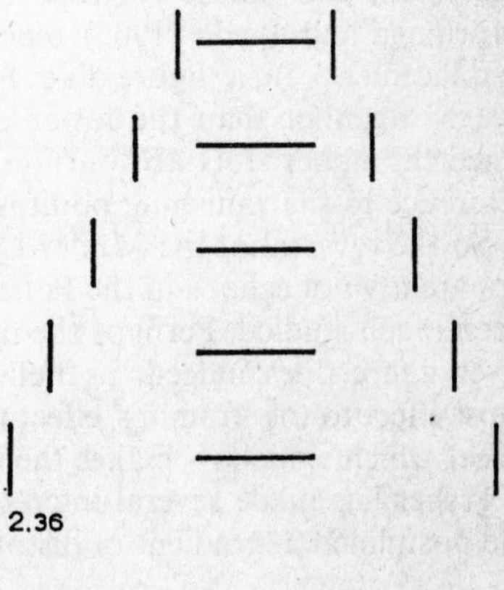

2.36

1968a) argued that the same principle operated in this illusion as in the Müller-Lyer illusion. He pointed out that the Fig. 2.32 can be taken either as a Müller-Lyer figure or as four Ponzo figures. He noted that the central horizontal line in the left-hand half of the figure appeared shorter than the upper and lower horizontal lines, and in the right-hand half of the figure it looked longer than the upper and lower horizontal lines. This is the Ponzo effect. But the Müller-Lyer effect entails a comparison between the central line in the left-hand half of the figure and the central line in the right-hand half. The apparent lengths of these lines usually differ because each is judged in its context. The central line in the left-hand figure is seen as being further away from the vanishing point of the relevant converging lines than other possible horizontal lines between those converging lines. The central line in the right-hand figure is seen as being nearer to the vanishing point of the relevant converging lines than all possible horizontal lines between those lines.

Fisher does not, however, explain, in terms of the Ponzo effect, the fact that the Müller-Lyer figure with ingoing fins gives two opposite effects depending on the completeness of the shaft. According to the work reported earlier, the inflexion should be where the space between the ends of the shaft and the apices of the fins is equal to $\frac{1}{5}$ of the length of the fins. Thus one can imagine a shaft ending just further from the apices than this distance (and therefore overestimated) and another line, the same length, parallel to the shaft and close to it, ending nearer to the converging lines of the fins than the critical distance (and therefore underestimated). Thus the line further from the vanishing point is apparently lengthened and the line nearer to the vanishing point is apparently shortened. This would be such a reversal in the Ponzo effect. Wagner (1969) deliberately attempted to obtain this reversal, in a way very like that just described, and failed. No report of such a reversal has appeared. Morinaga and Ikeda (1965) report what they call the 'paradox of displacement' in a figure like Fig. 2.33. The upper dots appear nearer together than the lower dots. Again no reversal is needed since the upper dots are outside the lines and their position with reference to the vanishing point is indeterminate.

So the reversal of the Müller-Lyer effect with incomplete shafts is apparently not echoed in the Ponzo effect, though the matter has not been much studied. Perhaps the presence of the angle in the Müller-Lyer figure does indeed, as Fellows suggested, add an additional 'fins' effect to the 'framing' effect produced by the lines, and it is this effect which somehow makes the difference.

Fisher has made several interesting studies of the Ponzo illusion. He postulated a 'gradient of distortion' from a maximum, where the converging lines are closest, to a minimum where they are furthest apart. He demonstrated (1968b) that if many lines were placed in an angle (Fig. 2.34) the amount of distortion of any line varies with its distance from the apex. Moreover, if only half the angle is used as in Fig. 2.35, precisely half the distortion occurs. This is a clear demonstration of the distorting effect of a single line which seemed to be operating in Morinaga's 'paradox of displacement' above. Fisher (1967b) had previously shown that detection of small squares exposed for 8 m/sec within the arms of a 60° angle was not as good nearer the apex as further away from it. This is just another indication that angles affect the area about them; and clearly, though there is little direct evidence, plain lines do the same. Fisher (1969a) throws some light on this point, leading again to the suggestion made earlier that the Ponzo illusion depends on some sort of framing effect. He presented a display like Fig. 2.36 and asked subjects to adjust all other bars so that they appeared equal to the top one. Subjects adjusted the bars so that they were progressively longer going down the series of lines. This means that when actually equal they would appear progressively shorter. Fisher varied several parameters of the figure, including the angle of the two imaginary lines joining the centres of the vertical lines. The effect was maximal when this angle was 45° and decreased with increasing angle up to 105°, the largest angle studied. This is another way of saying that, for the range of separations of vertical and horizontal lines used, the effect decreased with increasing separation. This point was demonstrated also by Gregory (1968) using a conventional Ponzo figure; the size of the illusion decreased with increasing separation of the horizontal lines from the converging lines.

The idea involved in the framing effect can be extended to include variations in the size and complexity of the 'frame'. This is implicit in Cleary's (1966) observation that the Ponzo figure can be seen as an example of the more general principle embodied in Fig. 2.37. This is seen if one imagines the horizontal lines in a standard Ponzo figure to be equivalent to the central sections of the two lines of Fig. 2.37 and the spaces between the horizontal lines and the converging lines in the Ponzo figure as equivalent to the outer sections of the lines in Fig. 2.37. This latter figure is generally regarded as an example of a principle of 'contrast' and it will be considered with figures like it in the next section.

This review seems to indicate that we have as remarkably little detailed information about the Ponzo illusion as about the Müller-Lyer illusion. Fisher, who has produced exact and detailed work, criticises previous writers for not doing so, and with justification.

CONTRAST ILLUSIONS IN SECTIONS OF A DIVIDED LINE

Proximity of a judged line to lines around it seems to be accompanied by distortion. So far we have dealt with distorting lines which form an angle with the judged line. This section deals with the effects of framing lines which are continuous with the judged line. They are usually seen as contrast effects and are certainly easy to see as some form of contrast.

Even the simple lines of Figs. 2.37, 2.38 and 2.39 give quite complex patterns of distortion when their dimensions are varied. Fig. 2.38 has a simple comparison figure. The other two each contain two figures which are probably distorted in opposite directions (the centre sections in Fig. 2.37 and inner sections in 2.39), just as the shafts of the two components of the Müller-Lyer illusion are distorted in different directions. Fig. 2.37 is therefore the one usually studied. This is done by comparing the centre section of the upper line with a plain line.

Oyama (1960) reports a good deal of Japanese work on this type of figure, usually using dots or short vertical lines and omitting the horizontal lines. The size of the figure seems to be relevant, overestimation of the centre section usually occurring with smaller figures. But this is little stressed and writers are prepared to state maxima of distortion for figures of various proportions without worrying about their absolute size. Thus several writers reported by Oyama agree that maximum overestimation of the centre section is found where the ratio of the entire figure to the centre section is 2:1, that is the centre section is half as long as the whole figure and it is bounded by sections each of which are a quarter of the whole line. Only Obonai (1954) gives any indication of what happens at smaller ratios (larger centre section). He found the usual maximum at the ratio of 2:1 and the overestimation then fell at still smaller ratios, but did not change to underestimation. In his investigations of the framing effect mentioned in the section on the Müller-Lyer illusion Fellows obtained an inflexion, at a ratio (putting it into the form used here) of 8:7, to underestimation. No such inflexion has been reported with this figure. Either it is quite different from the rectangle used by Fellows or the absence of the lines at the ends of the rectangle allows the point of inflexion to move so close to the end points that no investigator has yet tested a low enough ratio.

Increasing the ratio of the whole figure to the centre section beyond 2:1, according to work reviewed by Oyama, brings about an inflexion followed by maximum underestimation at 3:1, followed by inflexion again to overestimation with a maximum at 9:1, followed

2.37

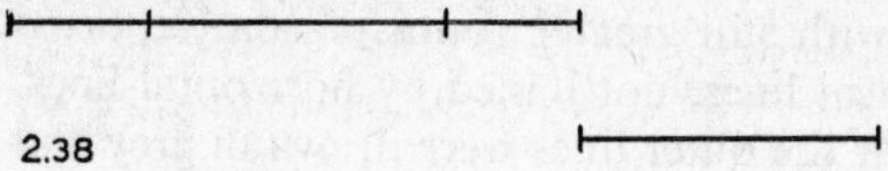

2.38

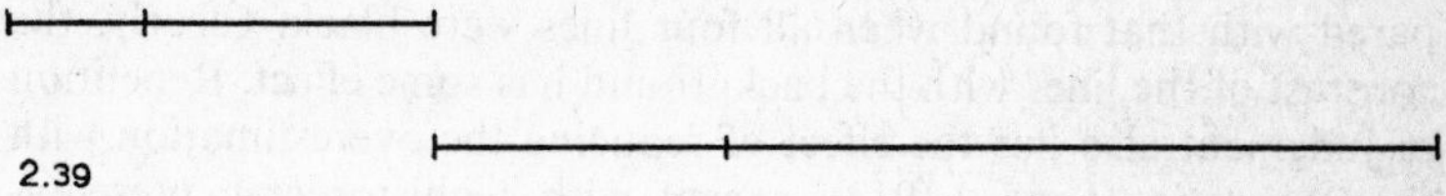

2.39

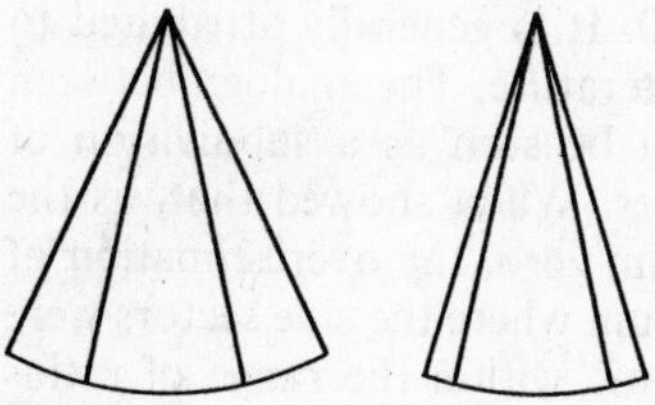

2.40

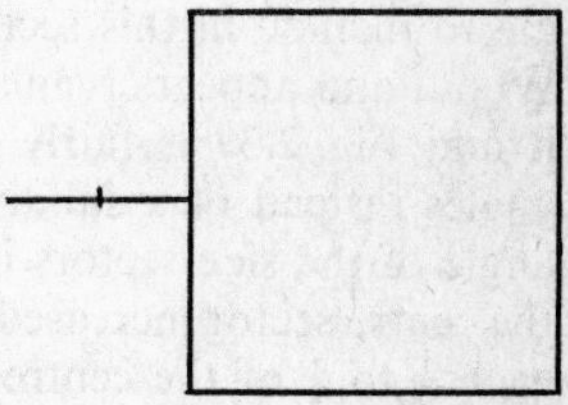

2.42

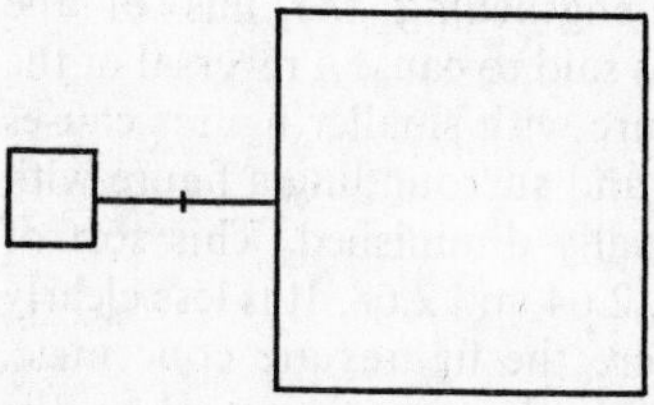

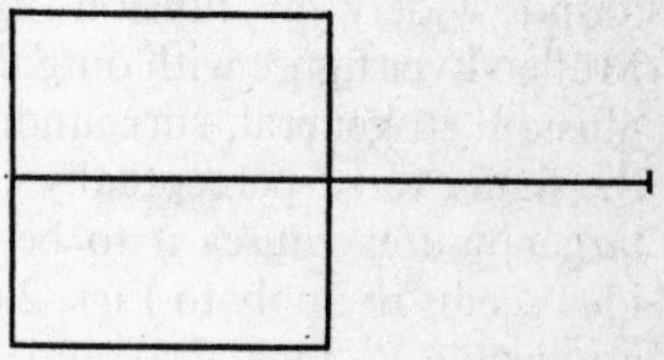

2.41

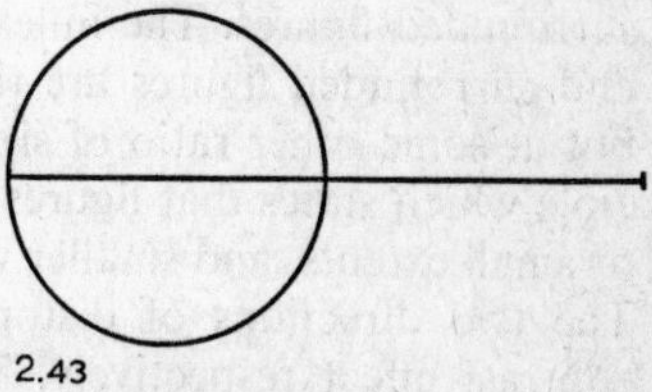

2.43

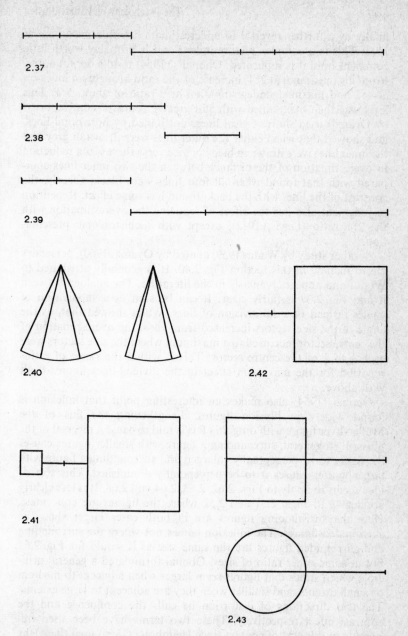

2.37 Müller-Lyer (1889) 2.38 Wundt (1898) 2.39 Piaget (1944)
2.40 Wundt (1898) 2.41 Baldwin (1895) 2.42 Baldwin (1895)
2.43 Titchener (1901)

finally by a further reversal to underestimation with a maximum at 11:1. This is a complex picture indeed and is probably worth little comment until it is replicated. Obonai's (1954) results do not agree. From his maximum at 2:1, increase of the ratio brought an inflexion at 4:1 and maximal underestimation at a ratio of about 5:1. This level was then maintained with still greater ratios. Wada (reported by Oyama) used short vertical lines, not joined by horizontal lines, and showed that when either the outer lines were drawn in grey and the inner lines were drawn in black or vice versa there was a reduction in overestimation of the distance between the two inner lines compared with that found when all four lines were black. Clearly, the contrast of the lines with the background has some effect. Repetition of judgment also has the effect of reducing the overestimation with the 2:1 ratio (Lewis, 1912), except with tachistoscopic presentation.

Another study by Wada (1959, quoted by Oyama, 1960), persuades me to include in this section Fig. 2.40. It is generally attributed to Wundt and appears regularly in the literature. The analogy between it and Fig. 2.37 is fairly clear. It can be seen as a subdivision of angles instead of a subdivision of lines. Wada showed that, as the angle of the side sectors increased from zero, the overestimation of the centre sector increased to a maximum where the side sectors were each $\frac{1}{3}$ to $\frac{1}{2}$ of the centre sector. This is within the range of ratios reported for the maximum effect in the divided-lines figures dealt with above.

Obonai (1954) also makes an interesting point that inflexion is found widely in illusion figures. Lengthening the fins of the Müller-Lyer figure with outgoing fins is said to cause a reversal of the illusion. In general, surrounding a figure with smaller figures causes the figure to be perceptually enlarged and surrounding a figure with larger figures causes it to be perceptually diminished. This sort of idea seems to apply to Figs. 2.62, 2.63, 2.64 and 2.68. It is less clearly applicable to Figs. 2.51 and 2.52 where the figures are concentric. Here the surrounding figures are in both cases larger than the surrounded figures. The inflexion comes not where the surrounding and surrounded figures are the same size as it would for Fig. 2.62 but at some other ratio of sizes. Obonai formulated a general principle which states that figures seem larger when adjacent to medium or small extents, and smaller when they are adjacent to large extents. The two directions of distortion he calls the confluence and the contrast effect respectively. These two terms have been used frequently in this sort of context since Helmholtz (1856) used them (the term 'assimilation' has often been substituted for confluence) and clearly these processes have often been seen as in some way analogous to other contrast and enhancement phenomena, for example those of brightness.

It is interesting here just to make the speculative connection between ideas of contrast in size judgments and an experiment by Blakemore and Sutton (1969). Their subjects inspected gratings without fixation and then judged the frequency of gratings of higher frequency and of lower frequency. The higher frequencies were judged too high and the lower frequencies were judged too low. This appears to be a demonstration of successive contrast in size judgment; the illusions mentioned here could be seen as demonstrations of simultaneous contrast. The mechanism of such a process is difficult to imagine. Blakemore and Sutton suggest that size estimates are derived from frequencies of light and dark areas across the field by a set of perceptual units each of which is fairly frequency specific (Campbell, Cooper and Enroth-Cugell, 1969, have demonstrated the existence of such units in the cat and the monkey). A particular value on the size dimension would presumably stimulate some of these units maximally and others submaximally much as colour receptors are thought to be stimulated by a particular hue in a three-component theory of colour vision. Blakemore and Campbell (1969) showed that the band width of spatial frequency mechanisms in humans is probably just over an octave in cycles of black/white bands per degree of visual angle. They got subjects to fixate a given spatial frequency (grating) and found the contrast threshold for various frequencies above and below it. The effect of the fixation grating was reduced to one-half for gratings just over an octave away. The connection of this work to size-contrast effects in illusions would be an interesting experimental project.

However, the analogy has not been explored in detail by students of illusions and, though Obonai does present several detailed studies, they are concerned only with a few of the figures discussed by him and he does not suggest where, in general, the boundary between 'large' and 'medium' figures lies. His paper is nevertheless very useful in pointing out this simple variation in the configuration of many figures which will bring about a simple variation in distortion.

Figs. 2.56, 2.57, 2.63 and 2.64 all use combinations of contrast and assimilation. In Fig. 2.63, for example, the enlarging effect of smaller figures is set against the diminishing effect of larger figures; *both* the two processes are included. These figures will be treated in detail in a later section.

OTHER LINEAR CONTRAST EFFECTS

It is not unreasonable to extend the idea of contrast to Figs. 2.41 to

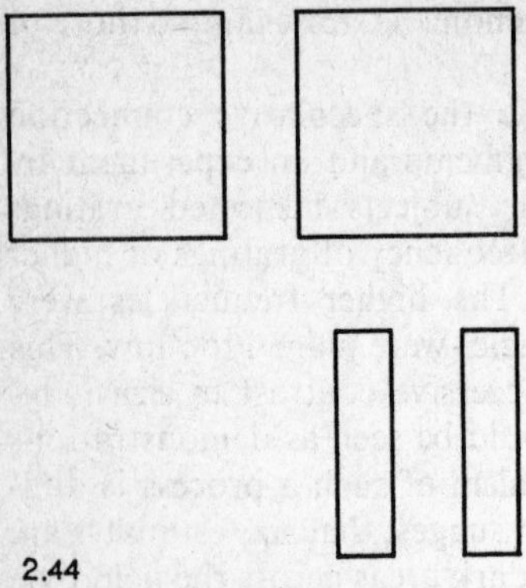

2.44

2.47

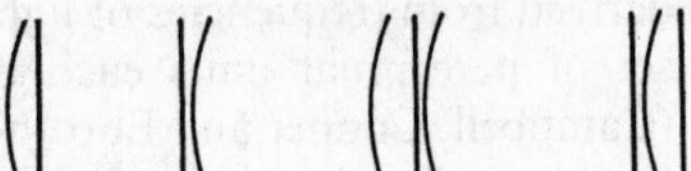

2.48

2.45

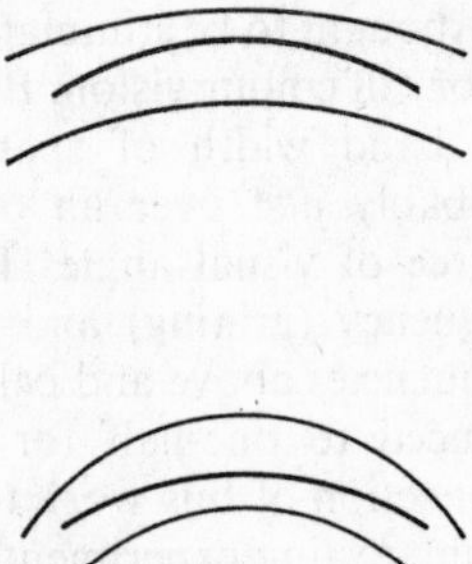

2.49

2.46

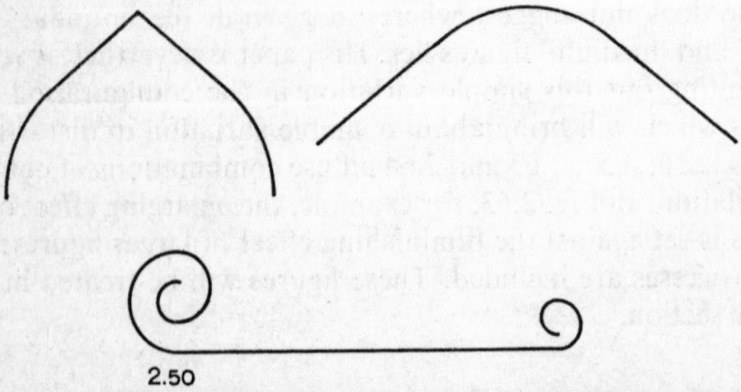

2.50

2.44 Müller-Lyer (1889) 2.45 Schumann (1900) 2.46 Schumann (1900)
2.47 Bourdon (1902) 2.48 Oyama (1960) 2.49 Lipps (1897)
2.50 Sanford (1903)

2.47. In the two figures included in Baldwin's (1895) study (Figs. 2.41 and 2.42) subjects had to bisect the horizontal line outside the square or squares. They placed the midpoint too far away from the larger square. This means that they underestimated the part of the line near to the larger square. A similarity in principle between these figures and Fig. 2.37 is easy to see. In this latter figure an extent bordered by larger extents is seen as smaller than an extent bordered by smaller extents. Figs. 2.41 and 2.42 show that when the extents are asymmetric the distortion is asymmetric. Figs. 2.44 to 2.47 are clearly all variations on this theme, though in Fig. 2.44 the effect is reversed. As was shown in the previous section, the ratio of the various extents is important in determining the direction of distortion.

Restle and Merryman (1969) investigated the effect on lines of different sizes of squares placed at their ends. Unlike Baldwin's study the squares in any one figure were equal. They found that the larger the squares the shorter the line appeared. This is compatible with Baldwin's results. But there is a problem here. The figure used by Restle and Merryman is not much unlike the outgoing Müller-Lyer type of figure with rectilinear ends (Fig. 2.4, lower fig.). The shaft of the latter is overestimated, whereas that of the figure used by Restle and Merryman seems to be underestimated. The explanation seems to be that Restle and Merryman never compared their line with a plain line; all their comparisons were between pairs of lines with different-sized squares at their ends. The distortions reported by Restle and Merryman were therefore probably not all different-sized overestimations. It is much more likely that, where the squares were small, the line was overestimated and, where the squares were large, the line was underestimated. The method of pair comparisons used by Restle and Merryman would quite hide this inflexion. It is the usual inflexion found in figures of the general type of Fig. 2.38 as the outer extents are increased from zero.

As a final point Figs. 2.48 and 2.49 seem intuitively to belong to this section. Little work has been done on them. Oyama (1960) reports Imai's work showing that, as the distance between the straight lines and the curves of Fig. 2.48 increased, their mutual effect on one another (the straight lines becoming apparently curved and the curves apparently straighter) was reduced. These effects are very like those reported by Gibson which are mentioned in Chapter 4.

Perhaps this is the best place to include Fig. 2.50 too. A very mild illusion, it seems to involve contrast. The straight parts of the various lines near to the beginnings of the curves seem slightly curved in the opposite direction. This is like Fig. 2.48 except that the curved and straight lines are placed end to end instead of side by side.

THE DELBŒUF ILLUSION AND THE TITCHENER CIRCLES

Attention has already been directed to some similar characteristics of these two sorts of figures (Figs. 2.51, 2.52, 2.62, 2.68). This point is not new; Zigler (1960) considered the Titchener circles as a modification of the Delbœuf figure. The relationship of the illusion to the relative sizes of the circles has been studied for both figures.

The Delbœuf illusion

The Delbœuf illusion in its original form consisted of the underestimation of the outer circle of a concentric pair and overestimation of the inner one. Figs. 2.51 to 2.60 are all examples of this effect.

Oyama (1960) reports work by Morinaga in 1955 showing that the maximum overestimation of the inner circle of a concentric pair occurred when the ratio of their diameters was 3:2. The illusion fell away steeply with decreasing ratios to reach zero when the ratio became equal to one (the circles coincided). Increasing the ratio also decreased the illusion to bring an inflexion to underestimation when the ratio was 5:1 or 6:1 (the situation shown in the upper left-hand figure of Fig. 2.51).

Other Japanese workers reported by the same author confirmed Morinaga's optimum ratio of 3:2 and showed that it applied both to the overestimation of the inner circle and the underestimation of the outer circle. These characteristics were also demonstrated in figures like Fig. 2.53. Piaget, Lambercier, Boesch and Albertini (1942) also confirmed the 3:2 ratio for overestimation of the inner circle.

Detailed studies by Ikeda and Obonai (1955) showed a maximum effect at a ratio of about 10:7; very similar to the 3:2 ratio reported by Morinaga. These authors found a ratio for the maximum underestimation of the outer circle of about 7:4, again not far from Morinaga's figure for the overestimation of the inner circle. The point of inflexion of estimation of the inner figure with increase in the ratio found by Ikeda and Obonai was at a ratio of about 2:1, a much lower value than that obtained by Morinaga.

The Delbœuf effect varies with brightness contrast of the lines with the background (Oyama, 1962) in a predictable way. Increasing contrast of the circle that is being estimated decreases the illusion, and increasing the contrast of the inducing circle (i.e. the other circle) increases the illusion. Alteration of hue contrast with no alteration of brightness contrast does not affect the illusion. The Delbœuf effect can work asymmetrically as is shown in Figs. 2.58 and 2.59. Bearing in mind the size ratio of 3:2 for the maximum overestimation of the inner figure and the maximum underestimation of the outer

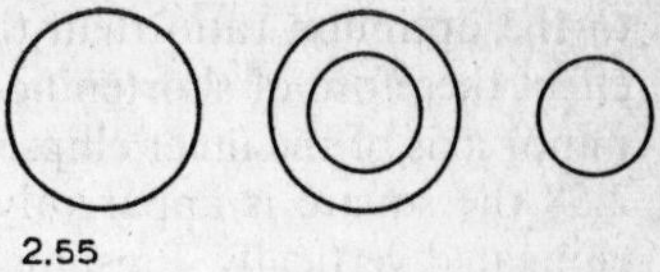
2.55

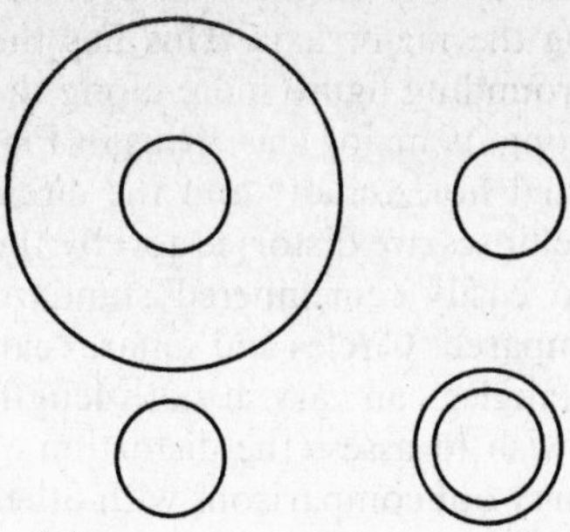
2.51

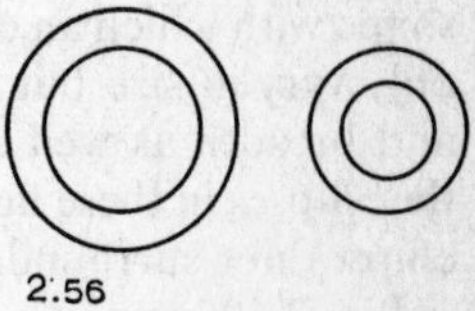
2.56

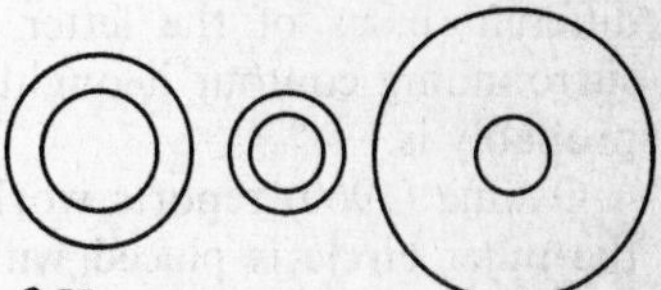
2.57

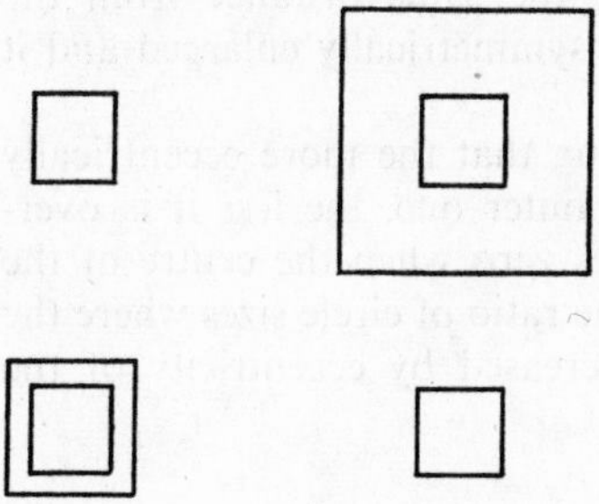
2.52

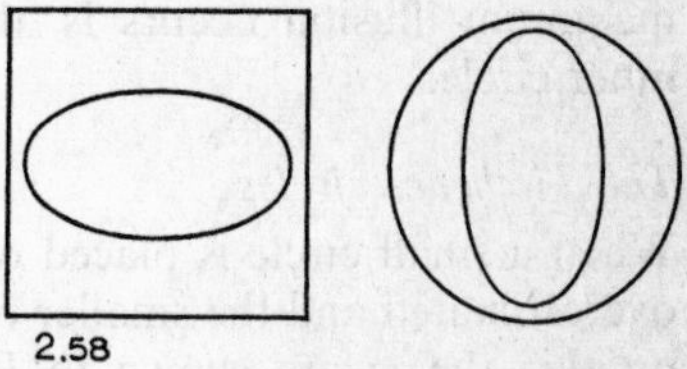
2.58

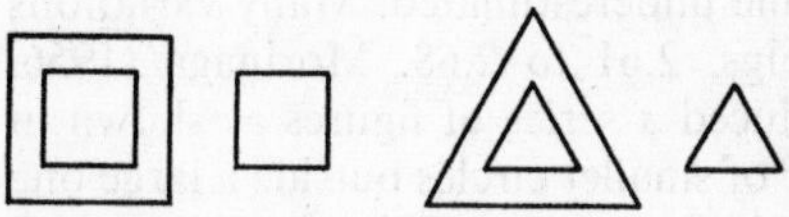
2.53

2.59

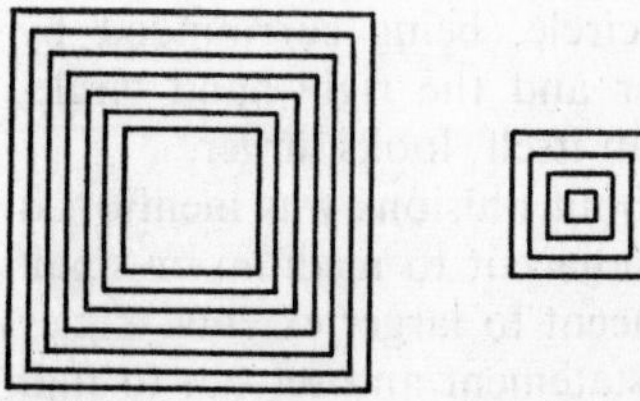
2.54

2.60

2.51 Obonai (1954) 2.52 Obonai (1954) 2.53 Oyama (1960)
2.54 Tolanski (1964) 2.55 Oyama (1960) 2.56 Delbœuf (1892)
2.57 Luckiesh (1922) 2.58 Sanford (1903) 2.59 Schumann (1900)
2.60 Sander (1926)

figure, clearly the ratio along the minor axis of each ellipse is closer to the optimum ratio than that along the major axis. This has the effect therefore of shortening the surrounding figure more along the minor axis of the inner ellipse than along its major axis. Thus in Fig. 2.58 the square is apparently elongated horizontally and the circle elongated vertically. Presumably the ellipses are distorted too by the surrounding figures, but there is no easily remembered standard shape with which an ellipse can be compared. Circles and squares can only vary in size but ellipses and rectangles can vary in both length and breadth as well as in size. If we wish to assess the distortion of the ellipses in these figures we must carry out comparisons with other ellipses not surrounded by figures.

Fig. 2.60 seems also to be an example of the Delbœuf effect. Since different parts of the letter are not the same distance from the surrounding contour it ought to be asymmetrically enlarged and it probably is.

Oyama (1960) reports work showing that the more eccentrically the inner circle is placed within the outer one, the less it is overestimated, and overestimation reaches zero when the centre of the inner circle lies on the outer circle. The ratio of circle sizes where the maximum illusion occurs is also decreased by eccentricity of the inner circle.

The Titchener circles

When a small circle is placed outside a larger one the larger one is overestimated and the smaller one underestimated. Many variations on this theme are shown in Figs. 2.61 to 2.68. Morinaga (1956, reported by Oyama, 1960) produced a series of figures as shown in Fig. 2.61. Increasing the number of smaller circles outside a large one increased the overestimation of the larger one. This effect decreased as the distance between the larger and smaller circles increased. The effect can best be seen by opposing the over- and underestimation as in Fig. 2.63, where the left-hand circle, being surrounded by circles larger than itself, looks smaller and the right-hand circle, being surrounded by circles smaller than itself, looks larger.

Obonai's (1954) general statement about illusions was mentioned earlier; that figures seem larger when adjacent to medium or small extents and smaller when they are adjacent to larger extents. Zigler (1960) criticised the vagueness of this statement and set out to find the inflexion between under- and overestimation. His subjects compared two 2 cm circles, one of which was surrounded by other circles of varying sizes. He found that estimation changed from exaggeration to diminution when the ratio of the diameters of the surrounded to the surrounding circles was 0·77. (This does not

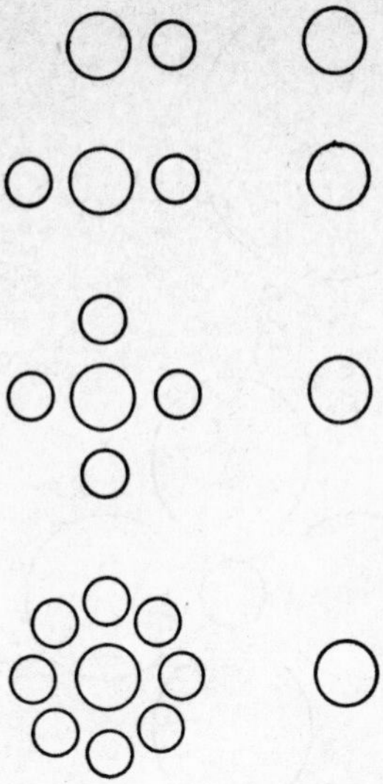

2.61

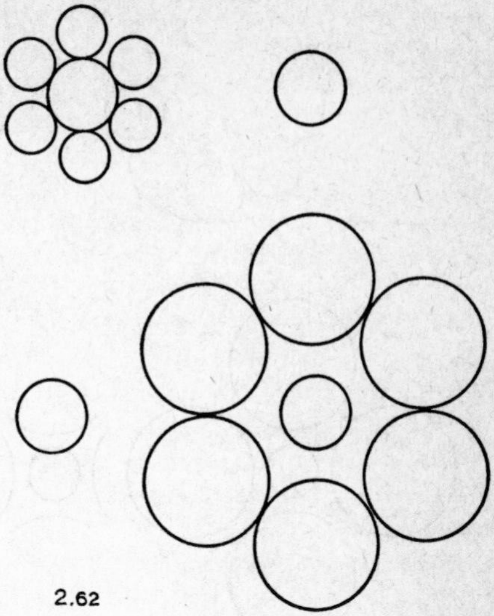

2.62

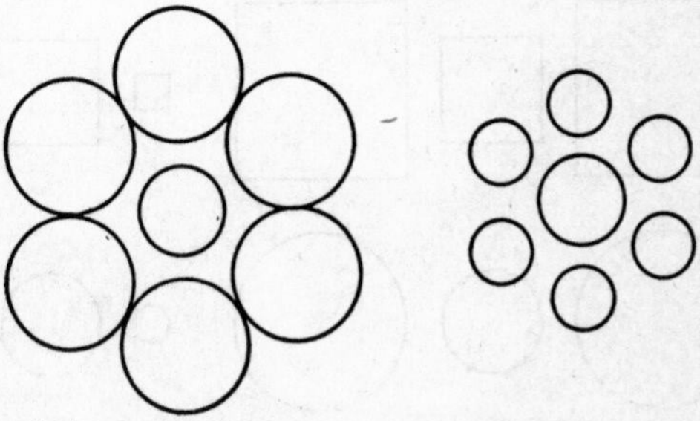

2.63

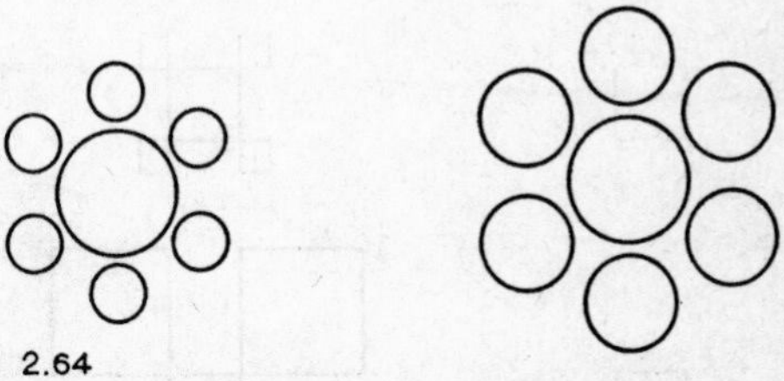

2.64

2.61 Oyama (1960) 2.62 2.63 Titchener circles (Wundt, 1898)
2.64 Lipps (1897)

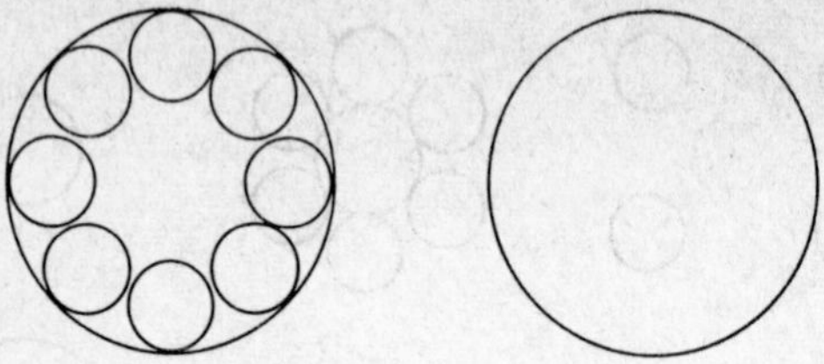

2.65

2.66

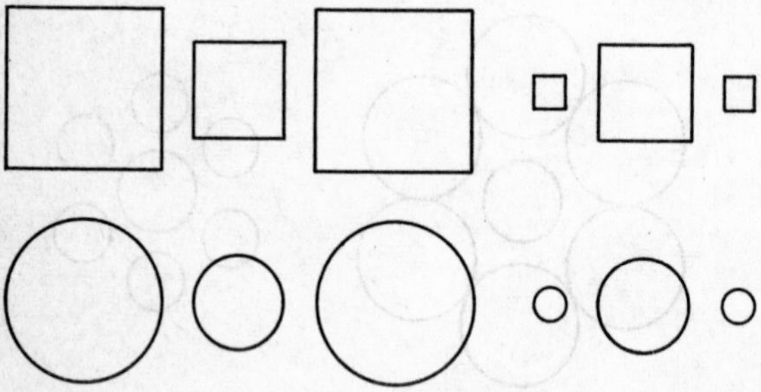

2.67

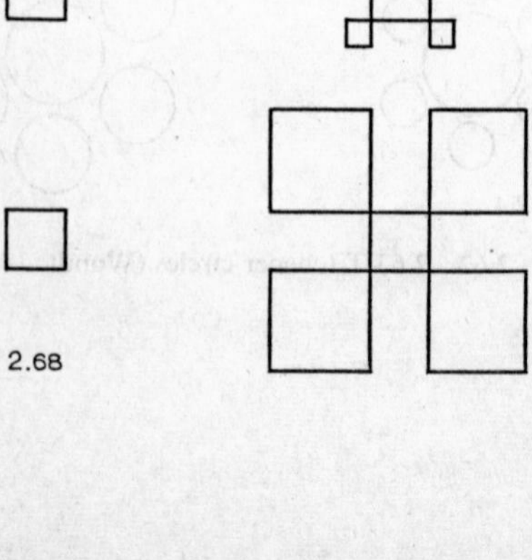

2.68

represent any ratio actually used. It is the value found for equality in the pair-comparison technique used by Zigler.) This means that the inflexion takes place when the surrounding circles are larger than the surrounded one. That inflexion does not take place when the circles are equal is a little surprising and suggests that the relative size of the circles is not the only factor in the illusion.

It is interesting to compare Zigler's ratio with ratios found for the Delbœuf figure. To make the comparison, one must calculate a ratio of the total width of the Titchener figure (the diameter of the surrounded circle plus twice the diameter of the surrounding circles) to the diameter of the surrounded circle. This assumes that the surrounding circles touch the surrounded circle. Where they do not do so, another variable is brought into the situation. Zigler's ratio thus converted is about 3·6:1. The figure given by Morinaga (1935, quoted by Oyama, 1960) for the point of inflexion in the Delbœuf figure is 5:1 or 6:1. These ratios are not far apart considering the differences between the two sorts of figures. The comparison can also be made of what happens when figures are filled with other figures either concentrically or eccentrically. In the Delbœuf effect a figure is underestimated when another is placed concentrically inside it. Morinaga showed that when a number of circles was placed eccentrically inside a larger one (Fig. 2.65) the latter was underestimated. The effect again is similar in the two situations.

Morinaga (1958, quoted by Oyama, 1960) made another observation which stresses the importance of the overall dimension of the Titchener figure. In a figure like the right-hand one of Fig. 2.66, where the inner arcs of the surrounding circles are missing, the effect (underestimation of the surrounded circle, since the ratio as calculated above exceeds 3·6:1) is unchanged, whereas when only those arcs are included, as in the middle figure of Fig. 2.66, the effect is reversed. This figure, with only the near arcs, resembles a Delbœuf figure with a size ratio well within the limits where the centre circle is overestimated, so this 'reversal' is to be expected. It is only fair to say, however, that Cooper and Weintraub (1970) failed to replicate this last part of Morinaga's work.

ILLUSIONS IN FILLED AND UNFILLED EXTENTS

The simplest and clearest form of this illusion is shown in Fig. 2.69 and is known as the Oppel–Kundt illusion. Oppel (1855) introduced it. The principle is that a filled extent is overestimated when com-

---

2.65 Oyama (1960) 2.66 Oyama (1960) 2.67 Lipps (1897)
2.68 Obonai (1954)

2.69

2.70

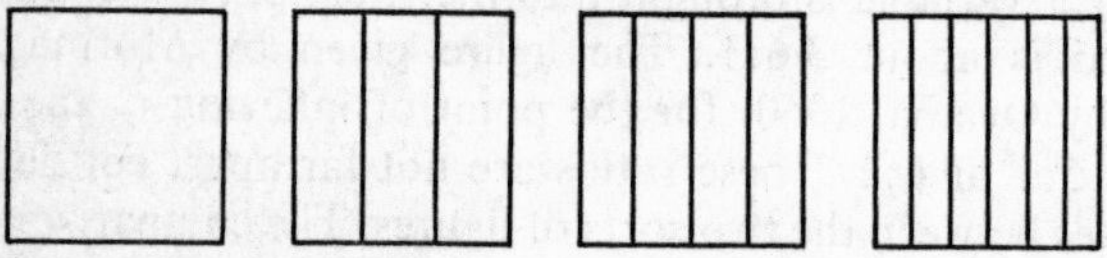

2.71

2.72

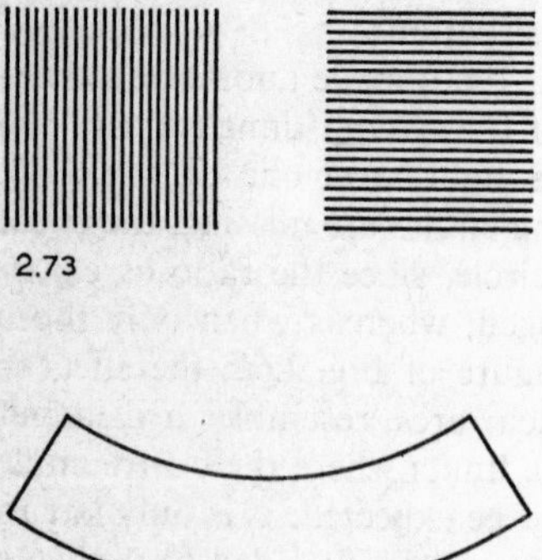

2.73

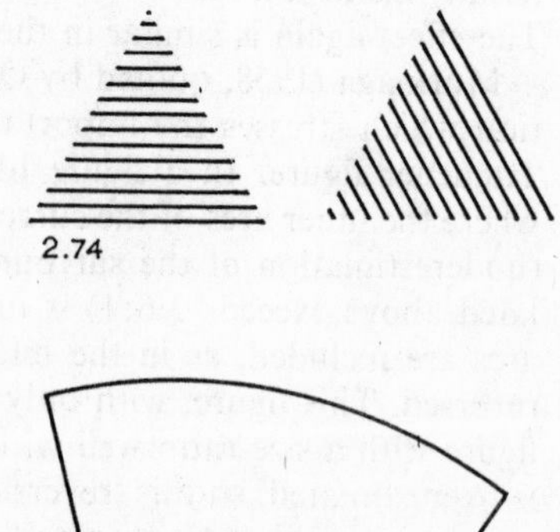

2.74

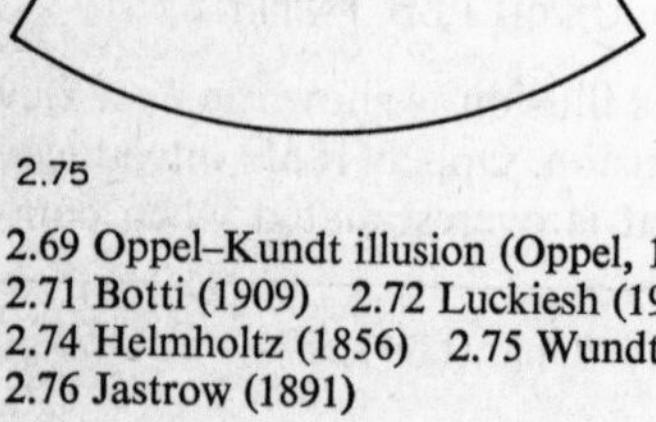

2.75

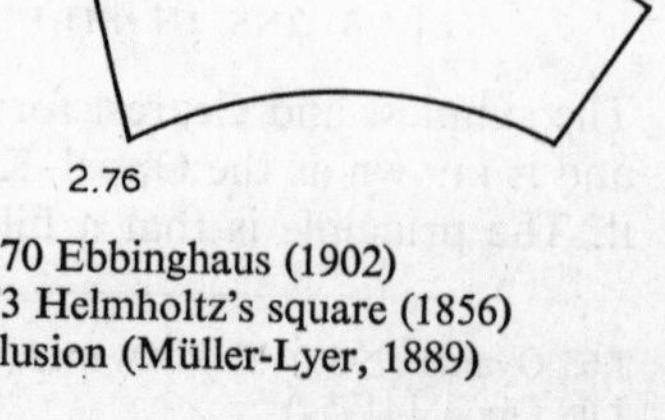

2.76

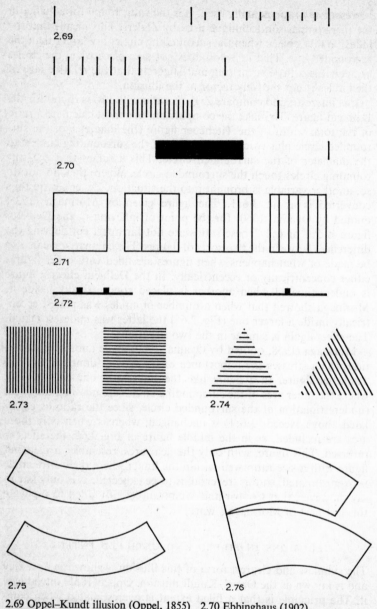

2.69 Oppel–Kundt illusion (Oppel, 1855) 2.70 Ebbinghaus (1902)
2.71 Botti (1909) 2.72 Luckiesh (1922) 2.73 Helmholtz's square (1856)
2.74 Helmholtz (1856) 2.75 Wundt's area illusion (Müller-Lyer, 1889)
2.76 Jastrow (1891)

pared with an equal unfilled extent. It is clear from Figs. 2.70, 2.71 and 2.72 that the mode of filling matters to the illusion. For example, in Fig. 2.70 many lines close together are less effective than few lines more widely spaced and more effective than a solid bar. In Fig. 2.72 there is scarcely any illusion at all. Piaget and Osterrieth (1953) demonstrated that the maximum effect was obtained with 9 to 14 lines in the filled intervals (10 to 15 divisions). The effect was maximal also when the lines were equally spaced. Slightly different results were reported by Obonai (1933) who obtained a maximum in the illusion which was flat from 7 lines up to 12 or 13. Equality of the lines in all respects seems to maximise the illusion; Oyama (1960) reports more of Wada's work which shows that, if lines in the filled extent are unequal in length, thickness or brightness, or are dotted, then the illusion is less than that obtained with lines equal in all respects.

The illusion is also affected by the size of the figure (and therefore probably by the viewing distance, since variation in this alters retinal size). Obonai (1954) demonstrated the usual illusion, but only for small figures of a rather special sort. His subjects compared the distance between a pair of horizontally arranged dots having a vertical line in the interval between them with a pair of dots without a line. When the dots were up to 3 cm apart (viewed at 5 metres) and the vertical line was less than 1·5 cm the normal illusion occurred and the filled extent was overestimated. Increase of either measurement brought an inflexion to underestimation which reached a plateau when the vertical line was about 3 cm long. This was so for all intervals between the dots, that is with a vertical line of 3 cm further increase of the distance between the dots made no difference.

Piaget and Bang (1961a) showed that fixation on different parts of the Oppel–Kundt figure gave different results. When subjects fixated the middle of the filled extent the usual illusion was obtained, when they fixated the centre of the figure the illusion was weaker and when they fixated the centre of the unfilled extent the illusion was reversed and the unfilled extent overestimated.

The so-called Helmholtz square is an example of this sort of illusion. It has been argued that the vertical–horizontal illusion takes a part in it, but that illusion exaggerates the length of vertical lines. The vertical lines in the Helmholtz square are perceptually shortened. This is the reverse of the vertical–horizontal effect. Figs. 2.73 and 2.74 show how the interrupted direction (that crossing the lines) appears longer than the uninterrupted direction (parallel with the lines). Not surprisingly, the Helmholtz square illusion, like the Oppel–Kundt illusion, varies with number of lines, width of lines and size of figure or distance from the observer.

Finally, of considerable interest to anyone seeking similarity in principle between these various illusions is Obonai's (1933) claim of similarity between this sort of illusion and a version of the Delbœuf illusion consisting of the left-hand and middle pair of circles in Fig. 2.55. If one drew diameters of the circles, these would form an Oppel–Kundt figure with two lines in the filled space (the diameter of the middle pair of circles). Obonai compared the overestimation of the outer circle, when the size of the inner circle was varied, with the overestimation of filled space, when the distance between the two filling lines was varied. The functions were very similar, both showing a maximum effect which fell away with alteration of the size of the circle or inner distance respectively in either direction. It is a clear possibility that the Delbœuf illusion is a two-dimensional version of this particular variant of the Oppel–Kundt illusion; the variant, that is, in which there are two lines in the filled space which are equidistant from the ends of the filled space. It would be interesting to study relationships between a version of the Oppel–Kundt figure with many filling lines and a version of the Delbœuf figure with many concentric circles.

MISJUDGMENT OF AREA

A puzzling set of illusions is represented by Figs. 2.75, 2.76, 2.77 and 2.78. Here, in spite of the fact that the two figures in each are equal, the one with its longer side towards its partner looks larger. Imai (1960, reported by Oyama, 1960) varied the dimensions and separation of the two parts of a display like Fig. 2.75. He found a maximum apparent difference of 10 per cent. Probably the contrasting lengths of the nearer edges are affecting the assessment of the areas of the pair. This points to a contrast effect of the sort we have been dealing with. If the final judgment of area were compounded from an estimate of the width of the figure and an estimate of its length, and if the latter estimate were an average of the maximum and minimum lengths, then, if one of these were distorted, the final estimate of area would be distorted. More knowledge about exactly what information we do use in judging area would be very helpful in considering this illusion.

Even simple figures like plain rectangles, lozenges (with all sides equal), parallelograms and trapezia are not immune from distortion. This is clear from Figs. 2.79 and 2.80 where the rectangle and the

---

2.77 Jastrow (1891) 2.78 Ponzo (1928) 2.79 Illusions in basic figures
2.80 Botti (1909) 2.81 Botti (1909) 2.82 Ebbinghaus (1902)
2.83 Wundt (1898) 2.84 Schumann square (Schumann, 1900)

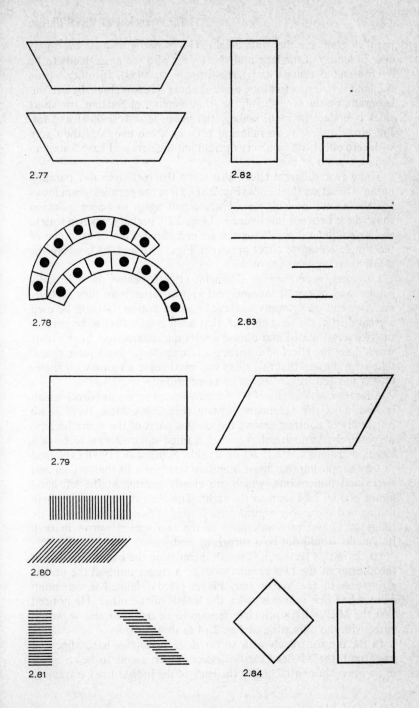

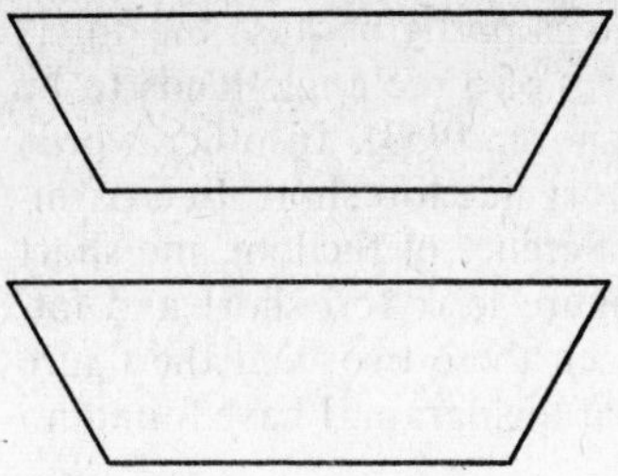
2.77

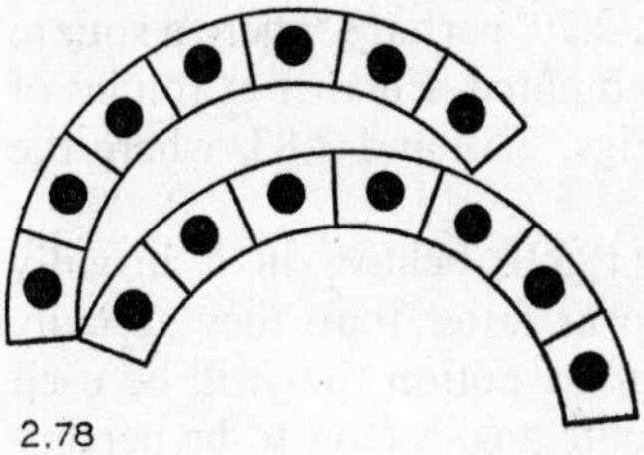
2.78

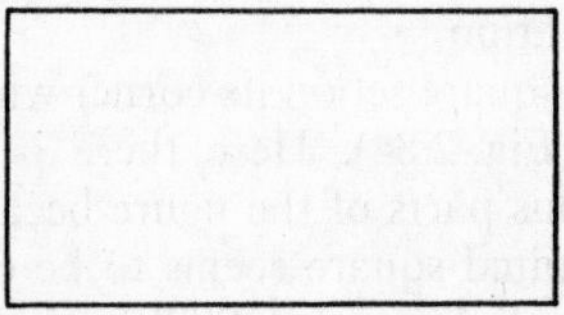
2.79

2.80

2.81

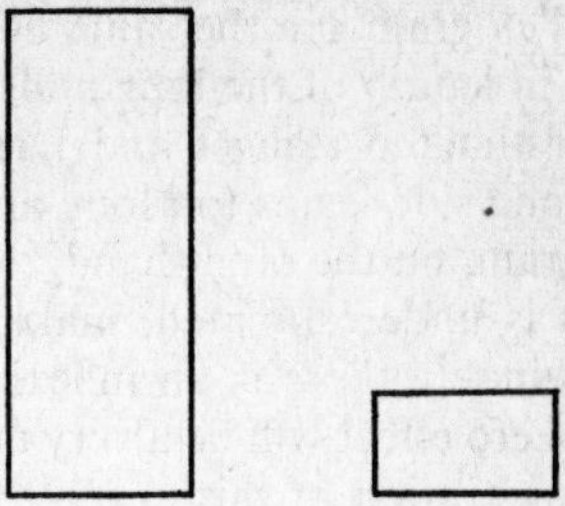
2.82

2.83

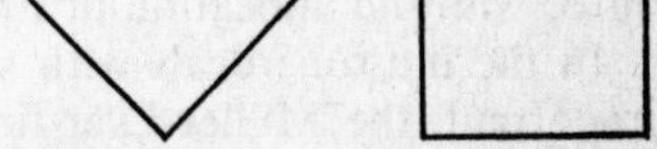
2.84

parallelogram are the same height. This is partly because the difference in length of the long and short sides of a rectangle tends to be overestimated (Piaget and Denis-Prinzhorn, 1953). In other words the long side seems too long and the short side too short. In a parallelogram, on the other hand, the size difference of the long and short sides is underestimated, making the figure look too short and fat. Presumably there is an inflexion between these two, and the figure with zero effect will be a very upright parallelogram. I have found no demonstration of this.

There is a different effect also when the rectangle and parallelogram are set on their ends (Fig. 2.81). Here the parallelogram looks a little too tall and narrow. There ought again to be an inflexion somewhere between this figure and Fig. 2.79, perhaps where a square and an equilateral parallelogram are compared. Further examples of the simple rectangle effect appear in Figs. 2.82 and 2.83, where the small figure appears too wide.

Lozenges, according to Ghoneim (1959), behave in a broadly similar way to parallelograms and appear fatter than they actually are. One can easily apply to these figures a notion that will be used a great deal in the next chapter, that acute angles tend to be perceptually overestimated and obtuse angles underestimated. Such errors would have the effect of distorting a lozenge towards a square shape. Ghoneim showed that this effect was maximal in a figure with angles of 45° and 135° regardless of its orientation.

A lozenge with angles of 90° forms a square set on its corner which is known as the Schumann square (Fig. 2.84). Here there is no possibility of contrast among the various parts of the figure because it is entirely symmetrical. Yet such a tilted square seems to be of a larger area than a square set on its side. Schumann (1900) explained this by supposing that most attention was given to the vertical and horizontal dimensions, which are clearly greater in the left-hand figure of Fig. 2.84 than in the right. This idea is very much worth testing and is another argument in favour of finding out how we do judge area. The preponderance of the two spatial norms in such judgments would not be a surprising find.

Lastly in this section it is worth mentioning the overestimation of the shorter of the two parallel sides of a trapezium and the underestimation of the longer one. Piaget (1961) claimed a maximum effect when one side was twice the length of the other. He noticed that the Müller-Lyer principle seemed to be involved and so would agree with the allocation of Fig. 2.14 to that category.

In the illusions dealt with so far three principles have appeared important, the Müller-Lyer fins effect (which seems to be an effect of an open figure attached to the ends of the judged line), a framing effect (which Fellows claimed was separate from the fins effect), and a contrast effect. It would seem to me useful to study the extent to which these really are separate effects. Is the fins effect merely an example of the framing effect in which the frame either forms less than a right angle with the judged line or forms a figure around the line which is narrow compared with its length? Is the contrast effect merely an example of a framing effect in which the frame itself is an extent? Is the fins effect for outgoing fins merely an example of contrast with open-ended figures forming the contrasting extents? Is the frame effect merely a contrast effect in which the spaces between the ends of the judged line and the frame are the contrasting extents?

THE MOON ILLUSION

Anyone who has already adopted one of the current explanations of the moon illusion will be surprised that it is placed here. It is usually considered to be an apparent distance phenomenon. However, the conclusion reached here is that size contrast forms a better explanation.

The moon at zenith appears smaller than the moon near the horizon. This is not due to atmospheric effects; the moon subtends the same visual angle, half a degree, in both situations. A photograph of the moon in each position would yield a circular patch of the same size, though a person looking at the two photographs might see something of the illusion. It is certainly detectable in the photographs published by Kaufman and Rock (1962a) of the moon near the horizon and near zenith. Indeed a misrepresentation of the size of the moon, perhaps related to the moon illusion, occurs, as Tolanski (1964) points out, in paintings. Here, especially when the moon is part of the dramatic effect of the painting, it is sometimes grossly enlarged. When it is painted its correct size, as near as Tolanski can ascertain, it can look absurdly small.

The moon illusion is large, the horizon moon appears 1·2 to 1·5 times larger than the zenith moon, and awareness of the illusion dates back early in history. One explanation of the illusion which is still current is attributed to Ptolemy. This explanation is that the horizon moon has near it in the visual field many objects and configurations which give an impression of distance (these are enumerated in every textbook on perception). The distance of the moon is equated with the most distant of these (it is not stated why this is, though there may be a case for taking it for granted) and is therefore seen as large compared with the zenith moon which has nothing near it in the visual field. The principle by which the horizon moon in this theory is apparently enlarged is now known as Emmert's law. It is best illustrated by thinking of an after-image being cast against screens placed at various distances from the observer. The after-image appears small on the nearest screen and progressively larger on progressively distant screens. If for some reason the observer were misled about the distance of one of the screens and it was further away than he thought, the after-image would still look to be of a size appropriate to the apparent distance. Thus apparent size is proportional to apparent distance.

Boring (1943) tested the apparent distance theory of the moon illusion by asking observers to compare the apparent distances of horizon and zenith moons. They judged the horizon moon to be the closer instead of the more distant of the two and this led Boring to reject the theory. He carried out experiments to test what he called the 'angle of regard' theory which proposed that the illusion stems from looking up at the zenith moon and not at the horizon moon. Subjects were asked to adjust a nearby disc so that it matched the size of the moon. The apparent size gauged in this way was plotted from horizon to zenith under different conditions. When observers raised only their eyes to look at the moon in higher positions the illusion was present. When they tilted their heads to look at the moon, there was no illusion. Also, when they lay on their backs to judge the apparent size of the moon so that the horizon moon was above their heads and the zenith moon was straight ahead, the illusion was reversed, provided again that they viewed the horizon moon by raising their eyes rather than by tilting their heads.

These results seem clear. They suggest that raising the eyes causes the illusion, and this is what Boring concluded. He could not say why this should happen. Neither did he explain why, in everyday viewing, the illusion seems to be fully present even when one is not particularly careful to keep the head level.

Ching, Peng and Fang (1963) obtained results very like Boring's but they were more detailed and viewing was done by adjusting the head posture rather than the tilt of the eyes. Observers adjusted a nearby balloon, by operating a valve, so that it appeared equal in size to balloons set at various distances along the horizontal. For all distances the apparent size of the distant balloon was greatest for subjects in a normal sitting posture, less for subjects lying prone or supine and raising their heads to view the balloons (the latter group would see the moon between their feet) and least for subjects lying supine on a dais and hanging their heads backwards over its edge to view the balloons. Size judgments seem to vary according to the unusualness of the posture. In the prone posture and the second supine posture of this experiment the body parts are in exactly the same position relative to one another; the difference between the postures is that they are different ways up.

These results and those of Boring show that size judgment differs in different postures and this could well be part of an explanation of the illusion in terms of apparent distance. Both the horizon and zenith moons, being apparently distant, will be perceptually enlarged, but the one judged on the horizontal will be enlarged more than the other.

Two studies show that the position of the stimulus also affects distance judgment. If head posture does indeed make a difference then it also at least makes a contribution to the total effect in these studies. Leibowitz and Hartman (1959) used a dark theatre with the observer sitting beneath a disc suspended in the roof 35 feet above. He had to adjust the distance of another disc of the same size horizontally in front of him so that it appeared to be at a distance equal to the disc above him. Observers adjusted the disc so that it was more than 35 feet away. In other words, when it was at the same distance it looked larger. The authors conclude that we are more accustomed to making distance judgments in the horizontal plane and we therefore make a greater size correction for a distant object of a given retinal size. The size-constancy correction is greater.

The study by Wood, Zinkus and Mountjoy (1968) is very similar except that they used, in one experiment, a size adjustment of a horizontally placed disc to match a disc above the observer's head, and, in another experiment, a height adjustment of a disc above the observer's head to match the distance of a horizontally placed disc. The horizontally placed disc was set too small (thus when actually equal it would appear too large) and the disc above the observer's head was set too low (thus when actually at the same distance as the other disc it would have appeared too far away or too small). These authors interpret their findings as evidence of a vestibular influence in the moon illusion.

It is interesting that of two almost identical studies one is taken as providing evidence of differences in constancy and the other as providing evidence of vestibular influences. Either or both may be the explanation, or indeed differences in the operation of constancy may be caused by vestibular activity. In these studies both effects were confounded.

Kaufman and Rock (1962a,b) and Rock and Kaufman (1962) reported a number of experiments. They took issue with Boring's 'angle of regard' theory and, even though they themselves were able to demonstrate a small effect of eye elevation, they favoured an apparent distance explanation.

They created an artificial moon by projecting a variable disc of light on to a half-silvered mirror which lay at an angle of 45° to the observer's line of sight. He could thus see both the scene through the mirror and the disc of light. The latter was superimposed on the scene. Using this equipment they first got observers to judge the distance of horizon and zenith 'moons' of various sizes. When the horizon moon was larger than the zenith moon it looked nearer, and when it was smaller it looked further away. This suggests that Boring's observations on the apparent size of the moon, which led him to reject the apparent distance explanation of the illusion, were merely artifacts of the illusion itself. The moon looked nearer at the horizon *because* it looked bigger.

They next got subjects to judge the apparent distance of the sky itself, without a moon, at horizon and at zenith. Nine out of ten observers judged the horizon sky to be more distant, and the writers go on to propose that the sky is seen as a flattened dome, the moon is seen as coincident with the surface of the dome and the moon illusion is due to the simple operation of Emmert's law. In other words, the moon has the same angular size at both horizon and zenith but is seen as nearer at zenith, and therefore smaller.

Much more convincing, however, are the observations of Kaufman and Rock on the importance of the horizon terrain for the illusion. A horizon moon with its background scene and a horizon moon with the scene masked out were each compared with a zenith moon. Only the horizon moon with its background scene gave the illusion. (The condition with the scene masked out, by the way, seems to contradict the results of Leibowitz and Hartman, but they were dealing with much smaller effects.)

Also, by a system of mirrors, they moved a moon with background terrain to the zenith and had observers compare it with a moon on the horizontal without the background. The moon with the background terrain still looked larger. This pits the effect of posture and position against the effect of background terrain, and the latter predominates. Clearly the posture/position effect is small. Another experiment compared the illusion produced by two different terrains, one in which the horizon was relatively near (a wooded landscape) and one in which it was distant (a prairie landscape). The illusion was greater for the latter condition. So not only does background terrain produce the illusion; more distant terrain is more effective.

This last evidence is much stronger than any argument that tries to use Emmert's law and the apparent distance of moon or sky. As Kammann (1967) pointed out, the explanation based on the importance of terrain is quite independent of the latter argument. Orbach and Solhkhan (1958) express this point well. They say that objects near the horizon, being distant and known objects, tend to be perceptually enlarged by the process of size constancy. This would mean that the horizon moon is quite incidentally enlarged because it happens to be close in the visual field to these other objects that are being enlarged. Rock and Ebenholtz (1959) had already produced evidence which makes it hardly necessary to invoke size constancy. Using a luminous line in a dark room they had shown that estimates of the size of this line were very much influenced by the size of a luminous frame round it. This was independent of apparent distance. In other words, the line being judged larger when in a smaller frame was not the result of the different-sized frames altering the apparent distance of the display; the influence was clear even with binocular viewing, which gave the observer accurate distance information for the frames. It was also independently shown that, when the frames were actually at different distances, those distances were fairly accurately gauged by subjects.

We are left now with two conflicting sets of information. One is that produced by Kaufman and Rock, that the distance of the horizon affects the illusion, and the other is that produced by Rock and Ebenholtz, that the effect on the apparent size of an object of other objects near to it has little to do with apparent distance. How then can the horizon's distance possibly affect the moon illusion? Restle (1970) has produced an argument which can incorporate both these facts. It is this argument which has made me place the moon illusion in this book along with illusions of size contrast. Restle explains the illusion in terms of the grain of the visual scene, a consequence of distance, and its effect on relative sizes within the field. Gibson's texture gradients are an example of the alteration with distance of the grain of a visual field.

Restle's basic assumption is that size is always judged relative to other extents in the visual field. This notion has become familiar during the earlier sections of this book. A natural scene, however, is much more complex than any of the configurations of lines we have considered so far. He uses the mathematical notation of adaption-level theory (Helson, 1964, and Corso, 1967, who gives a good brief account) to express the relationship of configuration of the visual field to the judgment of the size of one of its elements. The adaptation level is the 'weighted geometric mean of all relevant influences'. Restle considers the simplest possible case where the moon is viewed on a clear night over the sea. He considers that the only relevant influence here is the simple line of the horizon and writes expressions for the judgments of the size of the moon at horizon ($J_h(M)$) and at zenith ($J_z(M)$).

$$J_h(M) = MC^{s-1}\, S_h^{-s}$$
$$J_z(M) = MC^{s-1}\, S_z^{-s}$$

where M is the retinal size of the moon. C is a constant. (Its inclusion in both formulae expresses the notion that the rest of the visual field is the same for both horizon and zenith judgments.) S_h and S_z are the distances from the horizon and zenith moons respectively to the horizon. s is the 'probability that M will be compared with the inducing background object, and indicates the magnitude of illusory effects'.

Clearly the moon illusion is expressed by

$$\frac{J_h(M)}{J_z(M)} = \left(\frac{S_z}{S_h}\right)^s$$

And if the horizon moon is 1° above the horizon and the zenith moon is 90° above the horizon then

$$\left(\frac{S_z}{S_h}\right)^s = 90$$

Restle quotes data from Restle and Merryman (1968) which showed that the effect on a judged line of a gap between its ends and squares offset from its ends was between 0·03 and 0·09. When he substituted these values for s in the above equation, he obtained values of 1·15 and 1·5, both very like values for the moon illusion. The importance of this calculation is that Restle has taken values from a relevant line illusion and shown that they fit the moon illusion. However, he does this for only this very simple case. The rest of Restle's theorising is no more precise than any other. He claims that the horizon terrain for a distant horizon has a finer grain than that for a nearer horizon and thus is made up of smaller extents, which give a low value for the adaptation level (A). $J(M) = M/A$ and therefore $J(M)$ is large. Alternatively, in terms of my treatment of the Delbœuf and Titchener illusions, the extents near the horizon are smaller and therefore the moon looks larger by contrast. Restle's way of putting it will be clearly preferable only when he can show that adaptation-level expressions work for these more complex situations.

He goes on to suppose that the reduction of the illusion in a clouded sky, demonstrated by Kaufman and Rock, is due to the existence of grain and therefore of comparison extents in a clouded sky. Thus, for the zenith moon, instead of one massive extent stretching from the horizon to the moon and so setting a large adaptation level and a small value of $J(M)$, there are smaller extents which set a smaller adaptation level. He also accounts for the observation of Kaufman and Rock that the illusion is exaggerated when the horizon moon is viewed in amongst city buildings. Here the comparison extents almost surround the moon instead of being only below it. This gives a very low adaptation level. Again these accounts can be put in terms of size contrast. There is a great deal in common between the ideas of size contrast and adaptation level. It will be interesting to see in due course whether they are really divisible from one another at all.

In summary, then, an agreed explanation of the moon illusion does not exist. Differences in the application of size constancy appear to exist between stimuli judged in the horizontal and vertical planes. These differences seem to be partly due to posture effects and may also be due to the fact that we are more accustomed to applying size-constancy adjustments in the horizontal plane. These effects certainly seem to make a contribution but the main effect comes from the terrain at the horizon. Exactly how the terrain exerts its effect is not clear, but Restle's seems to be the sort of explanatory attempt that involves fewest difficulties, and the work of Rock and Ebenholtz fits well with it.

This chapter has described a broad division of illusions in which contrast effects have been more important than angles or orientation. The next chapter contains illusions in which the latter are relatively more important. True, the Müller-Lyer and Ponzo illusions could have been placed in either chapter, because both seem to depend at least partly on the existence of an angle in the configuration. In the case of the Müller-Lyer illusion, however, this only applies to certain versions and, in the case of the Ponzo figure, a contrast effect seems to be more important than an angular one.

Illusions among sections of a divided line (Fig. 2.37) and the Titchener circles (Fig. 2.63) all seem to involve contrast in either one or two dimensions and so does the misjudgment of area. It is harder to ascribe contrast to illusions in filled and unfilled extents, however (Fig. 2.69).

Two sorts of general principle pervade the illusions described in this chapter. One is the inflexion of illusion which takes place with many figures when the dimensions are gradually transformed. The Delbœuf illusion (Fig. 2.56) is one example of this and Fig. 2.37 is another. This alteration from contrast to so-called 'assimilation' needs much more detailed and exact study.

The other principle concerns configurations themselves. It is that illusion seems to be governed by two effects, an angle effect and a framing effect. The angle effect will be discussed at length in the next chapter. The framing effect is probably part of how contrast works. Putting a frame round a figure marks off extents beyond the figure which can then exert a contrast effect on the figure itself.

This emphasises the importance of the work of Blakemore and Sutton (1969), mentioned in the section on illusions between sections of a divided line. Spatial frequency in the visual field could possibly be the basis of size estimation. A great deal more psychophysical work is needed along the lines of that of Blakemore and Sutton. They used regular gratings; it would be fascinating to know how the visual system deals with irregular gratings, because in a sense Fig. 2.37 *is* an irregular grating.

3

THE GEOMETRICAL OPTICAL ILLUSIONS (II)

ILLUSIONS INVOLVING DISTORTION OF ANGLES AND DIRECTION

There is a very large group of illusions in which angles, particularly acute angles, seem to be a decisive factor in the illusion. Wundt (1898) drew attention to this and at first sight the principle seems very clear; acute angles seem to be perceptually enlarged and obtuse angles perceptually reduced. However, this principle has not been universally agreed, acute angles between 45° and 90° being the chief cause of disagreement, and in any case the illusions often happen when no actual angles are involved (for example Fig. 3.39). There are also more complex figures, for example the so-called twisted cord and shifted chequerboard illusions (Figs. 3.61 and 3.70), which seem to be based on the same principle but whose inclusion in this section may well be a matter for argument.

THE ZÖLLNER ILLUSION AND ITS VARIANTS

Some basic data

The most common version of this illusion is shown in Fig. 3.1 though Figs. 3.2 to 3.16 are all obvious variations of it. Benussi (1902) claimed that Montaigne was aware of the Zöllner illusion in the sixteenth century, but Zöllner (1860) produced the first detailed work on it. He used Fig. 3.2, a version with thick lines, and claimed that the maximum illusion occurred when the main (distorted) lines were at 45°. The illusion was minimal when these lines were vertical or horizontal. He found no effect of either the distance between the obliques or their number, a finding contradicted by Wallace and

Crampin (1969) who showed that increasing density of the obliques (that is, the number per inch) increased the illusion. Indeed Fig. 3.8 seems to bear out this contradiction since the vertical lines seem to be more tilted in the lower part of the figure than in the upper. Zöllner failed to find any effect of intensity of the lines or their relative width, findings again contradicted by later work, for example by Benussi (1902) who showed the effect of colour on the Zöllner illusion. Black lines gave the greatest effect followed by green, red, yellow and violet (giving equal effects), and grey. It is not unlikely that Benussi was actually dealing with different brightness contrasts and that hue itself was not an effective variable. However, Zöllner is contradicted by the comparison of black and grey lines alone.

Studies of the effect of altering the orientation of the whole figure appear in Table 3.1 and studies of the effect of altering the angle of the obliques to the main lines appear in Table 3.2.

Table 3.1

EFFECT OF ALTERATION OF ORIENTATION OF DISTORTED (MAIN) LINES ON THE SIZE OF ZÖLLNER-TYPE ILLUSIONS

Author	*Effect*	*Figure*
Zöllner (1860)	Max. at 45°; min. at 0° or 90°	Standard figure. Main lines at 45° to obliques
Judd and Courten (1905)	Max. at multiples of 45°	Standard figure. Main lines at 45° to obliques
Morinaga (1933)	Max. at multiples of 45°	Standard figure. Main lines at 45° to obliques

Wallace and Crampin (1969) confirmed Adam's (1964) observation that when the obliques lay at an angle of less than 2° to the long lines the illusion reversed. They put this down to a counteracting effect of the parts of the lines near the apices of the angles which cannot be visually separated from one another. Certainly odd things seem to happen to the lines at small angles (see Fig. 3.7 where the long lines seem to take on a stepwise form).

Maheux, Townsend and Gresock (1960) proposed that the perceptual system computes the direction of a line from information derived both from the angle it makes with other lines and the number of other lines crossing it. They used a set of parallel horizontal lines crossed by a single oblique line to demonstrate the increased 'stepping' effect in the line where the parallels were closer together, and they drew attention to the apparent rotation of each section of the oblique line about its midpoint. For more precise measurement these workers used a pair of horizontal parallel lines with an oblique line between them and just meeting them. They varied the distance between the parallels and the angle of the oblique and subjects were asked to adjust another line, some distance from the figure, so that it appeared to be precisely in line with the oblique. They found that the error of alignment was inversely related to the length of the oblique and also to the angle of the oblique. The former relationship

Table 3.2

EFFECT OF ALTERATION OF ANGLE BETWEEN DISTORTED (MAIN) LINES AND OBLIQUES ON THE SIZE OF ZÖLLNER-TYPE ILLUSIONS

(*'Positive' effect is an apparent enlargement of acute angle*)

Author	*Effect*	*Figure*
Morinaga (1933)	Max. at 20° to 30° falling sharply at <20° and gradually at >30° to reach zero at 90°	Zöllner figure
Wallace and Crampin (1969)	Max. at 15° to 20°, shape of function as Morinaga. Reversal at angles <2°	Zöllner figure. S adjusted one line to appear parallel to the other
Maheux, Townsend and Gresock (1960)	Max. at 10° (smallest angle studied) decreasing to 60° but rising again at 70° (largest angle studied)	Two parallels with one oblique between them only. S placed a separate line in line with the oblique
Hofmann and Bielchowsky (1909)	Max. at 20° decreasing to zero at 45°, reversal from 45° to 90°	Single line (either vertical or horizontal) with obliques. S adjusted line to appear vertical (or horizontal)
Gibson (1937a); Gibson and Radner (1937)	Max. at 10°, zero at 45°, reversal at >45°	Single line with obliques. S adjusted line to appear vertical
Day (1965)	Max. at 15°, zero at about 40°, reversal between 40° and 90°	Zöllner figure

was curvilinear, the effect increasing much more rapidly as the length of the oblique was reduced (i.e. as the parallels were brought closer together). The relationship of the effect with the angle of the oblique was linear from 10° to 60° but the value for 70° departed from linearity (it was too large). Thus these writers found a maximum at 10° (the smallest angle used) for this display in which the oblique was judged, whereas both Morinaga (1933) and Wallace and Crampin (1969) found a maximum at around 20° for the more common Zöllner figure with multiple obliques where the parallels were judged.

There are two differences in the experimental situations which may play a part in this disparity. One is the number of obliques (Maheux, Townsend and Gresock had only one) and the other is where the judgment was made. It was made on the parallels (which lay on the horizontal) in the work of Wallace and Crampin and on the oblique (with orientation varied and never very near the horizontal or vertical) in the work of Maheux, Townsend and Gresock. It will be seen later that this matter of orientation is important and the suggestion will be made that it could be relevant to the very different results reported in the last three studies shown in Table 3.2, in each of which was found an inflexion at 45° and a negative effect (apparent reduction of acute angles) with angles between 45° and 90°.

Distortion of the vertical and horizontal by the background

Day (1965) considers that the Zöllner illusion is a version of the phenomenon reported by Gibson (see Table 3.2). Gibson was particularly concerned with figural after-effects of tilted or curved lines which will be considered in the next chapter. However, he also observed simultaneous effects of tilted lines on the vertical of the kind mentioned above, and considered that these, like after-effects, were the result of 'adaptation' of the spatial norms. Usually the effect studied was that of a single tilted line on the adjustment of another line to the vertical, or the effect of a curved line on the appearance of a straight line. In the former case, when the test line was actually vertical, it appeared to be tilted slightly away from the vertical in the opposite direction to that of the tilted line. Thus, when it was adjusted to appear vertical it was set sloping slightly in the direction of the tilted line. Again, when a straight line was viewed in the presence of a curved line, the straight line looked slightly bowed in the opposite direction to the curve of the curved line.

3.1 Zöllner figure, common variant 3.2 Zöllner (1860) 3.3 Zöllner illusion (Hering's version, 1861) 3.4 Hering (1861) 3.5 Titchener (1901) 3.6 Zöllner variation 3.7 Zöllner illusion showing stepwise effect 3.8 Zöllner variation

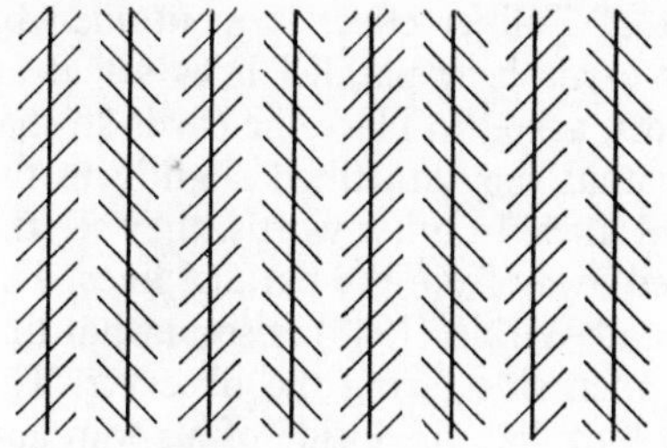

3.1

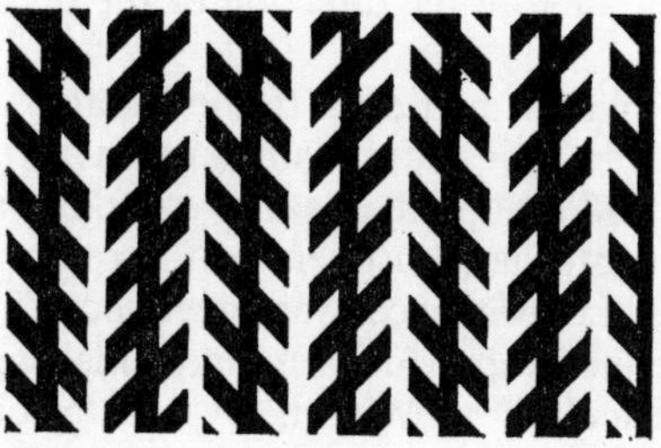

3.2

3.3

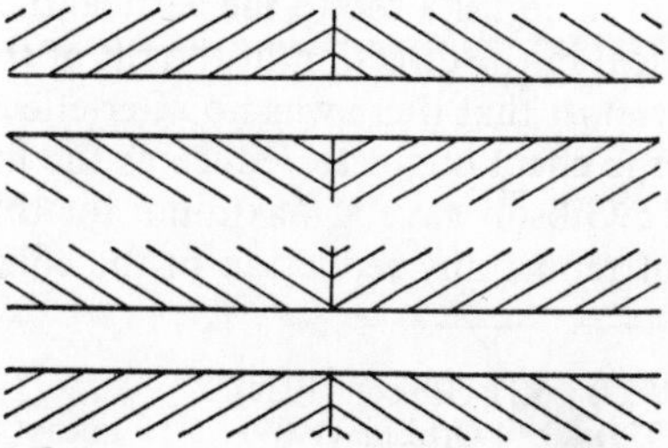

3.4

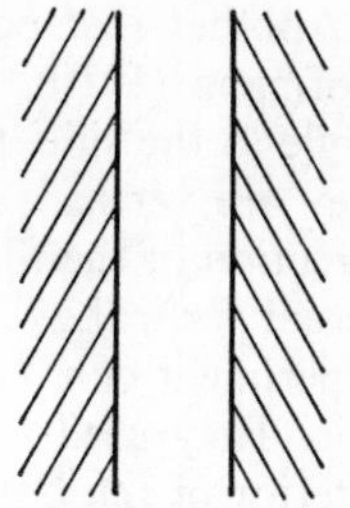

3.5

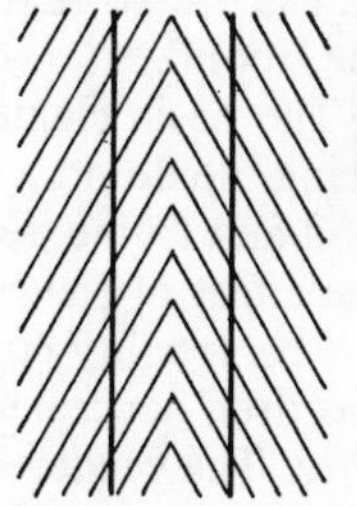

3.6

3.7

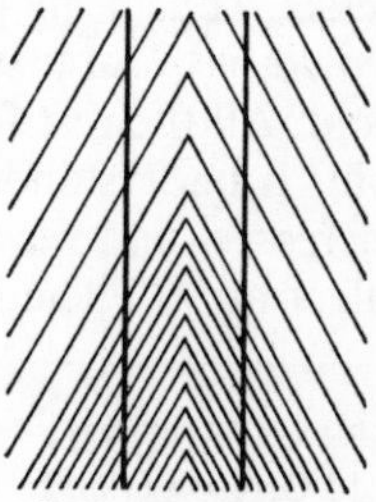

3.8

Another instance of this sort of Zöllner effect is mentioned by Hofmann (1910). If rectangular cards bear parallel lines set at an angle to the side, then the subjects, asked to place the cards so that they are vertical, place them so that they are tilted slightly in the direction of the tilt of the parallel lines. In other words, they see the actual vertical as apparently tilted away from the parallel lines. The experiment conducted by Asch and Witkin (1948) is somewhat like this. They used a box with an open side facing the observer. The interior of the box was made to look like the inside of a room and the whole 'room' could be tilted. When subjects were asked to adjust a bar on the far side of the 'room' so that it was vertical, they adjusted it so that it was slightly tilted in the direction of the tilt of the 'room'.

The basic elements of this situation, namely a frame capable of being tilted and a rod within it to be adjusted, became known as the 'rod and frame' test. Individual and group differences were found in the effect of the tilt of the frame on the adjustment of the rod and the personality continuum of 'field dependence' was suggested. This has itself generated considerable literature which cannot be included here. The reader is referred particularly to Witkin, Dyk, Faterson, Goodenough and Karp (1962).

Dixon and Dixon (1966) report what appears to be a straightforward example of Gibson's effect. It is an amusing description of a yacht, occupied by the Dixons, aground and listing as the tide left it. Water entered the cabin, and there is a clear impression that the subjects of this experiment could not be regarded as volunteers! They reported that the perceptual vertical seemed to lag behind the actual vertical in spite of things which were hanging in the cabin and ought to have rectified their sense of the vertical—these things simply seemed to be hanging out of the vertical. The inclinometer seemed to be in error and the water seemed to slope up towards the lee side of the heel of the vessel!

I believe that the perceptual vertical, in its lagging behind the actual vertical, was adapting, in Gibson's sense, to the slope of the vessel. Thus if the Dixons had had to adjust a rod to the vertical they would have set it out of the vertical in the direction of the tilt of the boat. All the rest follows. They report that there was no after-effect. This is understandable because the effect ought to reduce as the list increases, and reach zero at 45°; Gibson gave a maximum for this effect at 10°. The Dixons do not report any reduction in the effect

---

3.9 Luckiesh (1922) 3.10 Luckiesh (1922) 3.11 Orbison (1939) 3.12 Orbison (1939) 3.13 Orbison (1939) 3.14 Orbison (1939) 3.15 Lucas (in Fisher, 1968) 3.16 3.17 Schilder and Wechsler (1936)

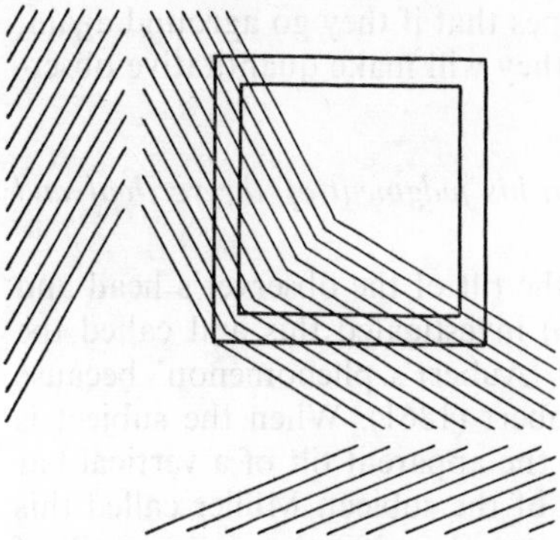

3.9

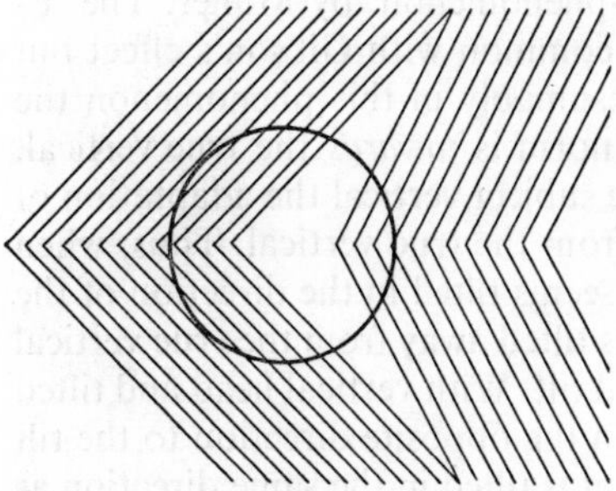

3.10

3.11

3.12

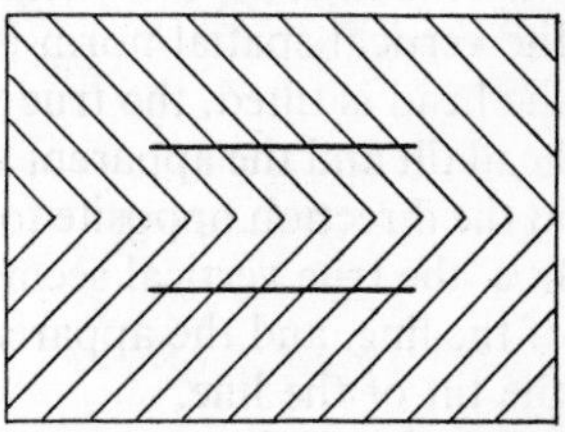

3.13

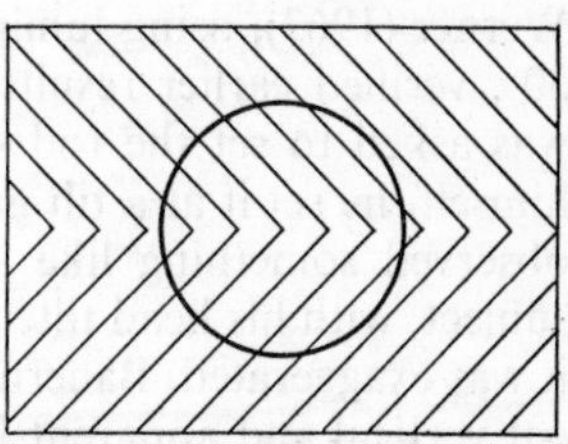

3.14

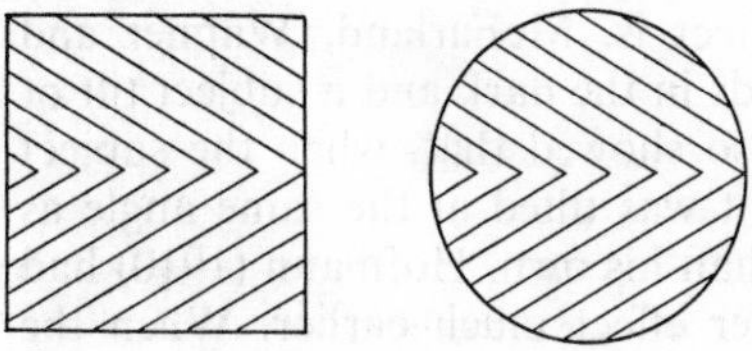

3.15

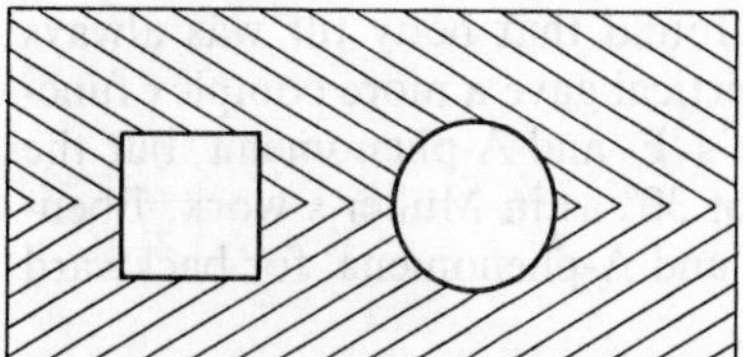

3.16

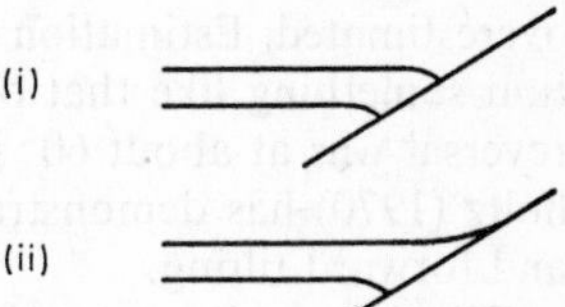

3.17

for angles larger than 10°. One hopes that if they go aground again, now accustomed to the situation, they will make quantitative observations!

The effect of tilting the observer on his judgment of the vertical and horizontal

In judging the slope of an object the tilt of the observer's head and body are important. Müller (1916) investigated this and called the peculiar misjudgments that occur 'Aubert's phenomenon' because they had also been studied by Aubert (1861). When the subject is tilted at small angles of up to 30°, the apparent tilt of a vertical bar is in the same direction as the tilt of the subject. Müller called this the 'E-phenomenon'. At tilts of greater than 30°, the apparent tilt of the vertical is in the opposite direction, namely, away from the tilt of the subject. This was called 'A-phenomenon' by Müller. The 'E-phenomenon' must have much in common with Gibson's effect but it is in the opposite direction. Presumably in this phenomenon the adaptation of the vertical spatial norm is *towards* the true vertical, whereas with the line tilted and the subject vertical the adaptation of the vertical spatial norm is *away* from the true vertical. Thus, when the head is tilted, the true vertical seems tilted in the direction of the head tilt and the apparent vertical is tilted away from the true vertical in the direction opposite to the head tilt. With vertical head and tilted line, the true vertical seems tilted in the opposite direction to the tilt of the line, and the apparent vertical is tilted in the same direction as the tilt of the line.

The fewer the cues as to the true vertical that are available to the subject the more marked this effect is. McFarland, Wapner and Werner (1962), using luminous rods in the dark and a subject tilt of 30°, verified earlier results and also showed that, when the subject was asked to set the rod so that it was tilted at the same angle as himself, he set it at a tilt greater than his own. Hofmann (1910) had observed something like this latter effect much earlier. When the subject, with his head tilted, judged the slope of a set of sloping lines it was exaggerated. Bauermeister (1964) investigated subjects' apparent vertical and apparent body tilt during tilting as far as 90° from the vertical in each direction. He found that body tilt was always overestimated. Estimation of the vertical gave a more complex function something like that of Müller's 'E- and A-phenomena' but the reversal was at about 60° instead of 30° as in Müller's work. Ebenholtz (1970) has demonstrated 'E- and A-phenomena' for backward and forward tilting.

Gibson's notions can clearly accommodate the overestimation of body tilt. The vertical spatial norm adapts towards the true vertical.

Thus a line on the *subject's* vertical meridian will appear less tilted than he. To appear at the same tilt as the subject, a line would actually have to tilt more than the subject. Wade (1968), however, was concerned with the role of the different sensory systems in judgment of the tilt. When the trunk was tilted but the head remained upright, apparent tilt was observed but it was in the opposite direction to the tilt of the body. This is to be expected, because to tilt the body clockwise leaving the head vertical is to tilt the head anticlockwise *with reference to the body*. Clearly Wade has demonstrated that stretch receptors in the neck play a part in the generation of apparent tilt. Wade (1970) later showed that the otolith organs also play a part by having supine subjects, with the head tilted with reference to the body, adjust a line so that it was parallel to the axis of the head. This sort of head tilt does not alter the direction of gravitational pull on the inner ear and no 'E-phenomenon' appeared. Wade (1969) suggests an additive model to describe how cues from the otolith organs, the neck and the trunk determine visual orientation.

Thus in judging the orientation of a line, the angles it makes with other lines, its orientation, and the orientation of the observer and his body parts, are all of them important. The process is a complex one, but perhaps one can begin to guess at what sort of process it is. I shall return to this in a later section.

Studies of the junctions of the lines in Zöllner figures

A fairly early study by Schilder and Wechsler (1936) makes some interesting detailed points which have received little attention. These writers refer to the apparent thickening of a line as it meets another, 'clubbing' as they call it. The effect increases as the angle between the lines is reduced from 90°. At first both edges of the line apparently turn in so as to make the angle larger (as in Fig. 3.17i). At angles of less than 15° one edge of the line turns in and one out (as in Fig. 3.17ii). The effect, they say, can be seen with a single pair of crossing lines but can best be seen where a group of parallel lines 1 mm thick and 1.5 mm apart meets a single oblique intercept 1 mm thick. They also observed that if a black area crossed such a group of parallels obliquely (as a black card laid across a set of parallel lines) then the ends of the lines near the edge of the card appeared turned down so as apparently to enlarge the angle between the parallels and the edge of the card. An extension of this, not mentioned by Schilder and Wechsler, is to lay such a black card next to an oblique line crossing the group of parallels. As the card is drawn away from, and parallel to, the oblique it has a curious effect on the small segments of the parallels thus exposed. They seem to turn down toward the edge of the card and become blacker. The effect persists until the card is 3 mm. away from the oblique.

Clearly, when one pays attention to the details of an angle some curious perceptual effects appear. Webster (1948) has pointed out that the effect of kinking where two lines cross can be seen at will as happening to either line, and there can be little doubt that, when an effect seems to be concentrated on a particular line, this is either because there is some good comparison by which its distortion can be judged, or else because it is crossed by many lines and so 'out-voted' by directional information coming from these lines.

THE ORBISON FIGURES

Orbison (1939) included figures like the Zöllner figure where the inducing lines (obliques) were straight and parallel. He also produced figures where the inducing lines were concentric circles or radial lines. The figures usually linked to his name are Figs. 3.18 and 3.19 but Figs. 3.20 to 3.32 are clearly of the same sort. Other figures with radial inducing lines have become known as the Hering figure (Fig. 3.33) and the Wundt figure (Fig. 3.34). Orbison advanced a theory to account for these illusions which was cast in the Gestalt mould. It proposed fields of force, presumably in the receiving perceptual apparatus, which were set up by the background patterns. Any line crossing these background lines would be distorted by the field in predictable ways. If, for example, the crossing lines were precisely at right angles to the concentric circles in Fig. 3.18 or the radial lines in Fig. 3.19 (that is, if they were radial lines or concentric circles respectively), then the forces would be perfectly balanced and there would be no distortion. But if the crossing lines did so at any angle less than a right angle then they would be distorted. The distortion would be in the direction of the lines where the forces are balanced. Thus in Fig. 3.18 the lines of the square are distorted in the direction of radial lines and in Fig. 3.19 the two parallel lines are distorted in the direction of concentric circles.

Such a theory is not worth much attention nowadays. It seems clear that perception is done by specialised units transmitting orientation, movement and so on. This simply does not fit in with the Gestalt idea of field forces, which clearly suggested a spatially organised field in the central nervous system. The organisation is not like this (see Hubel, 1963). The idea of a spatial field of

3.18 Orbison (1939) 3.19 Orbison (1939) 3.20 Ehrenstein (1925) 3.21 Orbison (1939) 3.22 Orbison (1939) 3.23 Orbison (1939) 3.24 Orbison (1939) 3.25 Ehrenstein (1925)

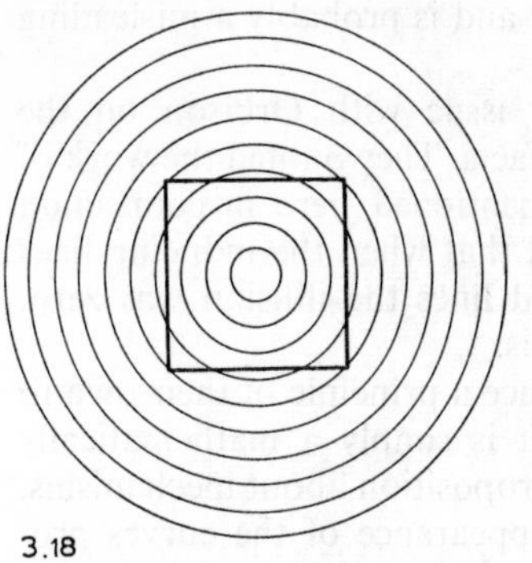

3.18

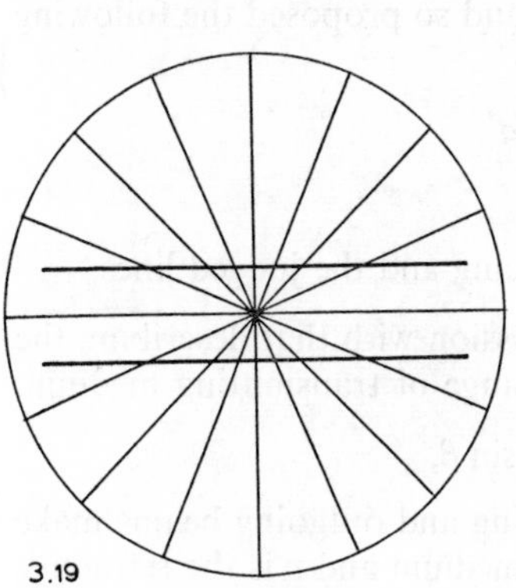

3.19

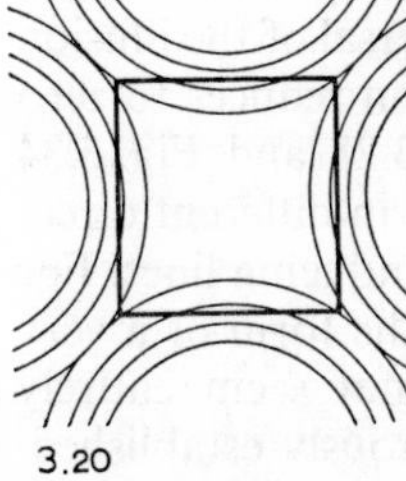

3.20

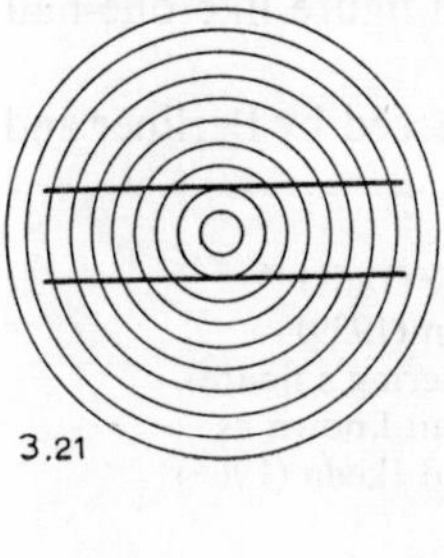

3.21

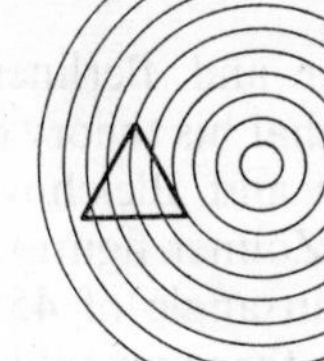

3.22

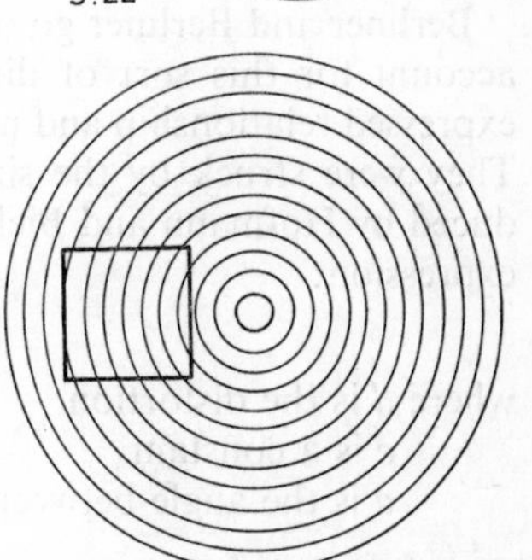

3.23

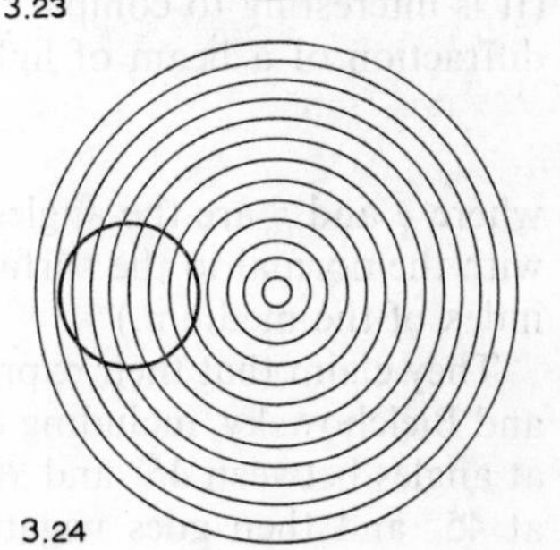

3.24

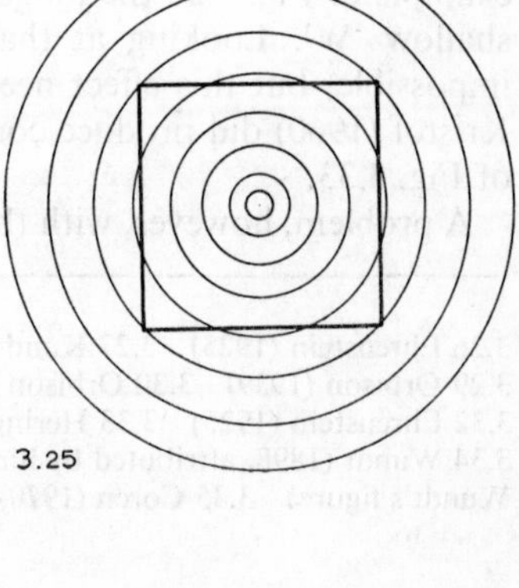

3.25

forces is therefore at most an analogy and is probably a misleading one.

Berliner and Berliner (1948) took issue with Orbison on the grounds that his theory did not fit the facts. They quoted the work of Hofmann and Bielchowsky (1909) (mentioned here in connection with the Zöllner figure) which showed that when the inducing lines were at an angle of 45° to the judged lines the illusion was zero. Orbison's theory would not predict this.

Berliner and Berliner go on to advance a principle of their own to account for this sort of distortion. It is simply a mathematically expressed relationship and makes no proposition about mechanisms. They were struck by the sinusoidal appearance of the curves produced by Hofmann and Bielchowsky and so proposed the following expression:

$$d = c \sin 4a$$

where d is the distortion
c is a constant
a is the angle between the inducing and the judged lines

(It is interesting to compare this expression with that describing the diffraction of a beam of light at a change of transmitting medium,

$$\sin \alpha = c \sin \beta,$$

where α and β are the angles the ingoing and outgoing beams make with the normal to the surface of the medium and c is the refractive index of the medium.)

They claim that their expression predicts the findings of Hofmann and Bielchowsky, including the observation of reversal of the illusion at angles between 45° and 90°. Clearly, if distortion reduces to zero at 45° and then goes negative, figures like Fig. 3.28 and Fig. 3.34 should show apparent bending of the judged lines in different directions according to the angle at which they cut the inducing lines. For example in Fig. 3.28 the judged line should take the form of a very shallow 'W'. Looking at that figure this does not seem entirely impossible, but this effect needs to be more rigorously established. Kristof (1960) did produce confirmation using a figure like one-half of Fig. 3.33.

A problem, however, with the expression proposed by Berliner and

---

3.26 Ehrenstein (1925) 3.27 Kundt (1863) 3.28 Hering (1861)
3.29 Orbison (1939) 3.30 Orbison (1939) 3.31 Orbison (1939)
3.32 Ehrenstein (1925) 3.33 Hering (1861, known as Hering's figure)
3.34 Wundt (1898, attributed by him to Hering, 1861, but known as Wundt's figure) 3.35 Coren (1970) 3.36 Morinaga and Ikeda (1965)

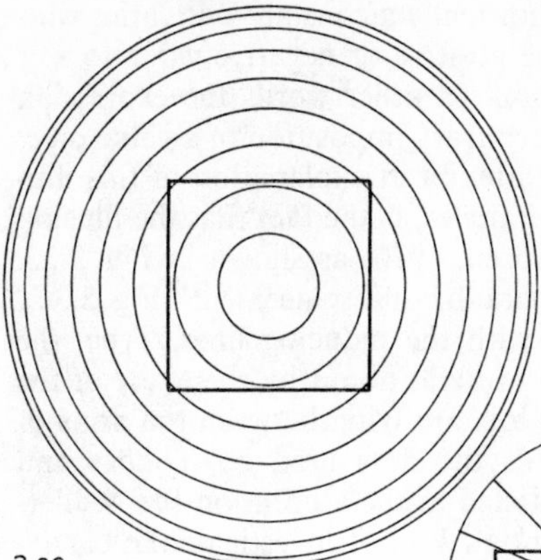

3.26

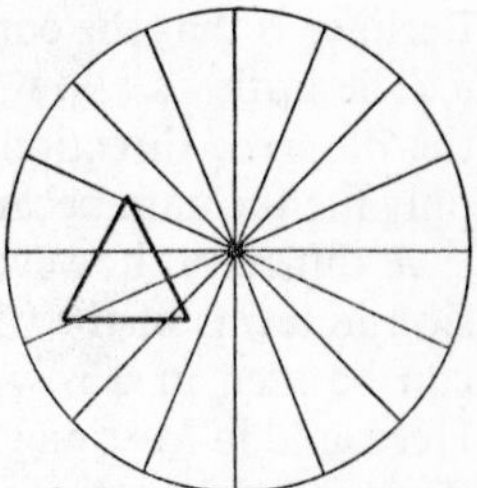

3.29

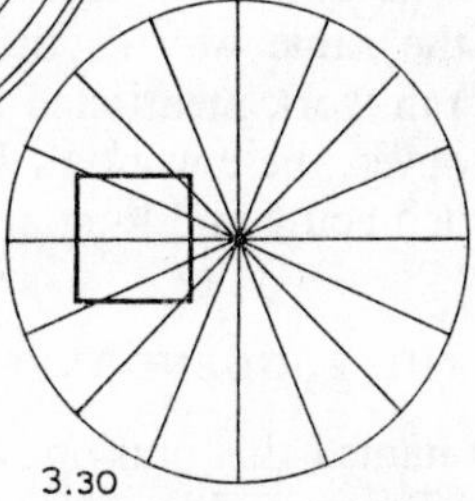

3.30

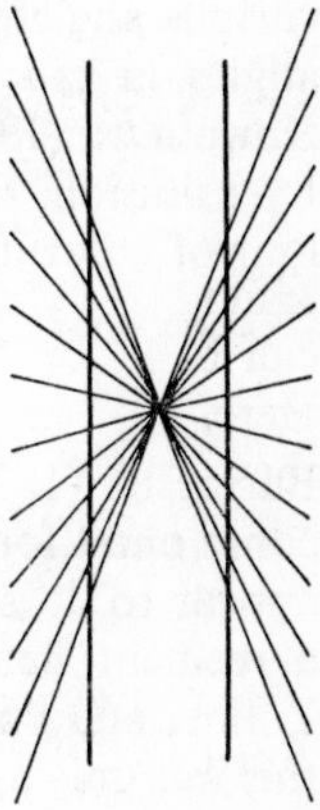

3.33

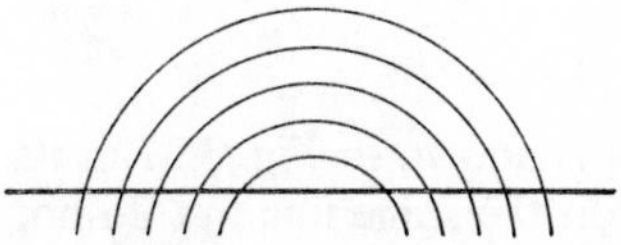

3.27

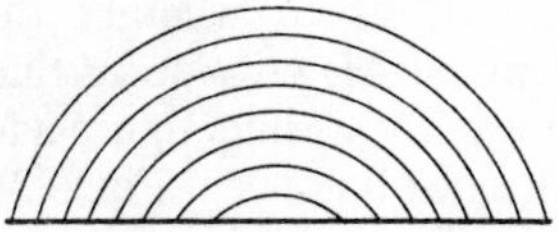

3.28

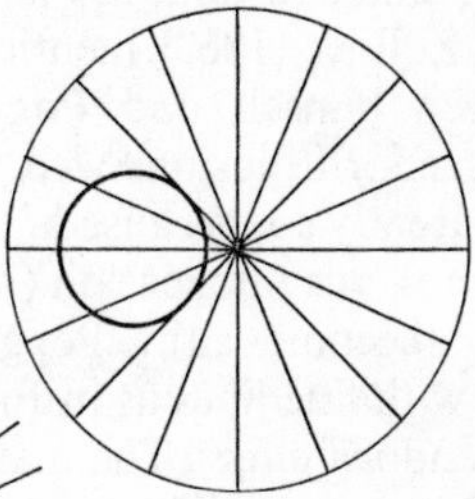

3.31

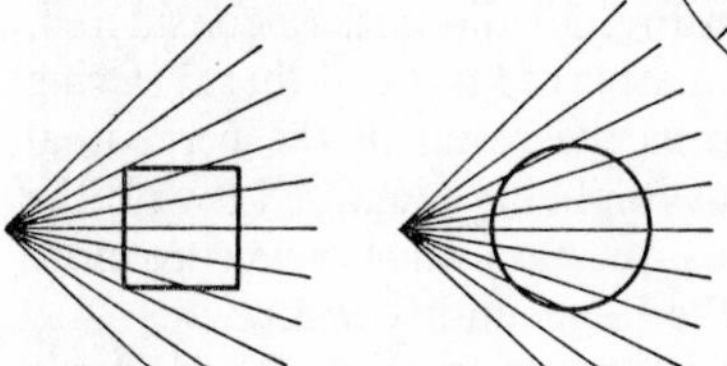

(a) (b)

3.32

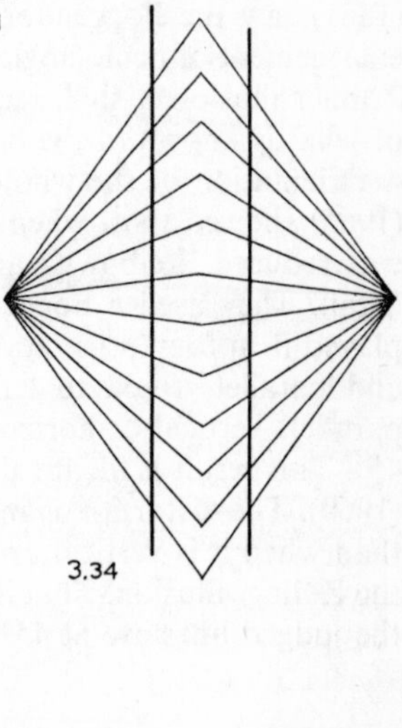

3.34

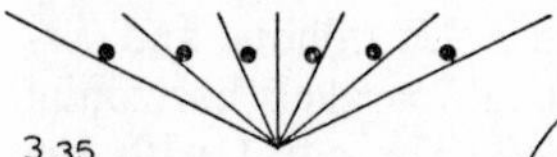

3.35

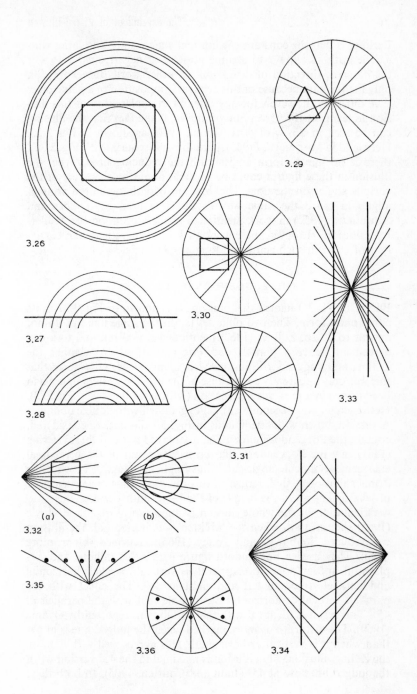

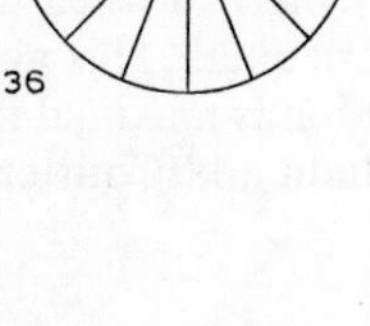

3.36

Berliner is that the constant *c* is not really a constant but varies with *a*. The authors allow *c* to assume positive or negative value to suit the *observed* direction of distortion. In other words the expression only fits the data because of this arbitrary imposition of a value on *c*.

A difficulty, however, for any attempt at explanation of this illusion in terms of the perception of angles, is the fact that the illusion can be seen in a row of dots (Coren, 1970) as shown in Fig. 3.35. Here, and in Morinaga's (1965) 'paradox of displacement' (Fig. 3.36), there is no line to form angles with the inducing lines. True, the illusion in these figures could be brought about by the effect of the various angles on the dots. The dots are lying between the arms of angles in much the same way as the dots used by Yokose and Kawamura (1952) in work mentioned in the section on the Müller-Lyer illusion. However, these workers did not investigate the behaviour of a dot in such acute and long-armed angles.

THE POGGENDORFF ILLUSION

Burmester (1896) named this illusion. It is shown in Fig. 3.37 in its commonest form. The two obliques lie on the same line but do not appear to do so. Zöllner (1860) mentioned it and referred to a disagreement between himself and Poggendorff as to whether the Zöllner and Poggendorff illusions were identical. He considered that this was only apparently so, because of the way the Zöllner figure had been drawn in a previous publication (with thick lines as in Fig. 3.2). Here each junction becomes a tiny Poggendorff with double obliques. A version drawn with fine lines as in Fig. 3.1 did not, he considered, contain the Poggendorff effect. The matter did not end there. Hering (1861) saw the Poggendorff illusion as the result of the perceptual enlargement of acute angles and thus implicitly identified it with the Zöllner illusion. I shall return to this question after reviewing more of what is known of the details of the Poggendorff effect.

Orientation of the whole illusion is important. Green and Hoyle (1965) showed that, when the 'oblique' was horizontal, the illusion was reduced. Leibowitz and Toffey (1966) confirmed this in more detail. They used a Poggendorff figure with a 45° oblique and displayed it in four orientations; parallels vertical, parallels horizontal and parallels tilted to left and right at 45°. The effect with the parallels vertical or horizontal was double that with the parallels at 45°. This result is identical with that of Obonai, reported by Oyama (1960). The distortion is more marked when the judged line is at 45° than when it is vertical or horizontal. This agrees well with data on the Zöllner illusion. That illusion is maximal in the 45° version when the judged lines are at 45° (Judd and Courten, 1905). In both these

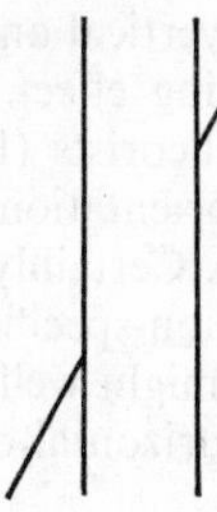
3.37

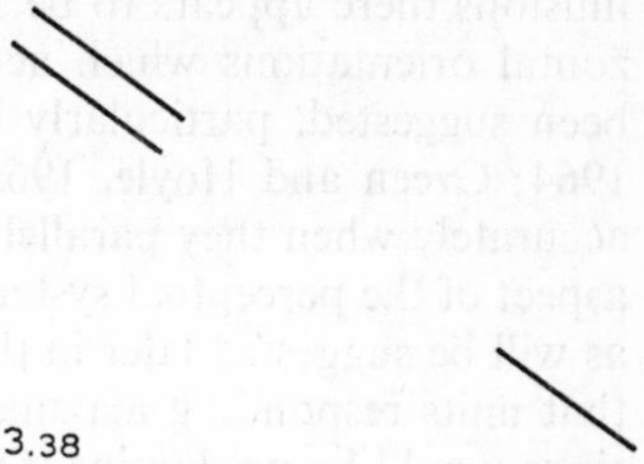
3.38

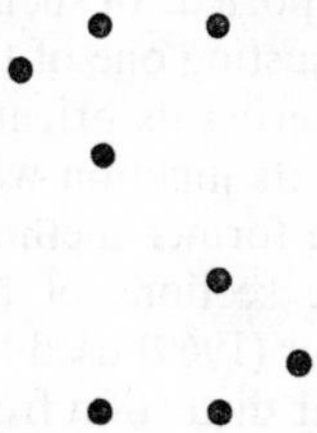
3.39

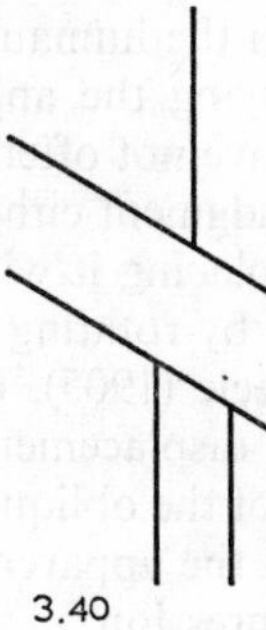
3.40

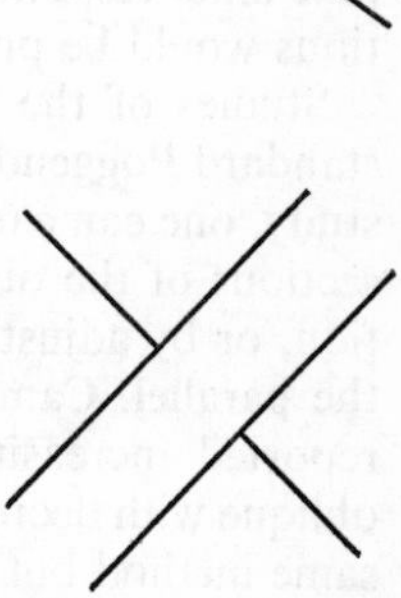
3.41

3.42

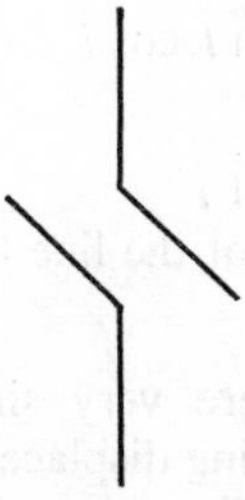
3.43

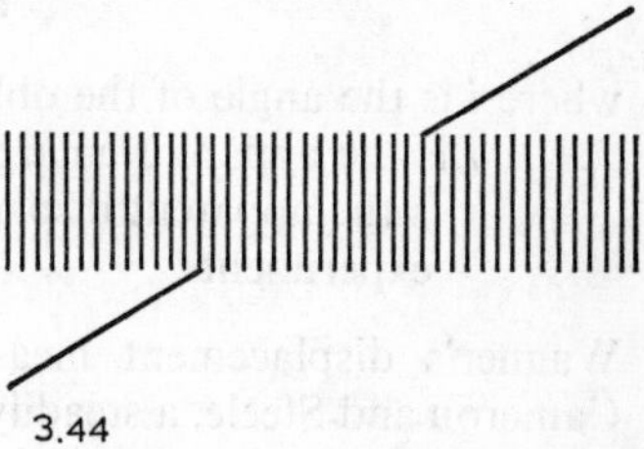
3.44

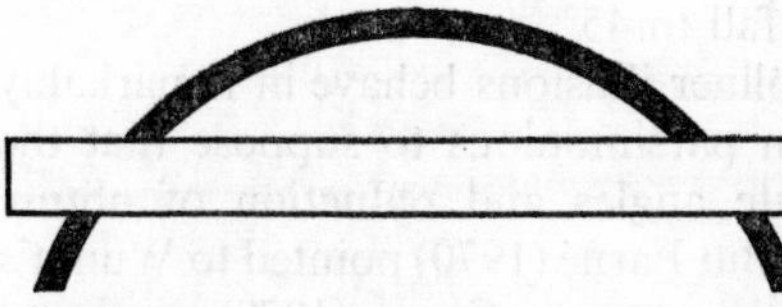
3.45

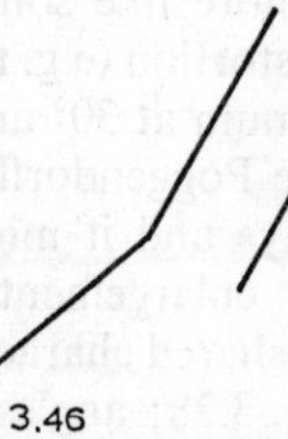
3.46

3.37 Poggendorff illusion (described by Zöllner, 1860) 3.38 Wundt (1893) 3.39 Coren (1970) 3.40 Tolanski (1964) 3.41 Fisher (1968) 3.42 Pressey and den Heyer (1968) 3.43 Pressey and den Heyer (1968) 3.44 Blix (1902) 3.45 Tolanski (1964) 3.46 Ebbinghaus (1902)

illusions there appears to be something about the vertical and horizontal orientations which acts against the distorting effect. It has been suggested, particularly by adaptation level theorists (Helson, 1964; Green and Hoyle, 1965), that we perceive orientations more accurately when they parallel these 'spatial norms'. Certainly if this aspect of the perceptual system is based on orientation-specific units, as will be suggested later in this chapter, then one might well expect that units responding maximally to vertical and horizontal orientations would be predominant in the human system.

Studies of the effect of varying the angle of the oblique in the standard Poggendorff figure have not often been reported. In such a study, one can carry out the judgment either by adjusting one of the sections of the oblique by displacing it without altering its orientation, or by adjusting it simply by rotating it about its junction with the parallel. Cameron and Steele (1905), using the former method, reported increasing apparent displacement of the sections of the oblique with decreasing angle of the oblique. Wagner (1969) used the same method but then derived the apparent angular distortion from his results by means of the expression:

$$\tan t = \frac{2x.\sin^2 i}{1-2x.\sin i.\cos i}$$

where i is the angle of the obliques

t is the apparent enlargement of i

x is the apparent displacement of the line found in the experiment

Wagner's displacement measures were very similar to those of Cameron and Steele, a steadily increasing displacement with decreasing angle. When converted to angular distortions, however, Wagner's data are more like some of the data from other figures involving angular distortion (e.g. the Zöllner figure). They show a rise from 10° to a maximum at 30° and then fall to 45°.

Thus the Poggendorff and Zöllner illusions behave in remarkably similar ways and it might seem parsimonious to suppose that the perceptual enlargement of acute angles and reduction of obtuse angles is a shared characteristic. But Farné (1970) pointed to Wundt's (1893) Fig. 3.38; angles are not necessary. Coren (1970) produced Fig. 3.39; lines are not even necessary. An illustration of Tolanski's (1960) is also difficult to accommodate. If the illusion is due to perceptual enlargement of angles, then the process should involve the rotation outwards of the arms of the angles. In Fig. 3.40 the upper vertical line, if continued downward, would go exactly halfway between the lower lines. This does not appear to be the case *but the lines seem all three still to be parallel.* This point is made by Pressey and den Heyer (1968). Fisher's (1968a) figure (Fig. 3.41) is similar in that the parallels are not vertical. Here the oblique seems out of line even though the angle is a right angle. Other work by Fisher, which will be reported in the next section, shows that the perceptual distortion of an angle depends on its orientation. This is clearly relevant to this figure and to changes with orientation in the angular distortions in general.

Restle (1969) also makes a difficulty for an interpretation simply in terms of acute angles by referring to Figs. 3.42 and 3.43. The former, according to him, gives the reverse of the usual Poggendorff effect, even though it contains acute angles, and the latter still gives the effect even though it contains no acute angles. However, it should be added that Pressey and den Heyer claimed only a smaller effect in Fig. 3.42 than in 3.43, not a reversal. It is interesting, and a comment on the progress we have made in understanding the geometrical illusions, that Judd (1899) made the same points as Restle for much the same reasons! Nevertheless, a point in favour of the view that the Poggendorff illusion is wholly accounted for by the manner of perception of angles is Koboyashi's (1956). He drew a figure in such a way that, very near the junctions of the obliques with the parallels, the obliques were bent, so that the final tiny portion made a smaller angle with the parallel than did the rest of the line. The illusion disappeared. In such a figure, presumably, the misleading contribution of the part of the lines near the apices of the angles to the total information about orientation of the lines, is altered. The parallels are therefore seen in their correct orientation. But in spite of this last study it seems to me that the bulk of the evidence points to two influences operating in the Poggendorff illusion, an angular effect and another one. The other one is perhaps best shown in Fig. 3.38 where the lower line seems to be shifted bodily, without change in orientation, and the illusion seems to be a misjudgment of the orientation of a sloping line which can take place in the absence of angles, or indeed of any other stimulus.

In conclusion, the three remaining figures of this type need a little comment. Blix's figure (Fig. 3.44) might be taken as evidence against the principle of the perceptual enlargement of acute angles because it gives the reverse of the usual effect. But this is only so if one regards the set of vertical bars as a plain rectangular area. This is not justified, because if the figure is reduced so that the separate vertical lines are hardly distinguishable and look indeed like a grey rectangular area, then the normal effect is seen. The reverse effect is seen only when the lines are plainly perceptually separable, in which case the obliques form an obtuse angle with them which is perceptually reduced. Fig. 3.45 is a more complex and slightly life-like example of the effect. It is not unlike Piaget's figure (Fig. 3.91) and each may have elements of both the Poggendorff illusion and the distortion of arcs. Fig. 3.46 is very like Restle's but shows how the effect is partly thrown on to the parallels when they no longer lie on one of the spatial norms.

SIMPLE ANGULAR FIGURES

Many studies have been done with simple angular figures which have often been understood as the basic elements of the more complex angular distortion figures such as the Zöllner and Poggendorff illusions. The reader must form his own opinion whether this interpretation is justified. As has already been shown, there are difficulties in this for the Poggendorff figure at least.

Ogasawara (1956, quoted by Oyama, 1960) obtained for Fig. 3.47 results very similar to those obtained by Morinaga (1933) for the Zöllner illusion. Subjects were required to adjust the upper line so that it appeared to lie on the same line as an arm of the angle. The angle was varied and a maximum error of alignment was found at 25°–30°, which reduced to zero at 90°. He also showed that when the lower oblique line was crossed by several parallel lines, instead of simply forming an angle with one of them, the illusion increased with the number of such parallel lines. It seems that the shape of the function of the illusion with variation of angle was the same however. Morinaga (1932) investigated the effect of orientation on Ebbinghaus's figure (3.48) and found that the illusion (the error in alignment of the dash with the oblique line) was maximal when both lines lay in the same quadrant, neither being on a spatial norm. This is predictable from other results quoted so far. Orientation of lines lying on spatial norms seems to be more accurately perceived and the maximum illusion for angular figures generally seems to be found with angles of less than 90°.

Jastrow's (1891) early study of angles emphasised the underestimation of obtuse angles and actually claimed that acute angles were underestimated too. He fitted this latter claim into an explanation of the Zöllner and Poggendorff figures in terms of angular underestimation by saying that when an obtuse and acute angle are adjacent, as they almost always are in these figures, the under-

3.47 Oyama (1960) 3.48 Ebbinghaus (1902) 3.49 Jastrow (1891) 3.50 Blix (1902) 3.51 Green and Hoyle (1965) 3.52 Wundt (1898) 3.53 Oppel (1855) 3.54 Titchener (1901) 3.55 Lipps (1897) 3.56 Lipps (1897) 3.57 Wundt (1898) 3.58 Jastrow (1891) 3.59 Helmholtz (1856) 3.60 Blix (1902)

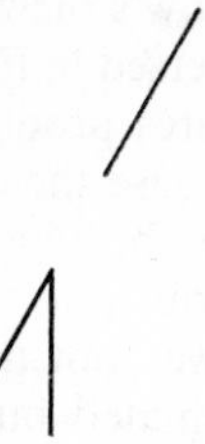
3.47

3.48
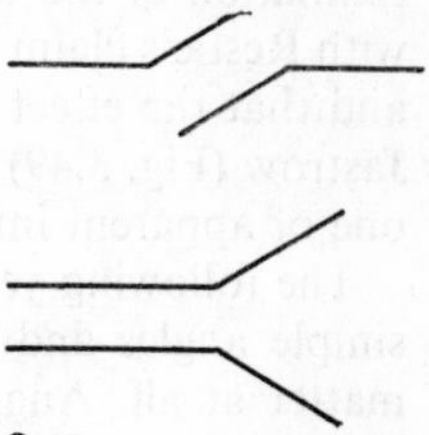
3.49
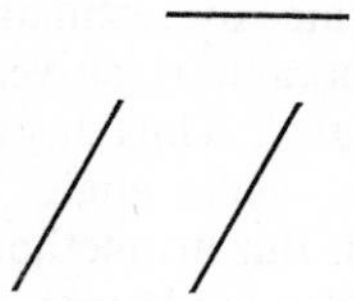
3.50
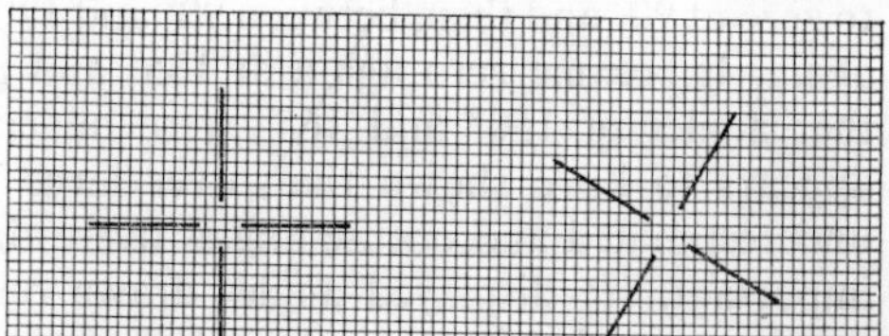
3.51

3.52
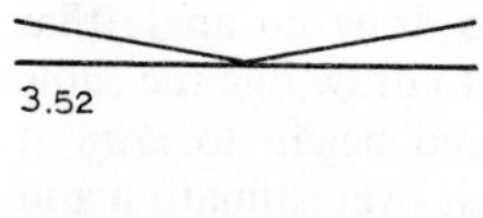
3.53
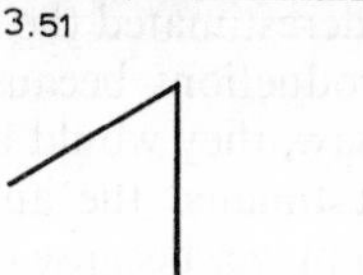
3.54

3.55
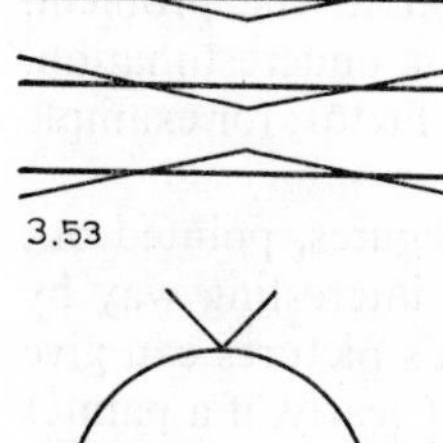
3.56
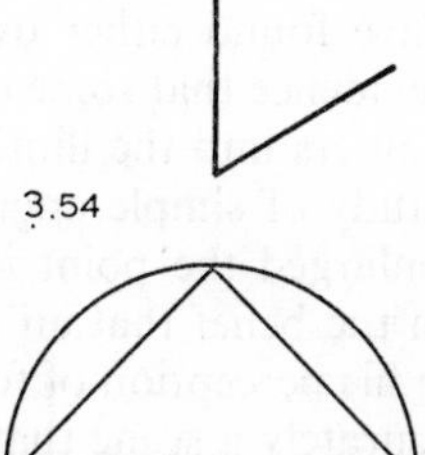
3.57
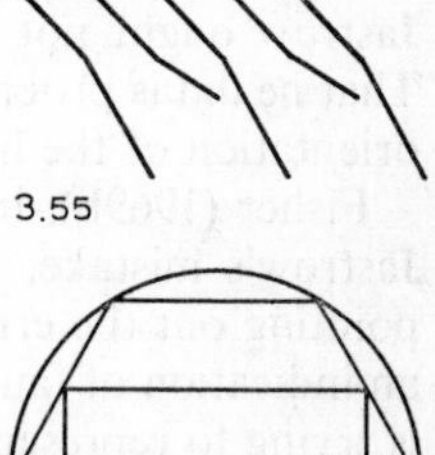
3.58
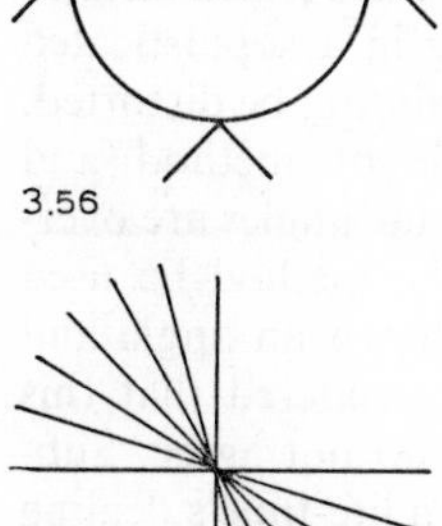
3.59
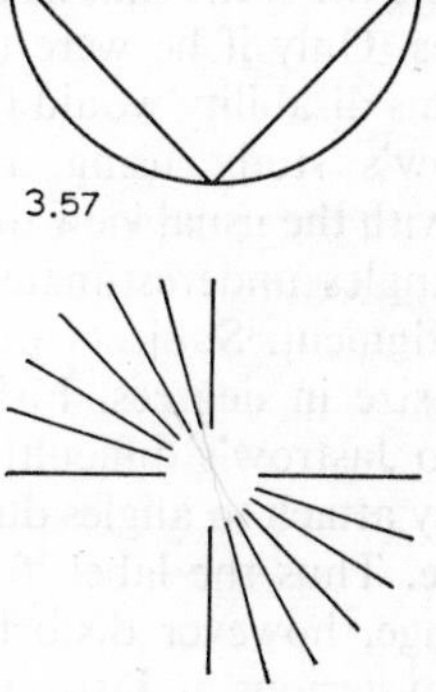
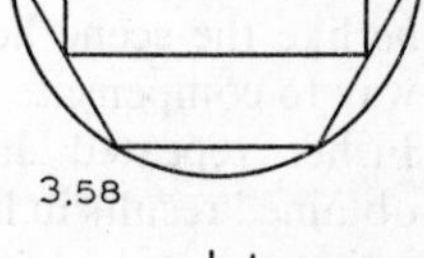
3.60

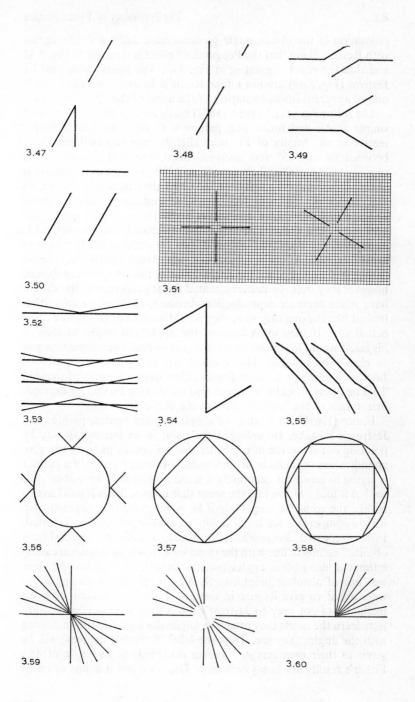

estimation of the obtuse angle predominates. Jastrow's view agrees with Restle's claim that the Poggendorff effect is reversed in Fig. 3.42 and that the effect is greatest in Fig. 3.43. The figures produced by Jastrow (Fig. 3.49) are not unlike Restle's. In each case the effect is one of apparent inward rotation of the arms of the obtuse angles.

The following year Jastrow (1892) made an experimental study of simple angles and found that judgment of them was not a simple matter at all. Angles of 15° were slightly overestimated but those between 30° and 75° were *under*estimated. The underestimation fell to zero at 90° and then, between 90° and 120°, became overestimation again. It became zero again at 135° and then became negative, so that angles of 150° and 165° were underestimated. Thus Jastrow appears to have shown that, over large ranges, acute angles are underestimated and obtuse angles overestimated. But his method is important. He displayed angles drawn on circular cards with one arm horizontal. After the subject had viewed each card it was covered and he had to reproduce the angle. Now by this procedure, subjects, however they over- or underestimated the angle perceptually, should have made accurate reproductions because, to draw an angle that looked like the one they saw, they would have to draw one the same actual size. If they overestimated the angle and began to *draw* it bigger, it would look even bigger because of their overestimation and so clearly be too big. This method will not get at the problem. Jastrow ought not to have found either over- or underestimation. That he did is probably evidence that some other factor, for example orientation of the lines, enters into the illusion.

Fisher (1969b), in a study of simple angular figures, pointed out Jastrow's mistake. He enlarged the point in an interesting way by pointing out the error in the belief that an artist's pictures can give an indication of faults in his perception of form. Clearly, if a painter is trying to represent accurately a scene that he sees, he will paint it so that it looks *to him* like the scene that he sees. Thus it will have to *be* like the scene he sees. Only if he were trying in a sophisticated way to compensate for his disability would the painting be distorted. Fisher repeated Jastrow's study using a different method and obtained results in line with the usual view that acute angles are overestimated and obtuse angles underestimated. The method he used was one of absolute judgment. Subjects were shown an angle and were asked to give its size in degrees. Fisher considered that this method was not prey to Jastrow's difficulties. I do not agree. Subjects learn the labels they attach to angles during a life-time's dealing with the angles they see. Thus the label 'forty-five degrees' will be given to their own image, however distorted, of an angle of 45°. Fisher's results are as mysterious as Jastrow's and it is just as much a mystery that they follow the majority opinion as that Jastrow's do not. Fisher's angles were side facing (that is their bisector would lie on the horizontal) but that was very little different from the orientation of Jastrow's angles. Fisher followed this experiment by one similar to Jastrow's, using reproduction of the angle by the subject. He obtained results like those of Jastrow and, in my opinion, they are as much a mystery as Jastrow's.

Beery (1968) made the same mistake even more obviously, because subjects merely reproduced an angle with the angle itself in view. He obtained results very like Jastrow's. The results reported by Blakemore, Carpenter and Georgeson (1970) are described in the next section. They showed overestimation of acute angles and a lesser underestimation of obtuse angles.

Fisher's study continued by turning to the question of orientation of the angles. For side-facing angles (bisector horizontal) he found overestimation between 0° and 90° falling to zero at these limits, and a very similar pattern, overestimation, for angles between 90° and 180°. For up- and down-facing angles (bisector vertical) he found overestimation up to 45° with inflexion then to underestimation which persisted as far as 125°. Here overestimation began again which fell to zero at 180°. This is a very interesting finding and may throw light on a discrepancy among studies of the Zöllner illusion mentioned in that section.

We have on the one hand studies like those of Hofmann and Bielchowski (1909), Gibson (1937a) and Day (1965) in which the maximum overestimation is at a small angle of 10°–20° followed by an inflexion at about 45° to reach a maximum under-estimation between 45° and 90°. On the other hand, the studies of Wallace and Crampin (1969) and Morinaga (1933) show a maximum at a slightly larger angle and overestimation continues to 90°. Maheux, Townsend and Gresock (1970) show a steady increase of overestimation to 60° and no inflexion. Now Fisher has demonstrated an inflexion for up- and down-facing angles at 45° but not for side-facing angles. Perhaps the orientation of the angles used is relevant. Were the angles used by Hofmann and Bielchowski, Gibson, and Day up- and down-facing? With the exception of the horizontal judgment in the study of Hofmann and Bielchowski, they were, because their displays all consisted of vertical or near-vertical lines crossed by sloping lines. The angles used by Wallace and by Maheux and others faced the side. Morinaga's, unfortunately for this argument, faced up and down.

So the effect of orientation is hard to tease out, especially with the doubts I have already expressed about Fisher's method, and it is complicated by the fact that, in the ordinary Zöllner illusion for example, although for small angles the acute angles face up and down, as the angles become larger they face more to the side. However, there is little doubt that two factors must be taken into account in thinking about the judgment of angles, one has to do with an effect taking place in the angle itself and the other has to do with its orientation. In the usual illusion figures these will interact in a complex way. There is certainly room for more research to disentangle these effects, and the notion of specifically tuned orientation analysers in the visual system may be relevant to their disentanglement. It may be, for example, that a majority of such analysers are tuned to vertical or horizontal orientations. Maffei and Campbell (1970) have demonstrated a greater evoked potential in humans for horizontal and vertical than for oblique gratings. This adds further complication to interactions between analysers of various specific tuning during complex visual stimulation, a notion which is amplified in the next section.

Three more studies of the effect of orientation ought just to be mentioned, though to connect them with work so far mentioned seems too speculative to be useful. Weene and Held (1966) asked subjects to place a line so that it bisected a right angle which was placed in various orientations. Subjects achieved very accurate bisection when the correct bisector was either vertical or horizontal but, when it was not, they made an error always towards the horizontal. In other words, they always set the line a little less steeply sloping than it actually was. Obonai and Asai (1957, reported by Oyama, 1960) obtained different results for a rather different situation. Subjects fixated a dot and then adjusted a line offset from the dot so that the two were in line. Subjects' errors in adjusting the line were always in the direction of the nearer spatial norm.

Weintraub and Virsu (1971) presented subjects with pairs of lines inclined at an angle to one another, but some distance apart (each lay 60 mm from the point of intersection and the display was viewed at 50 cm), and asked them to mark the point at which the lines, if extended, would meet. In one condition, the angle formed by the lines lay symmetrically across the subject's vertical and in the other condition one of the lines lay on the subject's vertical. Thus for small angles the conditions were very similar, but for large ones they became more and more different as the angle in the second condition became more and more side-facing. The results reflected this. For small angles, for both conditions, there was underestimation, with a maximum at the smallest angle used (5°), falling to an inflexion to overestimation between 45° and 60°. In the first condition, this overestimation of larger angles persisted to 180°, but in the second condition there was another inflexion between 90° and 120°. Weintraub and Virsu calculated that the error that subjects were making was one of perceiving the lines as closer to the nearer spatial norm than they actually were. It is interesting that, if one regards the display used here as an angular display, the distortions are in the opposite direction to that expected on the basis of studies of angles with actual apices. One way of separating orientation and angular effects may be to set the lines well apart as Weintraub and Virsu did.

Misalignment of sloping lines might well be the basis of Fig. 3.50 where the oblique lines are in line with the ends of the horizontal line but appear to be rotated towards the vertical. The figure (3.51) produced by Green and Hoyle (1965) is another example of this. The arms of the oblique (right-hand) cross all are apparently rotated in the direction of the nearer spatial norm. This effect can just be seen without the hatched background, but for some reason the background emphasises it. As will be seen later, Green and Hoyle use this figure in their argument for adaptation-level theory as a likely source of explanation of illusions. It is certainly a puzzling figure because the lines of the right-hand cross are rotated in precisely the opposite direction to what one would expect from the simple application of the principle of perceptual enlargement of acute angles. Take the upper arm of the right-hand cross, for example. It makes a small acute angle (about 30°) with the vertical background lines and a large acute angle with the horizontal background lines. Thus, the enlargement effect on the angle made by this line with the vertical lines should, by other evidence, be close to the maximum. In fact, the angle is perceptually reduced. Clearly, when there are 'inducing' lines in both directions their effects cancel out leaving only the effect which is found with no lines at all, namely that demonstrated by Obonai and Asai, apparent rotation towards the nearer spatial norm.

Green and Hoyle (1965) point out that the right-hand cross of Fig. 3.51 looks blacker than the left-hand cross. This would follow from work quoted in the next section showing the effect of fixating a grating on the contrast threshold of a differently oriented grating subsequently viewed. The contrast threshold of the test grating is raised if the orientation of the inspection grating is close to it. Thus, in Fig. 3.51 the contrast threshold would be higher for the left-hand cross because the background lines coincide in direction with it. This is not the case for the right-hand cross. The contrast threshold for this cross is lower and it therefore looks blacker.

To end this section, brief mention will be made of a number of other figures. Figs. 3.52, 3.53 and 3.54 seem to be straightforward examples of the perceptual enlargement of acute angles and complimentary diminution of obtuse angles. Fig. 3.55 is a less obvious instance. Here each line is like a section of a Zöllner figure containing a part of each of two parallels and an oblique joining them. The perceptual reduction of the obtuse angles leads to apparent rotation of the centre section which prevents the five centre sections from being seen as parallel. (This is exactly the same sort of rotation as is suggested for the Zöllner figure by Maheux, Townsend and Gresock, 1960.) This figure could also be seen as an example of the perceptual system taking a sort of average of directional information as in the Fraser (1908) figures (see pp. 91–4). Thus, the invocation of an angular effect is not really necessary here.

Figs. 3.56, 3.57 and 3.58 are slightly less straightforward examples of the same effect because one arm of each angle is a curve. The same principle suffices, however, to give the observed slight bulging of the circles. In Fig. 3.56 the effect apparently presses the circle inward near the apex of the angle and so makes it seem to bulge between the angles. In Figs. 3.57 and 3.58 the enlargement of the acute angles made by the circle cause it to bulge outward. This seems to be taking advantage of the vagueness of the concept of angular enlargement to predict the same effect from the operation of the principle in opposite directions, but a careful look at Figs. 3.56 and 3.57 will show that the circles do not seem to be the same shape. In Fig. 3.56 the circle looks rather square, whereas in Fig. 3.57 it seems to have kinks near the apices of the angles. This distinction would be a difficult one to test, but with computer-operated visual display such a test could now be possible, and ought to be done.

Figs. 3.59 and 3.60 could be placed either here or in the section on filled and unfilled extents. In these figures the perceptual overestimation of filled extents and the perceptual overestimation of acute angles are indistinguishable.

ORIENTATION ANALYSERS AND THE PERCEPTION OF ANGLES

The view has already begun to emerge that, in most of the illusions described in this chapter, two kinds of influence can be seen. One derives from the junction of two lines to form an angle and the other from the orientation of the lines themselves, particularly with reference to the spatial norms. In this section I shall amplify these two notions and it will be clear that I see them as principles likely to be involved in a successful explanation of illusions.

The idea, put forward by Maheux, Townsend and Gresock, of the building up of a notion of direction from various sorts of information is echoed and elaborated by Andrews (1967a,b) and by Wallace (1969). Both had available a great deal more physiological evidence of how orientation is perceived than was available to Maheux, Townsend and Gresock in 1960. Wallace's idea was that the apex of an angle has a distorting effect on its arms which decreases with distance from the apex, and that the perceived orientation of the arm of an angle will be the average of all the direction-information picked up from it. This will include some information relatively uninfluenced by the angle and some, near the apex, greatly influenced (in the direction of making the arm of, for example, an acute angle apparently form a larger angle than it really does). Wallace demonstrated the effect of distance from the apex by measuring the distortion in Zöllner figures where there was a gap between the inducing lines and the judged line. When the gap was greater than 1° of visual angle there was no effect. The illusion increased steadily as the gap decreased from 1° to zero.

There is good evidence of orientation-specific units in the perceptual system. McCollough's (1965) observations sparked off current interest in the topic. Her subjects fixated a horizontal grating under red light for a short interval followed by a vertical grating under green light for a similar interval. Presented immediately afterwards with a composite grating with vertical bars in one half and horizontal bars in the other, subjects saw only a green after-image colour in the horizontal grating and only a red after-image colour in the vertical grating. This seemed to show that different analysers were adapted by different orientations (and, by the way, that each of these analysers could deal with a large range of colour).

Later work using various threshold measures has elaborated this basic point. Campbell and Kulikowski (1966), for example, showed that the effect of one grating on the incremental threshold for another was maximal when they were at the same orientation, and was reduced to half the maximum value when their orientation differed by 12°. Houlihan and Sekuler (1968) studied the masking effect of a grating on a test line exposed for 10 m/sec after an interval of 10 m/sec from the switching off of the grating. There was no effect when the angle between the grating and the test line was more than 45°. Blakemore, Carpenter and Georgeson (1970) completed the connection between this sort of work and illusions. The work belongs in the section on simple angular figures, but is described here because of its relevance to this argument. Subjects viewed a simple side-facing angle and were asked to adjust a line, set apart from the angle, so that it appeared parallel to one of the arms. For acute angles the line was set too steep and for obtuse angles, though the effect was less, the line was set too level. In other words, subjects overestimated acute angles and to a lesser extent underestimated obtuse angles. The chief interest of these authors, however, is in directional analysers in the visual system. Accepting the notions of specifically tuned orientation analysers, they proposed that lateral in-

3.61

3.62

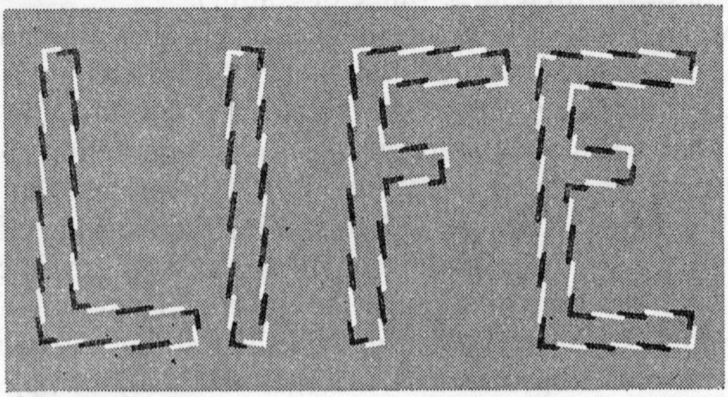

3.63

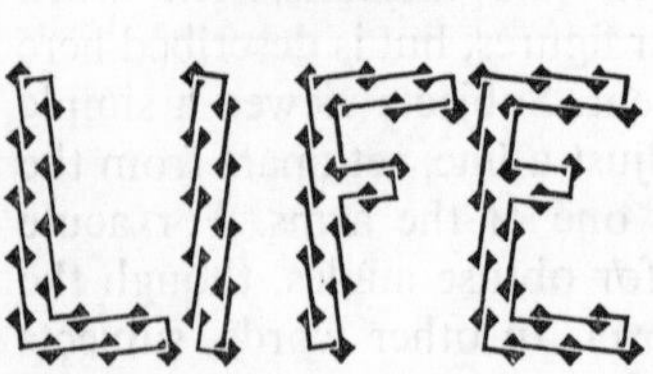

3.64 3.65

3.61–65 Fraser (1908)

hibition processes between analysers constitute the interactive effect of lines meeting at an angle. This is not lateral inhibition in the spatial sense as used theoretically by Ganz (see Chapter 5), but inhibition by one orientation receptor of other orientation receptors whose preferred orientation is close to its own. Thus, if the perceptual system computes the orientation of a stimulus from a population of differently tuned analysers, and some are artificially depressed and distort whatever critical parameter of the distribution the system uses, there will be a misjudgment of orientation.

Preliminary experiments in my own laboratory using a method very like that of the above authors confirm their results. They also show that the greater the length of the arm of the angle the less it is distorted. Thus, using an acute angle with one long and one short arm, when a line is placed by the subject in line with an arm but set apart from it, the placements for the short arm show a much greater apparent enlargement of the angle than those for the long arm.

Harris and Gibson (1968) suggest a simple mechanism which would perform the function of an orientation analyser. A unit would perform this function if it were connected to two points on the retina which were fairly widely separated and arranged so that, when an edge fell on or near both points, the unit fired. Edges falling on only one of the points, or neither, would not fire the unit. There is no obvious reason why the orientation analysers described by Hubel and Wiesel (Hubel, 1963) should not work in this way. Evans, Hoffman, Arnoult and Zinser (1968) describe a fascinating computer simulation of a process something like this which is worth reading. The explicit and detailed connection of all this work with the various illusion figures will be a notable programme of research.

We are left, then, with a notion of orientation units in the perceptual system tuned each to its own relatively limited band of orientations. Presumably any particular line fires a large population of such units, some maximally and some sub-maximally, very much in the same way as we imagine, in a three-colour theory of colour vision, a particular hue fires a similarly composed population of hue-specific units. This idea has been used before with reference to spatial frequency and size contrast. It is still a vague idea, but such common ground is likely to be very productive of research interest.

To all this can now be added the contribution of the spatial norms. The work of Maffei and Campbell (1970) was quoted earlier in which a greater evoked potential was demonstrated for horizontal and vertical than for oblique gratings. This reinforces the possibility that, of all the different tunings of orientation analysers, those corresponding to the spatial norms tend to predominate. Thus, when an oblique stimulus line is viewed, the average value used in

3.66

3.66 Fraser (1908)

the computation of orientation will be biased by predominance of activity from those analysers whose preferred orientations are the spatial norms. The average will be pushed towards the norm, hence the frequently observed distortion of the percept towards the norm.

The interaction of these two effects, angular effects and spatial norm effects, must be complex indeed, but it seems to me that they deserve study. In many figures they will interact with other effects, for example those of spatial frequency mentioned in Chapter 2; the use of extremely simple figures in investigation of all these effects will probably be advantageous.

3.67

3.67 Fraser (1908)

ILLUSIONS OF DIRECTION

Wallace's notion of how directional information is processed can be applied to two illusions which are probably the most forceful of all illusions. I shall deal first with Fraser's (1908) 'twisted cord' illusion, so called because it consists of something rather like a twisted cord on a chequered background. It can, in fact, be obtained by laying a twisted cord on a grey or coloured background of chequered material. The effect is that shown in Fig. 3.61. A glance at Fig. 3.62

shows that the check pattern alone, without the twisted cord, is not enough. Fig. 3.63, on the other hand, shows that the 'twisted cord' configuration alone gives some of the effect, but the more of the background that is included the greater the effect (Figs. 3.64 and 3.65). Fig. 3.64 shows the basic unit of all Fraser's figures, a line with a triangle at either end. This appears in both black and white in Fig. 3.61 and on the most forceful of all Fraser's figures, Fig. 3.66. Fraser calls this a 'directional unit' and clearly it is very effective in misleading the directional analysers of the visual system. In the earlier figures the 'directional unit' is sloping and slope is perceived. In Fig. 3.66 the lines of the directional units are sections of spirals, and spirals are perceived instead of the circles that exist. (Fraser gives detailed instructions for drawing this figure which can easily be followed by even a moderate draftsman.) The only way most people can convince themselves that this figure does indeed contain circles is by following them round with a finger. The spiral can be reduced to the same form as Fig. 3.64, though Fraser did not do this. It is shown in Fig. 3.68. It can also be reduced to the line form (Fig. 3.69) with a consequent reduction of the effect. Fraser produced several variations on Fig. 3.66, for example Fig. 3.67.

Why Fraser's 'directional units' should have the effect they do would make a fascinating study. Is a triangular end essential or will a semicircle do? Is there a shape which works better than either?

The second of these extremely effective illusions is that called by Pierce (1898) the 'illusion of the kindergarten patterns' because evidently it was fairly often seen when this particular pattern was made in weaving by kindergarten pupils. The effect is striking and rather difficult to describe (see Fig. 3.70). It is as if the columns of black and white rectangles strayed from the vertical by an angle of

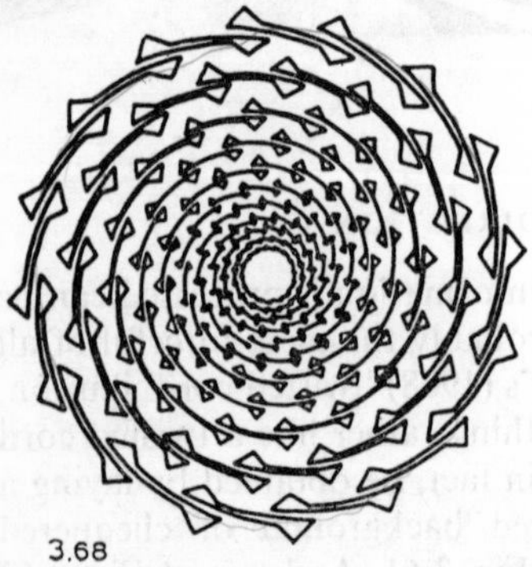

3.68

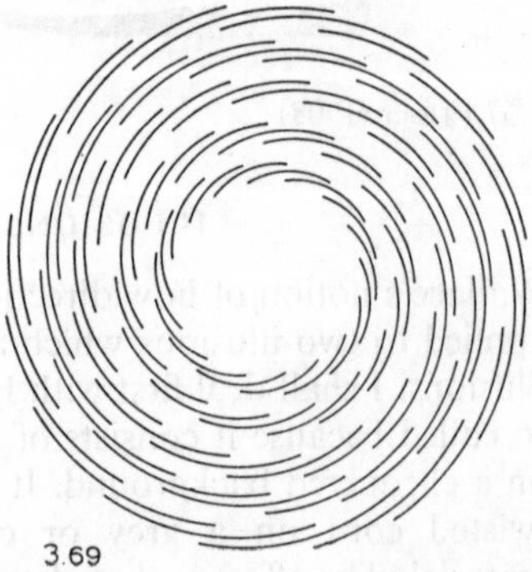

3.69

as much as 20°, but they do not do so at the point of fixation. This gives a rather unstable effect as the eye moves over the figure. It is as if the edges of the columns were sliding over and under one another. Letting the eyes go out of focus enhances the effect.

The illusion can be reduced to its basic element which is shown in Fig. 3.71. The effect is much less here, but it is one of perceived slope of the vertical lines outwards at the top and inwards at the bottom. The illusion has been called the Münsterberg illusion since Münsterberg (1897) produced one of the early theories accounting for it. He called it the *verschobene Schachbrettfigur* or 'shifted chequer-board figure'. It is also called the 'shifted quadrilaterals'.

Pierce considered that the illusion was due to 'irradiation' but did not define this term in detail. He saw the white areas as 'boring into' the black areas and so presumably moving the apparent positions of the contours. Such an effect is perfectly believable. It is this sort of effect that appears in Fig. 3.72 which was published by Helmholtz. Tolanski calls this the Helmholtz irradiation illusion. The small white square surrounded by black appears larger than the small black square surrounded by white, though they are in fact the same size. This effect could be seen as a consequence of asymmetrical intensification of edges by Mach bands (see Chapter 8). It bears some resemblance to Fig. 2.54, which is taken here as an example of the Delboeuf illusion. Fig. 3.73 is a more elaborate version.

Pierce saw this effect as operating asymmetrically. At the upper part of the line AB in Fig. 3.71 the white would 'bore' into the black and so push the black/white edge to the left. The line BC would in a similar way be pushed to the right, giving the whole line AC an apparent anticlockwise rotation. Since the same thing would happen in each section of the left-hand half of the figure, the whole central line would be apparently rotated anticlockwise. Conversely, the central line of the right-hand half of the figure would be rotated clockwise. A clear suggestion of the Zöllner figure can be seen here since lines joining the centres of each pair of attached squares would form parallel oblique hatching of the kind found in that figure. The illusion is in the right direction too.

By their very nature not many of the geometrical optical illusions contain large areas of black and white bordering one another. If Pierce's 'boring in' concept could be demonstrated on many more figures it would be interesting. As it is, it is limited as an explanation.

Fraser saw the 'twisted cord' illusions and the 'shifted chequer-board' as examples of the same sort of effect and showed how the former could be derived from the latter. The process of transition from one to another is seen in Plate I. Starting from the 'shifted chequerboard' (1) Fraser first introduces a grey vertical line between the squares (2). It is interesting that Pierce considered the illusion was much reduced by the introduction of a tiny space between the squares and the central line. Here the introduction of a grey line greatly emphasises the effect and also makes Pierce's idea of 'irradiation' being responsible for the illusion somewhat unconvincing. Fraser's next step (3) is to introduce an intermediate brightness into the background, the grey bands separating the columns of black and white squares. The next three transitions (4, 5 and 6) show how the shapes of the units can be altered leaving intact only the sides of the squares which were the adjoining sides. With semicircles and triangles the effect is further enhanced. The extension of the chequered pattern into the background is achieved next (7 and 8) so that the triangles appear as parts of squares of the chequered background. Fraser then begins to alter the nature of the vertical grey line, first by introducing black dashes between the white triangles (9), and then white dashes between the black triangles (10). The remaining sections of the grey line, now grey dashes, are next eliminated (11) and the black and white dashes are slightly rotated so as to join up precisely the black and white triangles respectively (12 to 14) thus completing the 'twisted cord' effect.

I have found no comment on this part of Fraser's work but it seems to me to be of great interest. The fact that one illusion can be turned into another is proof of nothing, but these illusions seem intuitively to have so much in common that this common ground could make an interesting study.

Two more much simpler illusions seem best included in this section. They are Schumann's figure (Fig. 3.74) and Lipps' figure (Fig. 3.75). In the former the lines are all vertical but do not seem so and it is a plausible idea that the perceived orientation of the lines is a result of a sort of perceptual pollution by the orientations of the *systems* of lines. A similar notion can be applied to Fig. 3.75 where the left-hand edges of the circles seem to lie on a curve although they are actually on a straight line.

This ends our consideration of illusions where the observer is misled about the direction of the stimulus. In general, angles seem to be of great importance, as in the Zöllner illusion, but there are numerous examples where angles are clearly absent and yet an illusion persists as in Coren's dot figures. Orientation of lines in this sort of illusion also seems to be an important factor which interacts with the angle effect. Even a set of figures in a line (like the squares in the

---

3.70 Illusion of the kindergarten patterns (Pierce, 1898) 3.71 Lipps (1897) and Münsterberg (1897) 3.72 Helmholtz (1856) 3.73
3.74 Schumann (1900) 3.75 Lipps (1897)

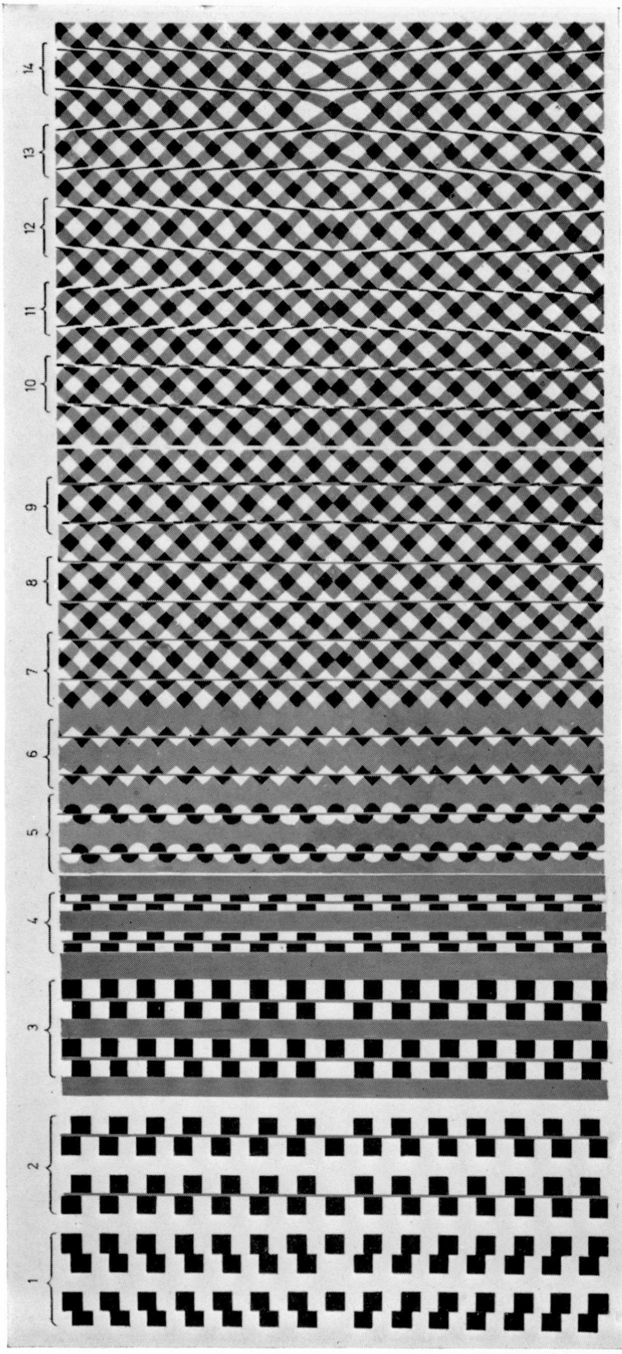

PLATE I

The twisted cord illusion (Fraser, 1908)

PLATE II

Cochran's photograph of his 'freemish' crate (see p. 172)

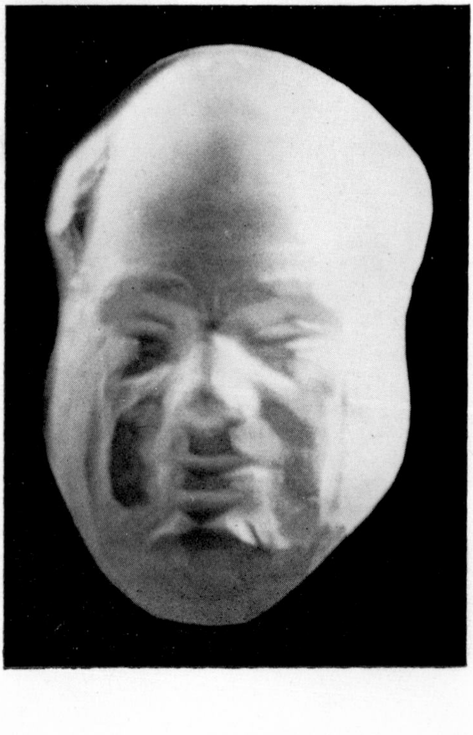

PLATE III

Photograph of a *receding* model face (see p. 176)

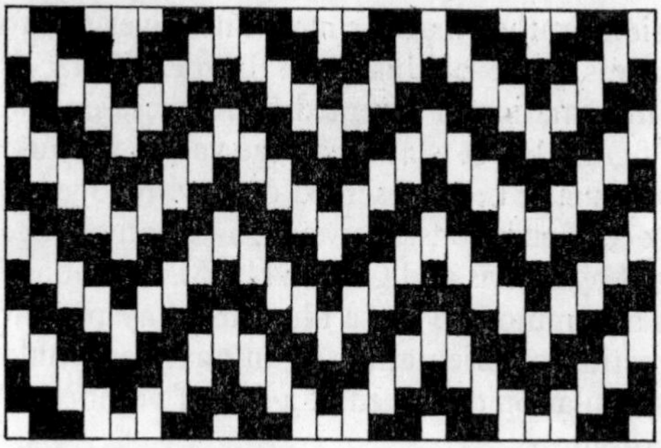

3.70

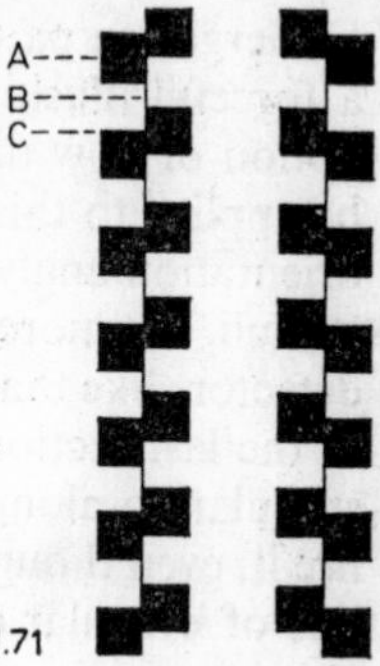

3.71

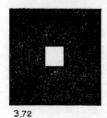

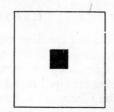

3.72

3.73

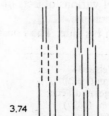

3.74

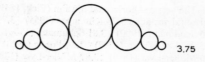

3.75

kindergarten pattern illusion), rather than a simple line, gives rise to a forceful illusion that seems to be of this general type. Wallace's notion of how direction information is accepted and processed can be applied to this sort of figure, but it is at this stage vague, because orientation analysers have usually been observed only with edges as stimuli, not more complex configurations. However, a notion of edge detectors like that proposed by Harris and Gibson (1968), mentioned in the last section, might accommodate these illusions. Any regular stimulation along the direction of orientation of an analyser would fire it, even though such stimulation consisted of a line of points or a line of irregular configurations.

OTHER ILLUSIONS

The second part of this chapter contains two or three broad classes of illusion and a few miscellaneous figures which have defied classification with any others. Of course there is no reason why all illusions should be capable of being arranged into groups. There very likely are many different illusion effects and so there is no reason why one effect should not have only a single representative among all the published illusion figures.

THE VERTICAL–HORIZONTAL ILLUSION

Orientation is not only important in the judgment of angles, it is important for lines. A vertical line is judged to be longer than a horizontal line of the same length. The middle figure of Fig. 3.76 is the one most often quoted as the vertical–horizontal illusion. Hicks and Rivers (1908) attribute the first observation of this illusion to Oppel (1855). It is a very commonly observable phenomenon. For example, Zanforlin (1967) claims that, if a person is asked to make a pile of identical coins so that it is as high as the diameter of one coin, he will make it 30 per cent too low. The hat picture (Fig. 3.77) is a commonplace example of this effect. Chapanis and Mankin (1967) had subjects estimate, on a horizontal scale, the height of various objects in photographs and claimed to find the illusion operating.

The illusion still happens if the subject lies on his side. The line,

---

3.76 The vertical–horizontal illusion (Fick, 1851) 3.77 Vertical–horizontal variant 3.78 Künnapas (1955) 3.79 Schumann (1900) 3.80 Schumann (1900) 3.81 Schumann (1900) 3.82 Piaget and Pène (1955) 3.83 Wundt (1898) 3.84 Ponzo (1928) 3.85 Lipps (1897) 3.86 Müller-Lyer (1889) 3.87 Müller-Lyer (1889) 3.88 Müller-Lyer (1889)

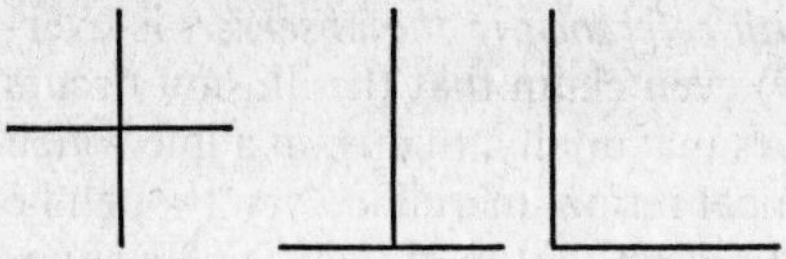

3,76

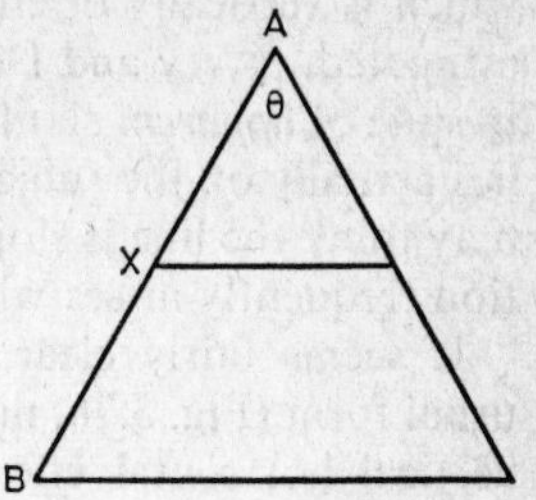

3.82

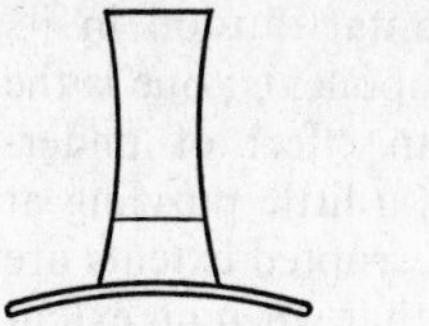

3.77

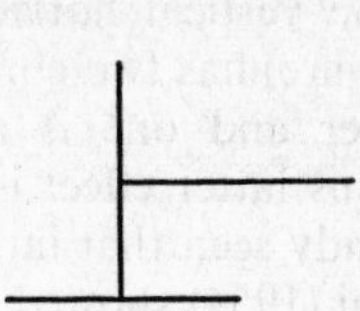

3.78

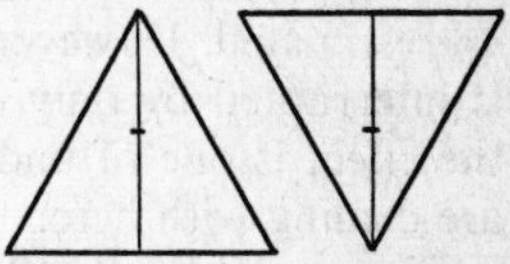

3.83

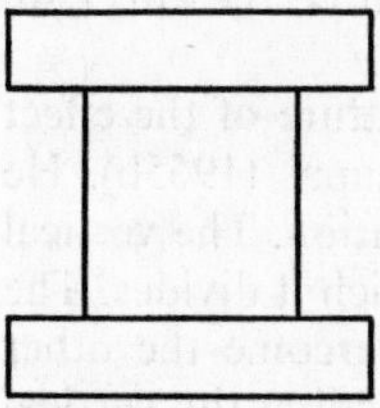

3.79

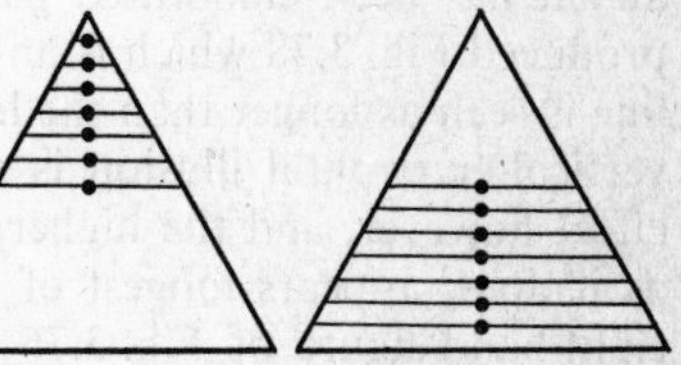

3.84

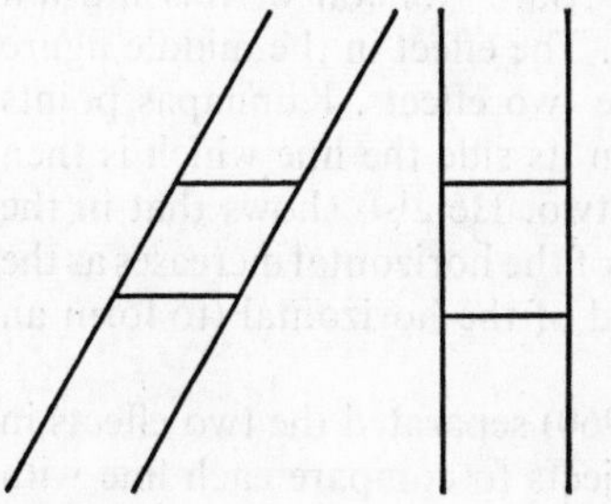

3.80

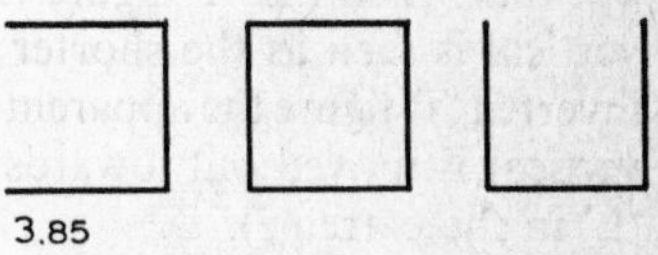

3.85

3.86

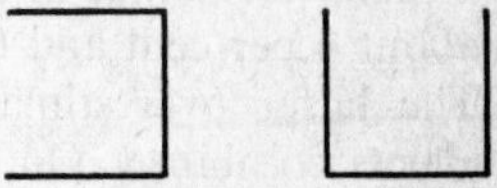

3.87

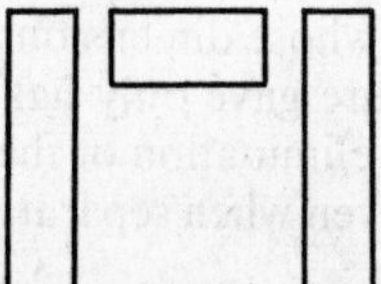

3.81

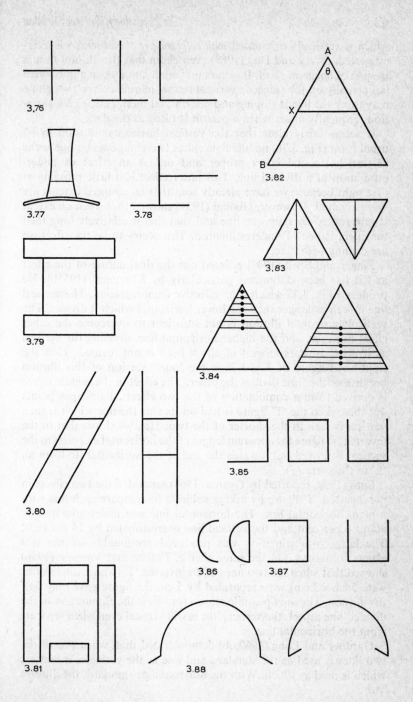

3.88

which is vertically orientated *with reference to the observer*, is overestimated. Avery and Day (1969) even claim that the illusion occurs in spite of *apparent* slant. It occurs maximally, that is, in a line which lies actually on the subject's vertical retinal meridian even though he may think the line is sloping and not on that meridian. Such a situation frequently arises when a person is tilted in the dark.

It seems fairly clear that the vertical–horizontal illusion in its usual form (Fig. 3.76, middle figure) has two components; one is the vertical–horizontal effect proper and one is an effect of underestimation of a divided line. This latter effect is a little puzzling at first sight because we have already seen that interrupted extents are *over*estimated. However, Obonai (1954) showed that when an extent is interrupted by only one line and that line is relatively long then the effect is one of underestimation. This seems to be the effect we are dealing with here.

Finger and Spelt (1947) pointed out the dual nature of the effect and it has been elaborated particularly by Künnapas (1955b). He produced Fig. 3.78 which is an effective demonstration. The vertical line is seen as longer than the lower horizontal which it divides. The vertical–horizontal illusion is not sufficient to overcome the other effect however, and the higher horizontal line, dividing the vertical as it does, appears longest of all; it itself is not divided. Thus the right-hand figure of Fig. 3.76 is the 'pure' version of this illusion because neither line divides the other. The effect in the middle figure is derived from a combination of the two effects. Künnapas points out that when the 'T' figure is laid on its side the line which is then vertical is seen as the shorter of the two. He also shows that in the inverted 'T' figure the apparent length of the horizontal increases as the vertical is moved out towards the end of the horizontal (to form an 'L' in the extreme).

Suto (1959, reported by Oyama, 1960) separated the two effects in the inverted 'T' figure by asking subjects to compare each line with a plain horizontal line. The horizontal line was underestimated by about 4 per cent and the vertical line overestimated by 14 per cent. The latter overestimation was produced presumably by the two effects combined. On the same theme, Fraisse and Vautrey (1956) showed that when the two lines of an inverted 'T' (whose dimensions were 3 cm × 3 cm) were separated by 5 cm the figure gave only half the illusion. The only possible reason for this is the elimination of the divided-line aspect, the vertical line is still vertical even when separate from the horizontal line.

Gardner and Long (1960a,b) demonstrated that, when one of the two lines is used as the standard and one as the variable, it matters which is used as which. With the horizontal as standard, the illusion is less than when the vertical is so used. These authors conclude that the 'error of the standard', a tendency to overestimate the line used as the standard, adds to the other effect in the one case and subtracts from it in the other. The term 'error of the standard' was apparently first used by Würsten (1947) and refers to the tendency always to overestimate the extent used as the standard. In Piaget's type of theory, details of which will be discussed in the chapter on theories of illusions (Chapter 6), this would be the result of the standard receiving a relatively large number of 'centrations', a term largely synonymous with 'fixations'.

According to Piaget, Matalon and Bang (1961), if the inverted 'T' figure is fixated then the illusion varies according to where it is fixated. Fixation of the vertical gives a greater illusion than fixation of the horizontal halfway between the junction with the vertical and the end. But Künnapas (1958) claimed that, in absolute terms, the illusion was greater without fixation.

An interesting attempt at explanation of this illusion is due to Künnapas. It is that the extent of the visual field is important in estimating lengths within it. The apparent length is greater, the greater the proportion of the visual field covered by the stimulus. He claimed that the visual field is greater horizontally than it is vertically, and that therefore a vertical line, extending as it does over a greater proportion of the vertical visual field than a horizontal line over the horizontal field, appears longer. First he showed, in 1957, that surrounding an 'L'-shaped figure with elliptical or rectangular frames in different orientations affected the overestimation of the vertical. It was less when the long axis of the frame was vertical than when it was horizontal. Künnapas' interpretation of these findings was that the vertical–horizontal illusion was due to the asymmetry of the normal visual field; it was larger in the horizontal direction than in the vertical direction. Surrounding the figure with frames of this sort compensated for the asymmetry of the visual field. But if this is the cause of the illusion why was it only reduced? Why was it not reversed when the axis of the frame was vertical? The answer could be that frames are different from whole visual fields and would be expected to have only a partial effect. Certainly if this effect is merely a framing effect it is in the right direction. Künnapas himself (1955a), using horizontal lines in square frames, showed that a line in a frame is overestimated. It is overestimated less as the frame gets larger, that is the frame has less and less effect as it gets larger. Thus the parts of the frame at the ends of the long axis should have a less enlarging effect on the 'L' figure than those at the ends of the short axis and the vertically orientated frames in the experiment would reduce the illusion because the horizontal would be more affected by the frame than the vertical. However, the largest square frames in Künnapas' (1955a) experiment did not have very much effect, so it would be surprising if the 'frame' imposed by the edges of the visual field had enough effect to cause the illusion, because they are too far away. If the visual field is a factor it does not seem to be the usual framing effect.

Künnapas (1959) produced more evidence on his theme by making subjects wear spectacles which varied the shape of their visual field. Subjects were in fact looking through elliptical holes with various ratios of major to minor axis. As the horizontal axis of the elliptical hole (the major axis) was shortened the overestimation of the vertical line of an 'L'-shaped figure was reduced. By the time the ellipse had become a circle the overestimation had still not reached zero, however, as it should have done if this theory were correct and if this were a good test of it. Overestimation continued to fall as the ellipse lengthened in the vertical direction.

This later experiment thus suffers from the same difficulties of interpretation as the first. Künnapas has demonstrated an interesting effect of framing on the vertical–horizontal illusion but results have not been exactly as his visual-field theory would predict. One can only conclude either that the theory does not hold or that it has not yet been tested because the experiments Künnapas has done have altered the frames in which stimuli were viewed but have not done anything equivalent to truly altering the shape of the visual field. This is a fascinating theory still needing a crucial test.

Three figures produced by Schumann (1900) seem to fit into this category (Figs. 3.79, 3.80 and 3.81). The central area of each, though square (or in one case an equal-sided parallelogram) looks elongated in the vertical direction. If the figure is rotated through 90° the central area looks elongated in the new vertical direction. It seems that a plain square is too stable a configuration perceptually to suffer from the vertical–horizontal illusion but, if it is embedded in other material, then it becomes susceptible. I have met no case where a circle, similarly stable presumably, has been made by its surroundings to appear elliptical in an analogous way.

BISECTION OF THE HEIGHT OF A TRIANGLE

When one attempts to draw a horizontal line across an isosceles or equilateral triangle so that it is halfway up the triangle (that is, it

---

3.89 Tolanski (1964) 3.90 Tolanski (1964) 3.91 Müller-Lyer (1889)
3.92 Piaget and Vurpillot (1956) 3.93 Wundt (1898) 3.94 Loeb (1895)
3.95 Bourdon (1902) 3.96 Ponzo (1928) 3.97 Ponzo (1928)
3.98 Luckiesh (1922)

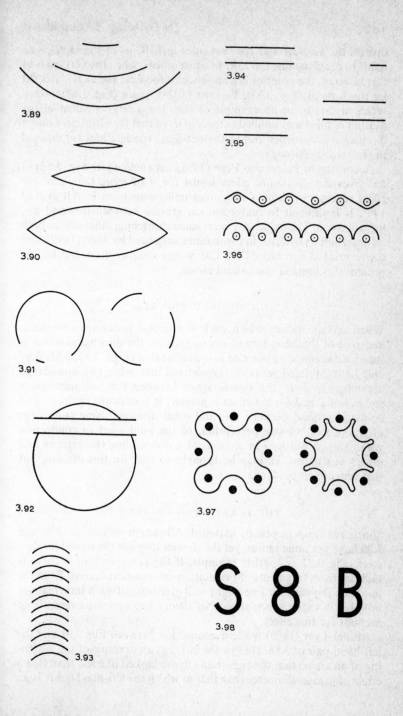

3.89

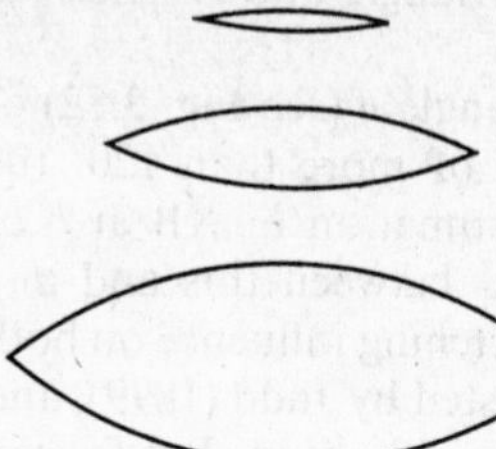

3.90

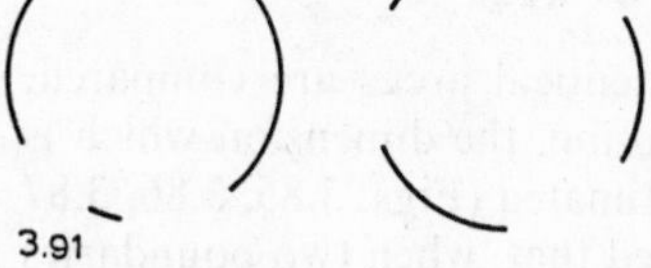

3.91

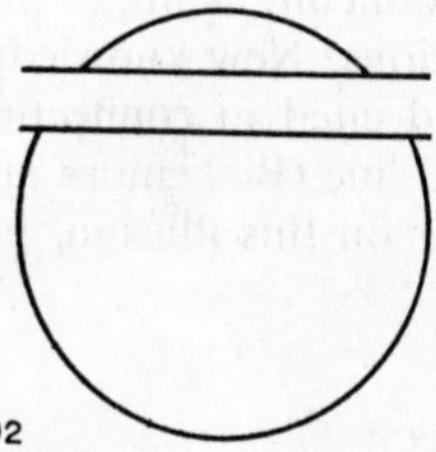

3.92

3.93

3.94

3.95

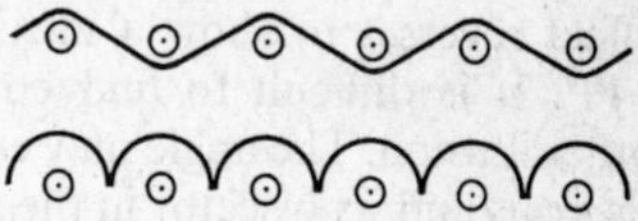

3.96

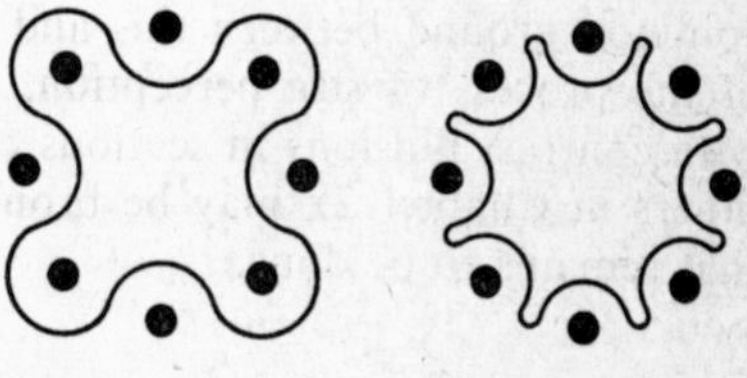

3.97

3.98

divides the vertical and the two sides in half, as in Fig. 3.82), one tends to draw the line too low. In other words, when the vertical is in fact bisected, the point of bisection seems too near the angle bisected by the vertical (Fig. 3.83). Ponzo's (1928) figure (Fig. 3.84), which seems at first to be an example of this, has a large element of the illusion of filled and unfilled extents in it, so that the effect now under discussion is cancelled out in the left-hand triangle and emphasised in the right-hand one.

According to Piaget and Pène (1955), an angle θ (see Fig. 3.82) of 55° gives the maximum effect whilst for θ of more than 120° the effect reverses to show a maximum underestimation of XB at θ of 140°. It is difficult to find common ground between this and any other illusion. The angle may exert some shortening influence on both its arms and its bisector in the manner suggested by Judd (1899), and the reversal at θ of more than 120° would roughly fit in. But for the present this illusion must stand alone.

UNBOUNDED FIGURES

When certain figures which enclose identical areas are compared, and part of the boundary of one is missing, the dimension which is thereby undefined at one end is overestimated (Figs. 3.85, 3.86, 3.87 and 3.88). Müller-Lyer (1889) considered that, when two boundaries are missing, as in the square space between the two incomplete squares of Fig. 3.87, the effect is greater. It is difficult, again, to find common ground between this and other illusions. New knowledge of the process of size perception, of the kind cited in connection with contrast illusions in sections of a divided line (Blakemore and others in Chapter 2), may be brought to bear on this illusion, but that remains to be done.

THE FLATTENING OF ARCS

Short arcs are perceptually flattened. All the curves in Figs. 3.89 and 3.90 have the same radius, yet the shorter they are the straighter they seem. Fig. 3.91 is another example. If the perception of a curve is built up from fragments of orientation-information derived from the line then the shortest line might well give least of such information, but this is vague speculation. No theory has appeared recently to account for this effect.

Müller-Lyer (1889) made a connection between Fig. 3.91 and the left-hand pair of 3.86. He saw the latter as an example of the flattening of an arc so that the right-hand figure looked like less than half a circle of greater diameter than that of which the left-hand figure is an arc, so that the left-hand figure looked more 'vaulted' than the right-hand figure. Since the ends of the arc appear to be the same distance apart in each, he assumed that the left-hand, more 'vaulted', arc must appear the longer. This led him to consider this figure, and even more so Fig. 3.88, as examples of the Müller-Lyer figure with the shaft bent round in a semicircle. The left-hand figure in Fig. 3.88 looks more vaulted and therefore longer, just as it would if the arc were straightened out to form half of a Müller-Lyer figure with outgoing fins. By assuming that the process of increasing the vaulting of the arc makes it seem to be an arc of a smaller diameter, Müller-Lyer finally accounts for the common observation that rods or balls of a given diameter look too small. This is the only mention I have been able to find of a very forceful and common illusion. Müller-Lyer's argument, unfortunately, seems to me fanciful.

Piaget and Vurpillot (1956) reported work on the under- and overestimation of chords. They showed that if the depth of the arc supporting the chord (measured along a line passing through the centre of the circle and perpendicular to the chord) is less than three-quarters of the diameter of the circle then the chord is underestimated, and if the depth of the arc is more than three-quarters of the diameter of the circle the chord is overestimated. This is due, according to Piaget (1961), to the distortion of the arcs themselves. Deeper (longer) arcs seem flattened, and shallower (shorter) arcs have their curvature apparently increased. Fig. 3.92 illustrates both these points. This last observation disagrees with most other work and Virsu (1971b) suggested why.

Since the subjects of Piaget and Vurpillot estimated chords, their judgments, Virsu maintained, were tainted by a version of the Müller-Lyer illusion with ingoing fins which would be formed by the chord and the adjacent parts of the arc (this is Müller-Lyer's point, mentioned above). Virsu's results, obtained by asking subjects to compare each arc with a set of circles and to choose the appropriate circle, showed the curvature of all arcs to be underestimated and the underestimation to be an exponential function of arc length (greatest with small arcs). Virsu offered an explanation in terms of eye movements which is elaborated in Chapter 6. The eyes tend to move in straight paths. According to Virsu, the preparedness of the eyes so to move causes the underestimation of curvature, presumably because the correction of the movement by visual feedback comes relatively late.

Wundt's figure (Fig. 3.93) is mentioned here only because it is composed of arcs. As far as one can see, it has nothing in common with any other figure. The effect is that the figure as a whole seems wider at the top than at the bottom.

ERRORS IN LINING UP THE EDGES OF TWO FIGURES

Related clearly to figural after-effects, as will be seen later, is the illusion seen in Figs. 3.94 and 3.95, where two of the lines in each figure do in fact lie on the same line but do not appear to do so. The reader should look at Chapter 5 for a description of figural after-effects. Clearly, judging by Figs. 3.94 and 3.95, the after-effect of a previously exposed figure is not necessary for the two lines to appear out of line. This simultaneous 'after-effect' is well recognised and features, of course, in the attempts to show that illusions and after-effects are the same process. These are discussed later. Figs. 3.96 and 3.97 seem to be of the same sort. In Fig. 3.97 the dots are apparently 'pushed' out of their circular formation.

INVERSION OF LETTERS

The letters of Fig. 3.98 are some of those which, when printed in the usual way, look symmetrical about their middle, that is the same width at the top and the bottom. However, when they are inverted they no longer look like that. I have found no serious attempt to account for this.

4

THE GEOMETRICAL OPTICAL ILLUSIONS (III): SOME SUBJECT VARIABLES AND SOME SPECIAL STUDIES

AGE AND THE GEOMETRICAL OPTICAL ILLUSIONS

A fairly large volume of work has been done on the variations of geometrical optical illusions with age, notably since the early 1940s, by Piaget and various co-workers in Geneva. Wohlwill (1960) reviews work in detail up to that time and this paper is an important one. Wohlwill mentions studies using the Delbœuf figure, the Titchener circles, the Müller-Lyer illusion, the vertical–horizontal illusion, the Sander parallelogram, the Poggendorff illusion, the Oppel–Kundt illusion, the judgment of angles, the judgment of length of chords of a circle, the comparison of width and length of a rectangle, and the Ponzo illusion.

There is a very clear general trend of a decrease of illusion between early childhood and adulthood. There is a little evidence (Piaget, Lambercier, Boesch and von Albertini, 1942) that this applies to both directions of the illusion when there is an inflexion. These workers showed that, in the case of the Delbœuf figure, children showed both greater overestimation than adults of the inner circle when it was not much smaller than the outer circle, and greater underestimation when it was much smaller than the outer one. Thus, both 'assimilation' and 'contrast' were exaggerated in children.

However, there are exceptions to the general trend. Leibowitz and Heisel (1958) showed that the Ponzo illusion *increased* between the ages of 4 and 7 years. Leibowitz and Judisch (1967) confirmed this with an age range of 3½ to 88 years. There was an increase from 3½ to 13 years and then the effect remained level up to 50 years. This was confirmed in a surprising study by Parrish, Lundy and Leibowitz (1968) using hypnotic age regression. Subjects regressed to an early age in this way showed an increase in the Poggendorff effect and a decrease in the Ponzo effect.

Another important difficulty in concluding that there is a general downward trend in illusions between childhood and adulthood was presented by two studies of the Müller-Lyer effect, by Walters (1942) and by Wapner and Werner (1957), both of which showed a fall from early childhood to the end of the first decade and then a rise from 15 to 19 years. As Wohlwill pointed out, these writers were unusual in including adolescents in their study and there could possibly be a rise and fall in the illusion in between childhood and adulthood which has simply been missed by everyone else. A more clear-cut departure from the general trend is the finding of Wapner and Werner that the illusion of the Titchener circles increases with age. This leads these workers to the conclusion, different from that suggested by Piaget's data, that contrast increases with age.

Both Fraisse and Vautrey (1956) and Würsten (1947) produced data for the vertical–horizontal illusion which did not fall in with the general downward trend of illusions with age. They showed a rise in early childhood up to about 10 years of age and then a fall to adulthood. In the case of Fraisse and Vautrey the trend was very small and was not tested statistically. Hanley and Zerbolio (1965) found a very flat function of this illusion with age but it was a significantly increasing one. In other words, according to these authors this illusion is very like the Ponzo illusion in its trend with age. They also confirm the increase of the Ponzo effect with age.

It is, perhaps, not sensible at this stage to try to evaluate claims like those of Fraisse and Vautrey of typical changes *within* childhood. Psychophysical observations of this sort with small children clearly must be difficult and any trend ought to be much better established before attempts are made to incorporate them in theory. We are left then with the general trend of decrease of illusion between childhood and adulthood with the possible exceptions of the Ponzo and vertical–horizontal illusions.

Wohlwill (1960) contrasts the views of Piaget and of Wapner and Werner on the nature of the change which brings about a difference in illusions between children and adults. Piaget favoured a process where the individual learns to use his perceptual apparatus and therefore does so more efficiently as the years go by. Wapner and Werner couched their views in terms of 'sensory-tonic field theory', a theory which postulates interplay of fields of force and does not demand increase of veridicality of perception with age. There is a view, which takes something from each of these, which regards the child as possessed of a perceptual system which has certain optimising processes, such as the sharpening of a contour on the retina by the dark side causing brightening of the bright side and the bright side causing darkening of the dark side (facilitation and inhibition). During development, the individual learns to make the best of these processes in the sense of using them to get the most accurate perception and avoiding the sorts of distortion they might produce (see Ganz's theory in the following chapter). It was this latter sort of process that Gregory (1967) was imagining when he declared that 'seeing machines', computer simulations of perception, will have illusions.

However, Pollack (1970) was not talking about such a process of acquisition of ability to use the perceptual system. He maintained that the actual brightness contrast threshold increased with age and that this caused a decrease in the Müller-Lyer illusion. Wickelgren (1965) had shown that increased brightness contrast of the lines and the background increased the Müller-Lyer illusion, and Pollack showed that both brightness contrast and the Müller-Lyer effect decreased with age and that if the illusion was drawn in colour in such a way that only colour contrast and not brightness contrast was involved, then this decline with age from a high level in childhood was not observed. Pollack (1969) guessed at the physiological reasons for the decline in contrast sensitivity with age. It could, he considered, be due to permanent adaptation of the retina to patterned stimulation, increase in lenticular density and pigmentation, increase in retinal pigmentation or decrease in pupil size. All but the first of these have been shown to happen with increasing age. It would be interesting to extend Pollack's findings to a greater range of illusion figures.

Papert (1964) suggested that children's search strategy makes a difference to the illusion effects. He examined the time courses of misjudgment of the vertical when the line which was to be adjusted by the subject was crossed by one line at an angle of 10° and when it was crossed by a number of parallel lines at the same angle. The distortion was measured for a range of short exposures by tachistoscope and with free inspection. Now in the work of Piaget and his associates (Piaget, Matalon and Bang, 1961; Piaget, Bang and Matalon, 1958; and several other investigations, see Piaget, 1961) a very common finding with tachistoscopic presentation has been that the illusion increases from very brief exposures to a maximum at between 0·2 sec and 0·5 sec, decreasing then with longer exposures to an asymptote. Moreover, children show a higher maximum than adults. Piaget and Bang (1961a) showed, with the Oppel–Kundt illusion, that the adults' maximum was at 0·2 sec and the children's at 0·5 sec.

Papert found that the figure with a single oblique produced a function of exposure time and distortion which increased to a maximum and then fell away. The maximum was very close in value to the distortion found for the other figure (with several obliques) in free inspection, not exposed by tachistoscope. Papert argued that if the illusion were the result of some sort of interaction of contours in the visual system then the interaction would build up until it was modified by the disturbance caused by the displacement of the image over the retina by an eye movement. The eye moves in a complex manner even during fixation (see Yarbus, 1967). One important type of movement, the saccade, is largely horizontal in direction. In the first figure such eye movement is likely to move the vertical line to a completely fresh area of the retina, whereas in the second the vertical line is likely only to be moved on to an area which has been stimulated by some of the other obliques (which cover quite a wide area). There is evidence that interaction in the visual system takes a little time to establish. Hartline (1969) claimed this for retinal inhibition measured physiologically and Mathews (1968) demonstrated that the raising of the threshold for a spot of light by the presence of a nearby contour had a distinctive time course. Inhibition appeared after 50 to 100 m/sec and reached a maximum at 400 m/sec.

Thus in Papert's figures one can think of interaction building up until it is disturbed by an eye movement, the degree of disturbance depending on the state of the new area of retina on to which the vertical line is thrown. If it has already been affected by sloping lines, as in the second figure (multiple obliques), the interaction, and therefore the distortion, will reach instantaneously the level to which it climbs only after hundreds of milliseconds with the first figure. Papert claims that results like those of Piaget and Bang (1961a) mentioned above, typical of other results produced by Piaget's group with a variety of illusions, can be explained by the fact that children's eye movements are less frequent than those of adults. If all illusions depend to some extent on eye movement as described then the 'temporal maximum', as Piaget calls it, will be determined by the interval of time spent viewing the display before the onset of the first eye movement.

Papert's work needs replication before it can be confidently accepted. In saying that children's eye movements are less frequent it oversimplifies the difference between adult and child eye movements. Piaget and Bang (1961b) write of lack of skill at fixating in the two children they observed, which caused small eye movements not seen in adults. They also found that the children took longer to locate a target. This latter disability could account nearly as well for the difference in temporal maxima as Papert's theory. The explanation would be in terms of time to locate the target instead of time to the first eye movement.

In conclusion, it would be well just to emphasise the bearing which developmental studies of illusions have on explanatory attempts. If illusions are seen as consequences of skill in using the perceptual system, so that for example search patterns (Piaget's view) or size constancy (Gregory's view; see Chapter 5), which become more developed with age, lead to distortion, then illusions should increase with age. If illusions are seen as consequences of the mode of construction of the perceptual system, so that for example retinal interaction or brightness contrast (the effects of which will be increasingly discounted with age, resulting generally in veridical perception) lead to distortion, then illusions should decrease with age.

But these are only the simplest possibilities. Pollack (1969) suggests that, in figural after-effects, a process of the second sort is predominant until about the age of 10, causing a decrease of the effect, and one of the first sort then takes over and brings about a subsequent increase. This sort of argument might be applicable to the results mentioned earlier in this section, of Walters (1942) with the Müller-Lyer figure and of Wapner and Werner (1957) with the Müller-Lyer and Titchener figures, but a good deal more work would be needed to establish such a notion as fact.

CROSS-CULTURAL STUDIES OF ILLUSIONS

A number of interesting studies which have compared the extents of illusions in different cultures seem worthy of separate treatment, particularly as they have achieved some theoretical importance because they have been taken as demonstrating the acquisition by learning of susceptibility to illusions.

Rivers (1905) showed that Europeans were more susceptible to the Müller-Lyer illusion and less to the vertical–horizontal illusion than were Murray Islanders and members of the Toda tribe of Southern India. However, the study which seemed to begin current interest in the topic was that of Segall, Campbell and Herskovits (1963). They compared one Philippine and twelve African groups with people of European stock on the Müller-Lyer illusion, the Sander parallelogram (Fig. 2.23) and the vertical–horizontal illusion. They found that the non-Europeans showed much less illusion effect on the first two figures, and greater effect for the vertical–horizontal illusion. To explain this they have used the fact that the non-Europeans largely lived in round houses on flat plain and scrubland. They consider that the European's illusion is due to his seeing the Müller-Lyer and Sander figures as representations, seen in perspective, of figures which actually contain right angles. Perspective theories will be reviewed in Chapter 6. The reader is very likely familiar already with them. They suggest that, for example, the Müller-Lyer figure is seen as a trestle viewed either from underneath (the outgoing figure) or from above (the ingoing figure) and the size distortions are perceptual adjustments for apparent distance. Now Segall, Campbell and Herskovits argue that this sort of adjustment will be much more marked in people who live in a 'carpentered world' where the customary visual input consists of rectangles and straight lines. People living in round houses in an environment containing relatively few rectangular stimuli will not have learned to make such adjustments.

They will however have learned that a vertical line in their visual field most often represents a line on the ground receding from them (for example, a stick lying on the ground or the boundary, not necessarily exactly straight, between two differently textured surfaces). They therefore see a vertical line as a receding line on the ground and, making a perceptual adjustment, see this line closer to its 'true' length, which is much longer than its vertical projection. They have more exposure to distance, living on plains, than most town dwellers and therefore this is an illusion to which they are particularly prone. This second part of their hypothesis is much more tentative than the first, but still the authors do not seem to allow that African tribesmen must thrust sticks into the ground quite often (perhaps even in the construction of their round huts), or see vertical grasses, and therefore not be quite bereft of experience of actually vertical lines! It is difficult to guess why their perceptual systems should not work according to their experience of these rather than of the rather rarer (surely) experience of receding, fairly straight contours on the ground.

Segall, Campbell and Herskovits, also, give insufficient emphasis to other differences between the Africans and Europeans. Chiefly these are educational differences, particularly differences in experience with drawings on paper, and physiological differences between the races themselves.

Other writers have taken up these points, but before mentioning these Fisher's (1968d) point ought to be made. He showed angle illusions with curved lines, for example the Zöllner figure with curved obliques, which still gave rise to the illusion. These were not obvious perspective representations of three-dimensional configurations, nor indeed are many of the versions mentioned earlier of the Müller-Lyer effect. The 'carpentered world' hypothesis falls with the rebuttal of theories of illusions which rely on perspective or constancy, and I believe that such rebuttal has been published (see Chapter 6).

Educational experience is likely to be closely related to experience of drawings on paper and Hudson had shown as early as 1960 that such experience affected the perception of perspective drawings and photographs. His subjects were white and coloured children and adults. Some of each were illiterate and some had had a certain amount of education. The illiterates tended to see only two dimensions in the material presented to them, whereas those with some education tended to see depth in the displays. This dichotomy of seeing two or three dimensions cuts across the dichotomy of black or white skin. The environmental experience of the illiterate subjects was not different from the rest however, so this work only demonstrates an additional influence of educational experience; it does not invalidate claims about the effects on illusions of perceptual environment. Moreover, it says nothing about illusions unless one has accepted a perspective explanation of illusions, and Wober (1970) cast doubt on the relationship between susceptibility to illusions and appreciation of perspective when he demonstrated a zero correlation between the vertical–horizontal illusion and the ability to infer three dimensions from pictures. (His subjects were Nigerian workers and clerks.) So although education seems to enhance people's ability to extract three dimensions from pictures it does not seem, on this evidence, that it is likely *because of this* to influence illusions. In other words, if experience of lines on paper does influence illusions it does not do so because of the ability thereby derived to see three dimensions in drawings.

A study by Gregor and McPherson (1965) gives little support to the 'carpentered world' hypothesis. They found Australian aborigines living under considerable European influence in and among rectangular houses and huts and compared them with aborigines living in pre-colonial conditions. They also compared both these groups with a group of Europeans. The two aboriginal groups showed significantly less illusion on the Müller-Lyer figure and the Sander parallelogram than the Europeans, but the difference between the two aboriginal groups was not significant. The results for the vertical–horizontal illusion were rather similar, except that both aboriginal groups showed a greater effect than the European group. The difference between the aboriginal groups was again not significant. Thus, the race difference between the aboriginal and European groups seems to be more important than the differences in perceptual experience between the two aboriginal groups.

Jahoda (1966) tested African groups with different environments on the Müller-Lyer and vertical–horizontal illusions. One group, the Lobi and Dagomba tribes, lives in open parkland in round huts, and the other group, the Ashanti, lives in dense forest in roughly rectangular huts. The expectation was that the Lobis and Dagombas would show a greater vertical–horizontal effect and less Müller-Lyer effect. Neither expectation was realised.

In view of all this evidence, it is difficult to believe that perceptual environment really is the effective variable. Educational experience is another of the possibilities mentioned earlier. Jahoda and Stacey (1970) equated educational experience in two ethnic groups, Ghanaians and Scots. All had had lengthy education of a similar type; they were drawn from universities, training colleges and similar institutions. These authors used the Müller-Lyer figure, the Sander parallelogram, the Helmholtz square, the Wundt and Hering figures, and several others. There were significant differences between Scots and Ghanaians on most of the illusions (though not on the Müller-Lyer, which is an unfortunate disagreement with other studies). The Scots showed greater illusion on all the figures except the vertical–horizontal illusion and the Helmholtz square (Fig. 2.73) where they showed significantly less illusion. Jahoda and Stacey also did a separate analysis which separated out those in each culture who had special training in art or architecture. There were no consistent differences.

This work seems to show that differences in training and education cannot account for observed cross-cultural differences in illusions. We must thus discount as explanations both perceptual environment and educational experience and yet we clearly have a racial difference in susceptibility to illusions.

A rather surprising sort of explanation has been put by Pollack and Silvar (1967) which amounts to proposing a physiological difference between races. It connects neatly with Pollack's work on brightness contrast and illusions but also presents some difficulties. It showed that children with darker pigmentation of the fundus oculi showed less illusion with the Müller-Lyer figure with outgoing fins. Now these children were all drawn from the same middle-class school and so cultural variance was small. Skin colour and pigmentation of the fundus oculi correlate very highly. Thirteen out of fifteen of those with dark pigmentation were Negroes and nineteen out of twenty of those with light pigmentation were white. Since assessment of degree of pigmentation involves looking into the subject's eye with an ophthalmoscope it is difficult to do the assessment without knowing what colour his skin is. The degree of pigmentation, moreover, is a fairly difficult judgment to make and for this reason it would be a great advantage to be able to do it 'blind' (i.e. without knowing skin colour). Only then could one be perfectly sure that one was really studying pigmentation in the eye and not simply repeating the observations, made so often before, of ethnic differences in illusions.

However, the suggestion of Pollack and Silvar is a fascinating one, especially as there is a clear suggestion that the darkly pigmented eye is less sensitive to contrast. I have quoted earlier Wickelgren's (1965) findings that the Müller-Lyer effect increases with increased brightness contrast. On the other hand, it is surprising that racial differences in brightness contrast sensitivity, if they exist, have not been observed more directly in other fields. Also, although the reduced Müller-Lyer illusion in dark-skinned people is explained by this idea, the enhanced vertical–horizontal illusion is not.

Jahoda and Stacey (1970) consider that the importance of cross-cultural studies has been underestimated. They consider that such studies can throw light on the extent to which perceptual characteristics are learned by examining different groups in different environments. Such attempts have largely failed and Berry (1968) suggests that this is because racial differences have been confounded with developmental differences. This certainly does seem to have happened, but the work has also been impaired by a usually implicit assumption that the illusions are the result of some fairly sophisticated perceptual process like constancy or perspective. These have been shown to alter with age and, presuming that this alteration has been caused by experience (and is not simply maturation), it has been hoped to demonstrate that *different* experience will have caused different sorts of alteration. Now the evidence that illusions do indeed stem from constancy or perspective is equivocal and the supposition that perceptual changes with age can be modified by environment is not well supported. It is true that Blakemore and Cooper (1970) seem to have achieved considerable perceptual modification in kittens. They raised kittens in environments consisting solely of vertical or of horizontal stripes and subsequently found considerably more cortical cells which responded to the experienced orientation. But this extreme alteration of environment is quite outside the range of any differences to be found in naturally occurring human environments. Conclusions drawn from cross-cultural studies have therefore rested on a chain of assumption in which each link is weak.

ILLUSIONS IN ANIMALS

It seems well established that various non-human species have geometrical illusions. As early as 1924 Révész demonstrated Wundt's area illusion (Fig. 2.75) in hens. Over (1968) points out however that the hens may have been giving an undistorted response to retinal size since Révész first trained his hens to respond to the larger of two stimuli and then presented the illusion figure with the upper element *further away* from the hen than the lower one.

The chief difficulty of this sort of investigation of animals is knowing exactly what characteristics of the stimulus they are responding to. This is the trouble with one of Winslow's (1933) figures. He trained chicks to respond to the longer of two lines and then presented them with a vertical and a horizontal line, a line with ingoing fins and a plain line, and a line with outgoing fins and a plain line. They responded to the vertical line, the plain line and the line with outgoing fins respectively. The last case is the difficulty because the chicks may have been responding to the length of the whole figure rather than the length of the line embedded in it.

Dominguez (1954) confirmed the vertical–horizontal illusion and also demonstrated the Helmholtz square effect (Fig. 2.73) in rhesus, mangabey and cebus monkeys. Illusions were similar in extent to those experienced by humans, the length of the lines being misjudged by 2 to 3 per cent.

Dücker (1966) made an extensive study of contrast and angular distortion effects using the Titchener circles (Fig. 2.63), the Zöllner figure and two others very like Figs. 3.18 and 3.20. Illusions were demonstrated in fish, chicks, mistle-thrushes and guinea-pigs, though in some cases only a few *out of many animals* showed the effect. Animals were trained to respond, in the case of the Titchener circles, to the smaller or the larger central circle (both cases were tried); in the case of the Zöllner figure, to non-parallel lines as compared with parallel lines; and in the case of the other figures, to curved as compared with straight lines. Thus when they responded, for example, to figures in which the lines actually were parallel or figures in which the lines actually were straight they showed that they saw the lines as non-parallel or curved respectively. Dücker's evidence is very much weakened by the fact that by no means all his animals showed the illusions.

Work on animals seems to show a great deal of promise. For example, the question of the influence of 'carpentered' and 'uncarpentered' environments could be resolved by raising animals in such environments in the manner in which Blakemore and Cooper (1970) have raised kittens in environments composed wholly of horizontal or vertical lines.

ILLUSIONS VIEWED UNDER THE STEREOSCOPE

Recently a number of studies have been made in which, by means of a stereoscope, one half of an illusion has been presented to one eye and the other half has been presented to the other eye. Thus, for example, the main judged lines of the Zöllner figure would be presented to one eye and the obliques to the other. The purpose of most of these studies has been to determine the place in the perceptual system where the illusions are generated. Chiefly it has been hoped to show whether they are a retinal phenomenon or whether they are generated higher in the system.

If illusions are generated wholly in the part of the visual system lying below the point where combination of impulses from the two eyes takes place, then, it is argued, viewing by stereoscope should abolish them. For example, if illusions are due to interaction on the retina between lines falling on it, then they will be abolished by stereoscopic viewing. Both Ohwaki (1960) and Springbett (1961) report findings and conclusions of this sort. Ohwaki used the vertical–horizontal illusion, exposing the horizontal line to one eye and the vertical line to the other. He also used the Titchener circles, exposing the inducing circles to one eye and the test circle, with a comparison circle some way from it, to the other. Here, the subject would be given a fixation point for each eye and would be asked to superimpose one fixation point on the other by convergence of the eyes. The fixation points would be arranged so that when they were thus superimposed the test circle would be placed in the subject's view within the set of inducing circles. The test and comparison circles would then be compared by the subject. Ohwaki also studied the Helmholtz square and the Müller-Lyer and Poggendorff (Fig. 3.37) figures.

This description of how the stereoscopic combination is achieved will give the reader with experience of stereoscopes some idea of the problems of retinal rivalry likely to be encountered. In other words, in this sort of situation, where there is no possibility of combining the two displays to form a single three-dimensional view, it is very difficult for the subject to prevent his visual system from suppressing altogether at least a large part of the view of one or other eye.

In every figure at least a large minority of Ohwaki's subjects still saw some illusion in the stereoscopic presentation. The obvious conclusion seems to be that the illusion process is not retinal (or not completely retinal), but Ohwaki concludes that the illusion *is* destroyed, because there is statistically significant reduction, and that therefore it is a retinal phenomenon.

Springbett (1961) experienced great difficulty with retinal rivalry in this sort of work but in the moments when his subjects could see both displays superimposed they reported complete absence of the illusion. The exception was the Müller-Lyer in which the illusion persisted. It was an exception to the rivalry difficulty, too, because the line from one field and the fins from the other did not need to be superimposed in the composite view; the fins simply lay at the ends of the line. This double exception of the Müller-Lyer throws a little doubt on the work and indeed it is unusual in reporting complete abolition of illusion in stereoscopic viewing.

Day (1961) suggests that the reason for Springbett's results was a combination of rivalry difficulties and the absence of a comparison illusion figure viewed normally. This prevented Springbett's subjects, he says, from being able to make a report of *reduced* illusion in stereoscopic viewing. Day makes the point too that illusions can only be demonstrated to be a retinal process if they are quite abolished in these conditions. He also mentions that the Müller-Lyer figure, since it does not need a line (it works with the fins alone), is complete on one retina in the studies reported. It is not split between the two eyes.

Day demonstrates reduction in stereoscopic viewing of a large range of illusion figures and reports difficulty with rivalry. Schiller and Wiener (1962) presented illusion figures stereoscopically and tachistoscopically simultaneously. This overcame rivalry, they claimed, and also showed a reduction in the illusion effect. They concluded that the process was central. Perhaps a word of detail of the method used here would be helpful. They asked subjects to look through the stereoscope at fixation points and visually to superimpose one point on the other; then the two fields were briefly exposed, each being correctly placed with reference to the fixation point for the eye viewing it, so that the desired superimposition of the two fields would be achieved.

Papert (1961) reports a study with a similar objective, but a different and intriguing design. He set up two sheets of glass a few inches apart. One was marked with a random pattern of dots all over it. The other bore a dotted Müller-Lyer figure. When subjects looked with only one eye through both sheets of glass the Müller-Lyer figure was invisible; it merged with the random dot pattern. Binocularly, however, the Müller-Lyer figure could be seen and the illusion was present. Now Papert argues that since the figure could not be seen at all until after the process of binocular fusion, it could not be retinal. I cannot follow this argument. If the display is viewed monocularly, then neither the figure nor the illusion effect is seen. When it is viewed binocularly, both are seen. It is difficult to see why, say, the effect of an interactive process taking place on one retina should be filtered out by the process of binocular fusion. If distortion arose from a purely retinal effect there still seems to be no reason why it should not persist through the process of binocular fusion.

ILLUSIONS INVOLVING SUBLIMINAL STIMULI

There is a small but important literature on the influence in illusion figures of inducing lines which are below the level of conscious awareness. Dixon (1971) reviews these and my account owes much to his. The Müller-Lyer illusion with subliminal fins has been observed in several experiments since the turn of the century and it has been shown that when the arrow-heads are too faint for the subject to be aware of them there is still a measurable illusion. One experiment (Bressler, 1931) even showed that the effect decreased as the fins, already below threshold, were made still fainter.

Other experiments have used as an inducing stimulus a fan of lines like those in Fig. 3.32. These have been exposed subliminally as background to a test figure which has been compared with another figure which had no such background. An illusion has been observed.

These studies have not gone unchallenged. Other studies have failed to demonstrate illusions from subliminal stimuli. Perhaps the most instructive of these is that of Trimble and Eriksen (1966) because it used methods of signal-detection theory. No illusion was reported for the Müller-Lyer figure, if the luminance of the fins was low enough to give a $d' \leqslant 1$. But this says nothing of thresholds. There is no space here for explaining the details of detection theory, only to say that its very basis is a denial of the existence of thresholds in the classical sense. If stimuli are to be termed 'subliminal', then we must either work with some sort of convention of threshold or talk about subjects being 'consciously aware' of the stimulus. Trimble and Eriksen do neither of these things and so their argument is oblique to the issue.

Experiments on signal detection are, if anything, all in support of the notion of subliminal effects, since subjects in such experiments almost always report *feeling* as though they are guessing when in fact they are achieving better than chance detections. In other words, their behaviour is being influenced by the stimulus even though they would not admit being able to sense it.

The theoretical importance of subliminal illusory effects is recognised in this book implicitly rather than explicitly in that purely phenomenal explanations of illusions are not even discussed. If illusions can be caused by subliminal stimuli then no explanation of illusions can be entertained which sees illusions as the result of the observer's making a conscious adjustment to his response to the stimulus display. Several of the old theories reviewed by Boring (1942) would suffer this exclusion.

5

FIGURAL AFTER-EFFECTS

This book must include a chapter on figural after-effects because they are in many ways clear relatives of the geometric illusions and indeed it can be argued that they form a class of illusion in themselves as they are distortions of current perception caused by preceding stimulation. However, a very great deal has been written about them and therefore their treatment here cannot be complete. The reader is referred to such reviews as McEwan (1958) or Day, Pollack and Seagrim (1959). Discussion is necessary here because, in the following chapter, theories of illusions are reviewed which equate the processes underlying illusions with those responsible for figural after-effects. Such an equation is appealing because the two phenomena often seem to merge imperceptibly into one another. But when examined in detail this sort of theory has difficulty in accommodating all the data. This chapter will describe the two chief sorts of figural after-effects and the theories connected with them. It will consider whether they are really different and will then review some other well-known theories. Finally, a short section appears about the visual after-effects of head and body tilt.

GIBSON'S AFTER-EFFECTS

The first of the two sorts of figural after-effects was described by Gibson (Gibson, 1933; Gibson, 1937a,b; Gibson and Radner, 1937). When a tilted or curved line was inspected for some time (fixation was not necessary), the perceptual system showed apparent adaptation of its norms in the direction of the inspected tilt or curve. Thus if the subject was then presented with a vertical or straight line respectively he would see it as tilted or curved in the *opposite direction* to the inspection line. It is worth pointing out how it follows that if he were asked to *adjust* a test line to the apparent vertical then his setting would be tilted or curved *in the same direction* as the tilt or curve of the inspection line. In reading about these effects, the opposite directions of the appearance of tilt of the actual spatial norm, and the adjustment by the subject of the stimulus so that it apparently corresponds to the spatial norm, can be a source of confusion.

Gibson thought that this effect was due to adaptation of the perceptual spatial norms so that, as inspection progressed, a line slightly tilted from the vertical, for example, would appear more and more vertical. Gibson came to this work after studying the way subjects adapted to wearing goggles containing distorting lenses. He had found that after wearing such goggles for some time the distortions which are first observed apparently disappear or are much reduced. On discarding the goggles, straight lines appear distorted until the perceptual system has returned to its former state.

Gibson wrote: 'If a sensory process which has an opposite is made to persist by a constant application of its appropriate stimulus conditions, the quality will diminish in the direction of becoming neutral, and therewith the quality evoked by a stimulus for the dimension in question will be shifted temporarily toward the opposite or complimentary quality' (1937b, p. 223). He claimed that such a process was not confined to orientation but could be found in other qualities such as colour, brightness, temperature, movement, taste, kinaesthesis and pleasantness.

With a tilted line the maximum after-effect occurred with a tilt of 10° and with curves (Bales and Folansbee, 1935); gentle curves gave the maximum effect. The after-effect was maximal immediately after inspection and then diminished with time. Morant and Mikaelin (1960) provided further evidence of the nature of the effect by imposing the test figure on a different part of the visual field from the inspection figure. They still found an after-effect of a tilted inspection figure on a vertical test figure and even on a horizontal test figure.

The after-effect occurs also with lines or surfaces tilting or curving towards or away from the subject. Bergman and Gibson (1959) demonstrated the effect also for textured surfaces sloping away from the subject. The edges of these surfaces were not visible to the subject so the effect came from the texture alone and not from edge lines. During inspection, as usual, the surface slope seemed to diminish, and adjustment of the vertical was in error in the direction of the inspection slope, that is the true vertical appeared to be sloping in the opposite direction to the previous slope.

With a more complex stimulus still (the tilted miniature room used by Asch and Witkin, 1948), Austin, Singer and Day (1969) demonstrated an after-effect. After exposure to the tilted room, subjects were required to adjust a luminous rod in the dark. With a room tilt of 22° the after-effect was 4°. It lasted 15 minutes after a 5-minute exposure to the room.

Ikeda and Obonai (1953), using a curved inspection figure, made interesting observations of the effect of inspection time on the decay time of the after-effect. The after-effect took 10 seconds to reach zero after an inspection time of 1 second, and 80 seconds to reach zero after an inspection time of 240 seconds. The absolute size of the after-effect was *unaffected* by the length of the inspection provided that the test figure was presented immediately. Clearly, if there was a delay in presentation of the test figure, decay began during that delay and the decay function is different for different inspection times.

Culbert's (1954) study emphasises the kinship of this after-effect and the Zöllner figure. He exposed, for 2 minutes each, grids set at various angles and required subjects to set the horizontal after such exposure. He found a maximum effect on the horizontal when the set of parallel lines composing the grid was at an angle of 10° to the horizontal. This matches one of the two incompatible sorts of results obtained in the various studies of the Zöllner figure reported in Chapter 3.

KÖHLER'S FIGURAL AFTER-EFFECTS

Köhler did not accept Gibson's explanation of the after-effects reported by the latter. He saw such effects as merely examples of a more general sort of after-effect which he and Wallach (1944) called 'figural after-effects'. If a line is fixated for a time and then another line is placed in the visual field close to the position occupied by the fixated line, the second line will be apparently displaced. If a square is fixated and then replaced by a smaller square it will appear even smaller. In general, a contour occupying a position near one that has recently been occupied will be displaced. Fig. 5.1 illustrates a selection of the displays used by Köhler and Wallach.

Köhler's explanation of the phenomenon is probably already familiar to the reader. It involves the same hypothetical mechanisms as those used in his explanation of decrement in the Müller-Lyer illusion. When a stimulus arrives in the primary projection area of the cerebral cortex it generates 'electrotonus' in the area about the projection. This 'electrotonus' is an alteration of the polarisability of the tissue which makes it less sensitive to subsequent stimulation. Such tissue is 'satiated'. Thus when subsequent impulses arrive they are deflected into neighbouring areas and so they are perceived as being in a different place. 'Electrotonus' is greater with more intense stimuli, greater brightness contrast and longer exposure. It persists when its cause is removed but gradually decays.

Köhler and Wallach (1944) based their disagreement with Gibson on a particularly clear piece of evidence. They showed that if the inspection line was vertical and the test line was tilted there was still an after-effect. Why should a vertical inspection line cause alteration of the vertical spatial norm? This is clearly a difficulty for Gibson's theory.

Köhler and Wallach also found what they called the 'distance paradox'. This is the fact that the maximum displacement of a line does not occur when the inspection and test contours coincide but when they are a little way away from each other. Indeed, if the two contours do coincide, the tendency of the processes derived from the first to deflect the second would be exactly balanced in each direction and so no deflection would take place. They see the maximum as occurring where these tendencies have become quite unequal and yet where the test contour still falls on part of the field where satiation is strong.

Later work has elaborated on figural after-effects. Pollack (1958) showed that the after-effect was greater with greater brightness contrast. But it has also been shown that it does not completely depend on contrast, only on a visible contour. Day (1959) demonstrated this, using figures where there was only a hue difference between figures and background, no brightness difference. Crawford and Klingaman (1966) did the same, showing that blue gave the largest after-effect followed by orange and then grey.

The interplay of inspection time and interval between figures has now been mapped out in some detail. For example Oyama (1953) used a successive version of the Delbœuf figure where the inspection figure was a circle and the test figure was a smaller circle. The test circle was presented along with a comparison circle against which its apparent size was judged. As inspection time increased from 1 second, the size of the effect increased rapidly to reach an asymptote at between 15 and 20 seconds. After this, any further increase in inspection time had no influence on the size of the effect, only on the decay time which increased with increase in inspection time. If an interval was allowed between the inspection and test figures then inspection time did affect the size of the displacement, presumably because some decay took place during the interval. The latter showed a negatively accelerated increase with inspection time. This function is clearly determined by the different decay times for different inspection times. Thus, using plain bar figures (Fig. 5.1 bottom right) Hammer (1949) had observed the function of amount of distortion and inspection time, placing the asymptote at about 150 seconds. Duncan (1962) also confirmed Oyama's findings of the increase in decay time with increase in inspection time and the relatively small effect of the latter on the size of the initial after-effect.

Work has also been done with very short inspection times, down to 5 milliseconds, and short interstimulus intervals. Figural after-effects still appeared (Fehrer and Ganchrow, 1963; Farné, 1965). This clearly connects this field with the study of so-called 'meta-contrast' and 'backward masking', which will be mentioned again later but will not be treated in detail in this book. The interested reader is referred to Raab (1963) or Alpern (1952, 1953).

The question of where the after-effect originates in the visual system is an interesting one. Köhler and Wallach argue that it must be a central effect because it can be obtained when the inspection figure is viewed with one eye and the test figure with the other. But the input from the two retinae is superimposed in the visual system and so it is altogether likely that an after-effect which was caused by stimulation coming from one retina will still, even though the eye is closed, be superimposed on current input from the other.

Convincing evidence of the role of higher centres is presented by McEwan (1959) and Sutherland (1961). They both showed that a figural after-effect could be brought about by the *apparent* size of a figure not only by its retinal size. That is, if cues were provided, for example cues of distance, then the after-effect was appropriate to the apparent size of a figure rather than its retinal size. McEwan presented inspection figures and test figures which were all retinally equal; but some inspection figures were apparently larger and some apparently smaller than the test figures. After-effects were appropriate to the apparent sizes.

Kolehmainen and Cronhjort (1970) also showed that after-effects could be derived from apparent lines. They displayed illusion figures (Figs. 3.18, 3.32a and 3.33) as inspection figures and the distorted parts of these figures (parallel lines or squares) as test figures. The test figures were distorted in the opposite direction to the distortion observed in the full figures. This means that the apparent, distorted lines (the parallels or squares of the inspection figures) were causing the figural after-effect. When only the background lines were presented as the inspection figures the parallels or squares were distorted in after-effect in the same direction as in the illusion. Weitzman (1963) reported an interesting study using as an inspection figure a square divided down the middle by a contour resembling the profile of a human face. The test figure was a pair of dashes placed, by means of a suitable fixation point, each immediately below one half of the square. The experiment was done with the profile facing in each direction. Clearly, in each presentation there was a side of the square which was a figure and a side which was background against which the profile was viewed. There was always a greater figural after-effect, in the form of a greater displacement downward of the appropriate dash, on the 'figure' side of the square. Thus the test line near the 'figure' seems to be more displaced than that near the 'ground'. This seems to demonstrate that figural after-effects are influenced by the meaning of the display and

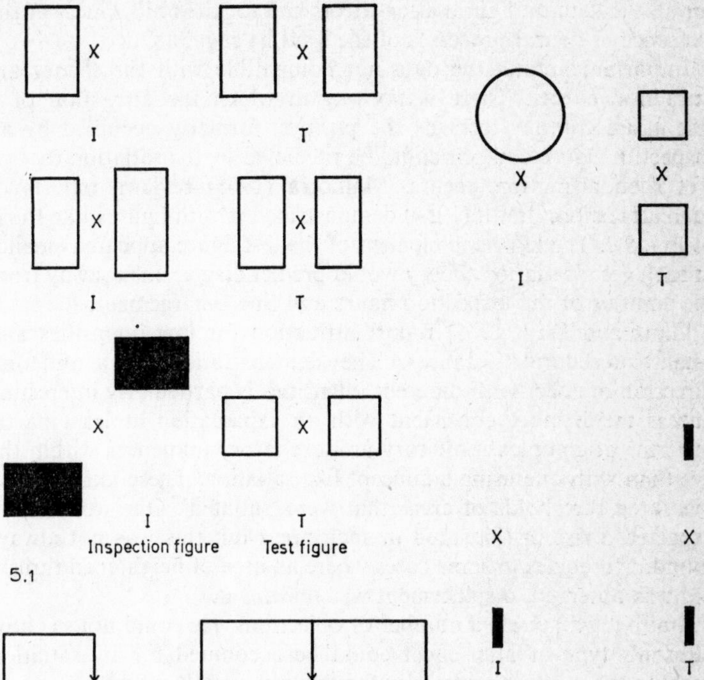

5.1

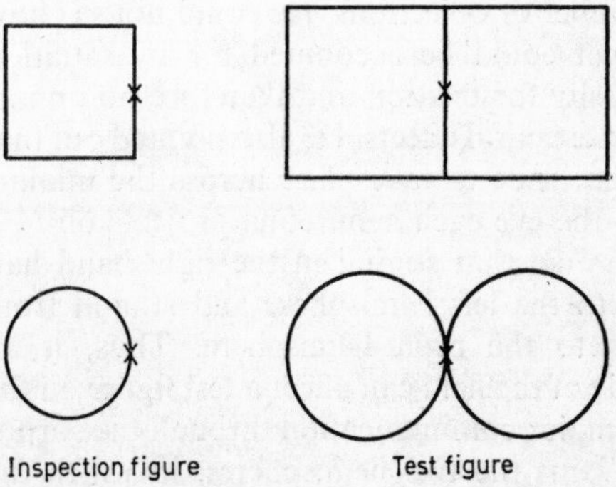

5.2

5.1 After Köhler and Wallach (1944) 5.2 After Smith (1954)

suggests that they are mediated at a high level in the visual system.

Claims that the effects are mediated higher in the system than the primary projection areas cause difficulties for Köhler's theory because he did not say how such higher processes could operate on satiation. Let us now look at other objections to Köhler's theory.

SHORTCOMINGS OF KÖHLER'S SATIATION THEORY

Köhler's theory has been criticised both for its failure to account for all the data on figural after-effects and for the unlikeliness of the existence of neural processes of the kind he suggests.

Important among the data not compatible with the theory are attraction effects. There is no way in which the attraction of a test figure contour towards the position formerly occupied by an inspection figure contour could be predicted by the satiation theory. Yet such attraction occurs. Malhotra (1968) reviews reports of such attraction. Smith (1954) demonstrated it with figures like those of Fig. 5.2. The left-hand element of the test figure appeared smaller in each case; satiation theory would predict displacement away from the contour of the inspection figure and thus enlargement.

Ganz and Day (1965) report attraction for low intensities and small interfigural distances. The demonstration of a different direction of effect with different intensities is particularly interesting and is much more consistent with an explanation at least partly in terms of complex inhibitory and excitatory influences within the eye than with one using a concept like satiation. These authors also measured thresholds of areas that were 'satiated'. One would have expected a rise in threshold in such areas but this was not always found. Moreover, in some cases where an area of heightened threshold was observed, displacement was *towards* it.

Smith (1948) made a number of objections. He could not see how Gibson's type of after-effect could be accounted for by satiation because there was no necessity for fixation and therefore no opportunity for situationally precise neural effects. He also pointed out that figural after-effects could be made to take place across the midline of the visual field. Now in the eye each hemiretina projects on to a different cortical hemisphere so that stimuli in the right-hand half of the visual field project to the left hemisphere and stimuli from the left-hand half project to the right hemisphere. Thus, if an inspection figure on one side of the field can affect a test figure on the other side there must be complex communication through the corpus callosum, the tract which joins the two hemispheres, in which the repulsion effect of the satiated area is transmitted.

The physiology of satiation theory has frequently been attacked.

For example, Lashley, Chow and Semmes (1951), after teaching monkeys a visual discrimination task, inserted gold foil or pins into the visual cortex to interfere with the 'figural currents'. They had no effect on the subsequent performance of the monkeys on the task. However, Köhler (1964) finds serious fault with these and other experiments of a similar sort. I do not wish to follow the controversy further. It seems sufficient here to say that the view that has been built up since the early 1960s of how the perception of lines and their position and orientation is carried out, a view that has been outlined earlier and is implicit in much of this book, does not seem consistent with Köhler's ideas of satiation. Moreover, even if it could be argued that the two views are indeed consistent, then the more recent view is still clearly more detailed and precise even in its present somewhat vague state.

Sutherland (1961) argues in a somewhat similar way. He shows that since the displacement effect reaches a maximum at a certain (small) interfigural distance then when inspection and test lines are not parallel they should appear bent (see Fig. 5.3). The observed distortion is nothing like this version of what would be expected on satiation theory. It is much more consistent with the notion of the orientation of a line being built up by the firing of a large population of directionally sensitive analysers. These are capable of becoming fatigued so that after viewing an inspection figure the perceived orientation of the test figure is derived from a biased population of analysers. Sutherland points out that the same sort of process could account for movement after-effects and we shall see later that there is much in what he says.

ARE GIBSON'S AND KÖHLER'S AFTER-EFFECTS DIFFERENT?

The question of whether we are dealing with one or two effects in Gibson's and Köhler's after-effects is an important one, particularly as the two reflect themes found in earlier chapters on illusions, namely orientation effects on the one hand and the perceptual displacement of one contour by another (as between the arms of an angle) on the other hand.

The two after-effects were examined by Morant and Harris (1965). They proposed theoretical curves describing the function of apparent tilt of a vertical test line caused by a tilted inspection line, with variation of the angle of tilt of the inspection line, for the two sorts of process. In the case of a 'satiation-like' process (Köhler), apparent tilt of the test line in the opposite direction to the tilt of the inspection line would reach a maximum at a fairly small angle of tilt of the

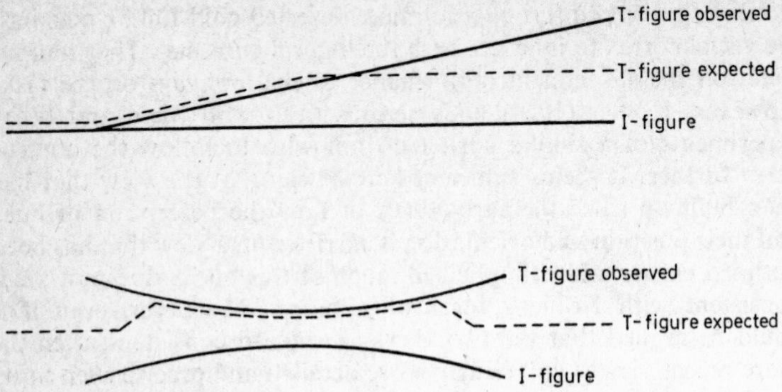

5.3

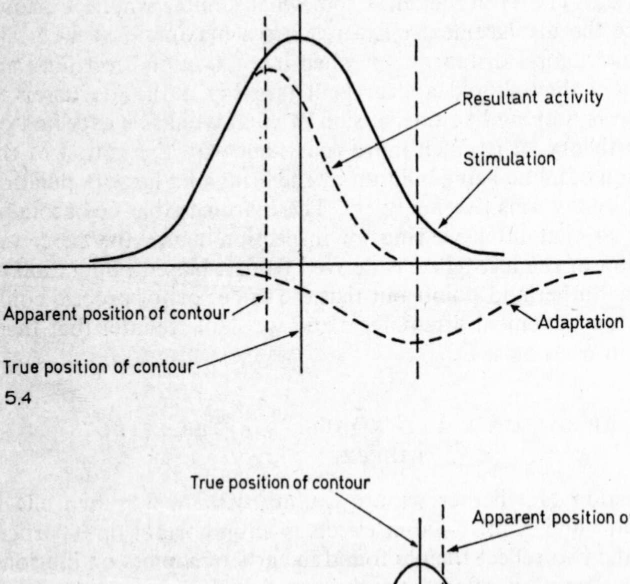

5.4

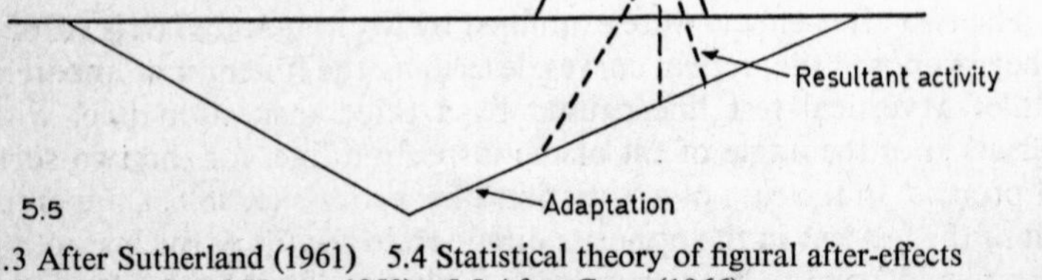

5.5

5.3 After Sutherland (1961) 5.4 Statistical theory of figural after-effects (after Osgood and Heyer, 1952) 5.5 After Ganz (1966) latter. The effect would then decline through greater angles of inspection line tilt through 45° to reach zero at 90°. With a 'normalisation-like' process (Gibson) the function would be broadly similar for smaller angles but at 45° the apparent tilt of the test line would begin to go in the same direction as the tilt of the inspection line because adaptation would be towards the horizontal spatial norm rather than the vertical one. The function between 45° and 90° would therefore be a mirror image of that between 0° and 90°.

In the first experiment of Morant and Harris, subjects fixated the middle of a tilted inspection line and then the middle of a test line which had to be set to appear vertical. Clearly, both satiation and normalisation can operate in this situation and indeed the function obtained was like the sum of the two functions described above. For angles of tilt of the inspection line below 45°, the function rose to a maximum and then fell. It passed through zero at more than 45°, remaining slightly negative until it returned to zero at 90°. In the second experiment, the tilted inspection line was presented to the left of the fixation point and the vertical test figure overlaid it, but adjustment was not of the vertical test figure but of a comparison line placed on the other side of the fixation point. This had to be adjusted so that it appeared vertical. Now if normalisation, which operates over a large distance in the visual field, were occurring, it would affect both test and comparison lines alike, so any *difference* in their apparent tilt must be due to satiation alone. So the authors argue, and they conclude that there are two different effects. Their data show that in the first situation there is a combination of both satiation and normalisation effects and, in the second, satiation acts alone.

Before the work of Morant and Harris mentioned above Prentice and Beardslee (1950) had also demonstrated the widespread nature of Gibson's effect. With the inspection figure on one side of a fixation point, and the test figure on the other, the effect still occurred.

Day (1962b) listed some notable differences between the Gibson and Köhler after-effects and was of the opinion that there were two separate processes. He claimed that the Köhler effect took place only up to a small separation of inspection and test contours (30 minutes of arc) and the extent of displacement was only 1 to 3 minutes of arc, whereas the Gibson effect took place with inter-figural separations of up to 12° and for an inspection figure tilted at an angle of 80 minutes there was an after-effect of 9 minutes. He also pointed out that the Gibson effect was not sensitive to contrast of the figures against their backgrounds, whereas the Köhler effect was fairly closely related to it. Finally, he mentioned the already obvious difference, that Gibson's subjects did not generally fixate whereas Köhler's subjects did.

Another source of differentiation between the two effects has been their time course. Papert (1964), in a study the details of which have been kindly amplified for me by Wilson (1969) who was associated with the work, used a line tilted at 10° for an inspection figure and one tilted at 12° for a test figure. Gibson's effect would cause the line to be rotated apparently towards the vertical and Köhler's effect would cause it to be rotated apparently away from the vertical, since the test line would fall on the side of the position of the inspection line farther from the vertical. For short inspection times, fractions of a second, the test line was apparently rotated away from the vertical (Köhler) and for longer inspection times, tens of seconds, it was rotated apparently towards the vertical (Gibson). Papert recommends the time course of after-effects and illusions as a likely source of fruitful study. Such work has been done for various sorts of after-effect, but little has yet been done for illusions as far as I have been able to discover. It seems to have been relatively neglected except by Piaget's group (Piaget, 1961).

Wilson (1965) also succeeded in demonstrating apparently separate effects. He found that a straight inspection line produced an after-effect which increased the curve of a curved test line. This would not be expected by adaptation, because there is no reason why a straight line should cause adaptation. A satiation effect would also be difficult to fit in with Wilson's results because when the inspection line was exactly the same as the test line he still found an after-effect.

The first of these demonstrations was similar to a demonstration, by Köhler and Wallach, that a vertical inspection line has an after-effect on a tilted test line. They used this to dismiss the idea that Gibson's effect was due to adaptation of spatial norms. Wilson decided to repeat this experiment and showed that although such an after-effect did occur, it was much smaller than the effect with the figures interchanged. The after-effect with a tilted inspection figure was 1·35 times that with a vertical one; Köhler and Wallach had claimed that the effects in two situations were identical. Wilson's results clearly suggest two processes, with a satiation type of process acting alone when the inspection line was vertical, and acting in combination with an adaptation type of process when the inspection line was tilted.

Wilson does not see these as separate types of process, however, but as short- and long-term effects of the same process of diminution of excitability in the visual system as a result of stimulation. The process is exactly that proposed by Osgood and Heyer (1952) and described in the next section, but Wilson thinks first of a short-term effect, which is the repulsion of a test line away from the position of the inspection line (see Fig. 5.4). Next, within a very short space of time, the test line itself begins to bring about neural adaptation and this works most rapidly on the part that was not already so adapted by the inspection figure (the part on the left in Fig. 5.4). This is because both adaptation and recovery are seen as negatively accelerated functions of time and excitation. When this is subtracted from the 'activity' curve (Fig. 5.4) the peak of that curve moves back towards the position of the inspection figure. This is the adaptation effect. All this certainly fits with Papert's (1964) results mentioned above and also with some of the very long-term changes observed in studies with distorting goggles. It is difficult, however, to reconcile Wilson's idea with studies showing that an inspection figure can cause adaptation effects of the Gibson type some distance across the visual field. It seems to demand that the test and inspection lines are within the range of separation required for the Köhler type of effect.

Over (1971) makes a case which in some ways resembles Wilson's. He proposes that both the Gibson and Köhler after-effects are due to neural inhibitory action. The former occur when non-topographic information is used by the perceptual system (for example, orientation information which says nothing about the position of the stimulus) and the latter when topographic information is used. This fits well with the way the Gibson effect takes place over large distances on the retina whereas the Köhler effect does not. Intuitively it also appears likely that, if there are separate analysers for different stimulus characteristics, then, since after-effects are general characteristics of perceptual function, each kind of analyser will have its own after-effect.

The evidence seems to indicate that the Gibson and Köhler after-effects can be observed separately but, more important for the practical problem of studying them, each is also likely to interfere in studies whose primary interest is the other. And this sort of difficulty will be a universal one in the study of perception if perception is achieved by the parallel processing of various characteristics of the display (orientation, movement, spatial frequency and so on).

OTHER THEORIES OF FIGURAL AFTER-EFFECTS

A number of theories have appeared since the work of Köhler and Wallach (1944) which have not made much of the distinction between the Gibson and Köhler effects and have generally dealt with the latter. Two will be discussed here; those of Osgood and Heyer (1952) and Ganz (1966a,b).

The statistical theory of Osgood and Heyer

This account of figural after-effects made use of a theory of visual acuity put forward by Marshall and Talbot (1942). A good brief version of it appears in Osgood (1953). Marshall and Talbot suppose that nystagmus and various sorts of interaction within the visual pathways, for example reciprocal overlap and lateral summation, all lead to a situation in which a line or contour on the retina is represented in the visual projection area as a normal distribution of activity. We are talking here about frequency of firing. The cells corresponding with the peak of the distribution will be firing with relatively high frequency and those in the tails of the distribution with relatively low frequency. The perceived position of a line, according to Osgood and Heyer, will be determined by the position of this peak and anything happening to shift the peak will shift the apparent position of the line. Now the cells in the system are capable of adaptation, which happens as a negatively accelerated function of the rate at which, and the time for which, they have been firing. This means that after a line has been fixated for a time there will be a normal distribution of adaptation at the appropriate point which, when stimulation ceases, will gradually flatten and disappear with time. Any new stimulation falling on this area during the period of adaptation will need to be much more intense to bring about the same frequency of firing as resulted from the first stimulus when the area was fresh. If the new stimulus is the same intensity as the old, then presumably it will look dimmer. But the position of the peak of the firing caused by the new stimulation is our chief interest. If there is already normally distributed adaptation, and new stimulation falls near, but is not coincident with it, then the new positive influence will summate with the existing negative influence to result in a distribution of activity whose peak is shifted. It thus lies, not where it would be expected to lie if there were no area of adaptation, but further away from the peak of the adaptation (see Fig. 5.4).

This theory accounted well for the temporal characteristics of Köhler's type of after-effect. Osgood and Heyer showed also that it could account for the distance paradox and various other figural after-effect phenomena. The distance paradox follows from the subtraction of the normal curve for neural adaptation by the inspection figure from the normal curve for stimulation by the test figure. As the peaks of the two distributions move closer together, the peak of the curve resulting from the subtraction first moves away from the peak of the stimulation (test) curve and, after reaching a maximum separation, returns towards it. This is the distance paradox. The reader can verify this by actually subtracting one normal distribution from another with its mean offset by different amounts.

Unfortunately, this theory does no better than satiation theory in dealing with the paradoxical attraction of contours reported by Smith (1954). Nor does it cope, as this latter writer had pointed out earlier (1952), with the situation where inspection and test contours coincide. Like Köhler's, this theory predicts no displacement, yet displacement takes place.

Several writers have questioned the role of nystagmus in the theory of Osgood and Heyer. This amounts to a criticism of Marshall and Talbot too. However, as Hochberg and Hay (1956) admit, to show that figural after-effects occur in the absence of nystagmus shows only that nystagmus is not a necessary condition. It may still be a sufficient one. It is only one source of the interlacing of activity which results in the final distribution. Hochberg and Hay eliminated any effect of nystagmus by presentation of the inspection figure by a single short intense flash. They still observed an after-effect. Krauskopf (1960) used a stabilised retinal image. The image was kept still on the retina by means of one of the contact-lens methods and still a figural after-effect could be observed. It is worth saying too that Ratliff (1952) had shown that nystagmus, far from being part of the acuity process, actually hindered it.

Deutsch (1956) showed clearly that the basic principle of the theory of Osgood and Heyer, that of the subtraction of the adaptation distribution from the excitation distribution could not account for both after-effect and acuity threshold data. If the peak of the excitation distribution is to be perceived as the locus of a line, then any *two* lines can only be distinguished from one another if the peaks of their distributions are distinct. Now according to the Osgood and Heyer theory, the distribution of adaptation (the mirror image of the excitation distribution of the inspection line) and the distribution of excitation of the test line are so close together that their peaks merge to form the resultant distribution which determines the apparent position of the test line. This means that the largest possible interfigural distance (between the inspection and the test figures) must be smaller than the threshold of separation of the two lines. This prediction does not fit the facts; figural after-effects are seen with interfigural distances of many times the acuity threshold.

Sutherland's (1961) argument also applies to this theory. If the effects were so localised immediately around contours then the result ought to be bending or kinking of the contours (see Fig. 5.3), not wholesale tilting. This argument was put against Köhler's theory earlier.

Thus the arguments against the theory advanced by Osgood and Heyer are as strong as those against Köhler's theory. Despite the appeal of extending the range of application of the theory of Marshall and Talbot, Osgood and Heyer do not seem to have overcome the chief objections to satiation theory. That being so, they have done little more than update the language of satiation theory to fit the physiology of Marshall and Talbot.

The lateral inhibition theory of Ganz

This theory, advanced by Ganz (1966,a,b) has some ideas in common with that of Osgood and Heyer in that it sees the position of a peak of excitation in the visual system as determining the apparent position of a line. The theory relies, however, for the shifting of a contour, not a process of adaptation, but on the widely accepted and well-documented notion of lateral inhibition. Ganz (1966a) reviewed a lot of evidence, both psychophysical and physiological, of the existence of such a process. There is no room for this here, but it is enough to say that lateral inhibition is a process whereby a unit in the system is so connected laterally that when it is stimulated it exerts an inhibitory influence upon units around it, depressing their response. Such a process will give rise to brightness contrast by intensifying the difference between a light and a dark area.

Lateral inhibition could be exerted, according to Ganz, either by a contour currently being put into the system or by the after-image of a contour no longer present in the field of view. He assumed that inhibition decreased linearly in strength with distance from the inhibiting contour. Unfortunately, Westheimer the following year (1967) reported finding that this was not so; indeed there was facilitation within 5 minutes of arc and inhibition occurred only at greater distances. Whilst Ganz's theory does not necessarily rest on the assumption of linearity of the function of inhibition and distance, the facilitation effect is not included in his theory.

Inhibition acts on the distribution caused by the test line, in a manner very similar to the way Osgood's adaptation acted (see Fig. 5.5). It subtracts asymmetrically from the test line's distribution of activity and so shifts its peak further away from the position of the inspection line.

Eye movement is of central importance in this theory because it is used to explain the distance paradox. Consider the viewing of the test figure when the after-image of the inspection figure is present on the retina. This after-image itself presumably would be spread somewhat by nystagmus during inspection, but as an after-image it would be stationary. Now during eye movements in viewing the test figure this figure would be moved about on the retina and therefore its position relative to the stationary after-image of the inspection figure would vary. Thus, the actual setting made by the subject on any one occasion might be either of two sorts of judgment. It might be the amount of contour shift for the current instantaneous position of the eye, or it might be the amount of shift derived from some sort of average of its immediately past positions. Either way several such settings would be expected to vary among themselves in a manner which is related to eye movements, and the greater the spread of eye movements the greater the variance of a set of such readings.

Our immediate interest, however, is in the situation where interfigural distance is small and eye movement therefore allows the image of the test figure to stray, at least now and then, over to the *other* side of the after-image of the inspection figure. On these occasions, the shift of the peak of the test figure brought about by the after-image will be in the opposite direction and so there will be an increased probability of the subject making a setting in the opposite direction. Since most conclusions are based on an average of many settings, decrease of interfigural distance will decrease the displacement of the *mean* setting. This is Ganz's explanation of the distance paradox. As interfigural distance decreases, the strength of lateral inhibition, and therefore the degree of contour shift, increases until the crossing over of the two images begins to reduce the displacement of the mean setting. Clearly there will be an interfigural distance where the net value of these two opposing effects is maximal, and with further decrease in interfigural distance the value will be reduced.

Ganz seems to have produced a plausible theory, but again there are difficulties. When inspection and test contours coincide Ganz's theory, just like the others, predicts no displacement. Eye movements may move the test figure about over the after-image of the inspection figure but the expected mean of the settings is zero. Observed after-effects with this arrangement are not zero. Also, reports of attraction displacement are as embarrassing to Ganz as to the others. Approach of the test contour to the inspection contour brings about a reduction of expected mean setting but this mean should only approach zero, it should not become negative.

It seems a pity that Westheimer's (1967) observations were not available to Ganz. It will be remembered that Westheimer showed facilitation close to a point of stimulation and inhibition further away from it. Incorporating this into his theory Ganz need not have invoked eye movements at all. Inhibition would have caused a shift of the test contour away from the inspection contour and facilitation would have caused a move towards it. This predicts the attraction found by Ganz and Day (1965) for very small interfigural distances. Also, since repulsion would increase to a maximum with decreasing interfigural distance and then decrease, it would accommodate the distance paradox.

However, it is unlikely that this would surmount a difficulty put by Willems (1967). He used as inspection figures various letters with parts missing. The test figure consisted in each case of the part that was missing and a comparison figure. The part was so placed relative to the fixation point that it fell precisely where, in the inspection figure, the gap had been. Figural after-effects were observed, that is, the small part did not appear to lie precisely in the gap. This means that the after-effect was induced by the *rest of the figure*. At the point at which the effect actually occurred, there had simply been no inspection line at all.

Neither Osgood and Heyer nor Ganz concern themselves with the type of after-effect reported by Gibson. I have described Wilson's (1965) attempt to incorporate them into the former theory. I have found no attempt to account for them in terms of Ganz's theory.

An important aspect of Ganz's theory, particularly in the present context, is the ease with which it appears to be extendable to account for geometrical optical illusions. This is considered separately among theories of illusions in Chapter 6. After-effects, in fact, are regarded as special cases of illusions where the inducing contour is the after-image of the inspection figure rather than, for example in the Zöllner figure, the currently present oblique lines.

The theories so far reviewed by no means exhaust the list of such theories. Pollack (1963) applies the 'sensory-tonic field' theory of Wapner and Werner (1957) to figural after-effects, and Helson's (1964) 'adaptation-level' theory is also clearly applicable. Motokawa, Nakagawa and Kohata (1957) have applied their notions of 'retinal induction' to figural after-effects. Taylor (1962b) has put forward a 'psychophysical' theory. Some of these theories are described among theories of illusions and the objections to them are discussed there. What has already begun to emerge, and will become more apparent when these other theories are considered, is that a wholly adequate explanation of figural after-effects has yet to appear.

VISUAL AFTER-EFFECTS OF HEAD AND BODY TILT

A small class of phenomena which fits most suitably here consists of the visual after-effects of head and body tilt. These are closely related to three other effects; namely, the after-effect of viewing a tilted line when the observer is vertical (this, of course, is Gibson's after-effect), the distortion of the direction of a line by a simultaneously present tilted line, and the distortion of the direction of a line caused by the observer's being himself *currently* tilted. These latter two effects were included along with illusions of angles and direction.

When the observer, in a vertical position after having been tilted for a period of time, is required to set a line so that it appears vertical, he sets it tilted in the same direction as his former tilt. The true vertical, therefore, appears to him to be tilted in the opposite direction to his former tilt. Such observations have been made by Day and Wade (1966), and in very much more detail by Wade and Day (1968a). They showed, by variation of the period of tilt, and of the interval between the end of tilt and making the adjustment of the vertical, that the after-effect both grows and decays exponentially and has an asymptote at a period of tilt of about 180 seconds. They used an angle of tilt of 30° throughout, this being the angle which gave maximum effect. Wade (1968) demonstrated that input from the neck muscles was important. His experiment, showing that tilting the body only (not the head) was equivalent to tilting the head alone in the opposite direction, was reported earlier in the section on illusions of angles and direction. It applied to the after-effect just as to the simultaneous effect.

Plainly Gibson's idea of adaptation of the spatial norms is applicable to these data. When he is tilted, the subject's vertical spatial norm adapts in the direction of his tilt, and so he sets his apparent vertical in that direction when returned to an even keel. However, most work has not dealt with such general theory.

Wade and Day (1968b) attempted to find whether proprioception was important in visual after-effect of tilt. When a subject's head has been tilted he makes an error in adjusting *it* to the vertical. If this is the source of the error in adjustment of a line to the vertical after head tilt, then as the angle of tilt increases, both the error in adjusting the head and the error in adjusting a line should increase also. Wade and Day found that the error in adjusting the line did indeed increase with increase of angle of tilt, but the error in adjusting the head decreased with larger angles. They concluded that proprioception did not play a major part.

Kinaesthetic effects were clearly shown to be important by Schneider and Bartley (1962). They fixed a frame on to subjects' heads and hung weights on one side or the other. In these conditions, subjects' adjustment of the apparent vertical sloped in the direction away from the weighted side. Having weights on one side of the head seems to be equivalent to tilting it towards the other side.

However the effect is mediated, it seems likely that it is a direct effect on seeing and not an adjustment after the act of perception has taken place. Horn and Hill (1969) produced interesting evidence relevant to this. When a cat's head was tilted they noticed a change in the orientation responded to by some of the simple receptive fields in the cortex. This seems to suggest that the after-effect is built into the very basic elements of perception.

The broad conclusion of this chapter is that we have not yet succeeded in formulating a widely acceptable theoretical account of figural after-effects. Accounts which try to make use of inhibitory processes in the visual system have seemed at first to be very promising, but have met objections serious enough to warrant their rejection. An account which uses the concepts of both inhibition and excitation in the visual system, operating over different distances in the visual field, does not appear yet to have been attempted, but might be fruitful, particularly because it might surmount the problem of attraction of the test contour towards the inspection contour. If such an account also used Over's (1971) distinction between topographic and non-topographic information from the visual field, it might well also successfully accommodate the two kinds of figural after-effect, those of Gibson and those of Köhler.

The experiments in the last section of the chapter were fairly straightforward attempts to find out what it is about tilting the observer that brings about a visual after-effect. Their authors did not concern themselves with theorising about the details of how the after-effect happens.

6

THEORIES OF THE GEOMETRICAL OPTICAL ILLUSIONS

The study of illusions began early in the history of psychology and the formation of theories followed closely. Boring (1942) recounts early theories, noting that twelve different theories of the Müller-Lyer illusion had appeared between 1889 and 1902. The seeds of some of the later theories are contained in these, but most would nowadays be seen as adding little to a mere description of the illusion. Thus Müller-Lyer himself explained the illusion in terms of the elongation of the arms of an obtuse angle as compared with those of an acute angle, while Brentano's explanation was in terms of the perceptual enlargement of acute angles and the reduction of obtuse angles. Others such as Delbœuf and Schumann argued in terms of the alteration of the overall judgment of the figures by various aspects of the fins. Wundt and Heymans based theories on eye movements and 'tendencies to eye movement' respectively, and Thiéry was the forerunner of 'perspective' theorists.

The ones amongst these which have the clearest echoes in later theories are those in which a specific sort of mechanism has been suggested, for example the distortion of angles or the operation of perspective. And a noticeable characteristic of later theories is the suggestion each contains of a mechanism by which illusions might be brought about. It is either a mechanism that has already been observed and which has been shown to operate in other aspects of perception and often has been demonstrated physiologically (for example, lateral inhibition); or it is a hypothetical mechanism expressed by means, perhaps, of a physical analogy. The theory of Eriksson (1970) is an example of the use of such a physical analogy, namely potential theory.

I shall review theories, beginning with those that propose a retinal mechanism and continuing with those that propose more complex mechanisms. Next, theories which are expressed as fairly simple relationships mathematically will be examined, and finally I shall try to evaluate adaptation level theory, which is one of those theories which propose a hypothetical mechanism of a much more general nature which accounts for illusions as well as a large group of other perceptual phenomena.

THEORIES WHICH PROPOSE RETINAL MECHANISMS

Motokawa's retinal induction theory

When an electric pulse is put across the eye between an electrode on the bridge of the nose and one on the temporal side of the eye an experience results of a brief flash of light. This is known as a 'phosphene'. Motokawa discovered that the strength of pulse required to create a phosphene varied with the immediately preceding stimulation of the eye. The quantity he actually measured was the phosphene threshold after two different stimuli had been applied, a monochromatic yellow patch of light, just clear of the fixation point, followed by a much smaller white test patch slightly offset from the yellow. From this was subtracted the phosphene threshold for the white patch alone and the result he called the 'contrast effect'. Now if the yellow patch took the form of a figure of some sort the contrast effect differed both according to what the particular figure was and according to the position of the test patch in relation to it. This description is only an outline of what was done. For details the reader should consult Motokawa (1950) or Motokawa and Akita (1957).

Motokawa found that the contrast effect was greatest when the white test patch was close to the position of the yellow figure and that it decreased with distance of the patch from the figure. The gradient of decrease, however, varied a great deal with the shape of the figure. In the case of the Müller-Lyer figure with outgoing fins, when such a gradient was plotted along a line bisecting the angle of the fins outside the figure, it was found that the gradient went down in two steps, one coinciding with the apex and one lying roughly on a line between the tips of the fins. Exactly the same was true for the figure with ingoing fins when the gradient was explored from the apex inwards along the shaft. Now Motokawa's idea was that such steps in the gradient would affect the perception of the ends of the shafts and therefore the shaft of the figure with outgoing fins would be seen as apparently longer and the shaft of the figure with ingoing fins as apparently shorter. But in both cases he ignores the step at the apex. Why the perceptual system should be affected by one step and not the other is obscure. Again, he gives no account of how the part near the apex should appear. Should the shaft appear to project beyond the apex in the outgoing figure? Ogasawara (1958) makes this sort of point in suggesting that if steep gradients of 'contrast effect' are seen as edges then the figure with outgoing fins should be seen as two solid triangles joined by a broad bar.

Motokawa also examined the Helmholtz square (Fig. 2.73) and found that a steep gradient occurred on the 'broken' side of the square (the side composed of the ends of lines) *inside* the square's boundary. This caused the illusion in the usual way. He also observed that the total field of induction for the square was smaller in the direction of the lines than in a direction perpendicular to them. He saw this as contributing to the illusion too. He also showed that the length of the field round a broken bar was greater than that round a complete bar of the same length. This is how he accounts for a version of the Oppel–Kundt illusion (Fig. 2.69) using, once again, total extent of induction field as his explanation rather than discontinuity of gradient.

Thus Motokawa did not examine a very large range of illusions and did not say very precisely how gradients or extents of induction fields could be used to explain illusions. Moreover, his work has proved difficult to repeat. Although Indow, Kuno and Yoshida (1958) confirmed some of his basic findings, Nakagawa (1958), using the Müller-Lyer figure with outgoing fins and no shaft, found no step in the gradient along the line bisecting the angle between the fins.

Western writers have also used Motokawa's technique, but have not studied illusion figures. Michaels (1960) explored the field of induction round a single yellow spot and found the effect to decrease exponentially away from the spot. The field was also asymmetric, being more extensive horizontally than vertically. It is interesting just to recall in this connection the work of Künnapas, mentioned earlier, with the vertical–horizontal illusion, in which he claimed that the visual field as a whole was more extensive horizontally than vertically. If the field in this fresh sense of an 'induction field' about a figure is asymmetric it might account for the data produced by Künnapas without running into some of the difficulties encountered by his original idea.

Howarth and Treisman (1958) failed to replicate many details of Motokawa's technique. They also substituted a bell for Motokawa's white test patch and found little effect of the substitution on the phosphene threshold. Their investigation did not include complex figures in the yellow induction phase of the technique, but there is a clear suggestion that in their experiment it would not have mattered where the white test patch was placed in relation to the yellow; it served merely as a warning stimulus for the phosphene pulse. This is a severe criticism of Motokawa's work and clearly a good deal more replication is needed. But this sort of study of the detail of the visual field about an illusion figure seems to me to be likely to be fruitful. Perhaps the phenomenon studied by Motokawa is an overcomplex one, the simple visual threshold for the white light might give results as good as the phosphene threshold. A great deal of detailed work remains to be done.

Chiang's diffraction theory

This theory, proposed by Chiang (1968), is a very restricted one. It deals with situations in which lines running close together affect one another. It applies therefore to the angular distortions and, he claims, to the Müller-Lyer figure, but does not deal with contrast. It might be applied to the framing effect if it were stated quantitatively but this has not been done. Moreover the theory has been so cogently criticised that it is likely to be short-lived.

Chiang likened the light coming into the eye from two lines to the light falling on to a screen from two slit sources in the study of diffraction patterns. The diffraction patterns of two such sources form distributions of light on the screen each of whose brightness in a direction perpendicular to the line can be described by a bell-shaped distribution. When the lines are brought near to one another their distributions will coalesce and will in fact summate. Now the distribution produced by this summation will be bimodal when the lines are well apart, but as they move closer the resultant distribution will form a single peak whilst the lines are still some way apart. This is a simple consequence of adding two such distributions. Chiang proposed that the pattern of two lines on the retina would be like such a diffraction pattern because of the blurring and diffusing effect of the media and the construction of the eye. The perceived locations of the lines would be at the peaks of the distributions, thus the two lines would apparently become one when the sum of their distributions formed a single peak. Consequently lines forming an angle would appear to converge to form a single line sooner that they actually did. Presumably this would lead to the perceptual enlargement of acute angles and therefore applies to the Wundt, Hering, Zöllner, Poggendorff, Orbison and many other figures. Its application to the Müller-Lyer is slightly different. Here the effect derives from an apparent shift of the apex brought about by the lines' premature convergence. This shift is in the direction away from that in which the arrow-head is pointing. Thus, the figure with ingoing fins appears shorter and the figure with outgoing fins appears longer.

This apparent shifting of the apex accounts for the apparent constriction where two lines cross at an acute angle. The cross so formed seems almost split into two separate acute angles so thin does the part which joins them appear. This said, however, Chiang's theory offers little more.

If illusions are the result of interactions at the retina they should not appear when inducing and distorted lines are presented to separate eyes in the stereoscope. They clearly do (see Chapter 4). Moreover, it is easy to find other versions of illusions mentioned by Chiang which do not fit his theory. Thus Pressey and den Heyer (1968) cite Figs. 3.42 and 3.43 which show that the figure with *obtuse* angles has the greater effect. It needs little thought to conclude that on Chiang's theory this should not be so. Indeed Restle (1969) claims that Fig. 3.43 gives the reverse of the usual Poggendorff effect. Pressey and den Heyer also cite Tolanski's figure (Fig. 3.40) where the top line appears shifted from its true position *without rotation*; Chiang's theory must postulate such rotation, though he does not go into detail about exactly how the effect near the apex enters into the complete perception of the whole line. In this connection these same authors quote the work of Mountjoy (1966) showing overestimation of the distance between the outer ends of the fins on the Müller-Lyer figure with ingoing fins. This again demands apparent rotation of the whole fin since it apparently is shifted one way at one end and the other way at the other. Chiang's omission of any sort of 'averaging' assumption inspires Cumming's (1968) criticism that there should be bends or breaks in the lines if the theory is correct. He advanced more telling points. Chiang's theory cannot account for decrement in illusions with repeated trials, cannot predict an illusion in Fig. 2.3 and 2.4 (the 'dumb-bell' and rectangular-ended versions of the Müller-Lyer) because there are no acute angles, cannot account for changes in illusion with changes in orientation of figures, and cannot account for the persistence of an illusion when the parts of the lines near the junctions are omitted. Such persistence is easily observed; indeed Coren (1970) has shown that a Müller-Lyer and a Poggendorff figure can be made only of dots and still show an illusion.

The very basis of Chiang's theory has been criticised too. Cumming (1968) points out that diffraction patterns would require the light from the two slit sources to be coherent. It would be so if it were all from the same source, but the light from an illusion display usually comes from all sorts of haphazard reflections of ambient light. The light should also be monochromatic: white light would make a much more complex diffraction pattern than Chiang describes. Coren (1969) used an artificial pupil and a chromatic filter to reduce the diffraction effects in the eyes of his subjects. He calculated that he had reduced the blur by 70 per cent, but the illusion was reduced by only 15·6 per cent.

In its short history Chiang's theory has not done well, and I propose now to leave it. It seems to me to have intrinsic interest even though it has been largely unsuccessful. The next group of theories to be considered are the theories in which eye movements are advanced as an important causative factor in illusions. Helmholtz (1856) cast the first serious doubt on such theories by showing that some illusions persisted when exposed by a flash of light, but conviction of the force of this argument has taken time to germinate!

EYE-MOVEMENT THEORIES

Many studies have been made of the movement of the eyes in viewing illusion figures, for example Judd (1905), Cameron and Steele (1905) and Judd and Courten (1905). The formulation put forward by Carr (1935) is the best known of the eye-movement theories formed with the advantage of knowledge of some experimental work on the subject. Carr did not subscribe exclusively to his theory but saw eye movements as at least contributing to the total illusion. He proposed that the eyes react to accessory lines and as a result pass more easily over unfilled than filled extents. This implies that almost any judgment of size must also be related to eye movements, though he did not say this. To this explanation of the filled/unfilled spaces illusion he added explanations of the Müller-Lyer, Poggendorff and Zöllner illusions. In the Müller-Lyer figure the eyes move more freely over the figure with outgoing fins than over the one with ingoing fins. He quoted Judd's findings that there is a hesitation in the eye movement over the latter figure at points on the shaft between the outer ends of the fins, which disappears after practice, just as the illusion disappears. In both the Poggendorff and Zöllner figures, deflections and hesitations in the eye movement are associated with the junctions of the oblique lines when the subject is instructed to move his eyes along the long lines of the figure. In both cases practice, which reduces the illusion, reduces the deflections and hesitations. Carr also mentions Lewis's (1908) demonstration that decrement with practice is much less with brief exposures of the illusion, the suggestion being that in this case the alteration of eye movement had no chance to occur.

Carr emphasised that all the work quoted shows only a correlation and not a causative relationship between eye movements and illusions. This is an important point made again by Yarbus (1967). He demonstrated once again that lateral eye movement had a smaller amplitude when the subject viewed the Müller-Lyer figure with ingoing fins than when he viewed the other figure. Yarbus also presented his subjects with a horizontal line crossed by an oblique and asked them to follow down the oblique with their eyes. They did this successfully as far as the junction with the horizontal and then their eyes moved off in a direction making a less acute angle with the horizontal than did the oblique. Yarbus concluded that illusions affect eye movements; a conclusion no less justifiable than its converse.

The most destructive evidence for this sort of theory however is provided by studies of stabilised retinal images. Pritchard (1958) used the contact-lens arrangement of Ditchburn and Ginsborg (1952) and showed that the Zöllner and one of the Ehrenberg (angular distortion) figures were little changed. Evans and Marsden (1966) made a more elaborate study using a flash to put a strong after-image on the retina. After-images in the shape of the Müller-Lyer, Poggendorff, Hering, Zöllner and Orbison figures were used together with the vertical–horizontal illusion, the Sander parallelogram and Wundt's area illusion. The illusions persisted in all these figures.

As a final point haptic illusions should be mentioned. Révész (1934) demonstrated that an illusion was obtained when figures were 'inspected' by tracing with the fingers over a raised outline and not seeing the figure at all. Illusions were also demonstrated without finger movement, the hand being laid passively on the figure. Over (1968) has taken an interest more recently in this sort of illusion and has repeated the work of Révész.

Clearly, eye movement is not necessary for illusions, though the relationship between the two is not by that fact divested of interest. A subtly difficult theory which fits best here has been advanced by Piaget. It is not wholeheartedly an eye-movement theory as will be evident later, but it slips into that role sufficiently often for it to be classified as one. It is at any rate a theory connecting characteristics of visual search with illusions.

PIAGET'S THEORY

Piaget (1961) accounts for what he calls the optico-geometric illusions by means of his 'law of relative centrations'. 'Centration' is a kind of centring of attention. It is not the centring of gaze although such fixation would usually entail centration. He and, to a greater extent, Vurpillot (1959) in her exposition of Piaget's 'law', seem to regard fixation as almost synonymous with 'centration'. 'Centration' on part of the field causes an overestimation of that part relative to the rest of the field.

Take, for example, two lines differing in length. If they differ only slightly, then, according to Vurpillot (1959), the difference will be underestimated. If they differ markedly then the difference will be overestimated. During inspection 'centration' will flit from line to line. Let us call the longer line A, and the shorter line B, and the overestimation during centration δA and δB. Now when $(A-B)>\delta B$:

During centration on A: $(A+\delta A)>B$ (since A itself is longer than B)
During centration on B: $(B+\delta B)<A$ (that is, adding δB to B is not sufficient to make it as long as A)

Thus, A will be overestimated when 'centration' is on either line. On the other hand when $(A-B)<\delta B$:

During centration on A: $(A+\delta A)>B$
During centration on B: $(B+\delta B)>A$

Thus, when 'centration' is on A it seems larger than B and when 'centration' is on B it seems larger than A. This is exactly what would happen if the lines were actually equal and so there is a tendency towards seeing these unequal lines as more nearly equal than they are. How the system distinguishes between a state of near equality and a state of complete equality is not explained. This is an elaboration of Vurpillot's (1959) explanation of the effect of 'centration'.

The final perception is in some sense an average of the effects of many 'centrations'. When no illusion has occurred, Piaget supposes that the overestimations and underestimations have cancelled one another out during the many 'centrations' involved in viewing a visual field; if an illusion does occur then they have not cancelled one another out. Such cancelling he calls 'decentration'. Much of the rest of his theorising consists of suggesting rules governing this averaging process. Different configurations bias the average to different extents and in different ways.

Various other hypothetical processes are described. Piaget sees the effect of 'centration' and 'decentration' as being mediated by what he calls 'encounters' and 'couplings'. Centration is made up of many 'encounters' between elements of the sensed field and elements of the sensory system. (These latter elements are not, for example, retinal receptors—they are abstract.) An act of 'centration', which takes place over a small period of time, consists of many still smaller intervals. During each of these intervals, a set of 'encounters' takes place between elements of the field and a proportion of all possible elements of the sensing system. The theory states that a greater number of 'encounters' will be made with field elements near the centre of 'centration' and that the perceived length of a line is determined by the number of 'encounters' of elements of the line. Thus, the portion of the line near the centre of 'centration' will tend to be overestimated. Moreover, the longer the 'centration' the more this overestimation will be.

This idea will probably work for one line, but it cannot predict what will happen when two lines are close together in the field and 'centration' is either between them or equally on each. This is the case in the example dealt with above. To account for misjudgments in this situation Piaget introduces the idea of 'coupling'. Apparently deliberately he leaves this concept very little defined. 'Encounters' of elements of the two lines have the capacity of cancelling one another out to various extents according to whether the 'coupling' is complete or incomplete. Many complete 'couplings' will lead to 'decentration' and therefore to veridical perception. Many incomplete 'couplings' will result in distorted perception. The completeness of 'couplings' depends on both the time of exposure and the difference in length between the lines.

Further elaboration of Piaget's theory would not be appropriate here. Much of the published work on Piaget has consisted of attempts at interpretation of his writings. This, in my opinion, is no compliment to Piaget, though Flavell (1963) gives a particularly good exposition.

Piaget's experimental work on illusions purports to validate his theory. It is reported fully in Piaget (1961), although most was published earlier elsewhere. He has studied the effect on the size of illusion (that is the amount of distortion) of varying the dimensions of different parts of the display. This sort of work is useful in that it helps to pick out the particular configurations which are effective in illusions and may even lead to the discovery of important similarities between illusion figures which are not obviously similar. Beyond this its theoretical importance is unclear and this is so particularly because it is not even clearly connected with Piaget's own theory.

He proceeds by deriving an expression for the amount of distortion in terms of various dimensions of the figure:

$$P = \frac{nL\,(L_1 - L_2)L_2}{SL_{\max}}$$

where:

P is the amount of illusion.

L_1 is the greater of the two lengths compared (e.g. the longer side of a rectangle)

L_2 is the shorter length
L_{max} is the greatest length of the whole figure
S is the surface (in the case of a rectangle this would be L_1L_2)
n is the number of separate comparisons (Piaget exemplifies this by reference to the Oppel–Kundt figure, where n is the number of subdivisions of the subdivided part of the line)
L is not clearly defined (it is called a 'reference length' and may be equal to L_1 or L_2)

This expression, he states, is derived from experimentation. Evidently experimental work has shown that if some of the various possible dimensions are used in this particular way then the data will fit the expression. To carry out fresh experiments as Piaget and his associates do and to find that again the results fit the expression shows that a constant experimental technique has been achieved and that sampling of subjects has not led to error, but it is difficult to see what more it has achieved. It would only bear on the theory if the expression had been derived from the theory.

Experiments relevant to Piaget's work are not all of this kind however. In some cases the hypotheses investigated stem clearly from the theory of 'centrations'. Several experiments are reported by Piaget (1961), done by him and his collaborators, on the effects of fixating different parts of a visual display. The section of the book in which these experiments are reported is called 'Effects of Centration', but the subject-matter is the effects of fixation. Results are mixed; sometimes fixation on a particular part of the field is associated with overestimation, sometimes not. In one experiment done by Fraisse, Ehrlich and Vurpillot (1956) subjects were instructed to fixate one part of the visual field but to give maximum attention to another. The part of the field given maximum attention was overestimated. Piaget (1961) reports an experiment with the Oppel–Kundt illusion (Fig. 2.69) displayed tachistoscopically. This showed that fixation of either the divided extent or the undivided extent caused it to be overestimated. Apparently fixation can be so placed as to overcome the illusion usually seen (overestimation of the divided extent). In other experiments results were less clear. For example, photographic records were made of the eye movement of subjects during inspection of two displays. Display (a) was a horizontal line 10 cm long divided into two sections, one of 2·5 cm on the left and one of 7·5 cm on the right. Offset to the right of this was another 7·5 cm line. Display (b) was also a divided 10 cm line with the 2·5 cm section on the right. Offset from this on the right was another 2·5 cm line. It was found that the right-hand section of the 10 cm line was fixated for most of the time in both (a) and (b). This section was overestimated in (a) and underestimated in (b). In other words, the illusion of a divided line operated regardless of fixation. This means either that 'centration' is not the same thing as fixation or that Piaget's theory has not worked. Paiget comes to the former conclusion. He says that 'centration' on the right-hand section of the line in (b) must have distributed more 'encounters' on the non-fixated part of the display. Evidently he sees the result of the experiment as confirming his hypothesis. Thus both possible results of the experiment would have confirmed the hypothesis. If fixation had resulted in overestimation this would have confirmed that 'centration' resulted in overestimation; when fixation does not result in overestimation, then encounters have somehow strayed away so as to produce overestimation in the non-fixated part of the display.

Now if an experiment is going to add to our knowledge in a formal way then at least one of the possible outcomes must be seen as failing to confirm the hypothesis under test. Unless this is so the experiment cannot be crucial, only vaguely exploratory. Yet this sort of conclusion is typical of several in this series of experiments. Research on Piaget's theory plainly can get no further until the term 'centration' is defined clearly enough for it to generate hypotheses which can be tested.

However, in spite of Piaget's treatment of his own experimental results, the kind of information they afford seems likely to be useful. It shows for example that visual fixation is an important variable in illusions especially when it coincides with direction of attention. Piaget has also demonstrated important differences in patterns of fixation between adults and children. Adults can fixate a point for a longer period than children and can find a given point more quickly. Children take longer to make a judgment, but spend a shorter time than adults on any point of fixation. Piaget has also examined the function relating extent of illusion to time of exposure using a tachistoscope. This function evidently also changes with age.

These various differences clearly implicate, in the generation of illusions, mechanisms both of scanning and of attention. It is clear from Piaget's work, and that of several others mentioned earlier, that eye movements as such are not crucial, since illusion remains when eye movements are eliminated, but attention and its distribution are clearly worthy of further investigation. Grindley and Townsend (1970) have shown that visual search can take place without eye movement. They exposed complex displays for only 40 m/sec and asked subjects to name part of the display, telling them exactly which part only after exposure. Subjects did this successfully. In the terms of Neisser (1967) they were reading off from the 'icon' of short-term visual memory.

VIRSU'S THEORY

Lastly, Virsu (1971a) has developed Festinger's idea of efferent readiness into a plausible theory of perceptual distortion. He suggests that tendency to eye movement, that is the output instructions for eye movement, not actual eye movement, can have a perceptual effect. This idea arises again later in connection with autokinesis; it arose before in the work of Heymans (1896). It avoids many of the arguments which have been put against eye-movement theories, but has the disadvantage that tendencies alone are difficult to demonstrate.

Virsu argues that the standard setting of the eye-movement system, the sort of movement that it is usually most ready to make, is linear and rectilinear, either horizontal or vertical. Thus, when a line is viewed which lies off the vertical or horizontal, an eye-movement correction must take place as the horizontal or vertical movement is shown, by feedback, to be scanning the target badly. Virsu is not explicit on this stage in the process. Presumably the correction is not well registered in the percept and so the target is seen as nearer the horizontal or the vertical than it really is. Fig. 3.38 is a good example of this. The results of Weintraub and Virsu (1971), described in the section on simple angular figures (Chapter 3), can also be interpreted in this way, especially their first condition. A downward-facing obtuse angle, for example, was overestimated, that is its arms were seen as lying closer to the horizontal than they actually did.

Weintraub and Virsu also recalled an earlier experiment with the perception of the curvature of arcs (Virsu, 1971b). Arcs that are so short, or so little curved as to be capable of being viewed without correction of a linear eye movement, will have their curvature underestimated. Short arcs certainly do have their curvature underestimated.

An extension of this idea to incorporate the Müller-Lyer figure brings in the observations of Kaufman and Richards (1969) and Richards and Kaufman (1969) that fixations tend to cluster about the centre of gravity of a figure. They proposed that the cause of the Müller-Lyer illusion was the anticipation by the visual system of eye movements being distributed between the centres of gravity of the arrow-heads rather than their extremes. The greater the distance of the centres of gravity of the arrow-heads from the ends of the figure the greater should be the illusion. Virsu varied this distance in two ways, by varying the visual angle (the viewing distance of the figure) and by varying the angle between the fins. The former results fit his predictions well and the latter do not.

Virsu's work is immaculate. He suggests a mathematical relationship which could describe the type of error he is proposing. He works out precisely the shapes of functions he could expect from experiments and then demonstrates these by simple and elegant experiments. But unfortunately he does not show any *necessary* connection between his theory in terms of expectation of eye movements and his initial mathematical relationship.

A theory like this, which is based on tendencies to movement, is exceedingly difficult to test, yet it is not nonsensical to entertain it. Later, in the section on autokinesis (Chapter 9), it will be seen that perceptual error can stem from the fact that the only non-visual information we have about the position of the eyes is what the system has 'told' them to do. Such information is important in discounting eye movement from the percept so that correct inference may be made about image movement. It would be fascinating if this characteristic of the system could be shown to be important also in the geometrical optical illusions.

THE THEORY OF KÖHLER AND WALLACH APPLIED TO ILLUSIONS

Two theories whose main objective was the explanation of figural after-effects, the theories of Köhler and Wallach (1944) and of Ganz (1966a,b), were also seen by their authors as capable of explaining illusions. The theories themselves and their shortcomings were described in Chapter 5. Their application to illusions will now be examined.

Köhler and Wallach considered that a currently present line created a 'satiated' area in much the same way as the inspection line in the figural after-effect situation. This satiated area repelled other activity and therefore lines separated by less than a certain distance would repel one another. Presumably because of the distance paradox, at even smaller separations they would repel one another less. The theory was not worked out in detail. Clearly it could only possibly be applied to a limited range of illusions, particularly contrast and framing effects. But if simultaneous effects of the kind these authors describe take place over much the same range of interfigural distance as figural after-effects (up to 30 minutes of arc according to Day, 1962b) then the great majority even of these illusions are excluded from the explanation. This is so especially because viewing distance makes little difference to illusions and yet it is possible with most figures to move them close enough to the eye for the crucial interfigural distances to exceed 30 minutes of arc. The explanation might suffice for illusions involving angular distortion, but even with these an assumption is required about how the effect of the angle is exerted over the whole line, and Köhler and Wallach do not give this.

Criticism of the theory has mainly involved decrement with practice of the Müller-Lyer illusion and was dealt with in the section on that subject in Chapter 2. The most important point was that satiation seemed to demand that the Müller-Lyer was fixated, yet decrement happened less with fixation than with free inspection. All the criticism in fact centres round the idea that a stimulus is fed into a particular location in the central nervous system. There is sufficient evidence now to support the idea of Kolers (1963) that perceptions are constructed by means of a number of different processes occurring at different times and places in the nervous system. If such evidence is acceptable, and I believe it is, then satiation theory is of no more than historical interest.

GANZ'S THEORY

Again this theory was described in Chapter 5, and again its application to illusions was much less well worked out than its application to figural after-effects. The way one line is seen by Ganz (1966a,b) as interacting with another is precisely the same as the way a line interacts with the after-image of a previously exposed inspection line. The lateral inhibition from one line depresses one side of the distribution of activity derived from the other, shifting its peak of activity and therefore its apparent position. Now it is possible for most illusion figures to be presented either as normal illusion figures or as figural after-effect figures. In the latter case one simply presents the inducing lines as the inspection figure (for example, the obliques of the Zöllner figure) and the test lines as the test figure (for example, the long lines of the Zöllner figure). When comparisons are made between such simultaneous and successive versions of illusion figures, some give the same effect, but others do not.

Ellis (1969), using successive versions of the Zöllner and Hering illusions with intervals of up to 0·5 sec, found distortion to be in the same direction as for the simultaneous display. Holt-Hansen (1961) even reported enhancement of the Hering illusion when the inducing and test line were alternated rapidly. However, Wagner (1969), although demonstrating for both the Ponzo and Poggendorff figures that the simultaneous and successive effects were in the same direction, showed significantly greater successive effects. Ganz's theory would predict the opposite.

Work on the Delbœuf illusion flatly contradicts Ganz. Ikeda

and Obonai (1955), in a detailed study using simultaneous and successive displays for a variety of ratios between the sizes of the circles, found that the functions for the two displays were practically mirror images of one another. The outer circle was underestimated in the simultaneous display and overestimated in the successive display. The inner circle was overestimated in the simultaneous display and underestimated in the successive display. Moreover, where there was a distinct difference in the extent of the effect (in the estimation of the inner circle), the successive effect was larger than the simultaneous effect. It is worth emphasising also that the simultaneous effect for both inner and outer circles is one of *attraction* of the contours. Ganz's theory cannot predict any of these results.

Seltzer and Sheridan (1965) report results rather similar. They exposed a white circle on a black background as the inspection figure to one eye and then asked subjects to judge the relative sizes of two smaller circles, one, the test circle, being centred on the inspection circle's position. For half the subjects the inspection circle was left on and for half it was switched off. In the former condition, the simultaneous version, the test circle was judged to be larger than its fellow and in the latter, the successive version, it was judged to be smaller. Spitz (1967) reported similar results using squares and circles and also bar figures.

Studies of individual differences tell the same story. Pressey and Koffman (1968) showed that susceptibility to figural after-effects was inversely related to susceptibility to the Poggendorff illusion.

There seems to be a difference between simultaneous and successive effects which Ganz's theory cannot account for. It is fair to say however that this applies mainly to figures like the Delbœuf figure. Angular distortions seem more often to behave in the simultaneous and successive versions as Ganz would predict; at least in *direction* of distortion. I myself have made a case for the limited application of Ganz's theory to the angular distortions (Robinson, 1968), but in many ways this is the less suitable application. The interaction of parallel contours clearly takes place all along such contours. The angular effect must take place only near the junction of lines, and additional assumptions of the kind made in my paper and elsewhere in this book are required to account for the rotation or distortion of the whole line.

A further difficulty for Ganz is that, if he is using known facts about lateral inhibition in the visual system to account for distortions, then the sizes of the distortions must be predictable from these facts. His theory encounters difficulties here too. Ganz himself (1966a, p. 132) sees contour interactions as taking place over a distance of up to 20 minutes of arc; yet, for example, Oyama (1962) showed that an illusion 15 minutes of arc in extent occurred in the Delbœuf figure at interfigural distances of 1·5°. This is more than three times the distance specified by Ganz.

Wagner (1968) found difficulty when he tried in detail to apply Ganz's theory to illusion figures. If the fins of a Müller-Lyer figure repel one another near the apex this should apparently shift the apex in the direction of the point of the arrow-head. This would have the effect of elongating the shaft of the ingoing figure and reducing the shaft of the outgoing figure; the reverse of the observed effect. It should also create apparent gaps at the ends of the shaft of the ingoing figure. Again, in the Ponzo illusion (Fig. 2.30) the line which approaches nearer to the inducing lines is the one which is overestimated. It should be shortened according to Ganz's theory.

The theory, in common with other theories involving interaction of contours, has difficulty with Coren's (1970) dot figures which show that both the Müller-Lyer and Poggendorff illusions are present in figures which simply do not contain lines. Angular distortion also occurs (Cumming, 1968) when the parts of the lines near their junctions are omitted, so that no lines approach near to one another. Coren is prepared to allow, against the dictates of parsimony, that probably lateral inhibition, constancy, optical aberration and eye movement all make a contribution to the causation of illusions. It does not seem that Ganz could claim more.

GREGORY'S THEORY AND OTHER THEORIES INVOLVING APPARENT DISTANCE

Perhaps the most consistent trend in theorising about the geometrical optical illusions has been to suppose that such figures are interpreted by the perceptual system as flat projections of three-dimensional displays. The system is then thought of as making certain sorts of corrections to the sizes or directions of the lines. Thiéry (1896) seems to have been the first explicitly to suggest this sort of theory. He suggested that the Müller-Lyer figure could be seen as a flat projection of a simple trestle viewed from directly above or directly below. Much more recently the idea was developed by Tausch (1954). He proposed that we learn to correct for depth in three-dimensional displays and this enables us more easily to see the 'real object'. Sometimes however there are cues in a two-dimensional display which trigger off this correction process and introduce a correction inappropriately. This is the distortion. Tausch saw the process mainly as one which tended to make acute angles more obtuse and obtuse angles more acute. This happens because, for example, when we view a rectangle from one side, its retinal image is a trapezium with the nearer angles appearing to be acute and those further away appearing obtuse. The effect Tausch describes brings each angle nearer to a right angle and therefore we are seeing the rectangle more nearly as it 'really is', that is, more nearly how it appears when it is in the fronto-parallel plane. Kristof (1961) advanced this sort of theory further by proposing explicitly that perspective triggered the constancy process, and that the illusion was the resultant of the contradiction between this effect and the obvious fact that the display was flat.

Still further development is due to Gregory (1963), who later produced more developed and detailed accounts (Gregory, 1968b, 1970). (More popular accounts have also appeared, for example Gregory 1966a, 1968a.) The volume of discussion aroused by the theory is very large. Gregory invokes size constancy to explain illusions. When an object is known to be distant it appears larger than would be expected on the basis of its retinal size. This enlargement Gregory calls 'constancy scaling' and he considers that it can be triggered in two different ways. One of them, 'primary constancy scaling', is set off by typical perspective features in the display itself. The observer knows that the display is flat because he can see the paper that it is drawn on, yet in spite of this the perspective features operate a fairly primitive automatic scaling process which enlarges the apparently distant parts of the display (the distance is 'apparent' to the system at a low level, not to the observer). Such perspective features in the Müller-Lyer figure would make the viewing of the ingoing figure like viewing the corner of a cube-shaped building from a fairly high viewpoint. The outgoing figure would be like the corner of a room viewed from within the room. The Ponzo figure would be like looking along a railway line (as in Fig. 6.9).

'Secondary constancy scaling' is the other concept described by Gregory. This is set by apparent distance and so involves fairly high-level awareness of cues of distance. It is this that is operating in Emmert's law which was described in Chapter 2. Thus 'primary constancy scaling' is a primitive process whereby the system adjusts the percept according to perspective features of the actual configuration of the lines in the display. 'Secondary constancy scaling' is a higher process (much more of a 'programming' and less of a 'hardware' event, in terms Gregory has employed) which adjusts apparent size by means of quite sophisticated and heterogeneous distance information; binocular disparity, parallax, overlap and so on. Gregory goes to some trouble to demonstrate the independence of these mechanisms, using the Necker cube (Fig. 6.1). This is a well-known 'reversible' figure and Gregory points out that when the cube is drawn on paper the two alternative depth interpretations do not appear to involve a change in the apparent sizes of the 'near' and 'far' faces. When a luminous Necker cube is viewed in the dark, however, reversal is accompanied by a change in the apparent relative sizes of the two faces. Gregory sees this latter situation as one in which the high-level appreciation of apparent distance can take place and therefore only 'secondary constancy scaling' can operate. My own difficulty with this argument is that I share the view of Hotopf (1966) that there is a clear difference in the apparent sizes of the faces of the Necker cube when it is drawn on paper, and that these change with the reversal of perspective of the cube. I cannot see that this is a good argument for the existence of two processes; the luminous version of the Necker cube probably gives a more pronounced apparent size difference between the two faces because the contradictory cues from the texture of the flat paper are absent.

A more forceful argument for the existence of two processes is contained in an ingenious device described by Gregory (1966a, 1970) for testing the apparent depth, on the basis of 'primary constancy scaling', of different parts of the display. It is, very briefly, an arrangement which allows both eyes, in the dark, to see a small light which can be adjusted in distance from the observer. Only one eye can see a luminous display of an illusion figure and, by means of a sheet of neutral tinted perspex at 45° to the line of sight, the light can be superimposed, in the observer's view, on the luminous display. Thus the light can be put at different points on the display and the observer asked to adjust it so that it appears to be in the same plane as the point on the display on which it is superimposed. Gregory thus mapped the apparent distance of the various parts of, for example, the Müller-Lyer display and showed that in the outgoing figure the ends of the fins were apparently less distant than the shaft and in the ingoing figure the ends of the fins were apparently further away than the shaft. Thus binocular disparity, one of the mechanisms involved in 'secondary constancy scaling', is used as a measure of the monocular depth effect which is the basis of 'primary constancy scaling'. This is a very clever idea.

Gregory regards the mechanism behind 'primary constancy scaling' as a special process, separate in kind from the various mechanisms feeding into 'secondary constancy scaling', binocular disparity, interposition and other well-known cues of distance.

6.1 Necker cube 6.2 Brown and Houssiadas (1965) 6.3 Fisher (1968c)
6.4 Zanforlin (1967) 6.5 Hotopf (1966)

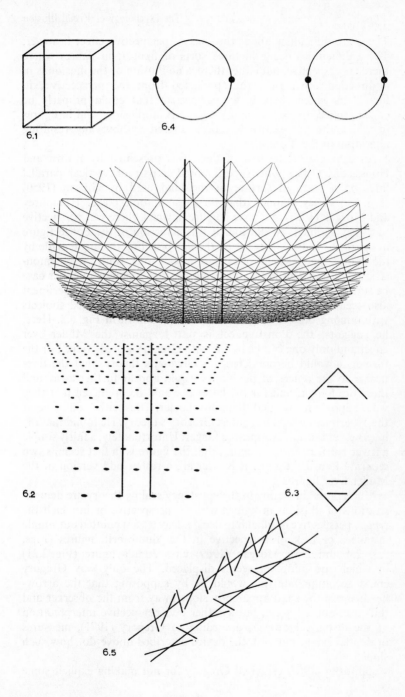

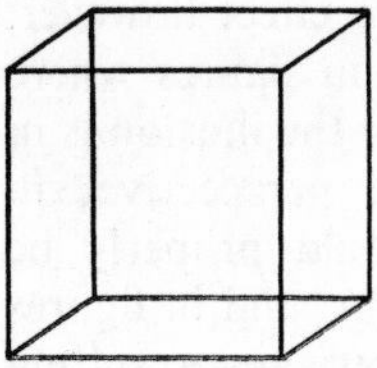

6.1

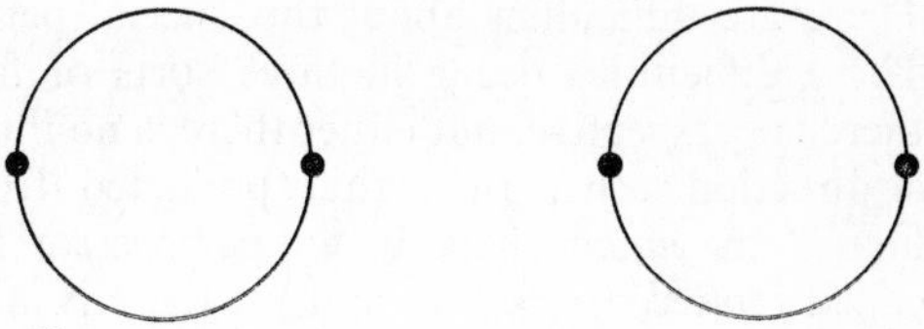

6.4

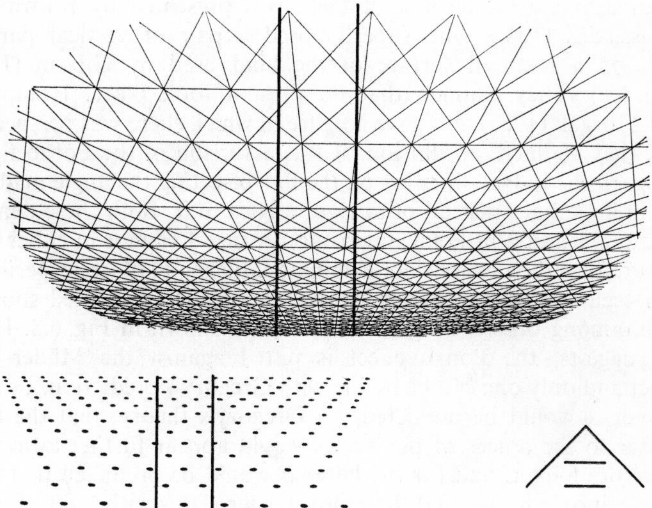

6.2

6.3

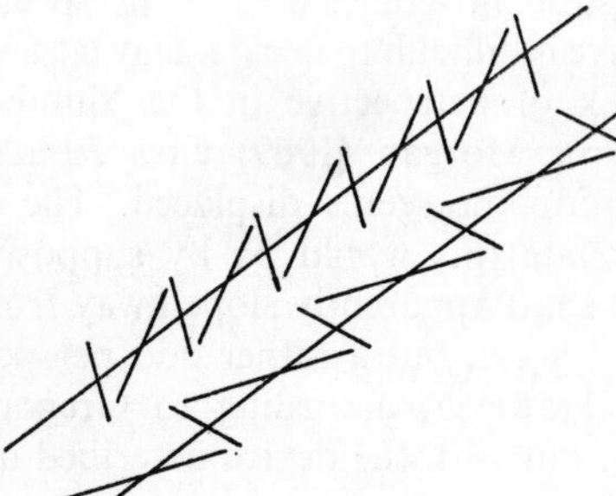

6.5

There are difficulties about this special perspective effect however. These difficulties occur in three sorts of figures: in figures where there is perspective, but either there is no illusion or the illusion is in a direction other than that predicted from the perspective; in figures in which there is no perspective that could properly be called *typical* perspective and yet there is an illusion; and in figures in which the perspective has been altered without any resulting alteration in the illusion.

An example of the first of these was presented by Brown and Houssiadas (1965) who superimposed a pair of vertical parallel lines on a textured surface of the kind used by Gibson (1950) (Fig. 6.2). They claimed that no illusion took place. Humphrey and Morgan (1965) also gave a figure in which there was perspective but, they claimed, no illusion. It was a version of the Ponzo figure in which the judged lines lay on the line bisecting the angle made by the oblique lines instead of at right angles to it. Both these demonstrations I find a little unconvincing because I cannot in either case be sure that the illusions are eliminated. Fisher's (1968e) experiment also seems to add relatively weak evidence. He presented subjects with, among others, a figure, like the one shown in Fig. 6.3. Here, he suggests, the Ponzo effect is pitted against the Müller-Lyer effect and only one can be in line with Gregory's prediction. For the former it would be predicted, on Gregory's theory, that the lines nearer to the apices of the angles would appear further away and therefore longer, and for the latter it would be predicted that they would appear nearer and therefore shorter. Thus, either outcome of the experiment would be against Gregory's theory. He found that the lines nearer the apices appeared longer. Unfortunately, a fairly simple answer is left open to Gregory, that the figure is in fact seen as two separate Ponzo illusions. It is after all, a rather odd version of the Müller-Lyer figure.

Much more damaging to the constancy scaling theory are demonstrations of illusions in figures with no perspective or in which the *typical* perspective is difficult to decide. Day (1965) pointed out simple instances of lack of perspective in the 'dumb-bell' figures (Figs. 2.3, 2.4 and 2.5). Morgan (1969) cites Judd's figure (Fig. 2.21) in which the midpoint seems displaced. The only way Gregory could accommodate this would be by supposing that the arrowheads made the shaft apparently slope away from the observer and thus use, not a typical, but a rather odd perspective interpretation of the display. However, according to Gregory (1971), measures of depth carried out with the device described above do show such slope.

Zanforlin (1967) criticised Gregory for not making explicit some acceptable method for determining the typical depth features of a display, pointing out that any figure can be seen as a projection of at least one figure-in-depth. This author adds Fig. 6.4 to the collection of illusion figures without perspective. Here the distance between the circles seems greater than the diameters (clearly this is a close relative of the 'dumb-bell' figure). Photographs of real objects are also presented which show illusions just the same. One shows two equal sticks and two equal circular wooden mats with diameters equal to the lengths of the sticks. The mats form a 'dumb-bell' shape with one stick lying along the diameter of one mat and the other placed end to end with the first and lying between the mats. The sticks appear to be of different lengths. Now clearly this is a representation of the objects photographed and not of some three-dimensional figure. Gregory could only object by appeal to his 'primary constancy scaling', claiming that it is set off, in spite of all the other cues, by the configuration of the outline of the display. The same goes for Zanforlin's pile of identical coins which is equal in height to the diameter of the coins and yet looks 30 per cent higher.

Hotopf (1966) produced Figs. 6.5 and 6.6 in which there is illusion but no easily decidable perspective. Also Fisher (1968c) made the obvious point that in the composite version of the Müller-Lyer figure, the depth location of the middle set of fins would be quite indeterminate because the ingoing end demands that they shall slope away from the observer and the outgoing end demands that they shall slope towards him. This paper also includes an interesting study taking advantage of the fact that the Müller-Lyer with ingoing fins and the Müller-Lyer with outgoing fins can both be seen as reversible figures. The extent of illusion was measured whilst subjects were seeing each of the two possible perspective interpretations of the two figures (the fact that this was possible suggests arbitrariness in Gregory's choice of one interpretation as 'typical'), and no difference in extent of illusion was found.

Green and Stacey (1966) have also tried altering a figure's perspective. They used one of the Orbison figures (Fig. 3.18) and, by altering the relative spacing of the concentric circles, got an effect of either looking into a tunnel or looking down on to a cone. They say that the distortion should alter with alteration of perspective. Now this involves distortions of lines and not alteration of their apparent length and the application of Gregory's theory, not described by him in detail, may not be obvious. One has to think of how the four lines forming the square in this figure would have to be drawn on the surface of, say, a cone so that, viewed from above, they would look like a square. The answer is that they would have to bow upwards towards the apex of the cone. Thus the visual system, when viewing the flat display, sees the lines as they 'really are', bowed in towards the centre. To draw the same thing on the inner wall of a tunnel, the line must also bow towards the centre. Thus Gregory's theory works for this figure and Green and Stacey are wrong. Where Gregory's theory does not work is in a figure like Fig. 3.19. Here the above sort of reasoning would still predict a bowing in of the line, whereas the line appears to bow out whether the figure is seen as protruding, receding or flat. Gregory (1966b) reported results with the Orbison figure (Fig. 3.18) using his device, mentioned earlier, for gauging apparent depths. If the circles were equally spaced, then the figure was seen as *flat*. This would predict no distortion, and Gregory went on to explain the distortion in terms of the formation of Müller-Lyer-type figures between the square and segments of the circles. Again, Gregory makes a surprising choice of typical perspective.

Fisher (1968e, 1970) also made use of alteration of perspective in his rebuttal of Gregory's theory. He showed Fig. 6.7 which can be seen either as a pyramid or a passage. However, the illusion seen in the Ponzo figures embedded in this figure would only be predicted in the 'passage' version. In the 'pyramid' version the line in each parallel pair lying nearer to the centre of the figure appears nearer, but still it appears larger. The converging lines within which these parallel lines lie seem to be a more important determinant of the illusion than perspective. In the later paper Fisher explored the idea of drawing Müller-Lyer figures as though they were constructed from pieces of material with a square section. By this means he could vary the apparent direction in depth of the fins (for example Fig. 6.8). It made no difference to the Müller-Lyer effect. Thus once again the illusion does not follow the obvious perspective features of the display, and Gregory's only course is to appeal to his primitive and automatic process of 'primary constancy scaling' as a process which can be sensitive to perspective interpretations which are much more abstruse than those available to conscious perception. Humphrey and Morgan (1965) make the point that 'a theory which appeals to the idea of automatic compensation for unconsciously perceived depth is in obvious danger of being irrefutable' (p. 744).

Even the strong evidence produced by Gregory, using his method of gauging apparent depth of a display, of the depth features of the Müller-Lyer figures has not apparently been easy for other workers to repeat. Sixteen out of twenty-five subjects of Hotopf (1965) saw a luminous Müller-Lyer figure as flat. This was in a simple view, not in a set-up like Gregory's, but Gregory had in fact claimed that such

6.6 Hotopf (1966) 6.7 Fisher (1970) 6.8 Fisher (1970)
6.9 After Gregory (1966a)

6.6

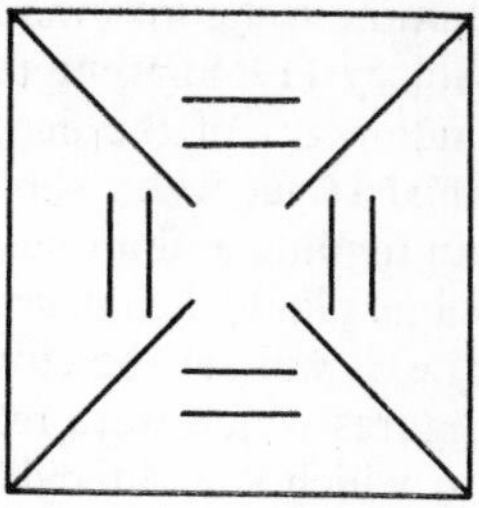

6.7

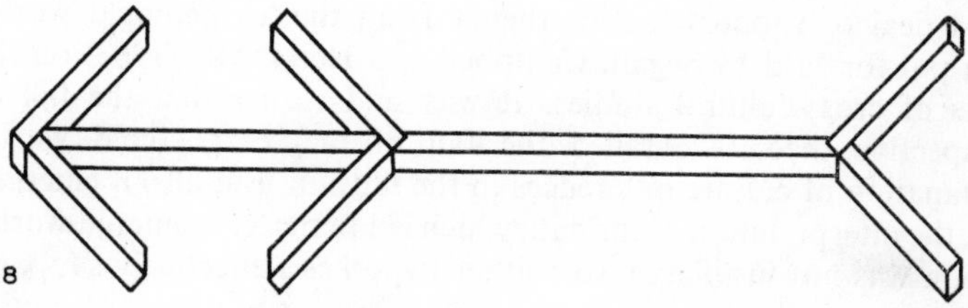

6.8

6.9

luminous figures were seen as apparently having depth. Pike and Stacey (1968) went further. They demonstrated that the subjects' judgments of the depths of the fins relative to the shaft were very mixed; yet when subjects adjusted the actual distance of shafts of an ingoing and an outgoing figure so that they appeared to be in the same plane, the *apparently* longer shaft was seen at a greater distance (i.e. it was set too close). The effect was present also in the 'control' figures which were rectangular-ended Müller-Lyer figures (Fig. 2.4) in which it is difficult to see perspective. Thus it seems much more likely that the apparent sizes of the shafts determine apparent distance than the other way round as Gregory claims. This idea gains further support from the findings of Stacey and Pike (1970) who showed that when the same sort of experiment was done with Müller-Lyer figures with incomplete shafts a reversal of apparent depth accompanied the well-known reversal of the illusion. In Gregory's terms the perspective cues were not altered.

As a final point it should be mentioned that Gregory invokes a good deal of support for his theory from the 'carpentered world' idea put forward by Segall, Campbell and Herskovits (1963) on the basis of cross-cultural studies. It was said earlier that the fall of perspective theories entailed the fall of the 'carpentered world' explanation of culture differences in the illusion. But also it emerged that the interpretation of the data which led to the 'carpentered world' notion was not justifiable, so neither hypothesis effectively supports the other.

However, in spite of all these arguments, Gregory's theory has a great deal of appeal. It uses a well-established perceptual principle and effects a connection between two large bodies of knowledge about perception. When we look at Gregory's picture of railway lines (Fig. 6.9) it is difficult to believe that apparent distance takes no part in the Ponzo effect therein. Indeed the same applies even to complex line drawings like Fig. 6.10. Yet Gregory specifically excludes apparent distance from 'primary constancy scaling' which he sees as a much more primitive process. The separateness of this process is what has caused most argument. Gregory's monocular depth gauging device certainly seems to show that one eye can deduce depth from a display of lines, but his critics find it difficult to accept this deduction of depth as a separate kind of process from the rest of depth perception, particularly as one which can operate on its own in a direction different from the rest of depth perception as Gregory claims for the Orbison figure.

It is easy to follow Hotopf (1965) in his supposition that illusions are multiply determined, with perspective corrections, contrast, orientation and probably many other influences all variously

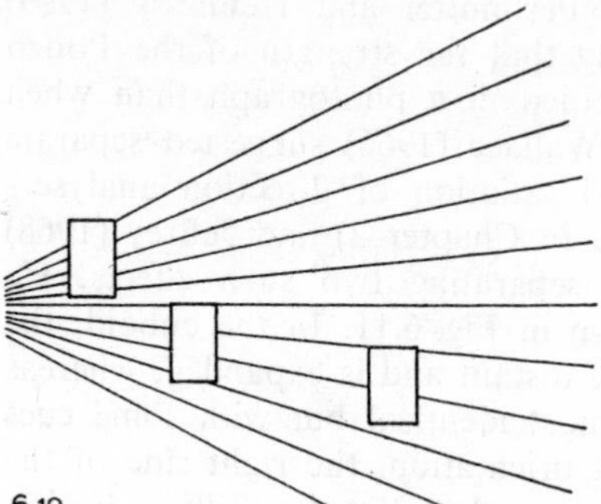

6.10

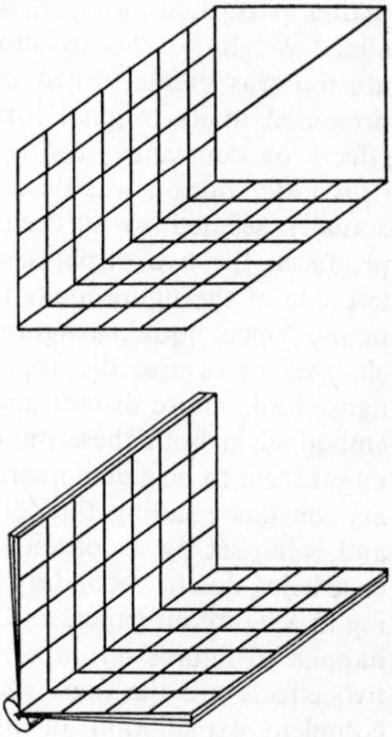

6.11

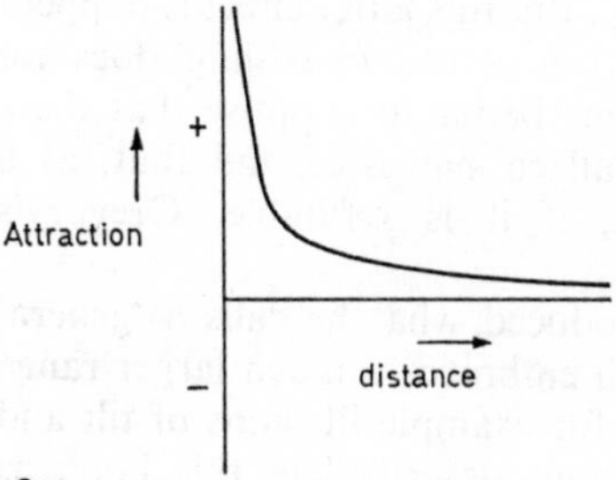

6.12

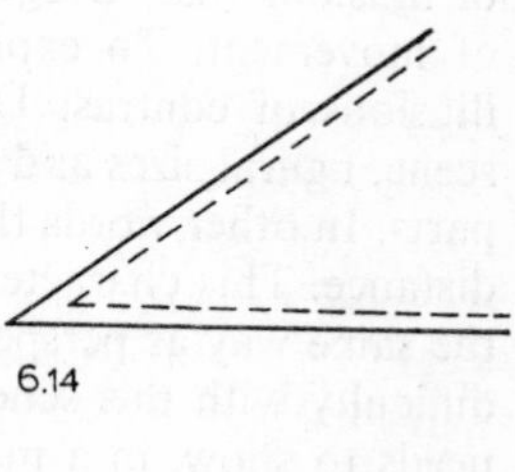

6.14

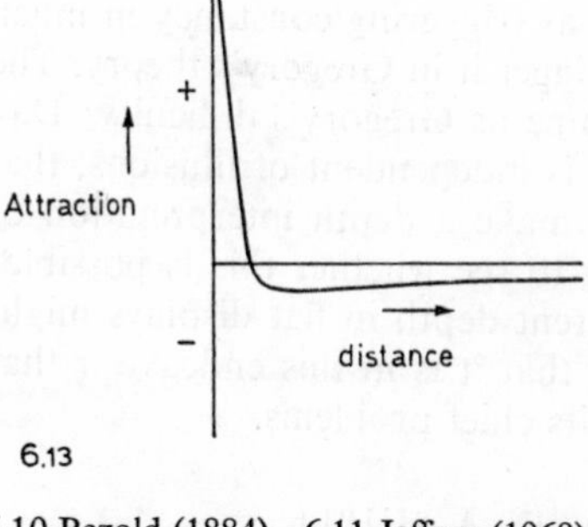

6.13

6.10 Bezold (1884) 6.11 Jeffrey (1968) 6.12 After Eriksson (1970) 6.13 After Eriksson (1970) 6.14 Eriksson (1970)

taking part. Leibowitz, Brislin, Perlmutter and Hennessy (1969) added weight to this by showing that the strength of the Ponzo illusion was greater when embodied in a photograph than when presented in its original form. Wallace (1966) suggested separate effects of constancy scaling and satiation of direction analysers (this latter notion was described in Chapter 3) and Jeffrey (1968) actually seemed to succeed in separating two such effects. He produced the two displays shown in Fig. 6.11. In the cuboid, the left side of the figure looks more distant and is expanded, whereas in the 'open book', a figure almost identical but with some cues changed to reverse the apparent orientation, the right side of the figure looks more distant and is expanded. Yet the Zöllner illusion embodied in both these figures *does not reverse.* At first sight this might seem to be a demonstration of Gregory's primary and secondary constancy scaling, the Zöllner effect being due to 'primary scaling' and being set by unconscious scaling processes and the size difference being due to 'secondary scaling'. But this latter effect is happening in a figure on paper, and 'secondary constancy scaling' does not happen to figures on paper. It seems better to suppose that these two effects are the ones which Wallace suggested and that, as a complete explanation of illusions, if it is refutable, Gregory's theory has been refuted.

Day (1972) has very recently produced what he calls a 'general constancy theory' of illusions which embraces a much larger range of illusions than Gregory's theory, for example illusions of tilt and of movement. To explain the illusions described in this book as illusions of contrast Day uses the fact that, in distant parts of a scene, figural sizes and interfigural distances are smaller than in near parts. In other words the 'grain' of the display becomes smaller with distance. This characteristic is seen as triggering constancy in much the same way as perspective cues trigger it in Gregory's theory. The difficulty with this scheme is the same as Gregory's difficulty; Day needs to show, in a manner which is independent of illusions, that the perceptual system does indeed make a depth interpretation of such displays. It will be interesting to see whether this is possible; Gregory's device for gauging apparent depth in flat displays might be used. It is fair to say, however, that it is in this endeavour that Gregory's theory has met some of its chief problems.

THEORIES BASED ON A SIMPLE HYPOTHETICAL RELATIONSHIP

Eriksson's field theory

Eriksson (1970) proposed a 'non-reductionist' theory which attempted to apply electrical potential theory to visual illusions. He did not set out to explain the illusions in the sense of showing that they are the result of the operation of any well-known mechanism. His was an attempt simply to find a single function or a small set of functions which would *describe* the perceptual result of the interaction of lines in the visual field. The proposal was that lines in the visual field affect one another as a function of the distance separating them. He suggested first the simple attraction function expressed in Fig. 6.12 but easily found it inadequate. However, with the addition of a further function (Fig. 6.13) which showed attraction only at small distances and repulsion at larger distances his 'theory' seems unusually successful.

With two functions he had the task of deciding which function operated in which situations, and proposed that the attraction function operated over empty distances or between configurations which are quite separate. The attraction–repulsion principle operated within filled distances or within configurations. Clearly there is a certain amount of vagueness in the specification of these two criteria; for example, how large does a gap have to be between two configurations before it ceases to be part of filled space and becomes the area separating two configurations? However, this could be determined empirically and Eriksson looked forward to a great deal of detailed experimental work to define both the exact shape of his functions and the appropriate situations for their operation.

The situation Eriksson suggested for the operation of his attraction–repulsion function is illustrated in the Oppel–Kundt illusion (Fig. 2.69). The integral of all the repulsion effects among the lines of the filled side would result in exaggeration of the length of that side. But this would happen only so long as the lines were more than a certain distance apart. If they were nearer, then each line would exert some attractive influence on the lines closest to it and the sum of all these effects would be a smaller apparent expansion of the filled space. Thus there is an optimum spacing of the lines in the filled extent for maximum apparent expansion, and in the extreme, the filled extent, a black bar, should seem shorter than the unfilled extent. Eriksson carried out an experiment which he took as demonstrating that a space filled with five lines appeared larger than one of the same length with only two lines defining its ends, and this in turn appeared longer than a solid black bar of the same length.

Eriksson next went on informally to apply his two principles to several illusions. In the Müller-Lyer figure he saw the attraction principle operating between the two arrow-heads and the attraction–

repulsion principle operating within each arrow-head. Thus the two arrow-heads would be attracted to each other in both figures but in the figure with ingoing fins the total effect would be greater because more parts of the fins approach one another more closely than is the case with the figure with outgoing fins (for which, by the way, the prediction is in the wrong direction). Within each arrow-head the attraction–repulsion function would have the effect, operating *within* each single fin, of shortening the fin. There would also be an attraction effect between each fin. All this would have the effect of apparently shifting the arrow-head bodily in the direction away from its apex and thus again contributing to the illusion. The operation of the two principles in this way thus predicts that the within-arrow-head effect is equal for the two figures but the between-arrow-head effect is greater for the ingoing figure. Indeed, any effect in the figure with outgoing fins depends on the within-arrow-head effect being large enough completely to swamp the between-arrow-head effect because the prediction from the latter is in the wrong direction for the outgoing figure. This ought also to mean that the total illusion should be greater for the ingoing than for the outgoing figure. The opposite is the case.

Eriksson also accounted for the Ponzo illusion by the simple attraction principle. The upper line, which appears longer, approaches closer to the inducing lines and is therefore more expanded than the lower line. The angle illusions were accounted for by supposing that attraction moved the apparent position of the lines as in Fig. 6.14, thus shifting the apparent position of the apex of an angle and enlarging it. A little thought will show how this would roughly predict the distortion in this sort of illusion generally.

Eriksson's theory avoids the difficulties of being tied to a mechanism (for example, lateral inhibition) which itself dictates the sizes and directions of illusions that ought to be found, but he has not applied his theory to illusion figures in any detail. The main danger is that he will find it impossible, when he specifies his two functions precisely, to get them to predict more than a very few illusions. Also if he continues to use two functions he must derive more explicit and detailed rules for deciding in which sort of configuration each operates.

Taylor's psychophysical theory

This is another theory centred on a relatively simple principle accompanied by a number of further assumptions which enable it to account for a greater range of observations. The basic principle (Taylor, 1962a,b) is that the perceived distance between two points is an increasing function of the discriminability of the distance between them. When further points are introduced between them, as in the Oppel–Kundt figure, if these points are themselves discriminable, the apparent distance between the first two points is increased. If the new points are not clearly discriminable then the apparent distance may be decreased. This roughly fits the data produced by Taylor. However, he also introduced what he called a 'weighting assumption', which says that an observer will use information from all available sources to make a judgment. Now this alters the theory from a simple one, which predicts fairly simple mathematically expressed relationships which can easily be tested, to one in which the relationships may be exceedingly complex. Before the theory can be assessed it needs to be applied to a wide variety of figures, and this has not yet been done, partly, one would suspect, because of the difficulty of specifying an 'available' source of information.

Pressey's assimilation theory

Pressey (1970, 1971) has advanced a theory based on the principle that, when a range of values is available to the senses, judgment of those values tends towards their mean, the smaller values being overestimated and the larger ones underestimated. Such a principle is fairly easy to apply to the Müller-Lyer figure (Brunot did it in 1893), and the description of that figure in Chapter 2 contained this idea. Pressey, however, extended it to account for Fig. 2.21 by supposing that judgment of the distance from the left-hand end of the figure to the midpoint is affected by all possible distances from points on the arrow-head to the midpoint. The judged distance is the longest of all these; the average distance is smaller and the judged distance is therefore underestimated. A similar argument accounts for the overestimation of the distance from the midpoint to the right-hand end of the figure.

The principle is also applied to the Hering and Wundt figures (Figs. 3.33 and 3.34). Here the sections of the radiating lines lying between the parallels and the nodes are seen as closer in length to their average than they actually are. A little thought will show that such a tendency would result in the distortion of the parallels.

One of the problems of extending this idea to other figures is the definition of the set of dimensions entering into each average. To simplify this problem, Pressey proposed 'attentive fields'. These are areas over which attention is distributed and it is from this that the average is obtained. Thus, for the Ponzo illusion (Fig. 2.30) Pressey presumes that the attentive field is restricted to the area between the two parallel lines. The diverging lines are then seen as forming half of an outgoing Müller-Lyer figure with the left-hand parallel line. This has a lengthening effect which leads to the Ponzo illusion.

Pressey proposes that the attentive field for Wundt's area illusion (Fig. 2.75) causes a greater influence of the central parts of the display. This means that the estimation of the area of the upper figure will contain a disproportionately high contribution from the longer side and so the area will be overestimated.

Pressey himself indicated that attentive fields for figures need to be defined and measured by a method which is independent of the figures, for example by measurement of eye movements, before the theory can be properly tested. His averaging assumption is an interesting idea, but it seems altogether likely that his attempt to widen the theory by the introduction of the idea of attentive fields will, by the time this book is published, have been shown to be misguided.

ADAPTATION-LEVEL THEORY

This is a large-scale psychological theory (Helson, 1964) which aims to encompass a much wider range of phenomena than theories reviewed so far. Helson himself mentioned illusions as due to 'spatial pooling' but did not develop the application further. Green and Hoyle (1965) and Green and Stacey (1966) saw adaptation level as a possible means of explanation of illusions. Adaptation level is a level of functioning peculiar to an individual at a particular moment. It depends on all current stimulation and also on past stimulation. A new stimulus which is more intense than the adaptation level will evoke one kind of response and one which is less intense will evoke another. In addition to evoking a response, such stimuli will also alter the adaptation level. Green and Stacey (1966) proposed a number of 'stored norms' which are features of the customary adaptation levels of observers. These are stored norms of right angles, of verticality and horizontality, of parallelness and of curvature, and they give rise to 'perceptual tendencies'. Features which come near to complying with these stored norms will be seen as actually doing so: thus, for example, large acute angles will tend to be seen as more nearly right angles than they really are; lines which are vertically or horizontally orientated will be more resistant to distortion than those which are obliquely orientated. These are well-known effects. Also, the norms are altered by stimulation; thus, in the view of Green and Hoyle (1964), the many obliques of the standard Zöllner figure 're-weight' the vertical spatial norm and so make the two long vertical lines seem not to be vertical.

As an explanation of illusions, adaptation level is difficult to assess, mainly because detailed consequences of the notions involved have not been worked out. For example, the number of obliques in a Zöllner figure and their length should make a difference. Also, the re-weighting should happen over some small space of time. Tachistoscopic studies could reveal what the relationship with time is. Adaptation level theory faces many of the same problems that Eriksson's theory faces, that it risks becoming more and more complex as assumptions are added to meet with specific findings. However, Restle (1970) has had some success with the moon illusion and the final outcome remains to be seen.

This ends our consideration of theories which have been advanced to account for illusions. One cannot disagree with Over (1968) that it is surprising that psychologists have achieved so little in this endeavour. Geometrical optical illusions were among the first phenomena to be seen as the proper interest of psychologists and that same interest has been maintained; yet no theory has been able to survive rigorous test. The reason for this may be that psychologists have rushed into theory without first collecting sufficient data on how illusions change with slight change in configuration, what the size of the illusion is under various conditions and so on. The taxonomy of illusions has been relatively neglected. Evidence of this is not difficult to find; gaps in our knowledge of common illusions were pointed out in the earlier chapters.

The large number and the variety of illusions give little reason to suppose anyway that they can be explained by a single principle. The most likely outcome is that a fairly small number of principles will be found which, working together, can account for the data. Such an outcome is probably not far off. As early as 1964 MacKay proposed different neural analysers signalling contour direction (orientation), contour velocity and contour location, and now this notion of the extraction of different features of the stimulus by different coding systems is well established. The various sorts of 'selective tuning' of analysers in such systems have been studied (see, for example, Pantle and Sekuler, 1968; Blakemore and Campbell, 1969; Blakemore, Carpenter and Georgeson, 1970). The operation of such analysers in more complex stimulus situations now needs to be studied. Blakemore, Carpenter and Georgeson stressed lateral inhibition between orientation analysers in accounting for the interaction of two lines meeting at an angle. They discounted adaptation, but it may be that adaptation of orientation analysers is the mechanism behind those figural after-effects which involve angles, such as those studied by Gibson. Inhibition and adaptation of *spatial* frequency analysers might account for illusion and after-effect respectively between parallel contours, and extremely complex interactions would then occur amongst all these. There is no reason why a concept like adaptation level should not be useful in working out the relationships involved.

To be successful a theory must deal with eye movements and fixation and must either show what contribution they make or demonstrate that they are irrelevant. The latter seems unlikely from evidence already quoted in earlier chapters and also from the work of Kaufman and Richards (1969) and Richards and Kaufman (1969). They showed that fixations tend to be controlled by the organisation of the percept rather than by cues from the periphery. Fixations hover around the 'centre of gravity' of a figure. Acute angles are also powerful attractants of fixation. Thus fixation is to a large extent stimulus-determined, but in spite of this it seems at present more likely that eye movement and fixation are modified by the perceived illusion rather than the other way round. In future experiments, therefore, they are likely in the first place to be regarded as interfering factors that have to be controlled so that the illusions which they may modify, but not primarily cause, can be effectively studied.

The different parts played by the two hemispheres may also contribute to the illusion process. The temporal half of each retina projects to the ipselateral cerebral hemisphere and the nasal half to the contralateral hemisphere. Thus from each retina half the image passes to the hemisphere on the same side and half to that on the other side. The conduction times for the two sorts of connection are slightly different. It would be surprising if this arrangement did not have some advantage in the pattern analysing process over conceivable simpler arrangements. It could be that the illusions are something we trade in for other gains; that we are equipped with a process of, for example, enhancement or clarification of percepts which usually operates successfully, but in odd cases, like the illusions, misleads us. It could also be that such a process relies partly on this particular linkage of the eyes to the brain.

7

ILLUSIONS OF DEPTH AND DISTANCE

Gregory (1967) made the point that pictures are 'impossible objects'. We shall come to 'impossible objects' shortly, but Gregory's point was that it ought really to be impossible for us to resolve the conflicting cues of, on the one hand, depth in the content of the picture and, on the other hand, flatness of the surface on which the picture is drawn. However, for some reason we find it perfectly easy to suppress the cues we wish to ignore and to see a picture in depth, though even so we can easily distinguish it from a real scene because, although it has many of the cues of depth, it does not have them all. Retinal disparity is generally the main cue missing. Retinal disparity can be introduced by means of the stereoscope. Many texts treat stereoscopy well and it will be largely omitted here, but an account should perhaps be given of a common stereoscopic effect which does not need a stereoscope in the usual sense. This is a powerful three-dimensional effect produced usually on coloured cards by a process known as 'autostereoscopic photography'. The subject is reviewed by Dudley (1952). The surface of such cards is covered by small vertical transparent ribs so that a cross-section of the card is like Fig. 7.1. These ribs are effectively a stereoscope. The photograph has been printed through such ribbing by laying the negatives over the ribbing which itself lies on the printing paper. Light is supplied, not from a diffuse source, but from each of two (or more) discreet sources in turn. Exposure to each source will print a narrow strip of picture for each rib. The final picture will contain information from each of two (or more) stereo negatives. These two sets of information are separated in viewing by the fact that what is seen from the direction of the arrow A (Fig. 7.1) is different from what is seen from the direction of the arrow B, and the two eyes view the picture in this sort of way. The two retinae thus have separate, and correctly disparate, information.

Ordinarily, however, the perception of depth in pictures is not an illusion in the same sense as those dealt with so far. It is the ordinary and correct interpretation of only slightly ambiguous cues of depth, whereas the geometrical optical illusions are not correct interpretations of straightness, size and so on. The phenomena I shall deal with here are therefore not the ones involving the simple interpretation of depth cues but the ones where the depth cues are ambiguous or misleading to the extent that unusual effects result.

ILLUSIONS OF DEPTH AND DISTANCE IN STATIONARY DISPLAYS

Ambiguous figures

Probably the most general of all figures whose depth is ambiguous was published by Hering (1879) and Wundt (1898) (Fig. 7.2). Sanford's figure is of the same sort (Fig. 7.3). In fact, a single line drawn on paper, because of the absence of retinal disparity, has an infinite number of possible depth interpretations. Wundt's crosses can be seen in an enormous variety of different orientations in space. Fig. 7.4 is yet another example. Looking at these figures one can watch the changes take place spontaneously as the perceptual system 'tries' to settle on a particular 'best' interpretation. In most of the material dealt with by the visual system there *is* a 'best' interpretation, but in these figures, and even more in 7.5, 7.6 and 7.7, there is not, and so the system carries on searching indefinitely. This happens even with completely random stimulation of the kind MacKay (1964) used. A photograph of sandpaper provides such stimulation and the observer's perceptual system quickly organises it. He reports that it looks like 'tufted' carpet, in other words it is formed into small irregularly shaped, but separate, areas. Relatively little is known about what brings about such repeated efforts at interpretation. It will be discussed again with reference to the Necker cube below because it is in this context that it has been studied most.

There are several interesting situations where, even though there is an obvious 'best' interpretation, one can easily persuade the system to accept an alternative one. Some years ago I occupied a tiny room in which the desk faced a window covered with translucent material with a regular dot pattern. One day, sitting at the

---

7.1 'Autostereoscopic photography' (after Dudley, 1952) 7.2 Wundt's crosses (Hering, 1879) 7.3 Sanford (1903) 7.4

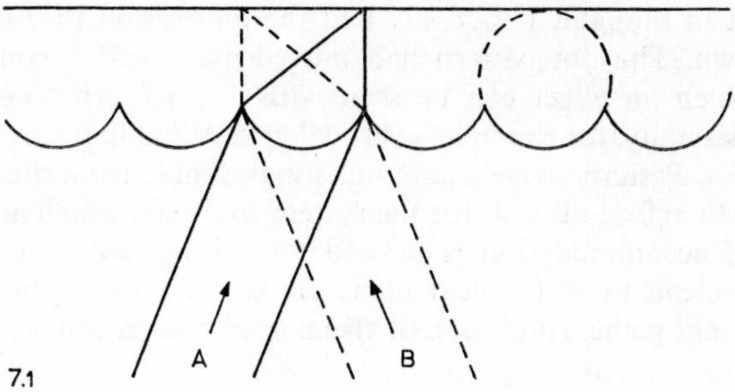

7.1

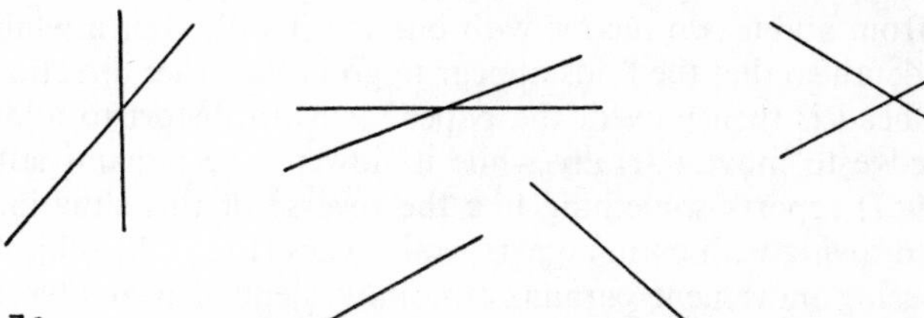
7.2

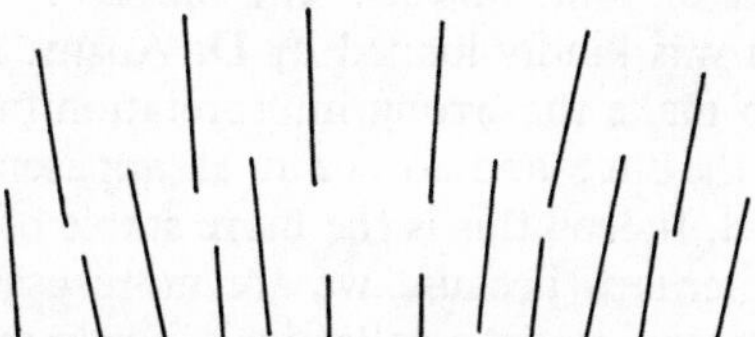
7.3

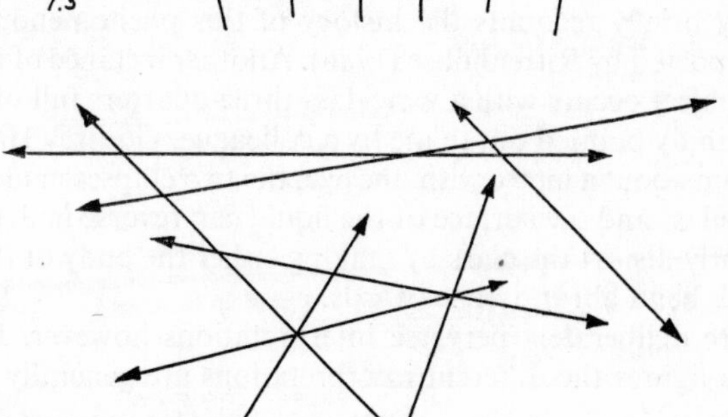
7.4

desk lost in thought, I suddenly had the impression that the room had grown. The dot pattern had moved away and become much larger. Such an effect can be seen with any pattern which is repetitive laterally, for example a vertical grid. What happens is shown in Fig. 7.8. Pattern elements are indistinguishable from one another and it is therefore difficult for the system to decide which are 'stereo pairs'. If accommodation is relaxed the wrong pairs are 'chosen' and two elements in the near plane are seen as one element in the more distant plane. Alteration of visual accommodation destroys the effect.

Sometimes solid objects can be persuaded to reverse in depth. If a piece of paper, folded into a zigzag and standing on its end, is viewed from about two metres with one eye it will, after a while, reverse in depth so that the folds appear to go in the other direction. When the head is then moved, the paper seems to distort to allow its upper edge to move laterally while its lower edge remains still. Jerison (1967) reports something like the reverse of this situation. Viewing a drawing with extreme perspective cues (Fig. 7.9), subjects reported seeing movement parallax (the movement of near objects against far ones when the head is moved) within the figure! The photograph in Plate II shows another instance of the apparent reversal in depth of solid objects. The mask of which the photograph was taken was kindly loaned by Dr Anstis. It is concave, yet it is very easy to make the wrong interpretation of the direction of illumination of the face and to see it as apparently standing out like a solid model. Indeed this is the more stable of the two possible interpretations, perhaps because we are more used to interpreting faces thus. I have tried to get a colleague's face in monocular view to change from the convex to the concave without success! Boring (1942) very briefly recounts the history of this phenomenon which was first reported by Rittenhouse (1786). Another instance of reversal in a solid object occurs with a wineglass three-quarters full of water. This was kindly pointed out to me by a colleague, Godfrey Harrison. Viewed from about a metre with one eye, the two ellipses made by the rim of the glass and the surface of the liquid can reverse in depth and so apparently distort the glass by making either the body of the glass or the stalk bend abruptly backwards.

These are deliberately perverse interpretations however. In truly ambiguous figures the different interpretations are generally neither

---

7.5 François Morellet, 'Screen painting 0°, 22·5°, 45°, 67·5°' (The Contemporaries, New York) 7.6 François Morellet, 'Tirets 0°–90°' (collection Jack Youngerman, The Contemporaries, New York)
7.7 Zip-a-tone pattern

7.5

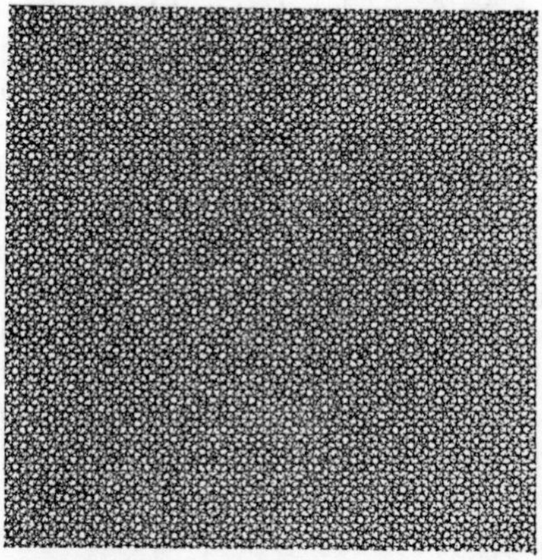

7.6

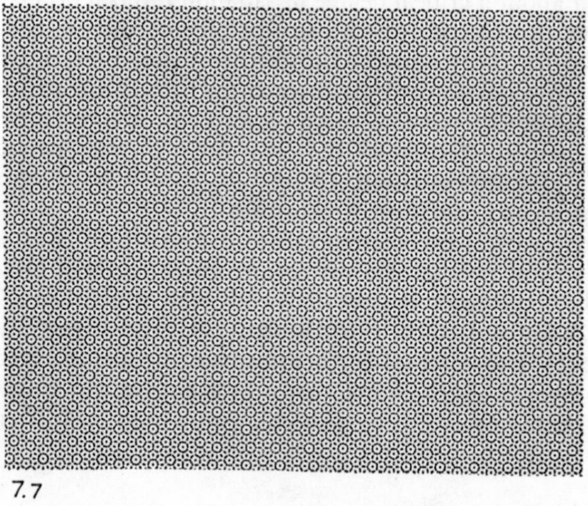

7.7

of them 'better' than the other. Fisher (1967c) pointed out the use of ambiguous pictures or ambiguous parts of pictures by Salvador Dali. He also produced a number of new ambiguous pictures (Fisher 1968f).

Some commonly studied figures are shown in Fig. 7.10. With these figures, the perceptual system behaves rather like a multistable oscillator, changing between two equally acceptable interpretations of the depth features. The rate of such spontaneous reversals has been shown to be reduced in psychotics (Eysenck, 1952) and in older people (Welford, 1958), and there has been a good deal of study using the reversal rate of ambiguous figures as a dependent variable. I shall confine my attention to a few of the studies of the reversal phenomenon itself.

An important study by Howard (1961) demonstrated that eye movement was not a factor by rotating two Necker cubes in opposite directions. Subjects viewing these reported the apparent direction of rotation to change in both cubes at the same time. It is difficult to see how eye movement could bring this about. Howard also showed that fatigue in fixation was not a factor by deliberately getting subjects to fixate another figure for some time before viewing a Necker cube. Reversal rate was unaltered. He also showed that viewing a Necker cube has no effect on the reversal rate of a different figure presented immediately afterwards, but that it does affect that of an identical cube. This effect, however, does not operate from one part of the retina to another. Howard concluded that the process is an auto-inhibitory one that is specific to a particular figure and, presumably, to a specific retinal location. This does not disagree with Gestalt notions which of course involve satiation. According to this view, when one interpretation of the figure has brought about a critical degree of satiation reversal occurs.

Olson and Orbach (1966), however, made the Gestalt position less tenable. They showed the Necker cube reversal rate to be greater with intermittent exposure at the rate of 109 exposures per minute than with continuous exposure. Thus, in unit time the intermittent condition exposed the cube for a shorter period, which should cause less satiation. Clearly any theory involving satiation must be a good deal more sophisticated.

Simon's (1967) explanation makes it possible to understand the abruptness of reversal. He stresses the serial nature of visual input. Saccadic suppression is now sufficiently well established (Volkman, 1962; Zuber and Stark, 1966; Wurtz, 1969) for us sensibly to suppose that visual input takes place in something like the 'frames' of a movie camera. Each 'frame' ends with an eye movement during which sensitivity is greatly reduced. Simon sees each 'frame' as a sort of perceptual act in which a fresh attempt at interpretation is made by the system. Thus one could think of several such attempts in succession resulting in the same percept until a process like adaptation has built up to a critical level. The next act would then bring about an abrupt change to a new interpretation. All this fits in with one's subjective impressions looking at Figs. 7.5, 7.6 and 7.7 where perceptual rearrangement seems to be linked with eye movements.

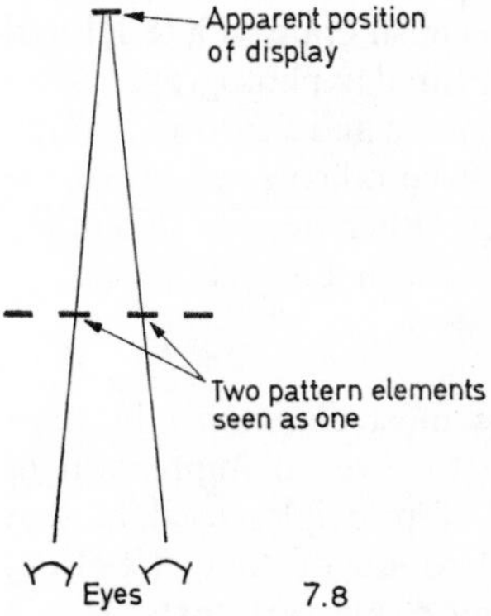

7.8

7.9

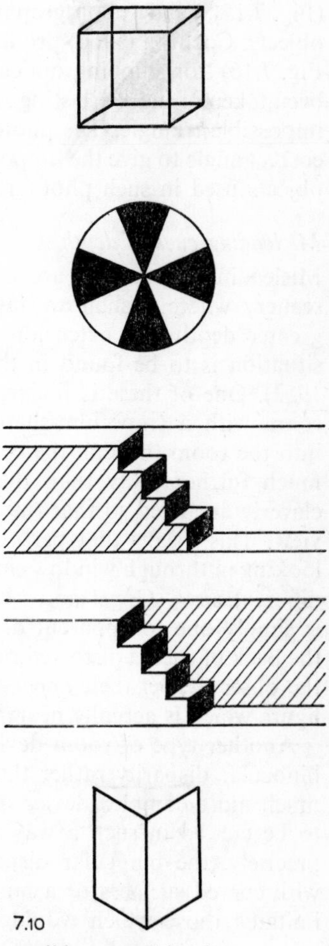

7.10

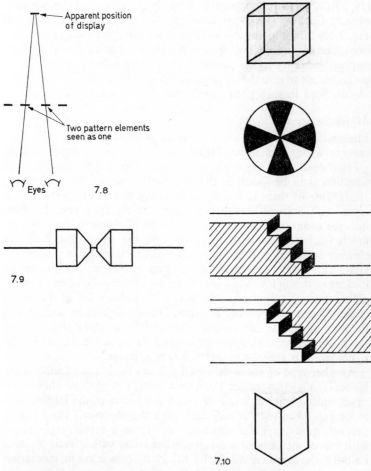

7.8 7.9 Jerison (1967) 7.10 Necker cube; reversible cross; Schröder staircase (Schröder, 1858); Mach book

Impossible figures

An amusing game can be played with perspective cues by making such cues in different parts of a display incompatible. Penrose and Penrose (1958) produced Figs. 7.11, 7.12 and 7.13. Schuster (1964) produced Fig. 7.14. Fisher (1968a) produced many more. Maurits Escher, the artist, has shown great interest in this sort of display and two of his fascinating and, to me, slightly disturbing lithographs are shown on the jacket and cover of this book and in the frontispiece. Gardner (1970) incorporated an 'impossible' figure into a picture (Fig. 7.15), and photographs have been taken of 'impossible' objects. Cochran (1966) produced the 'freemish crate' (Plate III and Fig. 7.16) 'for shipping optical illusions'. Similar photographs have been taken of the everlasting staircase (Penrose and Penrose) and the impossible triangle. The photograph must be taken at precisely the correct angle to give the 'impossible' effect. Other views of two of the objects used in such photographs are shown in Fig. 7.17.

Misleading cues of depth

Misleading depth cues are used perhaps most commonly in stage scenery where a shallow stage is made to give an impression of greater depth. An extension of the set of principles used in that situation is to be found in the distorted rooms of Ames (Ittelson, 1952). One of these is illustrated in many elementary texts. It is a room with a trapezium-shaped floor and an open end. Looking into the room through the open end, one of the far corners is very much further away than the other, yet the perspective cues are cleverly arranged so that the room looks rectangular in monocular view. This means that persons standing in the two far corners or looking in through windows in the far wall seem to be of enormously different sizes. Gogel and Mershon (1968) claimed that this effect is simply due to apparent distance. Human figures in windows at the back of such a distorted room are at different real distances from the observer, yet their *apparent* distance is the same. Therefore the figure which is actually nearer will appear larger.

Another type of room devised by Ames made use of misleading binocular disparity rather than misleading perspective. This was a much more complex device in that the surfaces of the interior had to be curved in such a way that, with the observer's head placed precisely, the binocular disparity cues from a much larger room with curved surfaces or a much smaller room with curved surfaces imitated those which would be expected from a room measuring

---

7.11–13 Penrose and Penrose (1958)

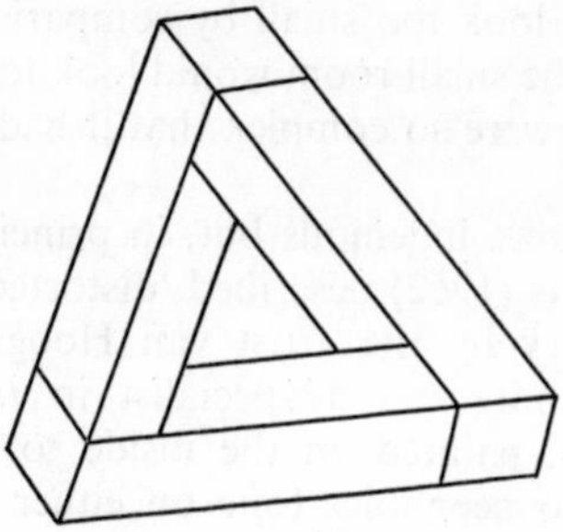

7.11

7.12

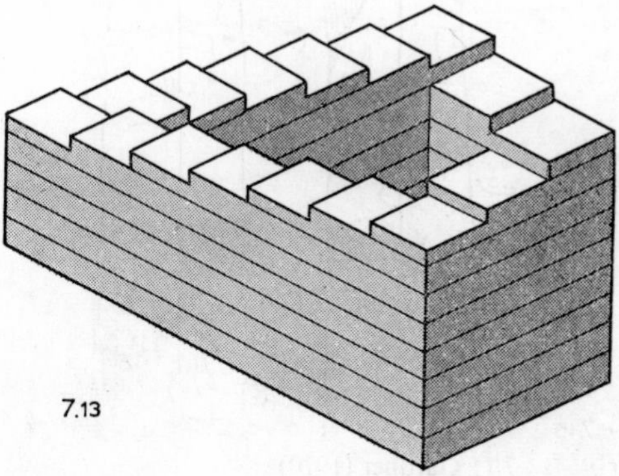

7.13

8 feet by 6 feet with plane surfaces. Thus a familiar object in the large room would look too small by comparison with the apparent room and one in the small room would look too large. The curves of this type of room were so complex that it had to be built by a firm of shipbuilders.

'Ames' rooms were ingenious but, in principle, not new. Van de Geer and de Natris (1962) described 'distorted rooms' made in the seventeenth century by the artist van Hoogstraaten (1627–78), a pupil of Rembrandt, and a specialist in *trompe l'œil* painting. These were boxes, painted on the inside to look like rooms and equipped with two peepholes (one on either side of the box; not together because the effect depends on monocular viewing). These authors describe one in the Bredius Museum in The Hague, a triangular box, and one in the National Gallery, London, a rectangular box. I have seen the latter and its effect is gained from painting

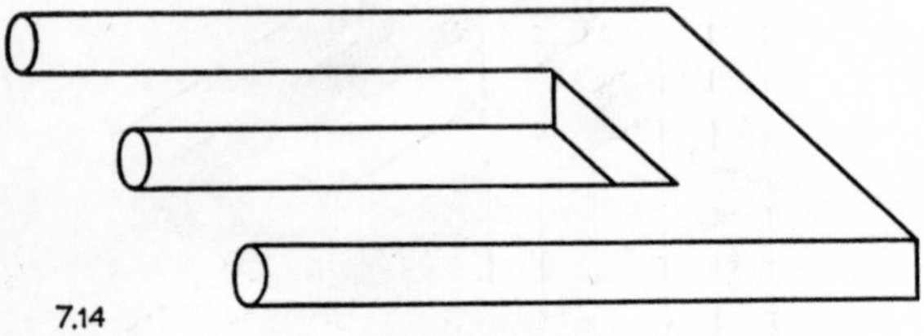

7.14

7.15

7.14 Schuster (1964) 7.15 Gardner (1970)

the walls of the box in such a way that the junction of the wall and floor of the apparent room is not coincident with the junction of the wall and floor of the box. The floor of the apparent room goes beyond the actual floor of the box. Thus the wall of the room is apparently beyond the actual side of the box. This means that anything painted on the side of the box *without* misleading cues as to distance seems to be standing or hanging away from the wall. The wall of the box forms an 'invisible' plane on which objects can be painted to give a powerful three-dimensional effect.

ILLUSIONS OF DEPTH AND DISTANCE IN MOVING DISPLAYS

Misinterpretation of depth occurs in both rotating and oscillating displays. In addition the direction of rotation of the former is easily mistaken. The reason for this is that a revolving figure quite easily becomes ambiguous in depth. Also, this is another situation in which the observer can, if he wishes, suppress cues and deliberately make the wrong interpretation of the display.

The stereokinetic effect

This effect occurs in figures which are displayed in rotation as if they lay on the turntable of a record player viewed from vertically above. Musatti (1929) gave the effect its name and attributed the first observation of it to Benussi. When interlocking rings or ellipses are rotated in such a way, it is easy to see them in depth as cylinders, hour-glass shapes and so on. A number of such displays are shown in Fig. 7.18. Metzger's (1953) figure resembling an elliptical clock face is particularly interesting. When rotated and viewed with one eye, this looks like a rotating circular face sloping away from the observer, and the arrow seems to stand out from the face. Fischer (1956) showed that the apparent depth in an apparent cylinder formed by the rotation of a pair of circles was linearly related to the separation of the two circles.

Wallach, Weisz and Adams (1956) described the phenomenon in more detail and without reference to apparent depth. When a single circle is rotated about its centre at about 20 rev/min they claimed that it did not appear to rotate. When two circles placed eccentrically were rotated they each appeared not to rotate but to slide over one another. This happened even if pairs of overlapping black discs were rotated with no visible contour at their junction. They seemed to slide over one another and an apparent edge appeared between them. Another such edge formed by a similar 'shearing' effect was formed when a scalloped circle and a plain circle concentric with it were rotated. Now the scalloped circle appeared to rotate presumably because, in its movement, it succeeded in firing movement detectors, whilst the plain circle did not. This resulted in an impression of shearing between the two.

There is an interesting distinction here between the impression of movement of a circle and the impression of rotation. When the circles are not concentric with the turntable they appear to move bodily but not to rotate. The scalloped circle is different in that it provides information about *rotation* in addition to movement bodily.

Wallach, Weisz and Adams prefer to restrict the term 'stereo-kinetic effect' to the case where, for example, a single rotating ellipse is seen like a plate spinning on its edge and viewed from above. This demands monocular observation and also, usually, suggestion from the experimenter. It is therefore distinguishable from the *pairs* of circles studied by Fischer. They prefer to include the latter with the phenomenon known as the 'kinetic depth effect' which is described below.

An important additional factor in stereokinesis was reported by Mefferd and Wieland (1967a). They rotated a luminous rod and a luminous ellipse about their centres in the way described above. At first the stimulus seemed simply to rotate and then began to appear either to advance towards the observer, or else expand, as it reached the vertical, and then to retreat, or else contract, as it reached the horizontal. Such expansion of the vertical and contraction of the horizontal we have met before. It is the vertical–horizontal illusion, and the authors see their work as support for the view of Künnapas (see Chapter 3). On further observation some variations occur. The axis of rotation may apparently change, or only one end of the figure may appear to advance and recede. These are both obviously the same effect acting asymmetrically. Clearly if a bar, for example, expands, it can be seen as expanding equally at each end or only at one end. In the latter case only that end would appear to advance and recede and the axis of rotation could appear closer to the opposite end. This is another example of a stimulus which is to a large extent ambiguous.

Mefferd and Wieland (1967b) studied other figures. A square rotating about its centre appeared to their subjects sometimes to be slanting and rectangular. A rectangle appeared to slant and become trapezoidal, or to undergo a process of expansion and contraction.

7.16 'Freemish crate' for 'shipping optical illusions' (after Cochran, 1966)
7.17*a* Gregory (1970) 7.17*b* Gregory (1970) 7.17*c* Gregory (1970)
7.17*d* Gardner (1970)

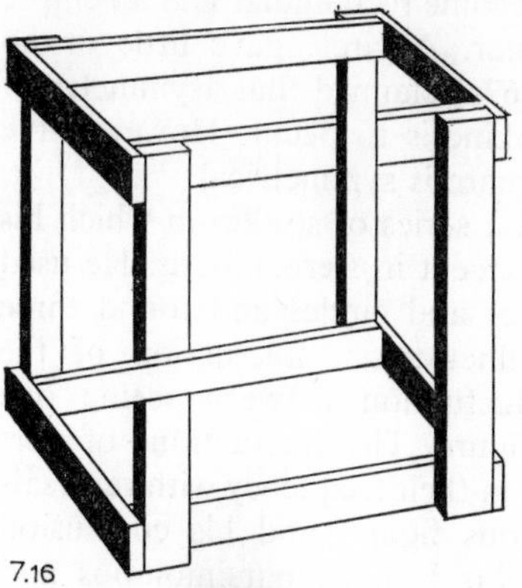
7.16

7.17a

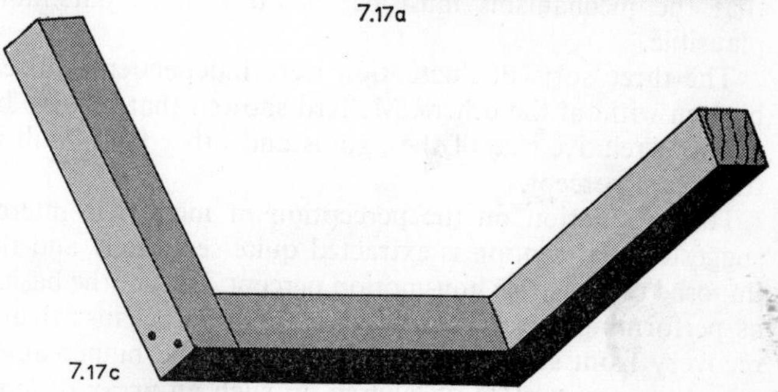
7.17c

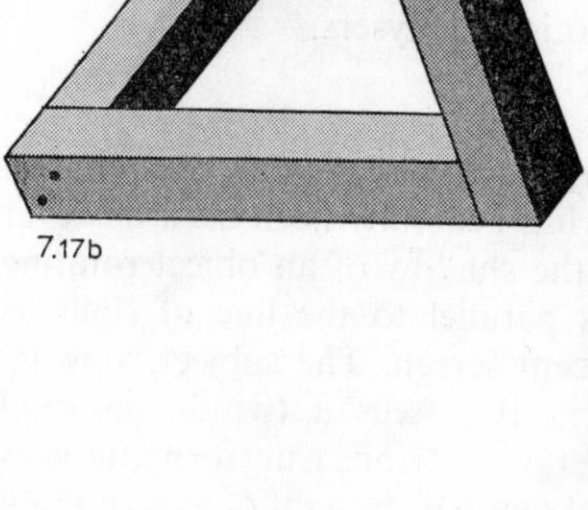
7.17b

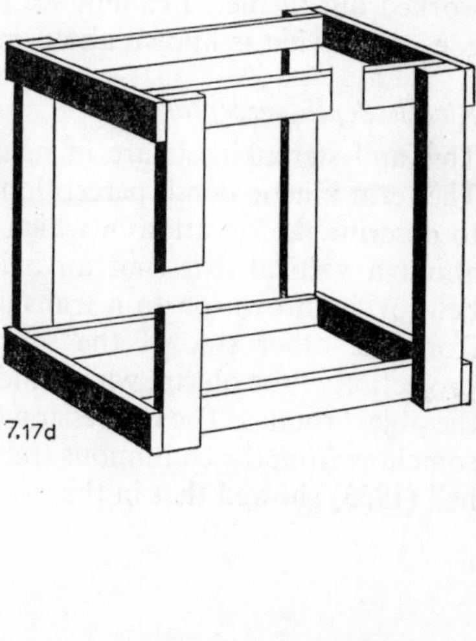
7.17d

A trapezoid appeared to slant and become rectangular and an ellipse seemed to slant and become circular. A circle gave little or no effect and Mefferd and Wieland (1967a) claimed that asymmetry of the figure was important for stereokinesis to occur. However, the square appeared to change and a square is symmetrical.

Mefferd (1968a,b,c,d,e,f) reported a series of studies in which his interest was the fluctuation of the percept in stereokinesis. He used luminous single and multiple ellipses and circles and found three types of fluctuation: perspective fluctuation, fluctuation of the apparent axis of rotation, and fluctuation between seeing one figure and seeing more than one figure. The fluctuations of perspective he found to correlate highly in their frequency with reversals of an ordinary stationary ambiguous figure, and his conclusion that the mechanisms must be similar is both parsimonious and plausible.

The three sorts of fluctuation were independent and each could happen without the others. Mefferd showed that relative brightness, fixation, relative size of the figures and other factors all influenced the actual percept.

His speculation on the perception of motion is interesting. He suggested that motion is extracted quite separately and then superimposed on the basic non-motion percept. He saw the basic receptors as performing a sort of condenser function because their complete recovery from stimulation is slow. Thus, the higher analysers can scan the current state of 'charge' in such an array of 'condensers'. Motion in a particular direction would presumably be signalled by such an analyser if a set of 'condensers' extending across the visual field were found to have a steadily increasing 'charge', since the 'charge' would have decayed the more the earlier in the set a particular 'condenser' lay. It would be interesting to see such an idea worked out further. I cannot see that it is incompatible, as far as it goes, with what is known about motion analysers.

Kinetic depth perception

This and stereokinesis are in many ways very similar phenomena. The term kinetic depth perception has generally been used however to describe the situation in which the shadow of an object rotating about a vertical axis (not an axis parallel to the line of sight as before), is thrown on to a translucent screen. The subject, viewing from the other side of the screen, thus sees a two-dimensional projection of the object, which undergoes various transformations as the object rotates. The impression of depth is thought of as stemming somehow from the continuous transformations. Wallach and O'Connell (1953) showed that in this sort of display using solid forms and

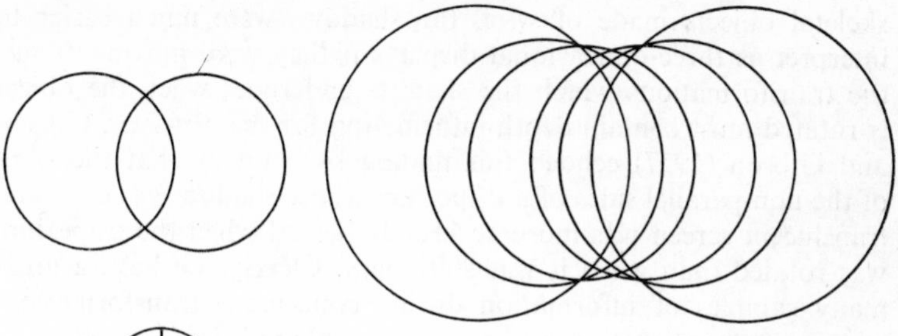

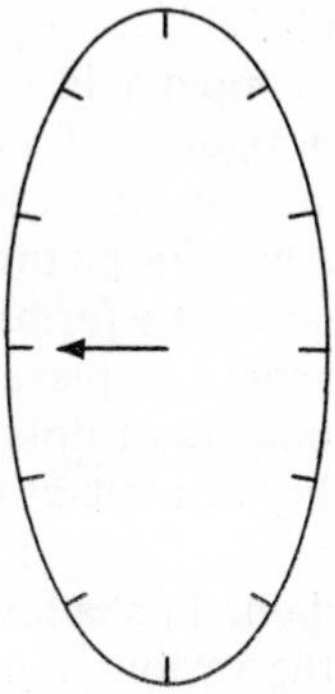

7.18

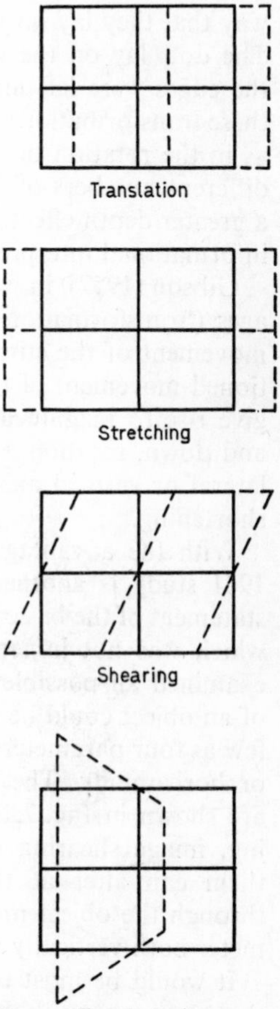

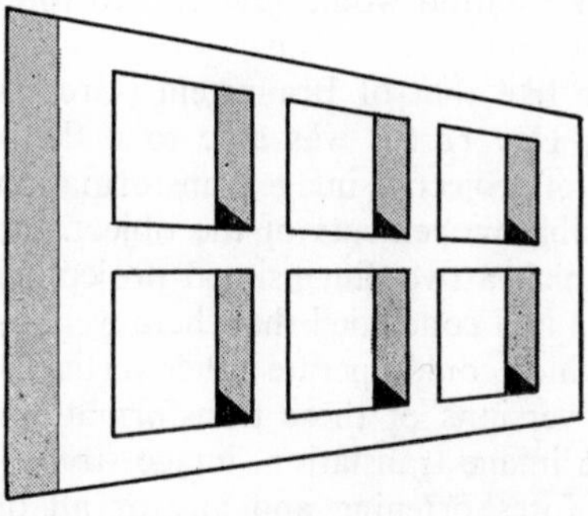

7.20

7.19

7.18 After Metzger (1953) 7.19 After Hay (1966) 7.20 Ames's window (Ames, 1951)

skeletal objects made of wire, the shadows were much easier to interpret as three-dimensional displays if they were moving. Thus, the transformations which the shadow undergoes when the object is rotated must contain depth information for the observer. Gibson and Gibson (1957) echoed this finding by showing that the slant of the non-parallel sides of a trapezium whose shadow was cast on a translucent screen was more accurately judged when the trapezium was rotated than when it was stationary. Clearly, we have a great many samples of information during continuous transformation, whereas without motion we have one sample only.

Braunstein (1962) generated sets of dots by computer in such a way that they lay on various perspective transformations of a cube. The dots lay on the surfaces of the cube and not on its edges, so the edges were left undefined. Braunstein made motion pictures of these transformations to give the effect of continuous transformation, as in the rotation of such a cube. Subjects compared displays with different numbers of dots. Those with larger numbers of dots gave a greater depth effect. This adds to the plausibility of a quantitative informational interpretation of the effect.

Gibson (1957), in writing about the cues available in shadow images ('transformations as stimuli') dealt with the various kinds of movement of the stimulus which would give rise to cues. He mentioned movement of the figure along the line of sight, which would give rise to magnification or reduction, movement sideways or up and down, rotation about the line of sight, and rotation about the lateral or vertical axis. The latter rotation would give rise to foreshortening.

With the advantage of studies like that of Braunstein (Green's 1961 study is another example), Hay (1966) was able to make a statement of the basic parameters of projective image transformation which was not in terms of possible movements of the object. He examined all possible ways in which a two-dimensional projection of an object could be transformed and concluded that there were as few as four parameters, each of which could operate either vertically or horizontally. The horizontal versions of these transformations are shown in Fig. 7.19. They are image translation, image stretching, image shearing and image foreshortening and any or all of them can alter at the same time. For example, magnification, through the object moving closer, alters the image-stretching parameter both vertically and horizontally.

It would be most interesting to know the relative importance of these parameters, how they are used in various situations and how their use develops. Much will soon be known, no doubt, because this is a very obvious use for computer-generated displays.

Ames's trapezoidal window and the reversal of rotary motion in depth
An object rotating on a vertical axis, especially if it is viewed with one eye, often apparently reverses its direction of rotation. Radar aerials in the middle distance are good objects on which to observe this. If the observer is not on a level with them then the new apparent plane of rotation is at an odd angle, not horizontal as it was before. The reversal may only persist for a half-turn and then revert to the original direction only to reverse again 180° later. This oscillatory motion was noticed long ago. Boring (1942) writes that Sinsteden noticed the phenomenon on a windmill and reported it in 1860. Kenyon (1898) saw a rotating fan doing it. He described oscillation and also other effects; the apparent 'flapping together' of the fan blades and also their apparent 'withdrawing and pushing out from the hanging rod'. Miles (1931), realising the importance of ambiguity in the image of the fan, used the shadow of a fan and noted the frequency of reports of the effects described by Kenyon by several subjects. His was a study, in fact, of the kinetic depth effect.

Ames (1951) provided a demonstration of reversal of rotary motion which captured widespread and long-term interest. He slowly rotated a trapezoidal frame which was painted on both sides with apparent shadows to look like a window frame (Fig. 7.20). This was rotated about a vertical axis and observers monocularly saw a rectangular window rotating to and fro. (This works binocularly too, probably by means of the suppression of cues mentioned earlier.) The apparent change of direction took place when the actual position of the window was approximately at right angles to the line of sight. Graham (1965) summarised these events well. He pointed out that the short end of the window appears to be in the two far quadrants of the rotation regardless of where it really is. If the actual rotation is clockwise, then, when the short end is in the nearer right-hand quadrant, it appears to be in the far right-hand quadrant and moving away from the observer (anticlockwise), and when it is in the nearer left-hand quadrant it seems to be in the far left-hand quadrant and moving towards the observer. If the short end is in either of the far quadrants, the actual direction of motion is perceived. Conversely, the long end apparently only traverses the near two quadrants. Ames gives a minute description and his account is worth reading.

When a small cube is attached rigidly by a short wire to the smaller end of the window it is seen in veridical rotation all the time and appears to float round the member to which it is attached, passing, at the appropriate time, through the window. A rod, rigidly fixed so that it lies at an angle to the window and passing through one of the 'panes', gives rise to a similar effect. When the motion of the window apparently reverses, that of the rod remains unchanged, and so it seems to be rotating in the opposite direction to the window. But as the rotation proceeds the apparently opposite rotation of the window and the rod becomes more and more 'impossible'. The rod appears to bend more and more until as the window crosses the line of sight (i.e. the smaller end, which is nearer, but looks farther, crosses from right to left), the rod suddenly 'snaps' straight. Again Ames (1951) explains all these effects in terms of the cues available from different parts of the display at different stages. The effects follow in a logical, if complex, way from the apparent and real perspective transformations of the various parts of the display.

Ames explained the phenomenon in terms of experience. We have a great deal of experience of rectangular objects and frequently deal with slanting views of them. Thus when we see a slanting trapezium we take it to be a slanting rectangle and make the 'best' interpretation on that assumption of the depth of the display and its direction of movement. When the short end is in one of the near quadrants this interpretation is misleading.

Various details have been examined since 1951. For example Zenhausen (1968) showed that when the window was actually oscillated it could appear to be in continuous rotation. Reduction of the ambiguity of a rotating figure by means of interposition of objects and the use of texture gradients was found by Canestrari and Farné (1969) to reduce the tendency to reverse. Zegers (1965) found that the number of reversals reported for a rotating plain trapezium increased with the slope of the top and bottom of the figure and also with the distance from the observer. This latter finding confirms Ames's similar finding. Zegers concluded that increasing viewing distance and slope of the trapezium both reduce the number of cues of real movement. He also showed that tilting the axis of rotation reduced the number of reversals and took it that this increased the number of such cues.

Epstein, Jansson and Johansson (1968) studied the factors affecting the amplitude of oscillation in a plain luminous trapezium. They found that decreasing the width-to-height ratio (this amounts again to altering the slope of the top and bottom) decreased the apparent amplitude of oscillations but increased report of their occurrence. Freeman and Pasnak (1968) studied factors determining the plane in which apparent reversal took place. As would be expected from the last two studies the slope of the top and bottom of the trapezium was important.

Mulholland (1958) found apparent reversal and oscillation in a much simpler figure. He rotated clockwise round a vertical axis a bar ¼ in. wide and 24 in. long with a black disc of ½ in. diameter at one end and a white disc of the same size at the other. Subjects reported several sorts of motion; veridical rotation, anticlockwise rotation, oscillation with black apparently passing in front, oscillation with white apparently passing in front, and apparent expansion and contraction of the bar without rotation. He varied the brightness of the background and, by altering the axis of rotation, introduced asymmetry. Oscillation was more frequently reported for less symmetrical displays, and the disc with the greater contrast tended to appear to pass in front.

Ames's explanation in terms of familiarity with transformations of a rectangle has not gone unchallenged. Pastore (1952) pointed out that apparent reversal happens for many figures, circles, ellipses, diamond shapes and even quite irregular figures. Certainly these last figures are not familiar in the sense that Ames's explanation would demand. Pastore suggests that perceived slant is the cue and that when perceived slant is different from actual slant the display apparently reverses in depth and therefore in direction of motion. I cannot see that this explanation is much different from that of Ames. It extends its application to other figures it is true, but applied to the trapezium it says only what Ames said, that apparent slant is misjudged. Ames differed only in trying to go further and say *why* slant is misjudged.

Day and Power (1963, 1965) put other arguments. Using rotation at 20 rev/min and monocular view they demonstrated apparent reversal in a trapezium; a rectangle with a window-frame pattern, with a pattern of vertical bars and with no pattern; an ellipse; a circle and an irregularly curved figure. To rebut Pastore's claim, they asked subjects to judge the apparent slant of several of these shapes, with or without surface patterns, stationary, and set at angles of 60° and 120° to the line of sight. Only the slant of the trapezium was misjudged, yet all the figures had shown apparent reversal of rotation. Thus, misjudgment of apparent slant is not a necessary condition for apparent reversal.

Day and Power see reversal as a fairly straightforward result of ambiguity. If the transformations are ambiguous as to direction of motion, then motion can apparently reverse. The situation is analogous to that of the stationary Necker cube with motion being ambiguous instead of perspective. Reducing cues to the actual direction of motion helps apparent reversal, though reversal can occur even in the presence of some contradictory cues (just as stationary figures can be persuaded to reverse in depth even when many cues of actual depth are present). No doubt ambiguous perspective can help apparent reversal of rotation too and indeed the trapezium reverses more readily than most other figures. Also in the case of Ames's window the pattern painted on the surface is actually misleading as to perspective and therefore adds further weight to the 'reverse' interpretation. This explanation is an appealing one because it unites all the phenomena dealt with in the chapter up to this point. All can be seen as situations in which cues are sufficiently reduced to leave the main judged characteristic ambiguous, or so nearly so that the observer can if he wishes ignore cues that would contradict the particular perceptual interpretation on which he has decided.

A great deal remains to be discovered, in the case of rotary motion, about what it is that becomes ambiguous. We do not yet know exactly what the cues of rotary motion are; what it is in continuous transformations that gives us information about motion in depth. Power (1967) discovered one cue, the lengthening and shortening of edges perpendicular to the axis of rotation, but Hay's (1966) work, mentioned in the last section, is applicable again here and goes much further.

It is a little odd, and a tribute to the force of the Ames window effect, that so much study has been done with such complex figures when the earliest observations of this sort of phenomenon were of very simple figures like the shadow used by Miles. The Ames window confounds the kinetic depth effect with misleading information about perspective given by the painted shadows on the frame and probably by the asymmetry of the trapezium itself. The study of the kinetic depth effect is probably the best beginning for a study of the apparent reversal, in monocular view, of rotary motion in real objects. The computer generation of artificial displays like that of Braunstein is probably the most powerful approach to this problem.

The Pulfrich pendulum

If a pendulum swinging from side to side is viewed through both eyes with a filter placed in front of one of them, then the pendulum seems to swing, not simply to and fro, but in such a way that the bob describes an ellipse. If the filter is over the right eye then the bob seems to be nearer the observer during its swing from left to right and further from him on the swing from right to left, that is the motion is anticlockwise when viewed from above. Pulfrich (1922) reported this phenomenon and used it for equating the brightnesses of different colours (heterochromatic photometry).

Pulfrich himself supposed that the filter caused a delay in the processing of the signal from the filtered eye, thus interfering with the correspondence of points on the two retinae in stereoscopic vision. This explanation has been elaborated since then and has not seriously been challenged. It would happen as follows. Consider a moment in time as the pendulum bob is swinging from right to left. If the filter is over the right eye then the right eye's view is a fraction of a second out of date. The bob will be seen by that eye to the right of its true position. But the binocular-fusion mechanism for some reason does not take into account the presence of the filter and assumes that the views of both eyes are contemporary. Now in stereoscopic vision, displacement of an image in the nasal direction on one retina compared with its position on the other gives an impression of approach, and relative displacement of the images temporally gives an impression of recession. This can be demonstrated by holding up the two forefingers centrally in front of the eyes, one about half a metre away and the other about a quarter, and fixating the far one. The two images of the nearer finger are each displaced nasally with reference to the far one; this can be discovered by closing each eye in turn. Conversely, when the nearer finger is fixated the two images of the far finger are displaced temporally relative to it. Thus, when the pendulum bob is moving from right to left and the right eye's view of the bob is displaced to the right this is a relative temporal shift and will make the bob seem further away than its true position.

The actual shape of the apparent path of the bob is determined by its varying speed. The faster the bob moves the greater will be its apparent displacement in depth. A pendulum's simple harmonic motion gives rise to the bob's apparently describing an elliptical path.

Lythgoe (1938) calculated a value for the delay for a given illumination of the pendulum. He also attempted to achieve a reduced brightness of the bob for one eye by other means than a filter. He shone an electric torch into one eye, thus presumably reducing the brightness of the bob to that eye by means of simultaneous contrast. The effect was reversed. He concluded that for some reason the shining of the light into the eye reduced its latency instead of increasing it but it was left to later workers to find the reason.

Lit (1949) made a detailed study of the phenomenon using an illuminated horizontal slit. In the upper half of the slit was a short vertical black bar which moved to and fro horizontally along the slit, the speed being constant for 90 per cent of its path. In the centre of the lower half of the slit was another short vertical bar which could be adjusted in depth. The task of the subject was to adjust the latter bar so that apparently it lay at the same depth as the moving bar. Of course in this arrangement the moving bar did not appear to move in an ellipse because it moved at constant speed, not like a pendulum. For 90 per cent of its path it appeared to move in a straight line in the observer's fronto-parallel plane, but the distance of its actual plane of movement was different from the apparent one. From the geometry of this situation, Lit produced a formula for calculating, from the Pulfrich effect, the delay in milliseconds caused by the lower intensity of input to the filtered eye. This was done for various distances of observation and various light levels. He found that the effect increased as the difference in retinal illumination (i.e. the density of the filter) increased. For a given difference in retinal illumination, the effect increased as overall illumination (the intensity of illumination of the slit) decreased.

However, as Lythgoe's work suggested, the intensity difference at the two eyes seems not to be the sole determinant of the magnitude of the Pulfrich effect. The shining of a light into one eye produced its effect, presumably by altering the state of adaptation of that eye. Engelking and Poos (1924) produced further evidence of this sort. They prepared their subjects by light adapting one eye and dark adapting the other. The Pulfrich effect was then obtained without a filter and its direction was as if the filter were over the dark adapted eye. Thus, although the stimulus *appears* brighter to the dark adapted eye still the latency for that eye must be greater. Rock and Fox (1949) again showed that dark adaptation has an effect similar to that of a filter. These authors also plotted the effect on the Pulfrich phenomenon of increasing the filter density. They found a steady increase up to their densest filter. The relationship was described by a compound log function:

$$\text{stereo effect} = k \log . \log \frac{1}{\text{filter transmission}}$$

which, however, broke down with the densest filter.

Diamond (1958) studied the effect of contrast. His stimulus was a rotating cross. A pointer below the cross, adjustable in depth, was adjusted by subjects so that it appeared to lie in the plane of the arms of the cross as they passed by it. By means of a half-silvered mirror, he arranged a bright annulus so that, in the view of one eye, it appeared to surround the stimulus. The effect was the opposite of that obtained with a filter over that eye and so was exactly like the effect obtained by light adapting one eye. Presumably the effect exerted by the annulus on the stimulus at its centre was very like one of light adaptation. In this case it would seem to be an excitatory influence because the delay for that eye, as indicated by the direction of the Pulfrich effect, was reduced.

Approaching the question slightly differently, Standing, Dodwell and Lang (1968) studied the effect of dark adaptation over time using a set-up with a filter. The Pulfrich effect increased over 20 minutes' viewing. They took this to be the result of dark adaptation in the filtered eye causing an intensification of the effect obtained with the filter.

Since rods and cones are at different states of adaptation at different light intensities, it might be expected that differences in the Pulfrich effect, found in different states of adaptation of the eye, might be traced to differences in the speed of action of these two sorts of primary receptor. Arden and Weale (1954) concluded that the phenomenon was due to delay in the rod mechanisms. They plotted the Pulfrich effect for various brightness differences when the stimulus was not on the fovea; the fixation point was to one side. They failed to find any Pulfrich effect using a red filter; the rods are insensitive to red. A blue-green filter, on the other hand, gave a marked effect; the rods are sensitive to blue-green.

This fits in neatly with the evidence of the effect of adaptation. In the dark adapted state presumably a greater proportion of the work is being done by rods and the extra delay involved could cause the Pulfrich effect. There are two difficulties, however. In work reported below, Wilson and Anstis (1969) used high light values, even in the filtered eye, at which rods would not be operating. Also it is easy to obtain the Pulfrich effect with a red filter.

The work of Wilson and Anstis is interesting both because of its unusual detail and because of the apparatus used. Subjects viewed two horizontal slits, illuminated from behind, monocularly. Instead of the filter being put over one eye it was put over one slit. The slits were one above the other and each contained a vertical shadow which moved together to and fro sinusoidally along the slit. Fixating a point between the slits, subjects saw the shadow in the dimmer slit apparently lagging behind the other. The phase of the movement of the two shadows was adjustable by the subject, and his task was to adjust the phase until the two seemed to move in phase. Thus, this ingenious device allows the delay to be read off directly in the form of the phase difference. Moreover the different delays in this situation took place within the same retina and any effects due to differences of adaptation must happen within the same retina too. The expression these authors derived from the relationship of delay to luminance was the power function:

$$D = aI^{-b} + D_o$$

Where D is the observed delay

I is the intensity compared with 1800ftL

D_0 is the estimated delay for the brightest light used
a and *b* are fitting parameters

They re-analysed Lit's (1949) data and claimed that it fitted this function well.

In later work Rogers and Anstis (1972) examined in detail the interrelationships of the three variables, delay, luminance and state of adaptation. The apparatus used was a modification of that used by Anstis and Wilson. The two slits were again used with the same filter arrangement, but one slit was presented to each eye through a stereoscope. The subjects' task was to adjust the phase of the shadow in the unfiltered slit so that the image formed by the fused shadows in stereoscopic view appeared to move in the fronto-parallel plane; that is, it appeared to move to right and left along a single horizontal path at right angles to the line of sight.

Rogers and Anstis produced a three-dimensional graph showing the interrelationships found. At all levels of adaptation, the maximum delay was found at the lowest luminances of the targets. (The difference between the luminances of the two slits was kept constant.) With increasing light adaptation at low luminances, the delay decreased. With increasing luminance of the targets, delay decreased, but then with very bright targets it *increased again*, except where light adaptation was at a very high level.

The outstanding point of these findings is the increase in the Pulfrich effect at high luminance levels. Even if the rods are heavily involved in the delay at low levels they could not be involved at high levels. It seems likely that another mechanism is brought into play at high light levels which increases visual delay, but such a mechanism would operate on the brighter eye first, increasing delay in that eye and so reducing the effect. Increase in delay in visual processing at high luminance levels needs further investigation.

An earlier method of producing the Pulfrich effect, which was used by Dvořak (1872), employs two episcotisters (rotating discs with sectors cut out). The subject views a pendulum, with one eye looking through each of the two episcotisters, which are in phase. Harker's (1967) demonstration is an interesting reminder that episcotisters can show the Pulfrich effect. The effect happens because, when the bob is at a position away from the centre on one side, the eye on the other side sees it first as the eposcotister gaps move round. This asynchrony gives rise to misjudgment of depth.

A lively report by Enright (1970) shows how easily the Pulfrich effect is observed. He recounts how his small son, after the manner of small sons, was looking out of a moving vehicle through sunglasses with one lens missing and noticed odd effects. With the lens over the 'leading' eye, the velocity of the vehicle seemed increased, with the lens over the 'following' eye it seemed reduced. Objects by the roadside seemed further away or nearer according to whether the leading or following eye was looking through the lens. The effect was most clear at slow speeds (10 to 20 m.p.h.) and where there were lots of objects at various distances from the road. I have tried this in a slow-moving train and the effect is surprising. With the filter over the following eye, one has the impression of being in a miniature train because one seems to be so very close to the track. Similar effects of apparently altered distance, in viewing with a filter over one eye, can be seen in objects moving across a cinema screen or even a television screen, though the latter is rather small to give rise to sufficient lateral movement. The effects can be quite bizarre since only moving stimuli alter in depth. Thus, in a scene where patches of light move across a wall, for example, the patches of light do not seem to lie in the same plane as the wall.

In conclusion, an unusual occurrence of this sort of effect reported by MacKay and Stroud (1968) ought to be mentioned. They observed that, when a tetrahedron made of the bars used in crystal models was rotated at about six revolutions per second, a pattern of dark lines appeared inside it. This happens because when the figure is rotated there is a blur of the bars composing it. The blurred images of the bars on the front of the figure and the blurred images of the bars on the back add to give a joint brightness, except where bars on the front cross over bars on the back. Here each front bar occludes a back bar (or a section of it if the bars are not parallel) and so a small patch has only the brightness of the front bar. This will give rise to a number of dark lines. The two eyes, from their different viewpoints, will see the coincidence of front and back bars in apparently different places. This disparity will cause the dark lines to be located by the stereoscopic mechanism somewhere within the tetrahedron.

In summary, the Pulfrich effect seems to be caused by delay in the processing of visual information from one of the two eyes. Such delay is brought about by reduction of the intensity of stimulation of one eye or by dark-adaptation of one eye. The effect seems to depend on three variables: adaptation, intensity difference and absolute intensity. The function relating absolute intensity, adaptation and the extent of the Pulfrich effect shows maxima at low and at very high absolute intensities. Increase of visual delay with lower intensities is well known if not precisely understood, but increase of delay with higher intensities is a surprising observation.

The illusions described in this chapter all involve the information used by the visual system to infer the relative distance of a stimulus or part of a stimulus. In knowing this we know a good deal more than we know about the geometrical-optical illusions, but there are gaps still in our knowledge of illusions involving depth perception. For example, we do not yet know why the visual system spontaneously changes its depth interpretation of ambiguous figures; we do not know exactly what cues the system uses in interpreting certain sorts of transformations of a flat display as rotary motion in depth; we do not know the mechanism by which filters or adaptation alter the delay in visual processing.

8

ILLUSIONS FROM BRIGHTNESS CONTRAST

Brightness contrast itself is such an ubiquitous perceptual phenomenon that its simple operation, although sometimes giving rise to curious effects, would not usually be classed as an illusion. In any case the subject has been so well treated in textbooks on perception that no lengthy treatment is needed here. A number of situations involving brightness contrast do however give curious perceptual effects and I shall briefly describe some of these.

The usual effect of brightness contrast is that a bright surround makes an area appear darker and a dark surround makes an area appear lighter. It is generally supposed to result from lateral interaction effects of facilitation and inhibition in the visual system. Westheimer's (1967) work is a good example of the sort of study on which this supposition is built. He examined the threshold for a small spot within a light disc as the latter increased in size. Size increase lowered the threshold for the spot up to a disc size of 5 minutes of arc (facilitation), then further increase of disc size steadily raised the threshold for the spot (inhibition). Thus it was not until units well away from the spot were stimulated that lateral inhibition took place.

A figure described by Hermann (1870) (Fig. 8.1) is often included in collections of illusions. It seems likely that the shadows appearing at non-fixated junctions of the white bars can be explained by contrast. Where the white lines run between black areas their whiteness is enhanced, but at the junctions the black areas have less effect. Thus the junctions seem darker. Interactive effects are greater in the periphery of vision than at the fovea and so the effect is greater away from the point of fixation.

REVERSED CONTRAST

In 1874 von Bezold noticed that, if black or white arabesques were superimposed on a coloured background, then instead of the black pattern making the background seem lighter and the white pattern making it seem darker the reverse effect occurred. Burnham (1953) gives examples of this effect taken from Evans (1948).

Helson and Rohles (1959) showed by means of Fig. 8.2 that the effect could be obtained in monochrome. They varied the spacing of their black and white lines, which were 1 mm wide. They claimed that some effect remained even when the lines were 55 mm apart! Previously Helson (1943) had demonstrated the effect with Fig. 8.3. As the length of the black bars increases so the contrast effect changes.

What is apparently another example of reversed contrast, one I have not seen reported before, was pointed out to me by a colleague, Michael Wood. In two-cycle by two-cycle log–log graph paper (see Fig. 8.4) the top right-hand corner of the bottom left-hand quarter looks darker than the top right-hand corner of any of the other quarters, in spite of the fact that the other quarters all border on plain paper and so, in ordinary contrast, would look darker.

Most contributors on this topic seem to agree that for some reason in certain situations facilitation takes the place of the expected inhibition, and vice versa. There seems to be good evidence, for example that of Westheimer (see p. 195), that the process which operates in a particular situation is quite finely determined. It ought to be possible to investigate the point of changeover from contrast to reversed contrast by manipulation of the figure used by Helson and Rohles. Either the number of lines involved is critical or the dimensions of the lines and spaces. Such an investigation might show that the dimensions involved in Westheimer's study of raised and lowered thresholds are similar to those involved in the two kinds of contrast. Festinger, Coren and Rivers (1970) have varied the exposure conditions of figures with broad bands of grey, black and white, and narrow ones. In general, under normal viewing, the narrow bands produced reversed contrast and the broad bands normal contrast. However, these workers found that either form of contrast could be produced with either sort of figure when suitable exposure conditions (in terms of timing and movement) were used. They suppose that the general level of brightness is perceived by an averaging process over the whole field and information about changes within the field is superimposed on this. Perceived brightness of any particular part of the field will therefore be a function of

8.1

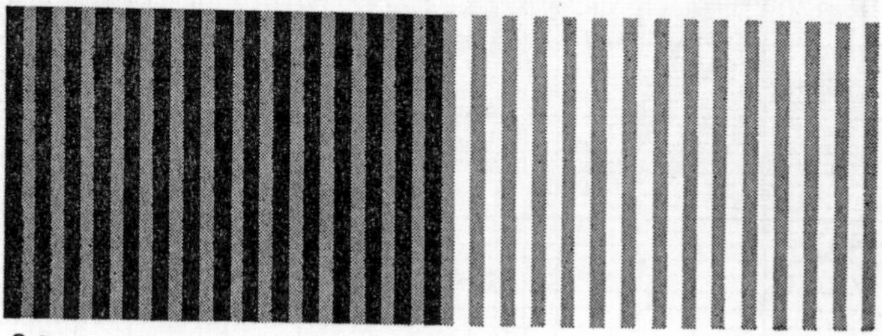

8.2

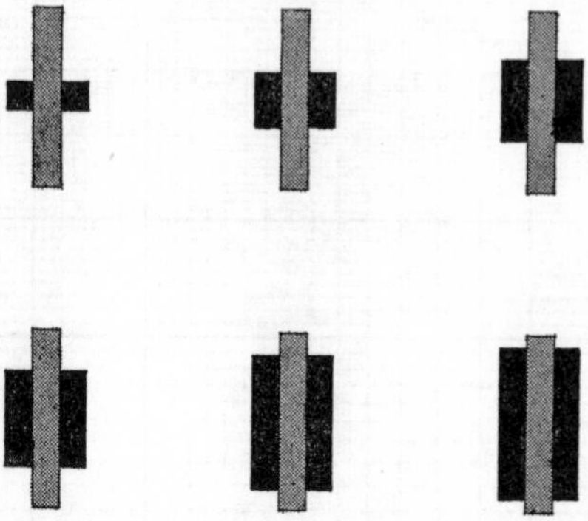

8.3

8.1 Hermann (1870) 8.2 After Helson and Rohles (1959) 8.3 After Helson (1943)

these two sets of information and this is why both the absolute brightness of the parts and their spatial frequency affect contrast.

MACH BANDS AND PERCEPTION OF CONTOURS

In his monograph on Mach bands, Ratliff (1965) includes a translation of a paper in which Mach reports the phenomenon. This was published in 1865. The specially interested reader should read Ratliff's work.

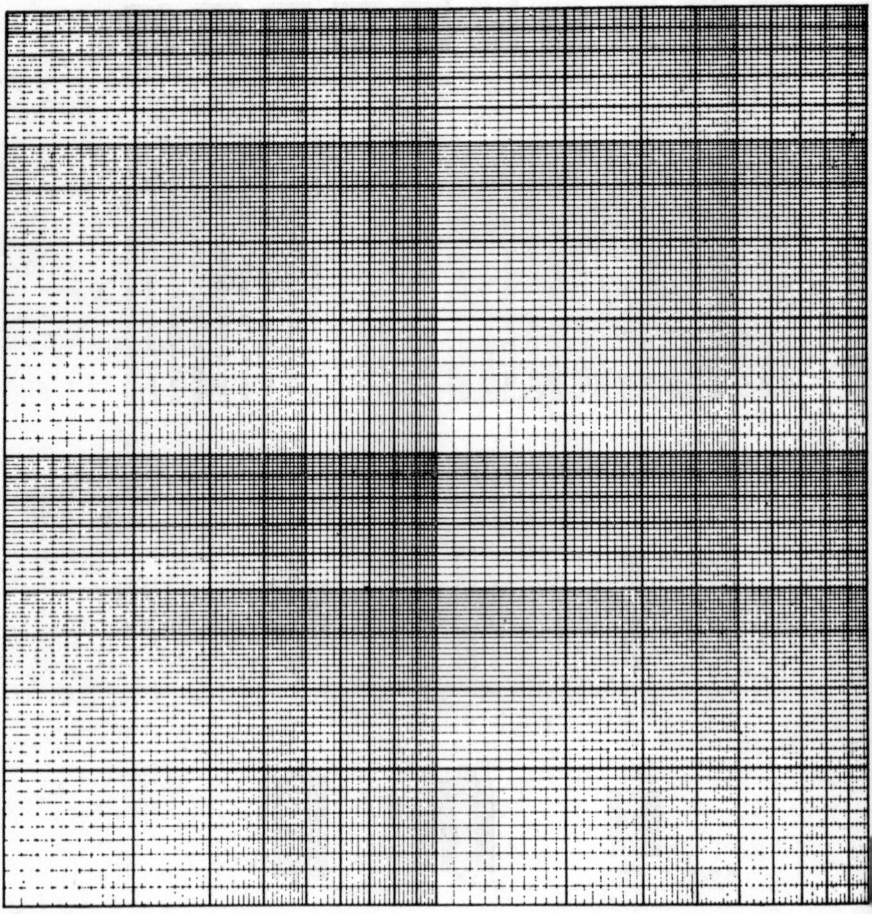

8.4

8.4 2 cycle log–log graph paper

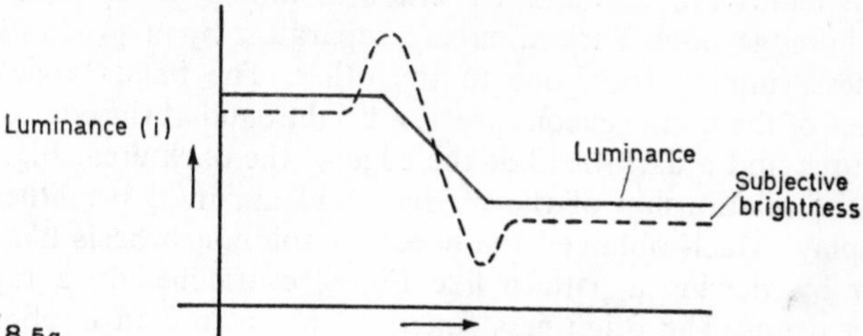

8.5a

8.5b

8.5c

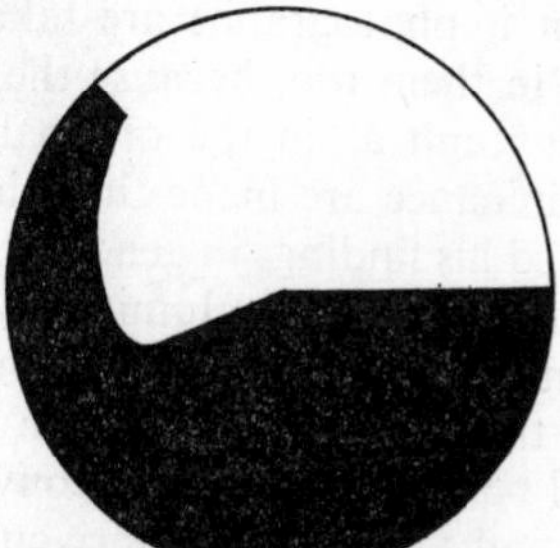
8.5d

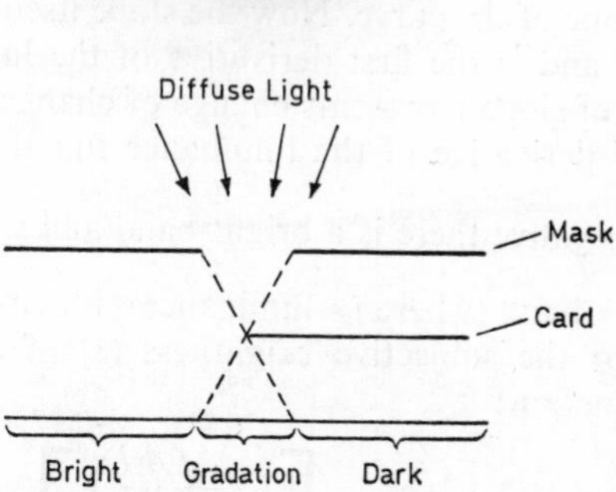

8.5e

8.5*a* 8.5*b* After Mach (1865) 8.5*c* After Mach (1865) 8.5*d* 8 5*e*

Mach bands are encountered where a homogeneous light area and a homogeneous dark area are separated by a gradation of brightness running from one to the other. The bands appear at the edges of the homogeneous areas, a bright band at the edge of the bright area and a dark band at the edge of the dark area. Fig. 8.5a shows the relationship of the physical and apparent brightness of the display. Mach obtained the effect by spinning wheels like Fig. 8.5b or by viewing a pattern like Fig. 8.5c attached to a rapidly rotating drum. The brightness function shown in 8.5a is obtained in this way. Another configuration giving the same function is shown in 8.5d. Here the inner and outer sections will form, when the disc spins, homogeneous areas of different brightness. The intermediate section will form a linear gradation of brightness if the curved side of the black area conforms to the expression $\theta = kr$, where θ is the central angle, r the radius and k the desired slope of the brightness gradation. Mach bands also appear in stationary displays, for example when an area, illuminated by a strip light about two feet away, has placed close above it (about two inches away) another card (see Fig. 8.5e). Here there is an area in between the bright and the dark which is progressively less illuminated going from left to right.

It is interesting that if photographs are taken of these displays Mach bands are seen in them too, because the light distribution is the same in the photograph as in the original display. When objective measures of luminance are made then the objective function is obtained. Mach stated his findings in general by saying that whereever there was an inflexion in the luminosity function across a surface (on which luminosity varies in only one direction) then a band will appear. If the inflexion is concave with respect to the abscissa, the band will be bright and if it is convex it will be dark.

Such humps and troughs in the luminance curve clearly represent changes of slope of the curve. Now the slope itself represents change in luminance and is the first derivative of the luminance function. Thus change of slope represents change of change of luminance and is the second derivative of the luminance function. It follows that where $\frac{d^2i}{dx^2}$ is negative there is a bright band and where $\frac{d^2i}{dx^2}$ is positive there is a dark band (where i=luminance). Mach gave the following expression for the subjective brightness (e) of a point along the luminance function:

$$e = \alpha \log \left[\frac{i}{\beta} \pm \gamma \frac{\left(\frac{d^2i}{dx^2}\right)^2}{i} \right]$$

where α, β and γ are constants and i is the luminance at the point in question.

This fits experimental results very well.

It is surprising that Mach, as early as the middle of the nineteenth century, proposed that these effects were brought about by interactive processes in the retina. It is easy to see informally how such processes could operate. If we consider only inhibition (it is easier still if we allow facilitation) and suppose that stimulated areas inhibit areas around them, we can see that points at the edge of the bright area near the beginning of the gradation will have much more inhibition from one side than from the other. The total amount of inhibition received by them will therefore be less than the total amount received by points well within the bright area. They will thus appear as a bright band. Points just within the dark area will receive inhibition from lighter areas and will thus differ from points well within the dark area and appear as a dark band. Fiorentini and Radici (1958) noted that the bright and dark bands are not equal. With higher rate of change (i.e. steeper gradient) the dark band grows darker but the light band remains the same. Also the positions of the two bands are not symmetrical with reference to the points of inflexion. The light band tends to straddle the inflexion whereas the dark band lies within the homogeneous dark area. This might follow if interactive effects were different on dark adapted and light adapted parts of the retina.

Mach bands have received rather less attention than they seem to deserve. Perhaps current interest in retinal interaction will focus more interest on to them. McDougall (1903) 'discovered' them again using a rotating disc bearing a rather rounded star-shaped figure. Von Békésy (1968) regards Mach bands as brightness 'overshoot' and 'undershoot' and evidently sees lateral inhibition and facilitation as their cause. He makes some interesting observations about the variation of bands with different fixations near a bright/dark border (i.e. not a gradation), pointing out that if we look at the white side a bright band appears just within the bright side and there is no dark band on the dark side, if we look at the dark side we see just the reverse, if we look at the edge then we see both Mach bands and if we allow our eyes to wander over the display we see neither band, only an intensification of the edge.

This consideration of Mach bands at abrupt edges puts into mind a possible explanation of so-called 'irradiation' effects (see Figs. 3.71, 3.72 and 3.73). If Mach bands are asymmetrically placed about a gradation then presumably they are asymmetrically placed about an abrupt edge and the intensification afforded by them is asymmetrical. Since the bright band straddles the inflexion it could

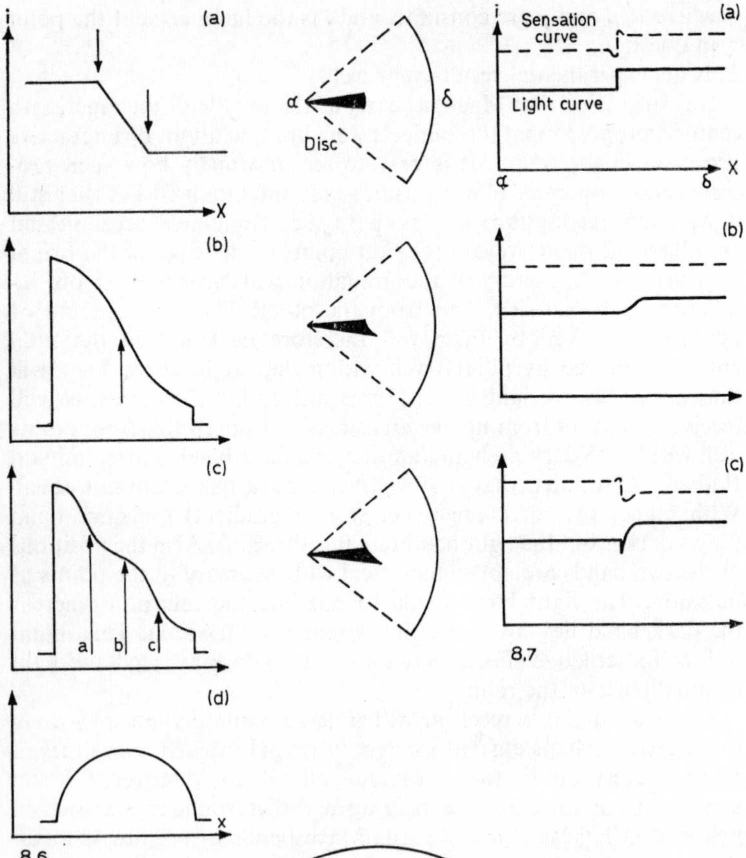

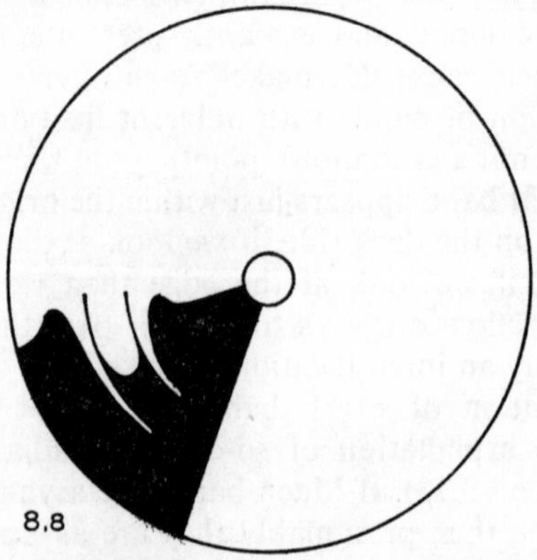

8.6*a,b,c,d* After Bergström (1966) 8.7*a,b,c* After O'Brien (1958)
8.8 Richards (1968)

account for the 'boring in' of the bright areas in Fig. 3.71 mentioned by Pierce and for the distortions of size in Figs. 3.72 and 3.73.

The relation of Mach bands to abrupt edges is an interesting one. Interactive effects on the retina have long been regarded as having an intensifying function, making contours more visible. McCollough (1955) points out that the width of Mach bands increases with decreasing maximum luminance of the gradation and decrease in its slope. Thus as the slope of the gradation increases, the width of the bands decreases until in the limit the slope is vertical, that is the edge is sharp, and the two bands are very narrow and serve to emphasise the edge.

Bergström (1966, 1967a,b) studied Mach bands in gradations without discontinuities. (His work also included a good review of mathematical theories which have been proposed to account for Mach bands.) For stimuli Bergström used areas in which the brightness varied in only one direction. The luminance functions of his displays are shown in Fig. 8.6. He asked his subjects where they saw light/dark borders and these points are marked with arrows on the functions shown. Thus in Fig. 8.6a they saw borders at the inflexions. In Fig. 8.6b, where the function is a smooth one, only one light/dark border was seen. In Fig. 8.6c three such borders were seen and in 8.6d none at all. In other words, this last stimulus, surprisingly, was seen as having the same brightness all the way across.

Bergström was interested in a paradox which had been observed by Mach. In Fig. 8.6c the strip between *a* and *b* was seen as darker than the strip between *b* and *c*. This is surprising because the luminance of the former is the greater. However, Mach's principle applies fairly well; a bright band is seen where the change of gradient of the luminance function is negative (i.e. for *bc* the value $\frac{d^2i}{dx^2}<0$) and a dark band is seen where the change of gradient is positive (i.e. for *ab* the value $\frac{d^2i}{dx^2}>0$). It is also interesting that the bright/dark borders in this display appeared at the inflexions of the change of gradient (i.e. where $\frac{d^2i}{dx^2}=0$). Where there was no such inflexion of change of gradient (Fig. 8.6d) no border was seen. In this figure the change of gradient is negative throughout.

The bright/dark relationship in Fig. 8.6*d* could be brought about by contrast of the bright area to the left of *a* and the dark area to the right of *c*. Indeed Bergström shows that one of these areas must be present for the effect to appear, but only one. The paradox does not occur if a stepwise function is used, like a version of Fig. 8.6c but going down in three steps rather than in curves. It seems then that this effect depends both on the two areas (*a* to *b* and *b* to *c*) having opposite signs for $\frac{d^2i}{dx^2}$ and at least one inducing area either brighter than *a* to *b* or darker than *b* to *c*. In other words the second differential of the brightness function cannot alone account for the paradox. Nevertheless Bergström concluded that his data are best fitted by Mach's theory. Another theory by Diamond (1960) fitted fairly well.

The importance of sharp discontinuities, contours, is well recognised. Within areas enclosed by a contour, processes tend to be subjectively equalised and contours tend to resist processes crossing them. The use of tissue paper to reduce the contour effects in elementary demonstrations of simultaneous brightness and colour contrast is a recognition of both these effects. The equalising process, coupled with some manipulation of luminance at a border, gives some rather odd perceptual effects reported by O'Brien (1958). His discs, compressed into quadrants, are shown in Fig. 8.7 accompanied by their luminance functions when rotated and the brightness function reported by observers. Fig. 8.7a produces an apparently darker disc surrounded by a brighter annulus with, perhaps, Mach bands visible. Fig. 8.7b produces an apparently uniform disc. This is rather like the last of Bergström's displays but it does contain an inflexion of the change of gradient. Displays without such an inflexion give greater uniformity, but it seems that the equalising process operates as long as there is no sharp discontinuity. In Fig. 8.7c the *sharp* discontinuity is reversed. The function drops sharply down from the dark side and then creeps gently up to a higher level. When the disc is viewed, the perceptual system picks up the *sharp* discontinuity and ignores the gentle one. The equalising process then ensures that the disc appears as a *darker* annulus with a *lighter* centre disc, the reverse of what the overall luminances would suggest. This is because the visual system has interpreted the luminance function at the discontinuity as a light/dark contour in the wrong direction.

Richards (1968) produced an interesting variation on this theme. His disc (Fig. 8.8) when spun is seen as a ring whose borders are formed by the two spikes on the edge of the black sector. The ring appears darker than the rest at larger visual angles (that is on close viewing) and lighter than the rest at smaller visual angles (viewing from further away). He reports that the change from one to the other is quite abrupt, taking place over as little as 20 per cent change of visual angle. Richards calls this an 'illusory reversal of brightness contrast'.

It is the right way round to fit in with some of the facts of brightness contrast and its reversals; thus when the 'grain' of the display is smaller (larger viewing distance) it is more like figures that show reversed brightness contrast (e.g. Fig. 8.2) and so the ring is apparently lightened by its surround. Viewed from a shorter distance, the ring covers a greater retinal area and is darkened. Richards refers to Graham (1965) where the view is developed that the visual system responds to spatial frequency of light variation across the retina and acts rather like a filter. It responds better to some frequencies and not at all to others. Thus, at larger visual angles the spikes fall within the right frequency and the slower variations are not picked up. This means that the brightness pattern seen is determined by the spikes, which give a reversed contour effect and hence a darker ring. At other, smaller, visual angles the lower frequency variations have moved into the critical frequency band and there is no response to the spikes. The system interprets the display in terms only of the slow variation, hence the appearance of a brighter ring.

This chapter, like the earlier chapters, has dealt with phenomena that have been known for a very long time. Although the general principle behind them, retinal interaction, is widely agreed the detail has not been worked out. Mach's theory fits much of the data very well but it is not known exactly how the visual mechanism works which produces data fitting Mach's formula.

In view of Westheimer's (1967) demonstration that facilitation and inhibition take place over different retinal distances the detailed spatial characteristics of contrast effects need more investigation. Perhaps such work should be done with figures, like those used by Bergström, without marked contours, since contour effects are powerful in perceptual organisation and override other interactive phenomena.

9

ILLUSIONS OF MOVEMENT FROM STATIONARY STIMULI

Although perception of motion derived from depth cues has already been discussed it is in this chapter and subsequent ones where illusions of motion are mostly to be found. Here I shall describe situations in which, although the stimulus never moves, the observer has a clear impression of movement.

AUTOKINESIS

An isolated light in an otherwise dark visual field appears to wander. Most reviewers (for example Royce, Carran, Aftanas, Lehman and Blumenthal, 1966, whose review is worth reading) agree that the earliest report of this phenomenon was by von Humboldt (1851). He noticed that a star appeared to move. Schweizer (1857) noticed individual differences in reports of the movement of a star and concluded that this 'Sternschwanken' was subjective. Aubert (1887) coined the name 'autokinesis'.

Only very few of the situations in which man is called upon to make complex perceptual judgments involve any possibility of autokinesis. The most obvious is night flying. Graybiel and Clark (1945) pointed out this danger and showed that observers sitting in a stationary Link Trainer in darkness all reported autokinesis from small lights. Moreover, when the lights actually moved at first, and then stopped, the observers could not tell when movement ceased. Clearly there are many situations in night flying where autokinesis could lead to dangerous error both in dealing with lights on the ground and, as Geldard (1953) pointed out, where pilots may watch the wing-tip lights of the next aircraft in formation flying. This latter author noted that flashing lights were less affected by autokinesis.

Although autokinesis is usually obtained using a single small light, it has been reported with both large and multiple stimuli. Luchins (1954) used squares varying in size from ¼ in. to 5 in. The larger the square the greater the latency of the effect (the time before movement was reported) and the smaller the amplitude of reported movement, but still large stimuli gave some effect. Edwards (1954, 1959) used arrays of dots, fairly dim and extending over visual angles of as much as 60°. All subjects reported autokinesis. When the brightness was increased latency was increased.

Geldard's claim that flashing lights are less susceptible to autokinesis appears to be contradicted by evidence reported by Elfner and Page (1964) that latency is reduced by intermittent light. However, the flash rates used here, 10Hz, were very much higher than those envisaged by Geldard. Spigel (1963) claimed that flash rates of less than 2Hz reduced autokinetic displacement and confirmed that 10Hz gave maximum enhancement.

It is well known that autokinesis is altered by higher-order variables. The work of Sherif (1935) is the best known. He showed that individual subjects tended to show a characteristic pattern but that subjects who had viewed in groups tended to show the pattern of the group, even when separated. Sherif also tried the effect of telling subjects that the light would move in a particular direction; they tended then to see the light move in that direction.

Rechtschaffen and Mednick (1955) report a flamboyant demonstration of the effect of suggestion which almost turns autokinesis into a projective test. They told subjects that the light would spell out words and, sure enough, subjects reported that it did. The words tended to be relevant to the subjects' preoccupations, so much so that one of them indignantly asked how the experimenters knew so much about her! It will be interesting to see this work repeated.

Suggestion within the display also has a strong effect. Toch (1962) presented stimuli in the shape of an arrow, a running man and a jumping deer. His subjects reported autokinesis primarily in the 'forward' direction of the stimuli.

Like so many of the phenomena described in this book autokinesis has no universally accepted explanation. The most persistently examined hypothesis has been that eye movements are responsible. The first experimental work on autokinesis was reported by Charpentier (1886) who set out to see whether eye movements were related to it. He arranged dots round the periphery so that when a central target dot was fixated the peripheral dots were just out of sight. They did not appear during autokinesis and Charpentier concluded that eye movements could not account for autokinesis. He favoured an explanation in terms of strain sensations from the eye muscles. These occurred during fixation and were taken by the perceptual system, he supposed, as evidence that the fixated object was moving. This would happen because such experience of strain was generally associated with object movement.

Carr (1910) reached broadly similar conclusions. He reported unusually large autokinetic movement of about 65° of visual angle whilst the subject's eye was observed directly by means of a weak light focussed on the eyeball. There was no relationship between eye movement and autokinesis and, besides, eye movements were much too small to account for such large autokinetic movement. If fixation was held to one side for a little while and then returned to the front, subsequent autokinesis went in that direction. This observation has been made many times since then. It seems that, if the eye muscles on one side are fatigued, then the unfatigued muscles on the other side will tend to pull the eye in that direction and so the target will appear to move in the direction of the original fixation. Carr also showed that, if the subject was asked to listen to and visualise a sound coming from one side, the autokinesis tended to go towards that side. This was an attempt to 'innervate' eye muscles without moving the eyes. Later work shows this to be an important observation, as will be seen below. This paper by Carr and another by Adams (1912) from the same laboratory are important early papers which give a great deal of basic information about autokinesis.

Guilford and Dallenbach (1928) photographed eye movements during autokinesis and concluded that they were not sufficiently large, numerous or regular to account for the effect. They tried to adapt Ferree's (1908) notion of 'streaming' of retinal fluids to explain autokinesis. 'Streaming' is a patterned movement of retinal fluids which Ferree supposed might have the function of removing metabolic waste products from the retina. Guilford and Dallenbach thought that if such streaming could be a stimulus then the target light would be seen against a moving background and would itself be taken as moving in the opposite direction. This theory has remained pretty well as vague as Guilford and Dallenbach left it.

An ingenious technique developed by Gregory (1959) again showed no large slow eye movements during autokinesis. He arranged a small red filter in line with the centre of a far-blue filter. Now far-blue (i.e. blue near the violet end of the spectrum) is not visible to the fovea and the whole stimulus was arranged so that it fairly well covered the fovea when the red patch was fixated. As long as the eye remained stationary, no blue was visible, but as soon as the eye moved slightly some of the blue surround went off the fovea and was seen. No blue was in fact seen during autokinesis, hence Gregory's conclusion.

However, although large eye movements have to be discounted as causes of autokinesis, small movements seem to be much more relevant. Skolnick (1940) induced nystagmus by irrigating the ear with cold water and this caused marked autokinesis in the direction opposite to the side of the irrigated ear. Thus, when small eye movements are deliberately induced something not distinguishable from autokinesis seems to occur. In many records of photographed eye movements Skolnick found the direction of autokinesis coinciding with the fast phase (flicking back phase) of nystagmus. A little thought will show that this is what would be expected. In nystagmus one views a stationary object and it seems to move, say, to the left because one's eyes are moving slowly to the right. After a while they flick back to the left and begin the slow movement to the right again and only the slow movement gives rise to apparent object movement, not the flick. Thus apparent movement is in the direction of the flick. Skolnick suggested that, just as the many eye movements of nystagmus perceptually summate to give apparent steady movement to objects in the visual field, so steady autokinesis is derived from many small eye movements.

Skolnick's findings were not limited to induced nystagmus. By direct observation of small eye movements he made a better-than-chance prediction of the presence of autokinesis. These findings are supported by the report of Crone and Lunel (1969) of a high correlation between small eye movements and autokinesis using an after-image method of observing eye movements.

Matin and MacKinnon (1964) gave support of a converse kind. They eliminated lateral eye movement by use of a stabilised retinal image. This almost eliminated autokinesis in the lateral direction, reduced it in a diagonal direction and barely affected it in the vertical direction. On the other hand, Brosgole (1968) reports the autokinetic movement of an after-image placed on the retina by means of a brief bright flash. In other words, the effect occurs with no movement whatever of the image with respect to the retina.

We appear to need a theory which will allow autokinesis in this latter condition and yet can still accommodate both the effect of partial stabilisation of the image, like that used by Matin and MacKinnon, and the commonly observed effect of straining the eyes to one side. This need seems most likely to be satisfied by a theory of the kind advanced by Gregory and Zangwill (1963). They proposed that autokinesis is due to spontaneous minor fluctuations in the neural system monitoring the outward signals controlling eye movement. Now such monitoring must be of great importance because no other non-visual information about the position of the eyes is available to the perceptual system than what it has 'told' them to do. Brindley and Merton (1960) clearly demonstrated this by anaesthetising the conjunctival sac so that the eye muscles could be seized with fine forceps and the eye pulled through up to 40° visual angle. This was done in the dark so that visual cues were not available and it was found that subjects had no notion of how the eye was being moved. They concluded that no non-visual information was available either from the eye or the muscles as to the position of the eye, and that what was fed into the percept was the output signal *to* the eyes, not anything *from* the eyes. The importance of such non-visual information is in the system's ability to separate movement of the stimulus from movement of the eyes and movement of the head. When a stimulus moves with reference to the retina, the percept of movement is modified to the extent that there is concurrent input from the neck showing that the head has moved. Similarly for the eye's movement, except that the modifying influence is what movement instructions have been sent to the eyes and not what evidence of movement has come from them.

Biologically I find the design of this sub-system very odd and agree with Gregory and Zangwill in their choice of it as one likely to produce anomalies, but their theory is not worked out in detail. Autokinesis stems presumably from the actual movement of the eye not corresponding exactly with the movement information given by the monitoring system to the perceptual system. Such movements would be expected to be very small and scattered. Yet the extent of autokinetic movement is large. Gregory and Zangwill would have to suppose that a tiny impression of movement builds up its own suggestion of movement and so perpetuates the impression of movement in that direction. This would not be unreasonable. Jordan (1968) has shown that, if during autokinesis the subject is asked to return his eyes to the front, he moves them in the opposite direction to the current autokinetic movement. Clearly, subjectively, the eyes have seemed to move. But if the monitoring system is inexact in the presence of only one small stimulus, why is it any more exact in normal daylight vision? Gregory (1966a) acknowledges this difficulty and suggests that the system assumes that large fields of view are stable. Why are large fields assumed to be stable? Gregory does not consider the interrelationship of impulses from peripheral and from central vision. It seems to me that the essential condition for the observation of autokinesis is relatively empty peripheral vision. The periphery is known to be a potent source of impulses which guide fixation and it seems likely that the final explanation of autokinesis will be one which implicates both the monitoring system described by Gregory and Zangwill and the paucity of fixation information in situations where autokinesis is observed.

THE OCULOGYRAL AND OCULOGRAVIC ILLUSIONS

The induction of autokinesis by means of nystagmus was mentioned earlier. There are two sorts of illusion clearly related to autokinesis, which result from stimulation of the visual system (through the mediation of the vestibular receptors) by various sorts of acceleration in conditions of reduced visual input. These illusions appear to be special sorts of autokinesis where the usual effect is influenced in its direction by acceleration stimuli.

The oculogyral illusion was named by Graybiel and Hupp (1946). It occurs when the observer and his visual field are rotated. This produces angular acceleration and the visual percept is influenced by activity of the semicircular canals. A small light in otherwise dark surroundings appears first to move in the direction of the fast phase of any nystagmus caused by the rotation, that is, in the direction opposite to that of the rotation. After a short time the direction of apparent movement reverses. The first phase is predictable from nystagmus. If the eye is moving slowly to the left and then jerking back to the right, then an object in the visual field will appear to move slowly to the right as the eyes move slowly to the left. The jerk of the eyes back to the right will not be perceived as movement of the object. But it has been claimed that nystagmus is not neccessary. Vogelsang (1961) gave four reasons for supposing this; nystagmus produced by irrigation of the ear with warm water produced the illusion in only 63 per cent of his subjects, the speed of the apparent movement of the light was nearer to the speed of turning sensation than to the speed of the slow phase of nystagmus, the illusion occurred with an after-image (produced by a flash) instead of a light and thus in the absence of any movement of the target on the retina, and in clinical states where nystagmus is absent the illusion is present.

Although the illusion is generally described as the result of ongoing acceleration, actual investigations of it seem usually to concern the *after-effect* of deceleration. Measurements are made after the rotation has ceased. Whiteside, Graybiel and Niven (1965) took up the problem of the role of nystagmus in a detailed study. They rotated subjects at 12 rev/min anticlockwise for one minute and then stopped them within the space of 5 seconds. A light used as target appeared at first to move to the right and then, after 20 to 30 seconds, to move to the left. The authors conclude that the first phase is due to nystagmus and stems from the movement of the light over the retina as described above. The second phase they see as the result of the monitoring of efferent activity, a view very like that of Gregory and Zangwill (1963). As nystagmus gradually dies out, the fixation mechanisms gradually assert themselves. It is the reflex efferent fixation impulses, antagonistic to the nystagmus movements, which are monitored and as they begin to predominate, they give rise to apparent movement in the opposite direction. Taking away the target light, and so removing the fixation stimulus, reintroduces nystagmus.

Observations by these authors using an after-image instead of a target light differ from those of Vogelsang. An effect certainly occurs, but it is in a direction opposite to that using a light. It begins with apparent movement of the image in the *same* direction as the rotation and then reverses. Whiteside, Graybiel and Niven suppose that this stems from the same efferent impulses though they do not go into detail. Presumably in the first, nystagmus phase, since there is no movement of the image on the retina, the efferent impulses which tend to cancel nystagmus will give rise to a sensation of movement in the opposite direction to the sensation of movement which accompanies nystagmus. However, in the absence of a light to serve as a stimulus to fixation impulses, it is difficult to see why the second, reverse, phase of apparent movement takes place.

When the observer undergoes linear acceleration, the oculogravic illusion occurs. This name was given to the effect by Graybiel (1952). Its exact nature depends on the direction of the acceleration. Like the oculogyral illusion, it affects stimuli which undergo no change of position in relation to the observer. It is mediated, at least in part, by the otolith organs. Since it occurs when the head is fixed, it does not seem to depend on input from the neck muscles. If acceleration is in a forward direction, as when an observer is sitting in an accelerating vehicle, then especially but not exclusively under reduced cue conditions (i.e. darkness), visible stimuli seem to rise steadily. If acceleration is in a backward direction, as when sitting facing the rear of an accelerating vehicle, stimuli seem to fall. If acceleration is from the side, as when an observer is sitting sideways in an accelerating vehicle or in a centrifuge facing forwards, then a vertical bar is judged as being tilted away from the direction of the acceleration, so that if the observer adjusts the bar to appear vertical he will adjust it so that it is tilted in the direction of the acceleration. If the acceleration is upwards or downwards, then the 'elevator illusion' occurs. This is an apparent upward or downward movement of the stimulus.

The apparent movement persists after the acceleration has ceased.

Whiteside and others group this illusion with the autokinetic and oculogyral illusions for the purpose of explanation. In forward or backward acceleration there is a tendency for the eyes to move in the direction opposite to the subject's felt tilt, that is the eyes tend to move downward in forward acceleration and upward in backward acceleration. Now this eye movement will itself give rise to the illusion. For example, in forward acceleration the involuntary downward eye movement will cause the stimulus apparently to move up. It is the equivalent of the first, nystagmus phase of the oculogyral illusion. Since Whiteside and others do not report a second, reversed, stage in the illusion, there is no need to postulate any effect from the monitoring of the antagonistic fixation impulses. It appears then that the explanation is slightly simpler than they allowed, though they did not comment on the distortion of the vertical in sideways acceleration. This seems to be a distortion of the kind met with earlier in this book where the spatial norm of verticality was altered by various means, in this case by sideways acceleration.

The oculogyral illusion and the various forms of the oculogravic illusion can be combined in exceedingly complex ways. Geldard (1953) describes how a relatively simple combination can occur. When a dim but structured target is viewed from a banking aircraft it appears to tilt and also to move bodily. The tilt is in the direction of the bank and can be as much as 15°. This tilting seems to be the oculogravic illusion for sideways acceleration and is presumably caused by centrifugal force as the aircraft turns. The bodily movement of the target is less predictable and probably depends on the steepness of the turn. During a turn in a banking aircraft, as well as the centrifugal force on the observer, there is also some angular (rotational) acceleration.

The second phase of the oculogyral illusion seems, then, to be a case of autokinesis with a special influence, falling into the same class as the case of autokinesis when the eyes have been strained to one side. The first phase of the oculogyral illusion and the oculogravic illusions of movement seem to be more directly due to the target moving across the retina when the retina involuntarily moves. Movement is therefore ascribed to the target. The oculogravic illusion of tilt seems to akin to other tilt effects.

ILLUSIONS OF MOVEMENT DURING FIXATION

Mere fixation for relatively short periods yields quite a number of movement effects which have been described by Honisett and Oldfield (1961). Subjects fixated a square or a random collection of straight and curved lines for three minutes and gave a continuous account of what they saw. A great many effects were reported. Apart from the familiar tendencies of parts of the display to be suppressed, subjects saw colours; rotation or up and down movement; pulsation, sway, drifts, twitches or jerks of parts of the display; elasticities and bulges like a rubber sheet; and parts of the display undergoing a sort of autokinesis with the rest of the display distorting to accommodate this. The authors suggest that there is a breakdown of stabilisation in the absence of eye movements.

Phenomena which appear to be in the same class are reported by Myers (1959) and White (1969). Both report the apparent breaking up of a bright line, viewed in the dark, into dashes which then appear to move up and down the line. Neither these authors nor Honisett and Oldfield attempted an explanation, and I have not found one.

ILLUSIONS OF MOVEMENT IN REPETITIVE PATTERNS

Many repetitive patterns give curious effects both in direct view and in after-image. In Fig. 9.1 curved shadows form a rosette over the display in normal viewing. In Fig. 9.2 one or more shadowy lines forming diameters seem to flicker round the display. In Fig. 9.3 there is a shimmering effect in each of the figures and in Fig. 9.4 there is what MacKay (1961a) describes as a 'curious trickling of wedge-shaped shadows up and down the blank stripes between the columns of parallel lines' (p. 340). When one of the first two figures is fixated at about the centre, there is a curious trembling effect which seems to be the equivalent of the shimmering effect seen in Fig. 9.3, and feels as though its origin is in the mechanics of the eye. It is especially noticeable in Fig. 9.1.

In Figs. 9.1 and 9.2 the pattern of shadows seems to be due to Moiré patterns (Oster and Nishijima, 1963, give a good description of these). They are patterns which appear when one repetitive design is not quite exactly superimposed on another. When Fig. 9.1 is superimposed on itself in this way curves are seen exactly like the shadows seen on viewing the single figure. Concentric circles (Fig. 9.2) form a Moiré pattern of lines. Whilst it seems generally accepted that the shadows are Moiré patterns, how they are formed is not so well agreed. The small eye tremors which take place all the time might move the display slightly on the retina so that it formed a Moiré pattern with its own after-image. Indeed the report by Evans and Marsden (1966), that the shadows did not occur

9.1 MacKay (1957)

9.1

when the concentric circles display was viewed as a stabilised retinal image, suggests that this is so.

However, the flash method of stabilisation used by Evans and Marsden would not distinguish between the effect of eye movements and the other cause that has been suggested for the phenomenon, namely momentary fluctuations in accommodation. The flash method impresses an image on the retina as an after-image. This would eliminate the shadow patterns no matter which of the two sorts of fluctuation caused them. MacKay (1957b) used the contact-lens method of stabilisation and observed the shadow patterns. In this method the image is stable on the retina but effects of variations in accommodation are not eliminated. This does seem to be evidence against eye movements being the cause of the shadow patterns and in favour of variations in accommodation.

MacKay (1957a) argues for fluctuations of accommodation as the cause and the evidence seems strong. The shadows do not occur when the cilary muscles, which alter the lens of the eye in the process of accommodation, are paralysed. MacKay notes the observation by Campbell and Robson (1958) that when the eyes are focussed at infinity the shadows vanish. This works promptly for all the displays mentioned so far. Eye movements do not stop when the eyes are so focussed.

Millodot (1968) cites more detail. He reminds us that Helmholtz (1856) ascribed the effect to accommodation because it altered in intensity with distance from the eye. Millodot presented concentric circle figures at different distances but always the same retinal size. He found that the effect was greatest at less than 1 m and very slight at 4 m. Now it is known (Arnulf and Dupuy, 1960) that fluctuations of accommodation are greater at greater accommodation (i.e. at close viewing). Eye movement would not be expected to give different effects at different distances when the retinal size of the display was constant.

Millodot also quotes observations by a subject who had no accommodation in one eye. He saw the shadows only with the other. Finally, according to this author, the frequency of movement of the shadows on Fig. 9.2 better matches the frequency of fluctuations of accommodation (Campbell, Robson and Westheimer, 1959, gave the dominant frequency for the latter as 0 to 0·5 Hz) than that of eye tremor (Yarbus, 1967, gave 30 to 90 Hz).

The weight of the evidence, then, seems to be in favour of fluctuations of accommodation as the cause of these effects and it seems generally to be assumed that the interactions from which the Moiré patterns originate take place at the retina. The situation need not be as simple as that however. Richards (1967) has claimed that

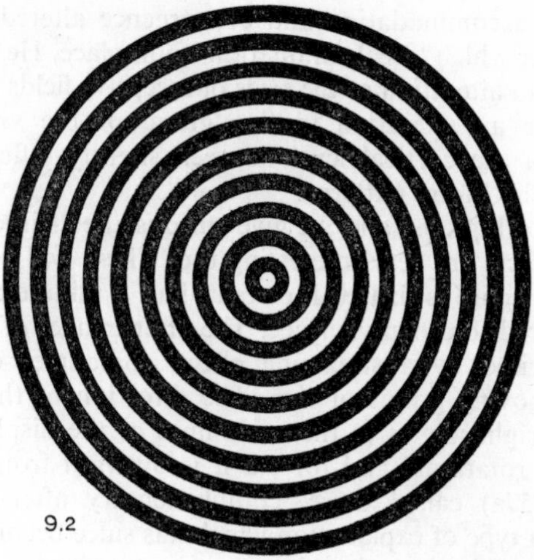

9.2

9.3

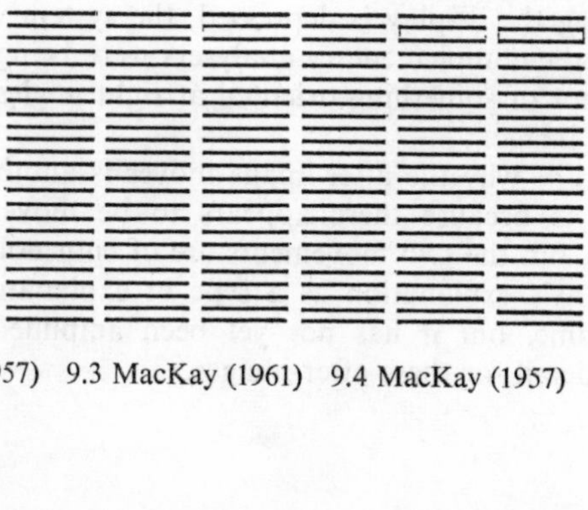

9.4

9.2 MacKay (1957) 9.3 MacKay (1961) 9.4 MacKay (1957)

alteration of accommodation and convergence altered the area of the retina over which 'areal summation' took place. He claimed that this entailed an alteration of the sizes of receptive fields at the cortex and therefore an alteration in the 'grain' of the visual system. Interaction at the cortical level between slightly different 'grains' might cause the Moiré patterns.

Not only do Figs. 9.1 and 9.2 give curious effects in direct vision, their after-effects are very interesting too. These will be seen if the centre of the figure is fixated for about half a minute and then the gaze transferred to a plain surface. The after-images of both figures are characterised by a streaming effect, sometimes described as resembling moving grains of rice. The direction of this streaming is always at right angles to the main lines of the display; thus for Fig. 9.1 it is rotational and for 9.2 it is outward from the centre. MacKay (1957a) called these 'complementary after-images' and put forward a type of explanation which has since become commonplace. This is the type of explanation in terms of separate units of the visual system analysing different characteristics of the stimulus. It has been used earlier in this book. MacKay spoke of 'directional satiation' by the positive image which gave rise to perception of complementary direction in the after-image. It is possible to use later evidence, not then available to MacKay, to amplify this view. Barlow and Hill (1963) noted that, when units in the rabbit's visual system which were sensitive to movement in a specific direction had been stimulated, their rate of discharge fell to below the level existing before stimulation. It is not unlikely that this overshoot is a common characteristic of many sorts of analysers. It may happen with the orientation analysers involved in perceiving these patterns. Now, if the percept is formed as a result of a process which scans the various orientation analysers and compares rates of activity in the various orientation sensitive units, it will mean much the same thing if one set of units is firing less than usual as that the complementary set is firing more than usual. Thus, when the after-image is viewed, if the firing rate of the set of analysers which has just been used for viewing the display is depressed, the system will interpret this as though the complementary analysers were being excited and so give a percept of something oriented at right angles to the lines of the primary image.

The question of why the after-image moves is another difficulty. Presumably it is because there appears to be movement in the primary image, but the two movements are of enormously different quality. MacKay's explanation as a type of explanation was well ahead of its time, but it has not yet been amplified sufficiently to account in detail for these after-images.

10

ILLUSIONS FROM MOVING STIMULI

In this chapter I shall describe three sorts of illusion which are associated with moving stimuli; distortions of the stimuli, apparent movement where no movement exists or which differs in some way from the real movement, and after-effects of movement.

THE DISTORTION OF MOVING STIMULI

Moving stimuli are sometimes distorted. Ansbacher (1944) reported that an arc of 30° drawn on a rotating disc appears to shrink when the disc is rotated at speeds somewhat below the flicker fusion threshold. It was found that most shrinkage occurred at 1·3 revolutions per second. Ansbacher favoured an explanation in terms of 'retinal overlap'. Presumably, at some critical speed, eye movement interacts with stimulus movement in such a way that two units of distance along the line are put on to one place on the retina.

This sort of overlap is best seen in situations where a stimulus is viewed as it passes behind a slit. A number of interesting distortions occur which Anstis and Atkinson (1967) put down to the 'painting' across the retina of the stimulus by eye movements. Their explanation was new in its detail but not in its broad outline, since Helmholtz (1856) attributed the effect to involuntary pursuit movements of the eye.

Zöllner (1862) reported a fairly detailed study. He called the effect anorthoscopic distortion. He arranged a situation in which a row of dots moved to and fro behind a vertical slit. The observer viewed the dots through the slit from a distance. When the dots moved slowly they appeared to be further apart than they actually were. At faster speeds the dots appeared to be closer together than they actually were and at very fast speeds they appeared correctly spaced. Zöllner accepted Helmholtz's explanation in terms of eye movements for the second and third condition but said that the first condition had a 'psychological explanation' which he did not specify. It is not difficult, however, to see how eye movements could account for all three. When the dots are moving slowly, pursuit eye movements will overtake the movement of the display and so the dots will be spread out over the retina. At faster speeds, the eye movements will lag behind the movement of the card behind the slit, and so the stimulus will tend to be overwritten on the retina as the dots pass by. At very fast speeds, no significant eye movement will have time to take place.

Anstis and Atkinson (1967) quote several interesting variations of the effect from a number of reports. These are shown in Fig. 10.1. They all represent the situation where the speed of stimulus movement is fast enough to cause compression. The ingenious experiments of these authors seem to verify the claims of Helmholtz. First, they asked subjects to view a circle moving sinusoidally behind a 2 mm wide slit at frequencies from 0·7 to 1·5Hz at the same time watching their eye movements. They noticed that the onset of tracking eye movements coincided with the subjects' reports of seeing an ellipse with its long axis vertical. Subjects gave further confirmation of this by reporting the movement to and fro of an after-image previously placed by flash on the retina. The amplitude of the tracking movements was four times the width of the slit.

Anstis and Atkinson next 'drove' the eye movements by means of a spot oscillating across the display in phase with the movement of the stimulus. The spot, on an oscilloscope, was superimposed by means of a transparent mirror set at 45° to the line of sight. Ellipses, with their long axes horizontal, were presented on a second oscilloscope behind the slit. They were Lissajous figures and could therefore be elongated or shortened by the subject simply by his turning a knob. Ellipses were presented of various lengths of long axis. All were made to oscillate at 1 Hz over 1·3 times their own long axis. Subjects had to adjust each ellipse until it became apparently a circle whilst following with their eyes the spot which was moving in phase. In fact the adjustment they made was one of elongating the short (vertical) axis until it appeared equal to the horizontal axis. The amplitude of the movement of the spot was set at various values and each shape of ellipse was viewed with each amplitude of eye movement. The results showed clearly that the apparent shape of the ellipse depended simply on eye movement. Since at greater amplitudes the eyes covered the display faster, one can say that the

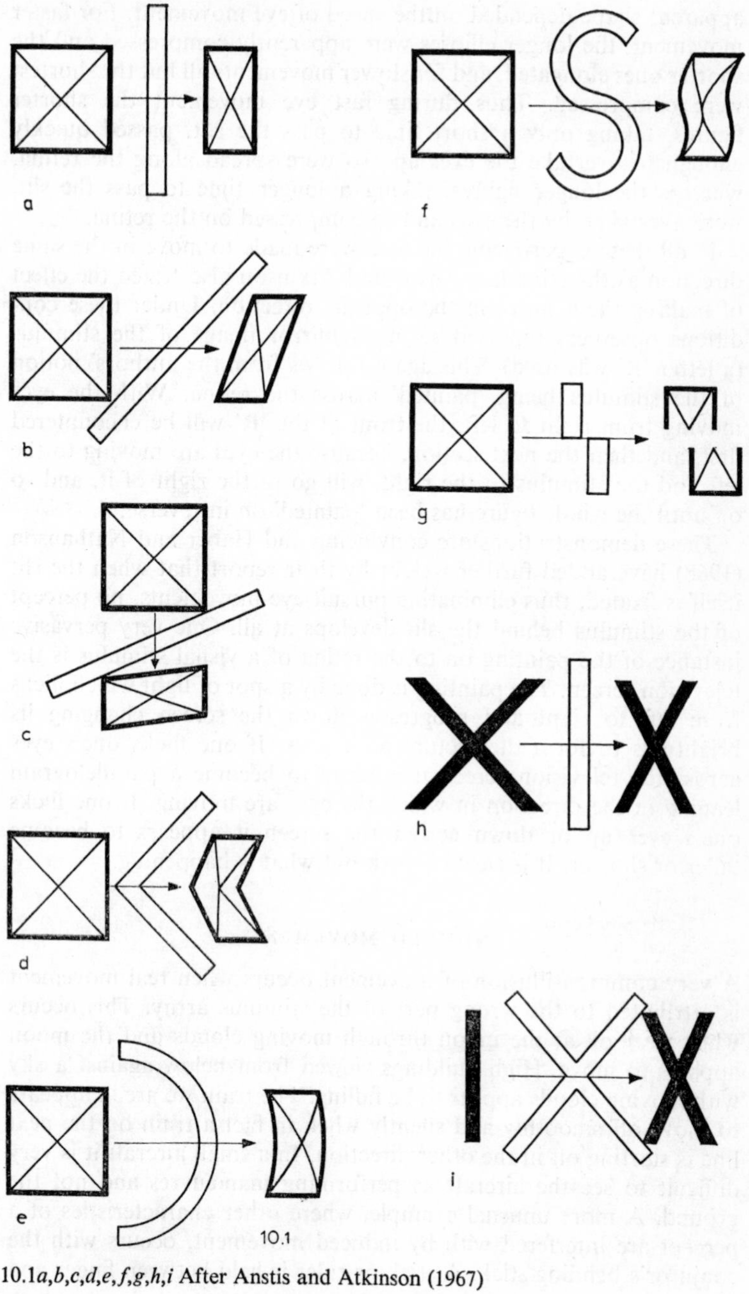

10.1*a,b,c,d,e,f,g,h,i* After Anstis and Atkinson (1967)

apparent shape depended on the speed of eye movement. For faster movement, the longer ellipses were apparently compressed and the shorter ones elongated, and for slower movements all but the shortest were compressed. Thus during fast eye movement the shorter figures, taking only a short time to pass the slit, passed quickly enough to overtake the eyes and so were spread along the retina, whereas the longer figures, taking a longer time to pass the slit, were overtaken by the eyes and so compressed on the retina.

In all these experiments the eyes were made to move in the same direction as the stimulus. Anstis and Atkinson also tested the effect of making them move in the opposite direction. Under these conditions observers reported seeing a mirror image of the stimulus (a letter 'R' was used). This again follows from the authors' notion of the stimulus being 'painted' across the retina. With the eyes moving from right to left, the front of the 'R' will be encountered first, and then the next section, because the eyes are moving to the left and the stimulus to the right, will go to the right of it, and so on until the whole figure has been 'painted' on in reverse.

These demonstrations are convincing and Haber and Nathanson (1968) have added further weight by their report that when the slit itself is fixated, thus eliminating pursuit eye movements, no percept of the stimulus behind the slit develops at all. One very pervasive instance of the painting on to the retina of a visual stimulus is the television screen. The painting is done by a spot of light which flicks from left to right and progresses down the screen changing its brightness to form the picture as it goes. If one flicks one's eyes across the television screen it appears to become a parallelogram leaning in the direction in which the eyes are moving. If one flicks one's eyes up or down across the screen it appears to become taller or shorter. It is easy to work out what is happening.

INDUCED MOVEMENT

A very common illusion of movement occurs when real movement is attributed to the wrong part of the stimulus array. This occurs when we look at the moon through moving clouds and the moon appears to move. High buildings viewed from below against a sky with moving clouds appear to be falling. The train we are in appears to move off smoothly and silently when in fact a train on the next line is starting off in the other direction. In a small aircraft it is very difficult to see the aircraft as performing manœuvres and not the ground. A more unusual example, where other characteristics of a percept are interfered with by induced movement, occurs with the conjuror's bending stick. A stick or ruler is held between finger and thumb and made to oscillate about a fulcrum at the point where it is held. At the same time the hand itself is moved up and down. The stick appears to be made of rubber and to bend about a point a little way from where it is held. This is because the movement of the hand is attributed to the stick as well as the movement of the stick and the only way the stick could perform the two sorts of movement simultaneously would be by bending.

As early as 1897 Stratton reported a phenomenon that strictly belongs to this class. He carried out a large number of experiments with inverting spectacles, wearing them for days at a time and studying the process of adjustment to them and readjustment to normal vision after taking them off. At this latter stage he reports attributing movement to objects when it was the head that had moved and not the object. In normal vision, as we have already seen, input from various non-visual receptors enters into the percept and cancels the effect of head movement. I shall not here be drawn into a discussion of this sort of mistaken interpretation of movement. Induced movement is generally taken to involve the interpretation of various movements within the visual field and does not include non-visual input.

Duncker (1929) carried out a large study on induced movement and his experiments set the style of many later studies. The basic display was a luminous dot within a frame in an otherwise dark environment. The frame was made to move to and fro but was not seen to do so. Instead the dot appeared to move. Duncker tried out a variety of patterns, sizes, speeds and other characteristics.

Wallach (1959) gives an interesting account using various displays. He points out that with two dots, one of which is moving, and no frame, almost any combination of movement may be seen. If one of the dots is on the rim of a rolling wheel and the other is at the hub, then the former appears to move in progressive circles round the latter. If only the dot at the rim is present, it appears to move along in a series of arches. The dot at the hub serves to give the impression of continuous smooth movement of the whole display. Wallach also showed that a dot within a frame is always seen as moving, whether actually the dot is moving, or the frame, or both. If a larger frame is put round the original frame, it takes on the frame function, so that if only the original frame is moving, then both the dot and the inner frame appear to move.

A puzzle arises from this arrangement if the outer frame, instead of moving to and fro, moves up and down while the inner frame moves from side to side. The subject then sees the outer frame as stationary and the inner frame as moving diagonally to and fro, but the point still appears to be moving horizontally to and fro.

Duncker had observed this and suggested 'separation of systems' as an explanation. The two systems of movement were somehow kept separate. Indeed they are! This is less an explanation than a restatement. However, Brosgole (1968) took it seriously enough to test it. He arranged two frames (rectangles 40 in. × 11½ in.) one above the other, each containing a dot. The two rectangular frames were made to move in opposite directions at 1 in. per second. Now these were quite separate systems and so Brosgole expected that each dot might appear to move. This did not happen. The rectangles appeared to move leaving the dots stationary, or one rectangle appeared stationary and the other rectangle and both dots appeared to move, but never did only the dots appear to move.

It is difficult to know exactly what Duncker meant by 'separation of systems', but certainly the apparent movement of stimuli seems to be determined only by their immediate frame. It would be interesting to study the effect of an outer frame placed very close to an inner frame on a dot within the inner frame, or the effect of an outer frame when the inner frame was a dotted, rather than a full line, or was very faint.

Induced movement is a very good example of the separateness of the perception of motion. We do not perceive moving objects; we perceive objects and we perceive motion and the system fits the two together in the best way it can. Usually, in a fully lit visual field, objects tend to move and the background to remain still. This is the interpretation that the system therefore uses in other situations where cues are scarcer. Other information is often used too. For example, Jensen (1960) induced 'backward' or 'forward' motion in small luminous patches shaped like ships or aircraft. It was much easier to induce 'forward' than backward motion.

Motion in depth can also be induced. Farné (1970) allowed subjects to view a screen with horizontal black and white stripes which oscillated through 90° about a vertical axis. They viewed this through a stationary sheet of glass which bore two widely spaced vertical white lines. After one or two preliminary percepts, subjects reported seeing the white lines, apparently rigidly connected, oscillating about a vertical axis.

ILLUSIONS AND AFTER-EFFECTS IN MOVING PATTERNS

Illusions in patterns during 'rinsing' movements

Thompson (1882) reported that if the concentric circles figure (Fig. 9.2) is moved about in the way one moves photographs when rinsing them in a shallow tray (so that all points on the figure describe circles of the same size), it appears to rotate. The apparent rotation is caused by regular movement of the shadow effect mentioned earlier which, when the figure is stationary, moves irregularly. Cobbold (1881) produced what seems to be an adequate explanation of this. He noted that what I have called a shadow is an area where the lines are less distinct and that there is always also a band where the lines are quite distinct. This latter band is always perpendicular to the current momentary direction of movement. These bands therefore move with the rinsing motion and cause the apparent rotation of the display. The suggestion was made later that the bands might be Moiré patterns. This may or may not be so, but one can still accept the notion that the bands cause the apparent rotation without knowing what causes the bands.

Bowditch and Hall (1882) produced a figure, the converse of which had been used by Thompson (1882) (Fig. 10.2). (Thompson's version consisted of six 'cog' figures surrounding a concentric circles figure.) Now with a rinsing motion the concentric figures seem to rotate in the same direction as the rinsing, but the central 'cog' figure seems to rotate in the opposite direction. They also described Figs. 10.3 and 10.4. In 10.3 the figure with ingoing cogs appears to rotate in the direction opposite to the rinsing movement and the figure with outgoing cogs appears to rotate in the same direction as the rinsing movement. In Fig. 10.4 the upper and lower 'racks' seem to move in opposite directions on rinsing. When the rinsing motion is anticlockwise, the upper rack appears to move to the right and the lower rack to the left.

Sanford (1903) developed a theory accounting for the movement of the 'cog' figures which seems plausible. He proposed that the cogs of Fig. 10.4 are more visible during their lateral movement than during their up or down movement because, at this latter stage, they tend to be confused with the after-image of the line. In fact, the clearest sight of a cog tooth on this reckoning occurs when the figure is moving over areas of the retina that have not been stimulated very recently. Thus, for Fig. 10.4 the upper rack is seen best when it is moving across the bottom of the circle it describes in the rinsing motion and the lower rack is best seen as it crosses the top, so that in anticlockwise rinsing the upper rack apparently moves to the right and the lower to the left. The same principle is applicable with a little thought to the two figures in Fig. 10.3.

Whilst a modern theorist would not be inclined to speak of after-images in the way Sanford did, it is possible to reformulate his theory, still, unfortunately, rather vaguely, in terms of directionally sensitive motion analysers. The cog teeth and the lines or circles to which they are attached are at right angles. Now if a line is moving in, say, a direction which is at 45° to its own orientation it could only be *seen* as doing this if its ends were in view. Without cues from the ends, end-on movement would not be visible. Motion analysers are likely to be sensitive only to the component of movement which is at right angles to the moving line. Thus the interpretation will for the most part be based on the stimulation in rapid

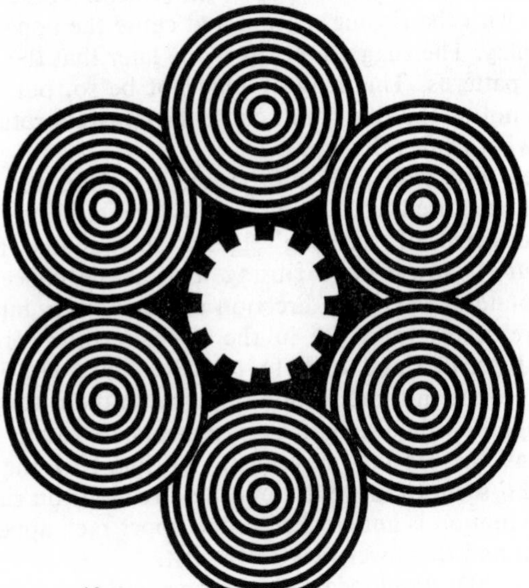

10.2

10.3

10.4

10.2–4 After Bowditch and Hall (1882)

succession of two sorts of directional analysers, by each cog tooth and the portion of line to which it is attached. The movement will thus be equivocal except where stimulation of mainly one sort of analyser occurs. This will be at the stage where the movement is perpendicular to any particular cog tooth. Taking as an example the teeth on the right-hand side of the figure with ingoing cogs in Fig. 10.3 during anticlockwise rinsing, these will be visible in least equivocal movement as they are moving *down* the left-hand side of the circle each describes in the rinsing motion. Thus the movement attributed to them will be downwards, that is clockwise. The same reasoning can be applied to any part of the figures. It would be interesting to see such a theory tested. One point that appears at first sight to be against it is that for a given speed of rinsing motion the circle with outgoing cogs seems to move more slowly than the circle with ingoing cogs. However, since the circles are the same diameter, the outgoing cogs move over a greater circumference than the ingoing cogs, and therefore will appear to cover a smaller proportion of it in the time. The movement therefore seems slower.

Illusions and after-effects in rotary and lateral movement

When a spiral is rotated it gives an impression of movement in a direction roughly at right angles to the tangents of the lines composing it. Thus a rotating barber's pole seems to move along and slowly round, and a flat spiral of the kind shown in Fig. 10.5 gives an impression of continuous expansion or contraction depending on the direction of rotation. (The examples shown in Fig. 10.5 are taken from Holland, 1965. More recently Wilson, 1972, has described a Fortran programme for the generation by computer of many different spirals of this kind.) The speculation of the last section can be continued here. A motion analyser with a particular 'preferred' direction ought to respond maximally to a contour moving in that direction but oriented at right angles to it. Motion of a straight line in a direction parallel to itself would not be perceived unless its ends were visible. Thus a straight line moving in the preferred direction but not oriented at right angles to it would not appear to move in the preferred direction but in a direction perpendicular to its orientation. In fact, a straight, long contour with no ends visible could only be seen to move in a direction perpendicular to its own orientation. (Imagine a line viewed through a small window in a screen. Whatever linear movement it makes, only movement at right angles to the line will be seen.) The direction of motion of curved lines, or of figures made up of contours in several different orientations, is presumably computed by taking some sort of average of the activity of a population of analysers with different 'preferred' directions. In the spirals, it is plausible that the result of the computation would give rise to the percept which actually occurs because most of the movement seen would be outward from the centre. Bidwell's (1899) observation is relevant here. He noticed that when a cross, with one limb vertical and the other oblique, was oscillated up and down, the oblique line seemed to move about on the vertical line. Clearly it was providing the more movement information of the two.

10.5

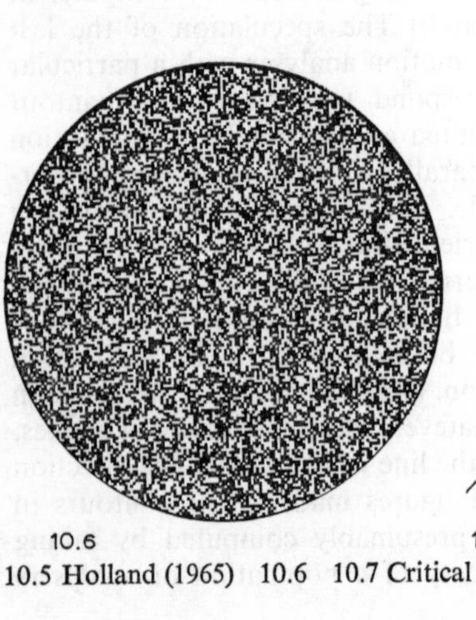

10.6

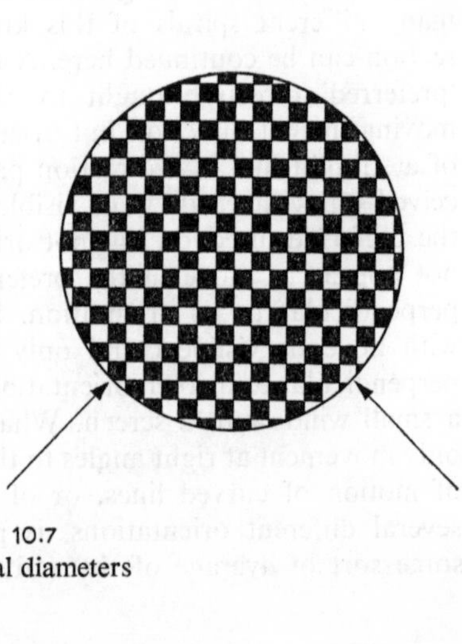

10.7

10.5 Holland (1965) 10.6 10.7 Critical diameters

It is not the primary movement in rotating spirals, however, that has captured interest, so much as the after-effect of their movement. This is known as the spiral after-effect and has been studied a good deal. There is room here for only a brief description of the main findings. The interested reader should consult Holland (1965).

The after-effect of movement was known to the ancient Greeks and was mentioned by Aristotle. The first modern reference to it appears to have been made by Purkinje (1823), a work which I have not been able to obtain, but which describes the occurrence of a movement after-effect after watching a military parade. Addams (1834) described such a linear after-effect after watching a waterfall, and the after-effect obtained in the laboratory from watching a continuously moving belt of black and white bands has become known as the 'waterfall' after-effect. Movement after-effect is probably most commonly observed nowadays immediately after stopping a car after a fairly long drive. In consists of an impression of movement in a direction opposite to that in which the perceived movement has been. Thompson (1882) demonstrated early that it was not due to eye movements by arranging two striped bands moving in opposite directions. The after-effects also moved in opposite directions.

Plateau (1849, 1850) is generally credited with the first report of the spiral after-effect and the inducing figure is sometimes called Plateau's spiral. Some are called Archimedes spirals (e.g. in Fig. 10.5, the top middle and right, and the bottom left).

The spiral after-effect is generally observed by viewing a stationary spiral after the moving one. Motion appears in the stationary spiral. In fact, unlike other after-images, movement after-effect does not appear on surfaces such as a blank screen or the sky. Texture is necessary. It is as though nothing can appear to move unless something is there which might actually do so! Moreover Day and Strelow (1971) have claimed that if the inducing figure has no background, for example when the figure alone is illuminated in the dark, then no after-effect occurs. Also, if the observer is not exposed to light after viewing the moving stimulus, the after-effect is preserved and is seen on subsequent exposure to light, even though this takes place after an interval long enough for the after-effect, in the light, to have decayed (Wohlgemuth, 1911).

If one eye is exposed to the moving display and then closed whilst the other eye views the test display, an after-effect is obtained. This interocular transfer is a complex and interesting phenomenon (see Dixon and Jeeves, 1970).

The duration of the after-effect increases with increase of brightness contrast between the parts of the display, increase of absolute brightness of the display, increase in duration of observation (maximum effect is obtained by about 2 minutes' observation) and decrease in the size of the display. Increase in velocity of the display from very slow speeds rapidly increases the duration of the after-effect, but at higher speeds it has much less effect.

The speed of the after-effect is also related to the speed of the display. Scott, Jordan and Powell (1963) reported the optimum speed of after-effect as 5 to 6 minutes of arc per second with display speeds of 114 to 228 minutes of arc per second. Dureman (1962) gave a graph of movement after-effect, for radial lines on a white disc, against log induction speed, showing an after-effect of 0·95° per second for a display speed of 9° per second and an after-effect of 1·3° per second for a display speed of 144° per second. Clearly in this latter display, which was like a rotary waterfall effect, much greater speeds could be used and resulted in much faster after-effects.

An interesting example of a movement after-effect is cited by Sumi (1966) which suggests that such after-effects could be more widespread in judgments of movement than is generally recognised. Sumi's display contained two lights which moved successively and independently along the arms of a letter 'L'. As the one in vertical movement arrived at the bottom, the one in horizontal movement set off from left to right. This latter light seemed to bow upwards in its path and Sumi supposed that this was an after-effect of the downward movement of the first light.

It has long been known that after-effects of movement can be obtained not only with real but also with apparent movement. Papert (1964) even obtained it with apparent movement in depth created by stereoscopic presentation of stimuli. He used random dot stereograms which were computer generated and therefore could be changed quickly. He progressively altered the disparity for a section of the display in such a way as to create the impression of a bar moving to and fro in depth. He observed an after-effect of this movement which was of short duration and was not simply related to duration of induction. He concluded, since the motion effect itself depended on binocular fusion, that this was only the central component of the usual movement after-effect, most of the latter being mediated at a more peripheral position in the perceptual system.

Anstis and Moulden (1970) took up this point of the locus of mediation of the after-effect of movement. They showed that it was an effect which took place both above and below the point of binocular fusion. In a stereoscope set-up they exposed the left eye to a sectored disc rotating to the left and the corresponding part of the retina of the right eye to a sectored disc rotating to the right. Subsequently each eye, viewing a stationary disc, saw its 'own' direction of after-effect. This would not happen if the activity essential for the after-effect was beyond the point of binocular fusion. In their second experiment these authors flashed lights in a circle to create apparent circular motion. There were two displays, one fed to each eye stereoscopically. The pattern of flashing of the lights was arranged so that neither single eye saw apparent motion, but both eyes together did. An after-effect was obtained. Thus the essential activity involved in the after-effect was beyond the point of binocular fusion.

I am not very surprised by these results. If it is true that visual characteristics, such as orientation, movement and so on, are processed separately, it would not be surprising if the motion analysers could get their information either direct from the eyes or through the binocular disparity processors. What one must be careful not to conclude from these results, is that everything below the binocular fusion level is retinal and that the process is therefore a *retinal* process. There has been some controversy on this point. Anstis and Moulden do not in so many words claim a retinal component and their review of the relevant literature suggests that such claims are weak. There is no reason even to suppose that binocular fusion is one link in a chain of processes. It may operate as one of several parallel and simultaneous processes none of which is 'above' or 'below' another.

Richards and Smith (1969) reported an ingenious experiment which seems to be strong evidence for the after-effect being mediated by the superior colliculus in the midbrain. This experiment took advantage of the fact that the proportion of the visual field which is impaired by a scotoma (due to injury of the cerebral cortex) varies with convergence, so that when a close object is viewed, the impaired proportion of the field is greater than when a distant object is viewed. These authors employed a spiral on a disc which was surrounded by an annulus also bearing a spiral pattern, but one going in the opposite direction. The after-effect of rotation of this display contained movement both inwards and outwards with, somewhere between them, corresponding to the border between the disc and the annulus, a ring of zero movement. The size of this ring of zero movement was the dependent variable in the experiment and it was shown not to change with change in convergence. Richards and Smith concluded that the effect was not therefore cortical and, since there is a good deal of evidence of directionally sensitive units in the superior colliculus, this was probably the locus of mediation of the after-effect.

A modern theory of movement after-effects, which owes much to an idea advanced by Barlow and Brindley (1963) is advanced by Sekuler and Pantle (1967). They propose that the visual system has directionally specific movement analysers and that, within any class of these, different ones respond maximally to different *speeds* of movement. After prolonged stimulation, analysers respond at a frequency below their baseline (frequency prior to stimulation). The amount of suppression depends on the stimulation; the recovery time (duration of after-effect) depends on the amount of suppression.

They make two other interesting points. A common finding is that with increasing display velocity, the duration of the after-effect increases to 2° to 4° per second and then decreases. This means that most stimulation is being achieved at display velocities in that range. It follows that there are most analysers with a 'preferred' velocity of about 3° per second.

The velocity of movement after-effect depends on both display duration and display velocity. This means that velocity of the after-effect is determined by the total stimulation of all analysers with a particular directional preference regardless of their velocity preferences, because if only those with the appropriate velocity preference were stimulated then display *duration* should not affect after-effect *velocity*. They consider that increasing display duration adds adaptation to analysers which are submaximally stimulated by the particular display velocity used and that these add to the velocity of the after-effect.

Probably the most powerful movement after-effect was devised by Dixon and Meisels (1966). It was a disc covered with small black and white squares (21,000 of them) distributed in a quasi-random manner. Fig. 10.6 is such a disc but not that used by them. This was rotated very slowly (2 rev/min) and yet gave rise to an exceedingly powerful after-effect which caused a test disc apparently to rotate but also caused a peculiar squirming movement in any subsequently viewed scene. The after-effect duration often exceeded the inspection time. The particular purpose of their work was to compare this 'high information' disc with a more redundant (repetitive) disc bearing a check pattern. The random patterned disc was clearly more effective. Dixon has kindly shown me this disc. The effect is certainly striking and he has shown (Dixon, 1967) that the threshold for seen movement is lower for this disc than for the chequered disc. It will even produce an after-effect when it is hardly moving at all. In this connection, in unpublished work with L. Hartley, Dixon has demonstrated larger amplitude-evoked potentials for random than for regular fields.

Dixon and Meisels also make some interesting observations of the appearance of these discs at higher rotation speeds. A change takes place between 2 and 20 rev/min in the chequered disc from shimmering white bands, of the kind which appear on the concentric circles figure described in the last chapter, to a grey cross, with its centre coinciding with that of the disc, rotating with the disc. When the randomly patterned disc is spun, there first appear vague swirling shapes which on further increase in speed of rotation change to 'contoured ovals or leaf-like figures'.

Dixon and Meisels do not attempt to account in detail for these patterns but they suggest the general manner in which they might occur. Viewing a disc, the visual system will deal with the displays in a particular way, responding appropriately as the various elements of the display pass by receptor elements. When the disc speeds up, there will be a time when movement is too rapid for the system to respond in the same way and so it begins to integrate over a larger area. The new situation has become, as it were, a freshly ambiguous display and a new interpretation must be imposed. Dixon and Meisels suggest that the grey cross represents a larger-scale periodicity which the system picks up when it can no longer respond to the smaller-scale periodicities of the checks. There are two important diameters on the display (Fig. 10.7) where a single colour is continuous across the disc. It is probably these that the system selects.

The greater complexity of the features of the random dot pattern is taken by the authors to indicate once again the high information content of the field. If the system is forming the simplest possible interpretation of the rotating display, then clearly the simplest interpretation of the more complex display is much more complex than that of the simpler display.

It would be an interesting exercise to try to construct various displays and predict what they would do at various speeds of rotation. The reader who has the use of a colour wheel might do this. It is conceivable that intelligent manipulation of the variables of this sort of display might throw light on some of the temporal characteristics of the visual system. Piaget and Lambercier (1951) actually used a change of percept of this sort in a study of visual fusion rates in children. They rotated a square eccentrically. At lower speeds, this appears to form a single cross, and at higher speeds it appears to form two superimposed crosses. The work of Richards (1968), mentioned in Chapter 8, is relevant here too.

11

ILLUSIONS FROM STIMULI IN RAPID SEQUENCE

The perceptual system has difficulty in coping with intermittent stimuli on a short time scale. This is not surprising because an important feature of the system is the integration of activity over short periods of time. Stimuli with which the system cannot fully cope (those devised by Dixon) were described in the last chapter. This happened because the stimuli moved over the retina too quickly and the system had to make what it could of them. In this chapter we shall see the perceptual results of the system's management of stimuli which only appear for a short space of time but do so in rapid sequences of various kinds.

APPARENT MOVEMENT

By far the best known of the results of intermittent stimulation is apparent movement. When a brief stimulus is followed by another stimulus after a short interval of time and within a short spatial interval, there is an impression of movement from the position of the first to that of the second. With several stimuli in the proper sequence a smooth, realistic movement can be achieved. Motion films are the best example, though even neon signs often achieve quite a realistic effect.

An interesting example of, as it were, apparent movement within apparent movement, might just be mentioned here. Wagon wheels in Western films appear to turn slowly backwards. This is a result of filming something in real and repetitive motion. Between the exposure of each frame by the camera the wheel has moved through almost, but not quite, a spoke interval (or two or three or more) and so the picture of the wheel on each successive frame is slightly behind the previous one. This gives the impression of slow backward rotation.

There is no space here for a detailed review of the literature on apparent movement. Graham's brief account is useful and appears in Stevens (1951) and Graham (1965) in almost identical form.

Stroboscopic movement, a more exact term for this phenomenon, was informally studied early in the nineteenth century. Boring (1942) gives an interesting account of this. Exner's (1875) experiments, using an electric spark as illumination, are an example of early experimental work. But it was an extensive study by Wertheimer (1912) which established the interest of psychologists in apparent movement. It did this because Wertheimer used the phenomenon to state the Gestalt case. He devised a means of presenting two stimuli tachistoscopically so that their duration and the interval between their exposures could be varied. The stimuli could be simultaneous, overlapping or successive and Wertheimer demonstrated the influence of changes in these and other parameters, such as shape and intensity. Simultaneity was reported by his subjects with intervals of 30 m/sec or less and succession with intervals of 200 m/sec or more. Between these occurred an optimum interval for apparent movement, and between that optimum and succession, Wertheimer reported what he called 'phi'. This was a pure sensation of movement that did not involve apparent object movement at all. On this Wertheimer based his claim that movement is a primary sensation and not based on particular transformations of other sensations.

Other kinds of apparent movement were described by Kenkel (1913). He called apparent movement between two spatial locations β movement. The apparent movement which occurred when the two elements of the Müller-Lyer illusion were exposed successively (expansion and contraction) he called α movement. Presumably one can give this name also to the apparent expansion and contraction observed when two *actually* different-sized stimuli are successively exposed. He designated as γ movement the apparent expansion and contraction which takes place when a stimulus is rapidly brightened and dimmed.

Korté (1915) added δ movement, which is the reversed β movement obtained when the second stimulus is much brighter than the first. Visual latency is probably the explanation of this. The second stimulus, being brighter, is perceived first. Anstis (1967) reports apparent movement of a field of unidirectionally graded brightness, for example a projection of an optical wedge, when the brightness of the whole is increased or decreased. This is a version of γ movement but involves no contours. There is apparent movement towards the dark end on brightening and towards the light end on dimming. He also reports a movement after-effect.

Korté published a set of 'laws' describing the interrelationships of stimulus luminances (*l*), durations (*t*) and separations in time (*i*) and space (*s*) in β movement.

1. With *i* and *t* constant optimal apparent movement can be maintained during increase of *s* if *l* is also increased.
2. With *s* and *t* constant, it can be maintained with decrease of *l* if *i* is increased.
3. With *l* and *t* constant, it can be maintained with increase of *s* if *i* is also increased.
4. With *l* and *s* constant, it can be maintained with decrease of *t* if *i* is increased.

His three remaining laws describe δ movement in a similar way.

It is surprising that in an authoritative book, published as late as 1965, Graham finds no more precise and detailed description of β movement than these laws. The situation involved is exactly specifiable in terms of sizes, distances, timing and intensities, yet these laws have not been relegated to history and replaced by precise, widely agreed functions describing the interrelationships. The literature on apparent movement abounds in the testing and discussion of, particularly, Gestalt theory, but the detailed spelling out of the phenomena has been relatively neglected.

More studies like that of Sgro (1963) are needed. He tested Korté's fourth law using a precisely specified situation and found that, for the values of *l* and *s* used, the function of *t* and *i* was linear up to a *t* value of 55 m/sec, and then progressively smaller increase of *i* was required for unit increase in *t*.

Apparent movement can be altered by subject variables. Wohlwill (1960) reviews age differences; Saucer (1958) and Saucer and Coppinger (1960) are examples of work dealing with differences in apparent movement perception in patients with mental disorder. Drugs affect it, for example Horne and Deabler (1962) showed that tranquillisers lowered the value of *i* required for optimal β movement.

With displays more complex than a simple pair of lights, individual variations of percept are even more marked, both between individuals and within one individual over a space of time. Let us take, for example, the display used by Brown and Voth (1937), four lights set in a diamond pattern. When the lights were flashed on and off in succession their subjects reported that the lights appeared to move in a circle the diameter of which was slightly smaller than the distance separating each opposite pair of lights. Brown and Voth explained this by the Gestalt concept of satiation, but most observers looking at such lights see other patterns of movement either besides or instead of the one they reported. Sylvester's (1960) subjects saw little circular motion with such a display. They reported the lights moving to and fro along the sides of the diamond or along the diagonals, and several other sorts of movement, all more powerful than the small amount of rotary movement that was seen.

Clearly, just as in the case of ambiguity in depth cues where there are several acceptable interpretations, the observer can accept in turn several interpretations of this display, in spite of the fact that the simplest interpretation of such a sequence seems to be movement round the figure, either diamond shaped or rotary movement.

When the movement is deliberately ambiguous, for example where there are three lights in a vertical line and the middle one is lit first, followed by the top and bottom ones simultaneously, other factors can determine the direction of motion seen. Toch and Ittelson (1956) presented lights shaped like bombs and like upward-pointing aircraft in this sort of display and their subjects reported apparent movement predominantly in the appropriate direction, that is downward for the bombs and upward for the aircraft.

At least implicit in the contributions on this subject by the Gestalt psychologists is the assumption that real movement and apparent movement are mediated by the same process. This is a reasonable view; that stimuli in certain sequences are sufficient to fire the ordinary movement analysing mechanisms. But the view has not gone unquestioned. Kolers (1963, 1964) made a strong case for a difference between real and apparent movement. The range of speed of perceptible apparent movement (15° to 20° per sec) is much smaller than that of real movement ($\frac{1}{2}$° to 125° per sec); the image moves across the retina in real but not in apparent movement; real movement produces a blurr; when the speeds of the two sorts of movement are subjectively matched, real movement is actually slower.

However, it seems to me that none of these is a strong argument for considering the two as separate. Taking them point by point: as long as the speed of apparent movement lies *within the range* of real movement, then the argument that stimuli in sequence can operate the movement analysers can stand. Secondly, the image need not move on the retina for apparent movement to be perceived. Rock and Ebenholtz (1962) demonstrated this by an ingenious arrangement in which the eyes moved in time with the alternation of the two apparent movement stimuli so that they both fell on the fovea. Apparent movement was perceived. Thirdly, whilst real movement can produce a blur, it *need* not do so. There is no need to regard blur as anything more than a by-product of the faster rates of real movement. Little blur occurs in real movement at a speed as low as 20° per sec, the maximum speed of apparent movement. Finally, since apparent movement is a relatively sparse stimulus for movement it could reasonably be expected that the stimulation of movement analysers would be less intense than for real movement and therefore that apparent movement over a particular distance in a particular time would appear slower than real movement.

Kolers next reported two experiments. In the first a vertical bar crossed a display in either real or apparent movement. In its path a smaller vertical bar was exposed briefly and the threshold of the subjects was obtained for seeing the smaller bar. During real movement of the larger bar, the threshold for the smaller bar was raised most when it was exposed just as the larger bar passed it. In apparent movement, the threshold for the smaller bar was unaffected. Now this certainly demonstrates that what happens on the retina in the two sorts of movement is different.

In another experiment Kolers reported that when an object was put into the space between two apparent movement stimuli the movement seemed to go round it or to bow under it. Thus real movement affects objects in its path, whereas apparent movement *is affected by* objects in its path.

However, if one thinks of the perceptual system as making an interpretation based on varied information, some being the movement of a stimulus over the retina, some being other stimuli on the retina, some being head movement, body movement or background movement, then the results of Kolers' experiments are not surprising. When the moving stimulus affects the object in its path, as in his real movement situation, then it will be interpreted as having moved in front of the object. Objects in real movement will affect the perception of objects in their paths by the usual processes of visual masking and by momentarily overlying them. On the other hand, if the stimulus does not track over the retina and an object in its path is not affected by it, then the interpretation will be that the moving object has gone round the object in its path or under it; this is a situation that the system has interpreted many times before. It does not seem to me that the fate of objects in the path of a moving stimulus bears on the problem of how movement is signalled.

There is interesting recent evidence about how two of the various sorts of movement, eye movement and movement-over-the-retina, are separated in the system. Mack (1970) made the movement of targets dependent on eye movement and was able to vary the amplitude of the target movement. When the discrepancy between target movement and eye movement was more than 20 per cent, the percept was one of target movement. When discrepancy was less than 5 per cent, the target rarely appeared to move. The operation of this system must involve input to the visual system about eye movements, and this has been demonstrated in cats by Lombrozo and Corazza (1971). They recorded a central visual discharge which seemed to be 'time-locked' to spontaneous eye movements. This discharge could provide the necessary information for the discounting of eye movement in the final percept.

What Kolers seems to be arguing is that the movement-over-the-retina component of the total situation is not the same for both real and apparent movement. This may be so, but it is clearly *only* a component in the total percept of either. His view is that the visual system registers movement over the retina in two different ways: one is when a stimulus actually does move over the retina (the real movement situation), and one is when two discreet stimuli occur within a critical period of time. This he calls the 'formation time' for a percept and gives its value at about 300 m/sec.

In spite of Kolers' view, however, it is not difficult to imagine how the two could be signalled by exactly the same analysers. Suppose that a directionally oriented movement analyser at the cortical level were fed from a string of cells dispersed in a line across the retina, and that it fired when these cells fired in order. Real movement would cause it to fire by stimulating the whole string of primary units and sequential stimuli would cause it to fire by stimulating only perhaps two of the primary units, in the correct order and within Kolers' 'formation time'.

Relevant to this point is an intriguing demonstration by MacKay (1958). This illustrates the principle that if an object, part of which is self-luminous, is moved about in stroboscopic illumination, then the self-luminous parts seem to move separately. They seem to move more. In demonstrations, MacKay uses a flashlamp with a grid attached to the front which obscures all but a small light. When waved about in the light from a stroboscope the small light in the centre of the grid seems to move about on the grid. Here we seem to have both 'apparent' (stroboscopic) and 'real' movement juxtaposed and a demonstration that 'real' movement is the more potent movement stimulus. There are amazing variations, such as a self-luminous ball attached to a stroboscopically lit bat.

A demonstration, by Dixon and Hammond (1972), also involves the combination of real and apparent movement, but in a very different way. Dixon sees it as an example of 'visual persistence' which is Sperling's (1960) term. If a simple line is put on an oscilloscope and the whole instrument is rotated about the line of sight then, instead of the single line, a fan of lines appears, all of the same brightness and radiating from the point on the line which is fixated. The same effect occurs when a rotating line is illuminated by a stroboscope, or when a disc with a slit in it is illuminated from behind by a stroboscope (Allport, 1970). Dixon believes that the most likely explanation for this is that, since a line on the oscilloscope is painted across at intervals by the passage of a bright dot and is not present all the time, it differs from a rotating line in continuous light. The latter, as it moves, will obliterate its former images by lateral inhibition. A line which appears only briefly at successive locations will not do this and so images will take longer to fade and will remain on the retina to form a fan with the distance between lines related to the frequency of passage of the dot and the speed of rotation. The difficulty about this explanation is that all the lines in the fan appear of equal brightness; they do not fade in the direction opposite to the rotation (but see Bidwell's 'recurrent vision', Chapter 11). The fanning out of the lines from the point of fixation follows from Anstis's idea of 'painting' on to the retina of a stimulus which is presented sequentially but rapidly (see Chapter 10). On an oscilloscope the stimulus is actually only a bright dot.

DYNAMIC VISUAL NOISE

Apparent movement can be obtained using a visual field without any form or pattern; not a blank visual field, but one in which the stimulation from moment to moment varies at random so that a stable percept can never form. This is something like a version, in apparent movement, of Dixon's random dot discs in real movement and has been called by MacKay 'dynamic visual noise'. In terms of quantified information, such a visual field is as highly informative as it is possible to be and it has curious effects on the perceptual system. MacKay (1961b, 1965) described such effects, which can be regarded as constantly moving ambiguous displays which the perceptual system interprets as best it can.

MacKay's demonstrations were made by mounting a photograph of sandpaper on a large disc and, as it rotated, making a film of a patch of it. Thus each frame of the film is filled with black and white specks of which the position is randomly determined. Most of the effects he described however work with the dynamic noise which appears on a television screen when the signal is very weak. Apparent movement presumably occurs because a speck in one frame of the film is next to the position occupied by a speck in the previous frame. Apparent movement will take place from the latter position to the former and such movement, often in longer sequences, will take place all over the display all the time.

Viewing the projected film, observers reported tiny particles in 'Brownian' movement, an appearance of 'boiling from a restricted central source'. This central source was always the point of fixation and indeed the movement near the point of fixation was much more lively than that in the periphery. This ties in with the observation of Piaget, Feller and McNear (1958) that objects appear to move more quickly as they pass over the fovea. In binocular viewing, the movement was always much more 'oily' and less 'sparkling' than in monocular viewing. If a frame, such as a wire loop, is moved to and fro close to the display, the movement of the particles enclosed by the frame is apparently reduced; they seem to stay within it whilst particles outside the loop seem to cling to it and move with it. It also causes a movement lagging behind it, like a fluid. When the frame stops moving the particles within it 'spring to life' and begin apparently to move like all the rest. This probably happens because, during the motion of the frame, part of the motion of the dots within it will be 'taken up' by their apparent movement with the frame. When the frame stops, all movement is again attributed by the perceptual system to the dots. If a finger tip is passed over the field it seems to leave a 'furrow' of reduced movement. This could be caused by a movement after-effect again 'taking up' some of the movement of the field.

Another interesting feature of this display MacKay calls the 'omega effect'. If only a strip is exposed, there is an apparent 'streaming' along the strip. If an annulus is exposed, there is apparent rotation at about ½ rev/sec. This speed is not affected by brightness or size, but seems at least partly to depend on the ratio of width to diameter of the annulus. The constancy of this speed is a very odd thing and deserves more attention that it seems to have attracted.

MacKay and Fiorentini (1966) report a further use of this display. They illuminated by means of a stroboscope a disc composed of a photograph of sandpaper rotating past a small window. The subject saw the photograph stroboscopically lit through the window. The display was thus just like the movie film described above, but in addition a flash was superimposed by means of a half-silvered mirror at 45° to the subject's line of sight. The frame repetition rate was 5 to 20 per second and the pause between the frame and the flash was 18 to 25 m/sec.

In this situation, instead of the usual 'Brownian movement', subjects saw writhing maggot-like objects forming chains and 'chain mesh' patterns. MacKay supposed that these were due to the contour detection mechanisms resonating and becoming hypersensitive. The idea of such systems resonating is unusual, but no alternative explanation has been proposed.

THE GENERAL EFFECTS OF STROBOSCOPIC ILLUMINATION

If one views a stroboscopically lit blank area, a large variety of coloured moving patterns is seen. Purkinje (1823) is said to have been the first to report this. He turned his face to the sun with eyes closed and passed his fingers, spread out, in front of his eyes. He described chequered, hexagonal, zigzag and rose-petal patterns. I shall briefly describe the work of three later writers on the subject, Brown and Gebhard (1948), Blum (1956) and Smythies (1959a,b, 1960).

The work of Brown and Gebhard is interesting particularly because it introduced the dichotomy of 'light phase' and 'dark phase' patterns. The 'light phase' patterns happen in the usual way, by direct stroboscopic illumination at flash rates of a little less than the flicker fusion threshold. If, however, this stimulation is fed to one eye only and the other is kept dark, then different patterns appear in the dark eye. These were called 'dark phase' patterns by Brown and Gebhard. They described a dominant pattern for each of the phases. The 'light phase' was characterised by fairly bright windmill or chequerboard patterns in yellow and blue, the 'dark phase' by irregular mosaics in violet and yellow-green. These two phases competed for predominance in a way which clearly suggested retinal rivalry and there is little doubt that the 'light phase' patterns originate in the system of the lit eye and the 'dark phase' patterns in the system of the dark eye.

In contrast with the rather limited range of imagery reported by Brown and Gebhard, Blum reported, for the 'light phase', a rich variety of colours, checks, ovals, discs, dots, mesh, spots, mottle, rays, lines, diamonds, spirals and many more. He also reported more meaningful images such as fire, waves, sky, balls, holes, wires and crosswords.

The very detailed study by Smythies included both the 'light phase' and the 'dark phase', though the latter was studied as an after-image situation following stroboscopic stimulation of both eyes. Smythies divided 'light phase' patterns into seven types: (1) unformed elements such as blobs, splodges, dots, streaks and mottles; (2) single lines or 'rainbows' crossing the field; (3) patterns based on parallel straight lines; (4) patterns based on radial straight lines; (5) other patterns based on straight lines, such as honeycombs, herring-bones, or zigzags; (6) patterns based on curved lines; (7) 'designs and formed images'. He describes also a large variety of different sorts of movement, some of which happen particularly to certain patterns.

Smythies found seven types of pattern in the 'dark phase' too. These were: (1) amorphous, generally swirling, red and green; (2) particulate, swirling small elements of various kinds; (3) stationary patterns described by terms like Paisley, marble, or leaf; (4) watery patterns, like sunlight through rippling water; (5) design patterns, for example 'Victorian wallpaper'; (6) vaguely animate patterns, a coiled octopus seen in deep water (only one subject reported this class of experience); (7) fully formed scenes.

The large variety of reported patterns raises the suspicion that the full range of possible reports may be much wider still. It seems likely that this sort of illumination stimulates the visual system haphazardly and that the system draws on visual memory for the elaboration of percepts. The patterns reported do have some common features in that they include at least borders and, usually, familiar shapes. Brown and Gebhard suppose, in this connection, that the visual system has 'configurational bias'. This supposition receives some support from later work on the visual system showing the separate processing of orientation and movement, but it has generally been reckoned that these need specific appropriate stimulation. They could only be fitted in here if they were presumed to fire, perhaps sub-maximally, under the amorphous stimulation provided by the stroboscope. This sort of stimulation might have the effect of amplifying any autonomous activity in the visual system; autonomous activity which could plausibly be regarded as giving rise to the patterns seen *whenever* one closes one's eyes. Such activity could originate either from general stimulation by light passing through the eyelids (and thus be not quite autonomous) or from the firing of units in the system at 'resting' rates. Nerve cells fire from time to time even when not stimulated.

SUBJECTIVE COLOURS

In 1894 and 1899 Bidwell described what he called 'recurrent vision'. He had noticed that when an object was illuminated by means of a flash produced by electric discharge, there was a positive after-image immediately (about 0·2 sec), followed after the same interval by another, and in some cases more. When a gas discharge tube was rotated at $\frac{1}{2}$ to $\frac{1}{3}$ rev/sec and illuminated by a rapid succession of flashes it appeared to be followed by a 'ghost' a few degrees behind. This was much dimmer than the discharge, blue or violet in colour, and it caught up to merge with the tube when the tube stopped.

Now this latter phenomenon may have been that reported by Dixon and described at the end of the last chapter, but most of Bidwell's investigations were without the strobe element of this situation and so 'Bidwell's ghost', as it came to be called, cannot simply be identified with Dixon's findings.

Bidwell investigated the effects of various coloured stimuli in the situation where a light was simply rotating. He shone a light on a rotating disc which had a hole near the rim. This hole was focussed on a screen, and the subject viewed the screen. He saw a patch of light describing a circle at about 0·75 rev/sec. When he did not look at the light it appeared to be followed by a 'ghost' which, at this speed of rotation, was about 50° (that is 0·2 sec) behind. A white light gave a violet 'ghost' and so, even more clearly, did a blue or green light. Orange or yellow gave a blue or greenish-blue 'ghost' and red gave none. These clearly are not negative after-images. Bidwell concluded that the 'ghost' was due to 'the violet nerve fibres' and that it took on other colours because of an 'illusory effect of contrast'. I have found no explanation of these colour effects. Perhaps they are related to the colour effects described below, but I cannot suggest exactly how.

Bidwell went on to recall an observation attributed to Charpentier (1892) in which, when a black disc with a white sector was rotated at about 0·75 rev/sec a shadow was seen on the white sector. It occurred about 15 m/sec after the passing of the black to white border and lasted for about 15 m/sec. If the sector was cut out to reveal a bright diffuser, then, says Bidwell, several such shadows could be seen by the 'acute and educated' observer. There was also a darker shadow on the black, again lasting about 15 m/sec just after the passing of the white to black border. Bidwell summarised all these findings in the graph shown in Fig. 11.1.

These observations of Bidwell have received surprisingly little attention. His 'ghost' became a party trick, but his more precise observations have been largely ignored. Perhaps now that the importance of timing in the visual system is being realised his work will begin to attract more interest. Ratliff, Hartline and Miller (1963) recalled his observation when they produced from ommatidia of

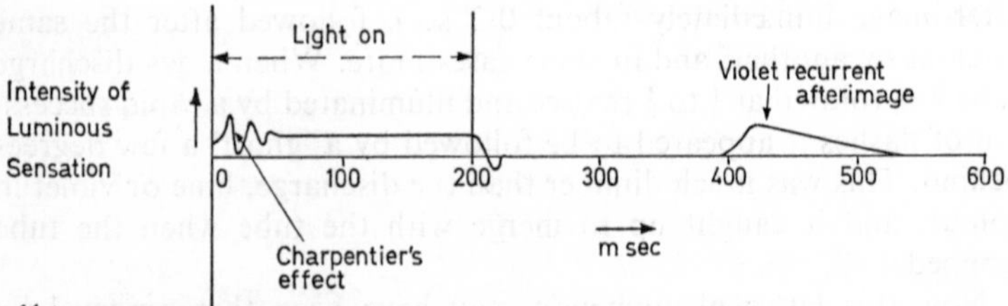

11.1

11.1 After Bidwell (1899)

Limulus a graph of frequency of discharge over a short space of time. This resembled the first 100 m/sec of Bidwell's function (Fig. 11.1) and they regarded their function as one of damped oscillation due to mutually inhibitory influence between ommatidia. It is not much of a flight of fancy to suppose that something like this might be operating in the human eye.

Another phenomenon, also often called 'Bidwell's ghost', but which Bidwell did not refer to as a 'ghost', was reported by Bidwell in 1896. He rotated a disc which was covered half with white paper and half with black velvet. A 45° sector was cut out, centred on the junction between black and white. When a colour stimulus was placed so that the passage of the cut-out sector exposed it, and it was followed by the white sector, it was seen correctly at low speeds, but when the speed was increased to 6 rev/sec, instead of the actual colours, colours complementary to them were seen. Bidwell performed variations on this theme, showing for example (1899) that a picture of a lady with blue hair and a violet sunflower was seen in more acceptable colours under these conditions.

This demonstration has excited more interest than the 'ghost', partly because it is clearly a case of backward visual masking. This is the capacity of a stimulus to inhibit the perception of a stimulus which has occurred immediately *before* it. This happens particularly if the second stimulus is the brighter of the two, and in this case is probably due to the shorter processing time required for the brighter stimulus. In this situation the white stimulus masks the coloured stimulus, leaving only the (longer lasting) complementary after-image. Backward masking is an extensive topic which cannot be treated here. The reader is referred to Alpern (1952, 1953) and Raab (1963).

Sperling (1960) explored Bidwell's phenomenon in detail, varying the parameters involved. He stated that the usual timing of stimuli used in studies of this effect was 80 m/sec dark, 20 m/sec colour and 60 m/sec white. Instead of a disc, he used a tachistoscope with two fields which were superimposed (by angled mirror) and so could vary at will all three parameters. With this equipment Sperling demonstrated that a hand could appear green and a dollar bill pink. If a black stimulus was used instead of a colour then the observed complementary image was of a white figure against a less white background. In his main study Sperling used a white stimulus (whose complementary image looked darker than its surround). His results specified the exact conditions of brightness and stimulus timing under which reversal (appearance of the complementary image) occurred. Wheeler and La Force (1967) report another such interesting study.

A few investigators have taken an interest in the effect of stimulant and depressant drugs on this phenomenon. Aiba (1960), for example, obtained a threshold for reversal of a red stimulus in the usual sequence, varying the intensity of the red stimulus. Amylobarbitone, a depressant, raised the threshold, that is the primary stimulus was more easily suppressed, and dexamphetamine lowered it. Kaplan (1960a,b) claimed large changes in the same threshold after subjects had drunk coffee, smoked a cigarette or taken stimulant or depressant drugs. As a test of small changes in the general state of the individual, it seems to me that this effect has considerable potential.

Another of Bidwell's (1897) observations using the same disc concerned the appearance of black objects instead of coloured ones through the gap in the disc. They appeared to have red borders. If the objects were thin lines then they appeared completely red and were not distinguishable from red lines. On increasing the intensity of the light on the disc, the borders appeared blue-green instead of red. In his 1897 paper Bidwell demonstrated that this last phenomenon was an after-image of the kind we have just considered. But why did the red colour appear in the first place, and why, also, when the direction of rotation of such a disc is reversed, do the lines appear blue?

This is exactly the same sort of phenomenon as Benham's 'artificial spectrum top'. This was a toy invented by Benham and described in *Nature* in 1894 by an unnamed writer. It bore a pattern like that of Fig. 11.2a and when spun it gave rise to the appearance of colours. A glance at the pattern will show that we have the same kind of situation again. As the disc rotates, any point on the retina will encounter a sequence of stimuli consisting in various orders of black, white and lines. In anticlockwise rotation just below fusion frequency, the disc shown in Fig. 11.2a looks like four sets of fine concentric circles. The outer set appears red as a result of the sequence; black/lines/white. The inner set appears blue as a result of the sequence; white/lines/black. The intermediate sets of lines are of indeterminate colour. Increasing the speed of rotation produces monochrome.

This coloured effect has been obtained with many displays, mostly rotating, some stationary. The colours are usually called

---

11.2*a* Benham's top (Anon, 1894) *b* Fechner (1838) *c* described by Smith (1860) *d* Helmholtz (1856) *e* Helmholtz (1856) *f* Brucke (1864) *g* Brucke (1864) *h* Finnegan and Moore (1895) *i* Finnegan and Moore (1895) *j* Bagley (1902) *k* Bagley (1902) *l* Baumann (1912) *m,n,o* After Erb and Dallenback (1939), described by Hurst (1895)

11.2

'Fechner colours' because they were reported by Fechner (1838) using a display like Fig. 11.2b. For the reader especially interested there are two good reviews of the subject, Cohen and Gordon (1949) and Erb and Dallenbach (1939). The former authors reported that the colours had been 'discovered', that is reported as a new observation, no less than twelve times! The twelfth was by B. F. Skinner (1932) who wrote 'so far as I am aware, no comparable effect has been reported'. His figure (Fig. 11.3a) was viewed stationary through a pinhole and so was in a sense new.

Stationary versions, like Skinner's, or like the one published by Luckiesh and Moss (1933), or indeed like the 'rays' or concentric circles figures of Chapter 9, all show desaturated wandering pinks and greens (though the subjects of Erb and Dallenbach reported primarily yellow and blue) in the white areas. Where possible these colours are formed roughly into bands oriented at right angles to the black lines.

For the rotating version of the phenomenon Fechner, although not the first discoverer, produced the first explanation in terms of the fall times for response of the various colour receptors. Several theories in similar terms have been independently advanced since. Probably the latest is due to Gregory (1969). This is the one which will be described here.

Gregory first pointed out that when the colours appear as borders on black figures their precise positions are not actually on the border. The red is just within the black and the blue is just outside the black. Now there is experimental evidence, for example that of Novak and Sperling (1963), that lateral inhibition for *white* light takes about 50 m/sec to develop. Gregory supposes that lateral inhibition for blue light builds up and dissipates more quickly than for red light. Thus, when a black figure is presented, lateral inhibition from the background will develop just within the black of the figure, but the stimulus appears for so short a time that only lateral inhibition of blue will have had time to develop before the arrival of the white stimulus. With blue inhibited, its complementary, red, is seen just within the black. In the situation where the black figure *follows* the white stimulus there has been time, during the white stimulus, for lateral inhibition to build up over the whole field. At the advent of the black figure lateral inhibition will fade all over the figure and *just within the background all round it*. The inhibition of blue will fade first, and therefore blue will be seen surrounding the figure.

This is a very plausible theory and no doubt it will soon be tested. One might ask why edge effects are not observed when the stimulus presented is coloured. In such a display the complementary colour is seen over the whole stimulus. The answer is that edge effects are indeed present. Reports of the appearance of the complementary colour are rather simplified. The complementary colour is certainly the predominant colour seen when the timing and brightness are right, but the edges change in colour from moment to moment and are not sharp. The image takes on some of the characteristics of images observed under stroboscopic illumination.

The creation of colour from black and white stimuli is remarkable and its possibilities for colour television were not missed. By suitable arrangement of the time sequence of brightening and darkening the dot, as it flicks across the screen, a coloured effect can be achieved. However, the range of colours is limited and their saturation is low. Also there seems to be some variation between individuals in whether or not, with a given set of conditions, colour is seen at all. This is not surprising in view of the demonstrated effect of quite mild doses of drugs on a phenomenon which is closely related (see Aiba, 1960; Kaplan, 1960, above). It would be a formidable difficulty for coloured television produced in this way if each viewer needed his own set with the stimulus timing individually adjusted!

Gregory's theory is not easily applied to the appearance of subjective colours during the viewing of stationary displays (Fig. 11.3). If the colours stem from movement of the stimulus over the retina

11.3*a* Skinner (1932) 11.3*b* Luckiesh and Moss (1933)

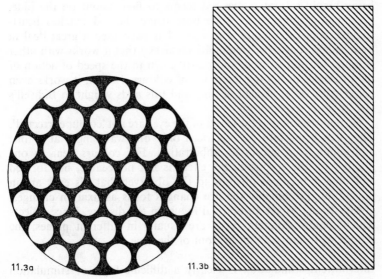

and therefore, by coincidence, the occurrence of appropriate sequences of stimulation, how does the movement occur? Erb and Dallenbach (1939) investigated the effects of eye movement and came to the rather obscure conclusion that 'Eye movement, though necessary, does not appear to be a sufficient or compulsory condition'.

Eye movement or, as in the case of the rays or the patterns of concentric circles, fluctuations in accommodation could cause movement of the stimulus on the retina. But the orientation of coloured bands at right angles to the lines in the figure presents a further problem. Again reference might be made to the after-effects of the figures of the rays and concentric circles and MacKay's notion of 'directional satiation', but I have not seen such ideas worked out.

THE 'FLUTTERING HEARTS' PHENOMENON

A curious effect of the juxtaposition of two highly saturated colours is included here since we are dealing with colour; intermittent stimulation is not involved though there is a slight impression of movement. The phenomenon was mentioned by Wheatstone (1844) and other early writers, and by the time Helmholtz (1856) mentioned it it had acquired the name of the 'fluttering hearts' phenomenon.

When red patches are put on a blue background, both colours being highly saturated, the red seems to float about on the blue. Presumably someone at some time made the red patches heart-shaped, hence the name. This effect has been used a great deal in 'psychedelic' patterns. Helmholtz remarked that it works with other colours, but not so well, and put it down to the speed of action of the processes mediating the different colours. In fact, it works even better with violet instead of blue and this adds weight to Bidwell's (1899) better explanation.

He pointed out that the lenses of the eyes are not 'colour corrected'. They can bring into precise focus only one wavelength at a time and suffer from chromatic abberration. For colours near to one another on the spectrum, the effect is not noticeable, but for red and blue it becomes obvious to the observer that his eyes are in difficulties. Presumably the eye changes focus as fixation changes, always trying to get an optimal focus on the display. Since objects which require different focus are usually in different planes, the red seems to move about in front of the blue.

Intermittent stimulation is clearly a difficult form of stimulation for the visual system to cope with. It fires various sorts of systems 'inappropriately', in the sense, for example, that it causes the perception of movement when nothing in the visual field is moving and, also, the perception of colour in a black and white display. Such illusory effects differ from the geometrical optical illusions in involving the perception of a quality which is non-existent rather than the distortion of a quality (size, straightness, etc.) which is actually to be found in the display.

EPILOGUE

This book has dealt with an enormous diversity of material which testifies to the occurrence of illusion in almost every aspect of visual activity. The various effects seem to have in common only the fact that they involve the observer in misinterpreting his visual field.

However, an interesting attitude towards illusions is that which regards them as the debt which the visual system pays for other advantages in the process of seeing. The system has developed in such a way that, under normal circumstances, the maximum amount of information is gained from the visual field. The special tricks that it plays usually serve this end remarkably well, but there are odd situations, usually ones which could not possibly have been important to primitive man, in which the tricks are turned against the system.

A little thought will show many of the effects mentioned to be examples of this. But some are only speculatively so, because their cause is unknown. Our understanding of illusions is still remarkably incomplete in spite of the volume of research that they have inspired. We know why some occur, but the causes of others are still beyond us. Indeed, the core of the subject, the geometrical optical illusions, perhaps engages the most doubt. This may be because the geometrical optical illusions have so often been used as tools for the investigation of more general theories rather than as phenomena worthy of investigation in their own right, but it does not seem to me to be unduly sensational to say that they are, at this moment, very little less mysterious to us than they were, in the middle of the nineteenth century, to Helmholtz.

BIBLIOGRAPHICAL REFERENCES

ADAM, J. 'A note on visual illusions of direction', *Austral. J. Psychol.*, 1964, **16**, 53–6.

ADAMS, H. F. 'Autokinetic sensations', *Psychol. Monogr.*, 1912, **14**, no. 2, 45 pp.

ADDAMS, R. 'An account of a peculiar optical phenomenon seen after having looked at a moving body', *Phil. Mag.*, 1834, 3 ser., 5, 373.

AIBA, S. 'The effects of stimulant and depressant drugs on the Bidwell phenomenon', *Brit. J. Psychol.*, 1960, **51**, 311–18.

ALLPORT, D. A. 'Temporal summation and phenomenal simultaneity: experiments with the radius display', *Quart. J. exp. Psychol.*, 1970, **22**, 686–701.

ALPERN, M. 'Metacontrast: historical introduction', *Amer. J. Optom.*, 1952, **29**, 631–46.

ALPERN, M. 'Metacontrast', *J. Opt. Soc. Amer.*, 1953, **43**, 648–57.

AMES, A. 'Visual perception and the rotating trapezoidal window', *Psychol. Monogr.*, 1951, **65**, no. 7 (whole no. 324).

ANDREWS, D. P. 'Perception of contour orientation in the central fovea, Pt. I: short lines', *Vision Res.*, 1967a, **1**, 975–97.

ANDREWS, D. P. 'Perception of contour orientation in the central fovea, Pt. II: spatial integration', *Vision Res.*, 1967b, **1**, 999–1013.

ANSBACHER, H. L. 'Distortion in the perception of real movement', *J. exp. Psychol.*, 1944, **34**, 1–23.

ANSTIS, S. M. 'Visual adaptation to gradual change of intensity', *Science*, 1967, **155**, 710–12.

ANSTIS, S. M., and ATKINSON, J. 'Distortions in moving figures viewed through a stationary slit', *Amer. J. Psychol.*, 1967, **80**, 572–85.

ANSTIS, S. M., and MOULDEN, B. P. 'After effect of seen movement: evidence for peripheral and central components', *Quart. J. exp. Psychol.*, 1970, **22**, 222–9.

ARDEN, G. V., and WEALE, R. A. 'Variations of the latent period of vision', *Proc. Roy. Soc.*, 1954, B, **142**, 258.

ARNULF, A., and DUPUY, O. 'Contribution à l'étude des microfluctuations d'accommodation de l'œil', *Rev. Opt. theor. instrum.*, 1960, **39**, 195–208.

ASCH, S. H., and WITKIN, H. A. 'Studies in space orientation: II. Perception of the upright with displaced visual fields and with body tilted', *J. exp. Psychol.*, 1948, **38**, 455–77.

AUBERT, H. 'Eine scheinbare bedentende Drehung von Objekten bei Neigung des Kopfes nach rechts oder links', *Virchows. Arch. Path. Anat. Physiol.*, 1861, **20**, 381–93.

AUBERT, H. 'Die Bervegungsempfindung', *Arch. ges. Physiol.*, 1887, **40**, 459–79.

AUSTIN, M., SINGER, G., and DAY, R. H. 'Visual orientation illusion following judgments with a tilted visual field', *Nature*, 1969, **221**, 583–4.

AVERY, G. C., and DAY, R. H. 'Basis of the horizontal–vertical illusion', *J. exp. Psychol.*, 1969, **81**, 376–80.

BAGLEY, F. W. 'An investigation of Fechner's colour', *Amer. J. Psychol.*, 1902, **13**, 488–525.

BALDWIN, J. M. 'The effect of size contrast upon judgements of position in the retinal field', *Psychol. Rev.*, 1895, **2**, 244–59.

BALES, J. F., and FOLLANSBEE, G. L. 'The after-effect of perception of curved lines', *J. exp. Psychol.*, 1935, **18**, 499–503.

BARLOW, H. B., and BRINDLEY, G. S. 'Inter-ocular transfer of movement after-effects during pressure blinding of the stimulated eye', *Nature*, 1963, **200**, 1347 only.

BARLOW, H. B., and HILL, R. M. 'Evidence for a physiological explanation of the waterfall phenomenon and figural after-effects', *Nature*, 1963, **200**, 1345–7.

BATES, M. 'A study of the Müller-Lyer illusion, with special reference to paradoxical movement and the effect of attitude', *Amer. J. Psychol.*, 1923, **34**, 46–72.

BAUERMEISTER, M. 'Effect of body tilt on apparent verticality, apparent body position, and their relation', *J. exp. Psychol.*, 1964, **67**, 142–7.

BAUMANN, C. 'Beiträge zur Physiologie des Sehens: IV. Subjektive Farbenerscheinungen', *Arch. ges. Physiol.*, 1912, **146**, 543–52.

BEERY, K. E. 'Estimation of angles', *Percept. Mot. Skills*, 1968, **26**, 11–14.

BÉKÉSY G. VON 'Brightness distribution across Mach bands measured with flicker photometry and the linearity of sensory nervous interaction', *J. Opt. Soc. Amer.*, 1968, **58**, 1–8

BENUSSI, V. 'Über den Einfluss der Farbe auf Grösse der Zöllnerischen Täuschung', *Z. für Psychol.*, 1902, **29**, 264–351 & 385–433.

BERGMAN, R. and GIBSON, J. J. 'The negative after-effect of the perception of a surface slanted in the third dimension', *Amer. J. Psychol.*, 1959, **72**, 364.

BERGSTRÖM, S. S. 'A paradox in the perception of luminance gradients. I', *Scand. J. Psychol.*, 1966, **7**, 209–24.

BERGSTRÖM, S. S. 'A paradox in the perception of luminance gradients. II', *Scand. J. Psychol.*, 1967a, **8**, 25–32.

BERGSTRÖM, S. S. 'A paradox in the perception of luminance gradients. III', *Scand. J. Psychol.*, 1967b, **8**, 33–7.

BERLINER, A., and BERLINER, S. 'The distortion of straight and curved lines in geometric fields', *Amer. J. Psychol.*, 1948, **61**, 153–66.

BERRY, J. W. 'Ecology, perceptual development and the Müller-Lyer illusion', *Brit. J. Psychol.*, 1968, **59**, 205–10.

BEZOLD, W. VON. *Die Farbenlehrer im Hinblick auf Kunst und Kunstgewerbe*, Brunswick, Westermann, 1874.

BEZOLD, W. VON. 'Eine perspektivische Täuschung', *Poggend. Annalen*, 1884, **23**, 351–2.

BIDWELL, S. 'On the recurrent images following visual impressions' *Proc Roy. Soc.*, 1894, **56**, 132–45.

BIDWELL, S. 'On subjective colour phenomena attending sudden changes of illumination', *Proc. Roy. Soc.*, 1896, **60**, 368–77.

BIDWELL, S. 'On the negative after-images following brief retinal excitation', *Proc. Roy. Soc.*, 1897, **61**, 268–71.

BIDWELL, S. 'Curiosities of Light and Sight', *Sonnenschein*, London, 1899.

BINET, A. 'La mesure des illusions visuelles chez les enfants', *Rev. Philos.*, 1895, **40**, 11–25.

BLAKEMORE, C., and CAMPBELL, F. W. 'On the existence of neurones in the human visual system selectively sensitive to the orientation and size of retinal images', *J. Physiol.*, 1969, **203**, 237–60.

BLAKEMORE, C., and SUTTON, P. 'Size adaptation: A new after-effect', *Science*, 1969, **166**, 245–7.

BLAKEMORE, C., CARPENTER, R. H. S., and GEORGESON, M. A. 'Lateral inhibition between orientation detectors in the human visual system', *Nature*, 1970, **228**, 37–9.

BLAKEMORE, C., and COOPER, G. 'Development of the brain depends on the visual environment', *Nature*, 1970, **228**, 477–8.

BLIX, M. 'Die sog. Poggendorff'sche optische Täuschungen', *Skand. Arch. Physiol.*, 1902, **13**, 193–228.

BLUM, A. C. 'Photic stimulation, imagery and alpha rhythm', *J. Ment. Sci.*, 1956, **102**, 160–7.

BORING, E. G. *Sensation and perception in the history of experimental psychology*, New York, Appleton-Century-Crofts, 1942.

BORING, E. G. 'The Moon illusion', *Amer. J. Physics*, 1943, **11**, 55–60.

BOTTI, L. 'Ricerche sperimentale sulle illusioni ottico-geometriche', *Memorie della Reale Acc. delle Scienze di Torino*, 1909, ser. II, vol. 60, 139–91.

BOURDON, B. *La perception visuelle de l'espace*, Paris, Reinwald, 1902.

BOWDITCH, H. P., and HALL, G. S. 'Optical illusions of motion', *J. Physiol.*, 1880–2, **3**, 297–307.

BRAUNSTEIN, M. L. 'The perception of depth through motion', *Psychol. Bull.*, 1962, **59**, 422–33.

BRESSLER, J. 'Illusion in the case of subliminal visual stimulation', *J. Gen. Psychol.*, 1931, **5**, 244–51.

BRENTANO, F. 'Über ein optisches Paradoxen', *Z. Psychol.*, 1892, 3, 349–58.

BRINDLEY, G. S., and MERTON, P. A. 'The absence of position sense in the human eye', *J. Physiol.*, 1960, **153**, 127–30.

BROSGOLE, L. 'The autokinesis of an after-image', *Psychonom. Sci.*, 1968, **12**. 233–4.

BROSGOLE, L. 'An analysis of induced motion', *Acta. Psychol.*, 1968, **28**, 1–44.

BROWN, C. R., and GEBHARD, J. W. 'Visual field articulation in the absence of spatial stimulus gradients', *J. exp. Psychol.*, 1948, **38**, 188–200.

BROWN, J. F., and VOTH, A. C. 'The path of seen movement as a function of the vector field', *Amer. J. Psychol.*, 1937, **49**, 543–63.

BROWN, L. B., and HOUSSIADAS, L. 'The perception of illusions as a constancy phenomenon', *Brit. J. Psychol.*, 1965, **56**, 135–41.

BRUCKE, G. 'Über die Nutzeffect intermitterender Netzhautreizungen', *Sitzungsberichte der Mathematisch-Naturwissenschaftlichen Classe der Kaiserlichen Akademie der Wissenschaften*, 1864, **49** (abteilung 2), 128–53.

BRUNOT, C. 'Les illusions d'optique', *Rev. sci. Paris*, 1893, 3 ser., **52**, 210–12.

BURMESTER, E. 'Beiträge zur experimentellen Bestimmung geometrisch-optischer Täuschungen', *Z. Psychol.*, 1896, **12**, 355–94.

BURNHAM, R. W. 'Bezold's color-mixture effect', *Amer. J. Psychol.*, 1953, **66**, 379.

CAMERON, E. H., and STEELE, W. M. 'The Poggendorff illusion', *Psychol. Monogr.*, 1905, **7**, 83–111.

CAMPBELL, F. W., and ROBSON, J. G. 'Moving images produced by regular stationary patterns', *Nature*, 1958, **181**, 362.

CAMPBELL, F. W., ROBSON, J. G., and WESTHEIMER, G. 'Fluctuations of accommodation under steady viewing conditions', *J. Physiol.*, 1959, **145**, 579–94.

CAMPBELL, F. W., and KULIKOWSKI, J. J. 'Orientation selectivity of the human visual system', *J. Physiol.*, 1966, **187**, 437–45.

CAMPBELL, F. W., COOPER, G. F., and ENROTH-CUGELL, C. 'The spatial selectivity of the visual cells of the cat', *J. Physiol.*, 1969, **203**, 223–35.

CANESTRARI, R., and FARNÉ, M. 'Depth cues and apparent oscillatory motion', *Percept. Mot. Skills*, 1969, **29**, 508–10.

CARR, H. A. 'The autokinetic sensation', *Psychol. Rev.*, 1910, **17**, 42–75.

CARR, H. A. *An introduction to space perception*, New York; Longmans, Green, 1935.

CHAPANIS, A., and MANKIN, D. A. 'The vertical–horizontal illusion in a visually rich environment', *Percept. Psychophys.*, 1967, **2**, 249–55.

CHARPENTIER, A. 'Sur une illusion visuelle', *Comptes rendus hebd. de l'Académie des sciences*, 1886, **102**, 1155–7.

CHARPENTIER, A. 'Sur le retard dans la perception des divers rayons spectraux', *Comptes rendus hebd. Sèances. Mem. Soc. Biol.*, 1892, **114**, 1423–6.

CHIANG, C. 'A new theory to explain geometrical illusions produced by crossing lines', *Percept. Psychophys.*, 1968, **3**, 174–6.

CHING, Chi-Cheng, PENG, Jui-Hseung, and FANG, Yun-Chiu. 'The effect of distance and posture of observer on the perception of size', *Acta Psychologica Sinica*, 1963, **22**, 20–30.

CLEARY, A. 'A binocular parallax theory of the geometric illusions', *Psychonom. Sci.*, 1966, **5**, 241–2.

COBBOLD, C. S. W., 'Observations on certain optical illusions of motion', *Brain*, 1881, **4**, 75–81.

COCHRAN, C. F. Letter to *Sci. Amer.*, 1966, **214**, June, p. 8.

COHEN, J., and GORDON, D. A. 'The Prevost–Fechner–Benham subjective colors', *Psychol. Bull.*, 1949, **46**, 97–133.

COOPER, L. A., and WEINTRAUB, D. J. 'Delbœuf-type circle illusions: interactions among luminance, temporal characteristics, and inducing-figure variations', *J. exp. Psychol.*, 1970, **85**, 75–82.

COREN, S. 'The influence of optical aberrations on the magnitude of the Poggendorff illusion', *Percept. Psychophys.*, 1969, **6**, 185–6.

COREN, S. 'Lateral inhibition and the Wundt–Hering illusion', *Psychonom. Sci.*, 1970, **18**, 341–2.

CORSO, J. F. *The experimental psychology of sensory behavior*, New York, Holt, Rinehart and Winston, 1967.

CRAWFORD, F. T., and KLINGAMAN, R. L. 'Figural after-effects as a function of hue', *J. exp. Psychol.*, 1966, **72**, 916–18.

CRONE, R. A., and LUNEL, H. F. E. V. 'Autokinesis and the perception of movement: The physiology of eccentric fixation', *Vision Res.*, 1969, **9**, 89–101.

CULBERT, S. S. 'Directional after-effects following systematic distortion of the visual field', *J. Psychol.*, 1954, **37**, 81–93.

CUMMING, G. D. 'A criticism of the diffraction theory of some geometrical illusions', *Percept. Psychophys.*, 1968, **4**, 375–6.

DAY, R. H. 'Hue differences and brightness differences as determinants of figural after-effects', *Brit. J. Psychol.*, 1959, **50**, 223–30.

DAY, R. H. 'On the stereoscopic observation of geometric illusions', *Percept. Mot. Skills*, 1961, **13**, 247–58.
DAY, R. H. 'The effects of repeated trials and prolonged fixation on error in the Müller-Lyer figure', *Psychol. Monogr.*, 1962a, **76**, no. 14 (whole no. 533).
DAY, R. H. 'Excitatory and inhibitory processes as the basis of contour shift and negative after-effect', *Psychologia*, 1962b, **5**, 185–93.
DAY, R. H. 'Inappropriate constancy explanation of spatial distortions', *Nature*, 1965, **207**, 891–3.
DAY, R. H. 'Visual spatial illusions: a general explanation'. *Science*, 1972, **175**, 1335–140.
DAY, R. H., POLLACK, R. H., and SEAGRIM, G. N., 'Figural after-effects: a critical review', *Aust. J. Psychol.*, 1959, **11**, 15–45.
DAY, R. H., and POWER, R. P. 'Frequency of apparent reversal of rotary motion in depth as a function of shape and pattern', *Aust. J. Psychol.*, 1963, **15**, 162–74.
DAY, R. H., and POWER, R. P. 'Apparent reversal (oscillation) of rotary motion in depth: An investigation and a general theory', *Psychol. Rev.*, 1965, **72**, 117–27.
DAY, R. H., and WADE, N. J. 'Visual spatial after-effect from prolonged head-tilt', *Science*, 1966, **154**, 1201–2.
DAY, R. H., and STRELOW, E. 'Reduction or disappearance of visual after-effect of movement in the absence of a patterned surround', *Nature*, 1971, **230**, 55–6.
DELBŒUF, J. L. R. 'Sur une nouvelle illusion d'optique', *Bull. de l'Acad. roy. de Belg.*, 1892, **24**, 545–58.
DENTON, G. G. 'The influence of visual pattern on perceived speed', Road Research Laboratory Report LR409, 1971.
DEUTSCH, J. A. 'The statistical theory of F.A.E.'s and acuity', *Brit. J. Psychol.*, 1956, **47**, 208–15.
DEWAR, R. E. 'The effect of angle between the oblique lines on the decrement of the Müller-Lyer illusion with extended practice', *Percept. Psychophys.*, 1967a, **2**, 426–8.
DEWAR, R. E. 'Stimulus determinants of the magnitude of the Müller-Lyer illusion', *Percept. Mot. Skills*, 1967b, **24**, 708–10.
DIAMOND, A. L. 'Simultaneous brightness contrast and the Pulfrich phenomenon', *J. Opt. Soc. Amer.*, 1958, **48**, 887–90.
DIAMOND, A. L. 'A theory of depression and enhancement in the brightness response', *Psychol. Rev.*, 1960, 67, 168–99.
DITCHBURN, R. W., and GINSBORG, B. L. 'Vision with a stabilised retinal image', *Nature*, 1952, **170**, 36–7.
DIXON, N. F. 'Effect of information content and size upon the absolute threshold for movement', *Percept. Mot. Skills*, 1967, **25**, 37–40.
DIXON, N. F. *Subliminal perception: the nature of a controversy*, London, McGraw-Hill, 1971
DIXON, N. F., and DIXON, P. M. '"Sloping water" and related framework illusions', *Quart. J. exp. Psychol.*, 1966, **18**, 369–70.
DIXON, N. F., and MEISELS, L. 'The effect of information content upon the perception and after-effects of a rotating field', *Quart. J. exp. Psychol.*, 1966, **18**, 310–18.
DIXON, N. F., and HAMMOND, E. J. 'The attenuation of visual persistence', *Brit. J. Psychol.*, 1972 (in press).
DIXON, N. F., and JEEVES, M. A. 'The interhemispheric transfer of movement after-effects: a comparison between acollosal and normal subjects', *Psychonom. Sci.*, 1970, **20**, 201–3.

DOMINGUEZ, K. E. 'A study of visual illusions in the monkey', *J. genet. Psychol.*, 1954, **85**, 105–27.

DÜCKER, G. 'Untersuchungen über geometrisch-optische Täuschungen bei Wirbeltieren', *Z. Tierpsychol.*, 1966, **23**, 452–96.

DUDLEY, L. P. *Stereoptics*, London, Macdonald & Co., 1951.

DUDLEY, L. P. 'The development of autostereoscopic photography', *Brit. J. Physiol. Opt.*, 1952, **9**, 123–44.

DUNCAN, C. P. 'Amount and rate of decay of visual figural after-effect as functions of type of inspection-stimulus and inspection-time', *Amer. J. Psychol.*, 1962, **75**, 242–50.

DUNCKER, K. 'Über induzierte Bewegung (ein Beitrag zur Theorie Optisch Wahrgenommener)', *Psychol. Forsch.*, 1929, **12**, 180–259.

DUREMAN, I. 'Factors influencing the apparent velocity of visual movement after-effects', *Scand. J. Psychol.*, 1962, **3**, 132–6.

DVOŘAK, V. 'Über Analoga der persönlichen Differenz zwischen beiden Augen und den Netzhautstellen desselben Auges', *Sitzber. d. k. böhm. Gesellsch. d. Wiss, in Prag.*, 1872, 65–74.

EBBINGHAUS, H. *Grundzüge der Psychologie*, Leipzig, Veit, 1902, vols. I & II.

EBENHOLTZ, S. 'Perception of the vertical with body tilt in the median plane', *J. exp. Psychol.*, 1970, **83**, 1–6.

EDWARDS, W. 'Autokinetic movement of very large stimuli', *J. exp. Psychol.*, 1954, **48**, 493–5.

EDWARDS, W. 'Information and autokinetic movement', *J. exp. Psychol.*, 1959, **57**, 89.

EHRENSTEIN, W. 'Versuche über die Beziehungen zwischen Bewegungs und Gestaltwahrnehmung', *Z. Psychol.*, 1925, **95**, 305–52.

ELFNER, L. F., and PAGE, H. A. 'Autokinetic movement as a function of light-dark-ratio (LDR)', *Psychonom. Sci.*, 1964, **1**, 59–60.

ELLIS, H. D. 'Illusions, after-effects and iconic memory', *Psychonom. Sci.*, 1969, **17**, 328–9.

ENGELKING, E., and POOS, F. 'Über die Bedeutung des Stereophänomens für die isochromen und heterochromen Helligkeitsvergleichung', *Arch. Ophthalmol.*, 1924, **114**, 340–79.

ENRIGHT, J. T. 'Distortions of apparent velocity: A new optical illusion', *Science*, 1970, **168**, 464–7.

EPSTEIN, W., JANSSON, G., and JOHANSSON, G. 'Perceived angles of oscillatory motion', *Percept. Psychophys.*, 1968, **3**, 12–16.

ERB, M. B., and DALLENBACH, K. M. 'Subjective colors from line patterns', *Amer. J. Psychol.*, 1939, **52**, 227–41.

ERIKSSON, E. S. 'A field theory of visual illusions', *Brit. J. Psychol.*, 1970, **61**, 451–66.

ERLEBACHER, A., and SEKULER, R. 'Explanation of the Müller-Lyer illusion: Confusion theory examined', *J. exp. Psychol.*, 1969, **80**, 462–7.

ESCHER, M. C. *The Graphic Work of M. C. Escher*, London, Oldbourne, 1961, 2nd ed,

EVANS, C. R., and MARSDEN, R. P. 'A study of the effect of perfect retinal stabilization on some well-known visual illusions, using the after-image as a method of compensating for eye movements', *Brit. J. Physiol. Opt.*, 1966, **23**, 242–8.

EVANS, R. M. *An introduction to color*, New York, Wiley, 1948.

EVANS, S. H., HOFFMAN, A. A., ARNOULT, M. D., and ZINSER, O. 'Pattern enhancement with schematic operators', *Behavioral Science*, 1968, **13**, 402–4.

EXNER, S. 'Über des Sehens von Bewegung und die Theorie des zusammengesetzten Auges'. *Sitzber. Akad. Wiss. Wien* (*Math.-nat. Kl., Abt.* 3), 1875, **72**, 156–90.

EYSENCK, H. J. *The scientific study of personality*, London, Routledge & Kegan Paul, 1952.

FARNÉ, M. 'Figural after-effects with short exposure time', *Psychol. Forsch.*, 1965, **28**, 519–34.

FARNÉ, M. 'On the Poggendorff illusion: a note to Cumming's criticism of Chung Chiang's theory', *Percept. Psychophys.*, 1970, **8**, 112 only.

FARNÉ, M. 'Induced motion in three dimensions', *Percept. Mot. Skills*, 1970, **30**, 426 only.

FECHNER, G. T. 'Über eine Scheibe zur Erzeugung subjektiver Farben', *Pogg. Ann. Physik, u. Chemie.*, 1838, **45** (121), 227–32.

FEHRER, E., and GANCHROW, D. 'Effects of exposure variables on figural after-effects under tachistoscopic presentation', *J. exp. Psychol.*, 1963, **66**, 506–13.

FELLOWS, B. J. 'Reversal of the Müller-Lyer illusion with changes in the length of the inter-fins line', *Quart. J. exp. Psychol.*, 1967, **19**, 208–14.

FELLOWS, B. J. 'The reverse Müller-Lyer illusion and "enclosure" ', *Brit. J. Psychol.*, 1968, **59**, 369–72.

FERREE, C. E. 'The streaming phenomenon', *Amer. J. Psychol.*, 1908, **19**, 484–503.

FESTINGER, L., WHITE, C. W., and ALLYN, M. R. 'Eye movements and decrement in the Müller-Lyer illusion', *Percept. Psychophys.*, 1968, **3**, 376–82.

FESTINGER, L., COREN, S., and RIVERS, G., 'The effect of attention on brightness contrast and assimilation', *Amer. J. Psychol.*, 1970, **83**, 189–207.

FICK, A. *De errone quodam optic asymmetria bulbi effecto*, Marburg, Koch, 1851.

FINNEGAN, J. M., and MOORE, B. 'The artificial spectrum top', *Nature*, 1895, **51**, 292–3.

FINGER, F. W., and SPELT, D. K. 'The illustration of the horizontal–vertical illusion', *J. exp. Psychol.*, 1947, **37**, 243–50.

FIORENTINI, A., and RADICI, T. 'Brightness, width and position of Mach Bands as a function of the rate of variation of the luminance gradient', *Atti. Fond. Giorgio. Ronchi.*, 1958, **13**, 145–55.

FISCHER, G. J. 'Factors affecting estimation of depth with variations of the stereo-kinetic effect', *Amer. J. Psychol.*, 1956, **69**, 252–7.

FISHER, G. H. 'A common principle relating to the Müller-Lyer and Ponzo illusions', *Amer. J. Psychol.*, 1967a, **80**, 626–31.

FISHER, G. H., 'Detection of visual stimuli located within angles', *Nature*, 1967b, **215**, 553–4.

FISHER, G. H. 'Ambiguous figure treatments in the art of Salvador Dali', *Percept. Psychophys.*, 1967c, **2**, 328–30.

FISHER, G. H. *The Frameworks for Perceptual Localization*, Dept. of Psychology, Newcastle-upon-Tyne, 1968a (Library of Congress Catalog Card no. 68–8554).

FISHER, G. H. 'Gradients of distortion seen in the context of the Ponzo illusion and other contours', *Quart. J. exp. Psychol.*, 1968b, **20**, 212–17.

FISHER, G. H. 'An experimental and theoretical appraisal of the inappropriate size-depth theories of illusions', *Brit. J. Psychol.*, 1968c, **59**, 373–83.

FISHER, G. H. 'An experimental comparison of rectilinear and curvilinear illusions', *Brit. J. Psychol.*, 1968d, **59**, 23–8.

FISHER, G. H. 'Illusions and size-constancy', *Amer. J. Psychol.*, 1968e, **81**, 2–20.

FISHER, G. H. 'Ambiguity of form: Old and new', *Percept. Psychophys.*, 1968f, **4**, 189–92.

FISHER, G. H. 'Towards a new explanation for the geometrical illusions: I. The properties of contours which induce illusory distortion', *Brit. J. Psychol.*, 1969a, **60**, 179–85.

FISHER, G. H. 'An experimental study of angular subtension', *Quart. J. exp. Psychol.*, 1969b, **21**, 356–66.

FISHER, G. H. 'An experimental and theoretical appraisal of the perspective and size-constancy theories of illusions', *Quart. J. exp. Psychol.*, 1970, **22**, 631–52.

FLAVELL, J. H. *The Developmental Psychology of Jean Piaget*, Princeton, van Nostrand, 1963.

FRAISSE, P., EHRLICH, S., and VURPILLOT, E. 'Études de la centration perceptive par la méthod tachistoscopique', *Arch. de Psychol.*, 1956, **35**, 193–214.

FRAISSE, P., and VAUTREY, P. 'The influence of age, sex and specialised training on the vertical–horizontal illusion', *Quart. J. exp. Psychol.*, 1956, **8**, 114–20.

FRASER, J. 'A new visual illusion of direction', *Brit. J. Psychol.*, 1908, **2**, 307–20.

FREEMAN, R. B., and PASNAK, R. 'Perspective determinants of the rotating trapezoid illusion', *J. exp. Psychol.*, 1968, **76**, 94–101.

GANZ, L. 'Mechanism of the F.A.E.'s', *Psychol. Rev.*, 1966a, **73**, 128–50.

GANZ, L. 'Is the figural after-effect an after-effect? A review of its intensity, onset, decay and transfer characteristics', *Psychol. Bull.*, 1966b, **66**, 151–65.

GANZ, L., and DAY, R. H. 'An analysis of the satiation–fatigue mechanisms of figural after-effects', *Amer. J. Psychol.*, 1965, **78**, 345–61.

GARDNER, M. 'Of optical illusions, from figures that are undecidable to hot dogs that float', *Sci. Amer.*, 1970, **222**, May, 124–7.

GARDNER, R. W., and LONG, R. I. 'Errors of the standard and illusion effects with the inverted T', *Percept. mot. Skills*, 1960a, **10**, 47–54.

GARDNER, R. W., and LONG, R. I. 'Errors of the standard and illusion effects with L-shaped figures', *Percept. mot. Skills*, 1960b, **10**, 107–9.

GARDNER, R. W., and LONG, R. I. 'Selective attention and the Müller-Lyer illusion', *Psychol. Rec.*, 1961, **11**, 317–20.

GEER, J. P. VAN DE, and NATRIS, P. J. A. DE. 'Dutch distorted rooms from the 17th century', *Acta Psychol.*, 1962, **20**, 101–3.

GELDARD, F. A. *The Human Senses*, New York, Wiley, 1953.

GHONEIM, S. 'Les déformations perceptives du losange de l'enfant à l'adulte', *Arch. de Psychologie*, 1959, **37**, 1–99.

GIBSON, J. J. 'Adaptation, after-effect and contrast in the perception of curved lines', *J. exp. Psychol.*, 1933, **16**, 1–31.

GIBSON, J. J. 'Adaptation, after-effect, and contrast in the perception of tilted lines: II. Simultaneous contrast and the areal restriction of the after-effect', *J. exp. Psychol.*, 1937a, **20**, 553–69.

GIBSON, J. J. 'Adaptation with negative after-effect', *Psychol. Rev.*, 1937b, **44**, 222–44.

GIBSON, J. J. *The perception of the visual world*, Boston, Houghton Mifflin, 1950.

GIBSON, J. J. 'Optical motions and transformations as stimuli for visual perception', *Psychol. Rev.*, 1957, **64**, 288–95.

GIBSON, J. J., and RADNER, M. 'Adaptation, after-effect and contrast in the perception of tilted lines: I. Quantitative studies', *J. exp. Psychol.*, 1937, **20**, 453–67.

GIBSON, J. J., and GIBSON, E. J. 'Conginuous perspective transformations and the perception of rigid motion', *J. exp. Psychol.*, 1957, **54**, 129–38.

GOGEL, W. C., and MERSHON, D. H. 'The perception of size in a distorted room', *Percept. Psychophys.*, 1968, **4**, 26–8.

GRAHAM, C. H. (Ed.). *Vision and visual perception*, New York, Wiley, 1965.

GRAYBIEL, A. 'Oculogravic illusion', *A.M.A. Arch. Ophthalmol.*, 1952, **48**, 605–15.

GRAYBIEL, A., and CLARK, B. 'The autokinetic illusion and its significance in night flying', *J. Aviat. Med.*, 1945, **16**, 111–51.

GRAYBIEL, A., and HUPP, D. I. 'The oculogyral illusion', *J. Aviat. Med.*, 1946, **17**, 3–27.

GREEN, B. F. 'Figure coherence in the kinetic depth effect,' *J. exp. Psychol.*, 1961, **62**, 272–82.

GREEN, R. T., and HOYLE, E. M. 'Adaptation level and the optico-geometric illusions', *Nature*, 1964, **201**, 1200–1.

GREEN, R. T., and Hoyle, G. M., 'The influence of spatial orientation on the Poggendorff Illusion', *Acta Psychol.*, 1965, **22**, 348–66.

GREEN, R. T., and STACEY, B. G. 'Misapplication of the misapplied constancy hypothesis', *Life Sciences*, 1966, **5**, 1871–80.

GREGOR, A. J., and MCPHERSON, D. A. 'A study of susceptibility to geometric illusion among cultural subgroups of Australian aborigines', *Psychologia Africana*, 1965, **11**, 1–13.

GREGORY, A. H. 'Bidwell's Disk and Benham's Top', Paper for review, XIX Internat. Cong. Psychol., 1969, London.

GREGORY, R. L. 'A blue filter technique for detecting eye movements during the autokinetic effect', *Quart. J. exp. Psychol.*, 1959, **11**, 113–14.

GREGORY, R. L. 'Distortion of visual space as inappropriate constancy scaling', *Nature*, 1963, **199**, 678–80.

GREGORY, R. L. *Eye and brain*, London, Weidenfeld & Nicolson, 1966a.

GREGORY, R. L. Reply to Wallace 'Optical Illusions', *Nature*, 1966b, **209**, 328.

GREGORY, R. L. 'Comments on the inappropriate constancy scaling theory of illusions and its implications', *Quart, J. exp. Psychol.*, 1967, **19**, 219–23.

GREGORY, R. L. 'Visual Illusions', *Sci. Amer.*, 1968a, **219**, November, 66–76.

GREGORY, R. L. 'Perceptual illusions and brain models', *Proc. Roy. Soc.*, 1968b, B, **171**, 279–96.

GREGORY, R. L. *The intelligent eye*, London, Weidenfeld & Nicolson, 1970.

GREGORY, R. L. Personal communication, 1971.

GREGORY, R. L., and ZANGWILL, O. L. 'The origin of the autokinetic effect', *Quart. J. exp. Psychol.*, 1963, **15**, 255–61.

GRINDLEY, G. C., and Townsend, V. 'Visual search without eye movement', *Quart. J. exp. Psychol.*, 1970, **22**, 62–7.

GUILFORD, J. P., and DALLENBACH, K. M. 'A study of the autokinetic sensation', *Amer. J. Psychol.*, 1928, **40**, 83–91.

HABER, R. N., and NATHANSON, L. S. 'Post-retinal storage? Some further observations on Parks' camel as seen through the eye of a needle', *Percept. Psychophys.*, 1968, **3**, 349–55.

HAMMER, E. R. 'Temporal factors in figural after-effects', *Amer. J. Psychol.*, 1949, **62**, 337–54.

HANLEY, C., and ZERBOLIO, D. J. 'Developmental changes in five illusions measured by the up-and-down method', *Child Develop.*, 1965, **36**, 437–52.

HARKER, G. S. 'A saccadic suppression explanation of the Pulfrich phenomenon', *Percept. Psychophys.*, 1967, **2**, 423–6.

HARRIS, C. S., and GIBSON, A. R. 'Is orientation-specific color adaptation in human vision due to edge detectors, afterimages or "dipoles"?', *Science*, 1968, **162**, 1506–7.

HARTLINE, H. K. 'Visual receptors and retinal interaction', *Science*, 1969, **164**, 270–8.

HAY, J. C. 'Optical motions and space perception: An extension of Gibson's analysis', *Psychol. Rev.*, 1966, **73**, 550–65.

HEISS, A. 'Zum Problem der isolierenden Abstraktion', *Neue psychol. Stud.*, 1930, **4**, 285–318.

HELMHOLTZ, H. VON. *Handbuch der Physiologischen Optik*, Leipzig, Voss. Part I (1856), Part II (1860), Part III (1866). The first two parts were published in the same volume as the third part in 1866. This was called the first edition. Translation by J. P. C. Southall of the third (1909) edition was published as *Treatise on Physiological Optics*, New York, Dover, 1962.

HELSON, H. 'Some factors and implications of color constancy', *J. opt. Soc. Amer.*, 1943, **33**, 555–67.

HELSON, H. *Adaptation-level Theory*, New York, Harper & Row, 1964.

HELSON, H., and ROHLES, F. H. 'A quantitative study of reversal of classical lightness-contrast', *Amer. J. Psychol.*, 1959, **72**, 530–8.

HERING, E. *Beitrage zur Psychologie*, vol 1, Leipzig, Engelman, 1861.

HERING, E. 'Der Raumsinn und die Bewegungen des Auges', *Handbuch der Physiologie*, Hermann, L. (Ed.), vol. III, p. I, 579, Leipzig, F. C. W. Fogel, 1879.

HERMANN, L. 'Eine Erscheinung simultanen Kontrastes', *Pflüg. Arch. ges. Physiol.*, 1870, **3**, 13–15.

HEYMANS, G. 'Quantitative Untersuchungen über das "optische Paradoxen"', *Z. Psychol.*, 1896, **9**, 221–55.

HICKS, G. D., and RIVERS, W. H. R. 'The illusion of compared horizontal and vertical lines', *Brit. J. Psychol.*, 1908, **2**, 243–60.

HOCHBERG, J. E., and HAY, J. 'Figural after-effect, after-image, and physiological nystagmus', *Amer. J. Psychol.*, 1956, **69**, 480–2.

HOFMANN, F. B. 'Über den Einfluss schräger Konturen auf die optische Lokalisation bei seitlicher Kopfneigung', *Arch. ges Physiol.*, 1910, **136**, 724–40.

HOFMANN, F. B., and BIELCHOWSKY, A. 'Über die Einstellung der scheinbaren Horizontalen und Vertikalen bei Betrachtung eines von schrägen Konturen erfülten Gesichtsfeldes', *Arch. ges. Physiol.*, 1909, **126**, 453–75.

HOLLAND, H. C. *International series of monographs in experimental psychology: II. The spiral after-effect*, London, Pergamon Press, 1965.

HOLT-HANSEN, K. 'Hering's illusion', *Brit. J. Psychol.*, 1961, **52**, 317–21.

HONISETT, J., and OLDFIELD, R. C. 'Movement and distortion in visual patterns during prolonged fixations', *Scand J. Psychol.*, 1961, **2**, 49–55.

HORN, G., and HILL, R. M. 'Modifications of receptive fields of cells in the visual cortex occurring spontaneously and associated with bodily tilt', *Nature*, 1969, **221**, 186–8.

HORNE, E. P., and DEABLER, H. L. 'Optimal beta motion in patients receiving insulin and chlorpromazine treatment', *J. gen. Psychol.*, 1962, **67**, 265–9.

HOTOPF, W. H. N. 'The size constancy theory of visual illusions', *Brit. J. Psychol.*, 1966, **57**, 307–18.

HOULIHAN, K., and SEKULER, R. W. 'Contour interactions in visual masking', *J. exp. Psychol.*, 1968, **77**, 281–5.

HOWARD, I. P. 'An investigation of a satiation process in the reversible perspective of revolving skeletal shapes', *Quart. J. exp. Psychol.*, 1961, **13**, 19–33.

HOWARTH, C. I., and TREISMAN, M. 'Validity of Motokawa's technique for investigating retinal function', *Nature*, 1958, **181**, 843–4.

HUBEL, D. H. 'The Visual cortex of the brain', *Sci. Amer.*, 1963, **209**, 54–62.

HUDSON, W. 'Pictorial depth perception in sub-cultural groups in Africa', *J. soc. Psychol.*, 1960, **52**, 183–208.

HUMBOLDT, A. VON. *Kosmos III*, Stuttgart & Augsburg, Cotta'sche Buchhandel, 1851.

HUMPHREY, N. K., and MORGAN, M. J. 'Constancy and the geometric illusions', *Nature*, 1965, **206**, 744–6.

HURST, C. H. 'A spectrum top and a complementary one', *Nature*, 1895, **51**, 510 only.

IKEDA, H., and OBONAI, T. 'The quantitative analysis of figural after-effects: I. The process of growth and decay of figural after-effects', *Jap. J. Psychol.*, 1953, **23**, 246–60; **24**, 59–66.

IKEDA, H., and OBONAI, T. 'Figural after-effect, retroactive effect and simultaneous illusion', *Jap. J. Psychol.*, 1955, **26**, 235–46.

INDOW, T., KUNO, K., and YOSHIDA, T. 'Studies on the induction in visual process taking electrical phosphene as an index: 2. Experiments on the propagation of the induction across the blind spot', *Psychologia*, 1958, **1**, 175–81.

ITTELSON, W. H. *The Ames demonstrations in perception*, Princeton, Princeton University Press, 1952.

JAHODA, G. 'Geometric illusions and environment: A study in Ghana', *Brit. J. Psychol.*, 1966, **57**, 193–9.

JAHODA, G., and STACEY, B. 'Susceptibility to geometrical illusions according to culture and professional training', *Percept. Psychophys.*, 1970, **7**, 179–84.

JASTROW, J. 'A study of Zöllner's figures and other related illusions', *Amer. J. Psychol.*, 1891, **4**, 381–98.

JASTROW, J. 'On the judgment of angles and positions of lines', *Amer. J. Psychol.*, 1892, **5**, 214–21.

JEFFREY, H. J. 'An enquiry into inappropriate constancy scaling', *Quart. J. exp. Psychol.*, 1968, **20**, 294–6.

JENSEN, G. D. 'Effect of past experience upon induced movement', *Percept. Mot. Skills*, 1960, **11**, 281–8.

JERISON, H. J. 'Apparent motion of a vista: an illusion of perspective', *Amer. J. Psychol.*, 1967, **80**, 448–53.

JORDAN, S. 'Autokinesis and felt eye-position', *Amer. J. Psychol.*, 1968, **81**, 497–512.

JUDD, C. H. 'A study of geometrical illusions', *Psychol. Rev.*, 1899, **6**, 241–61.

JUDD, C. H. 'Practice and its effects on the geometrical illusions', *Psychol. Rev.*, 1902, **9**, 27–39.

JUDD, C. H. 'The Müller-Lyer illusion', *Psychol. Monogr.*, 1905, **7**, 55–81.

JUDD, C. H., and COURTEN, H. C. 'The Zöllner illusion,' *Psychol. Monogr.*, 1905, **7**, 112–39.

JULESZ, B. 'Binocular depth perception without familiarity cues', *Science*, 1964, **145**, 356–62.

JULESZ, B. 'Texture and visual perception', *Sci. Amer.*, 1965, **212**, 38–48.

KAMMANN, R. 'The overestimation of vertical distance and slope and its role in the moon illusion', *Percept. Psychophys.*, 1967, **2**, 585–9.

KAPLAN, S. D. 'Autonomic visual regulation: Pt. I. The after-image spectral photometer; an apparatus for measuring visual excitation, inhibition, and differentiation in psychopharmacology', *Psychiat. Res. Rep.*, 1960a, **12**, 104–14.

KAPLAN, S. D. 'Autonomic visual regulation: Pt. II. Differential spectral sensitization to autonomic drugs in depression', *Psychiat. Res. Rep.*, 1960b, **12**, 115–18.

KAUFMAN, L., and ROCK, I. 'The moon illusion', *Sci. Amer.*, 1962a, **207**, 120–32.

KAUFMAN, L., and ROCK, I. 'The moon illusion: I', *Science*, 1962b, **136**, 953–61.

KAUFMAN, L., and RICHARDS, W. 'Spontaneous fixation tendencies for visual forms', *Percept. Psychophys.*, 1969, **5**, 85–8.

KENKEL, F. 'Untersuchungen über der Zusammenhang zwischen Erscheinungsgrösse und Erscheinungsbewegung bei einigen sogenannten optischen Täuschungen', *Z. Psychol.* 1913, **67**, 358–449.

KENYON, F. C. 'A curious optical illusion connected with an electric fan', *Science*, 1898, **8**, 371–2.

KOBOYASHI, T. 'Analytical study of displacement in visual perception: I', *Jap. Psychol. Res.*, 1956, no. 3, 37–44.

KÖHLER, W. 'Unsolved problems in the field of figural after-effects', *Psychol. Record*, 1964, **15**, 63–83.

KÖHLER, W., and WALLACH, H. 'Figural after-effects: An investigation of visual processes', *Proc. Amer. Philos. Soc.,* 1944, **88**, 269–357.

KÖHLER, W., and EMERY, D. A. 'Figural after-effects in the third dimension of visual space', *Amer. J. Psychol.*, 1947, **60**, 159–201.

KÖHLER, W., and FISHBACK, J. 'The destruction of the Müller-Lyer illusion in repeated trials: I. An examination of two theories', *J. exp. Psychol.*, 1950a, **40**, 267–281.

KÖHLER, W., and FISHBACK, J. 'The destruction of the Müller-Lyer illusion in repeated trials: II. Satiation patterns and memory traces', *J. exp. Psychol.*, 1950b, **40**, 398–410.

KOLEHMAINEN, K., and CRONHJORT, R. 'Apparent properties of inspection figures as determiners of figural after-effects', *Scand. J. Psychol.*, 1970, **11**, 103–8.

KOLERS, P. A. 'Some differences between real and apparent movement', *Vision Res.*, 1963, **3**, 191–206.

KOLERS, P. A. 'The illusion of movement', *Sci. Amer.*, 1964, **211**, no. 4, 98–106.

KORTÉ, A. 'Kinematoskopische Untersuchungen', *Z. Psychol.*, 1915, **72**, 193–296.

KRAUSKOPF, J. 'Figural after-effects with a stabilized image', *Amer. J. Psychol.*, 1960, **73**, 294–7.

KRISTOF, W. 'Ein Umschlag der Heringschen Täuschung bei Abwandlung der Vorlage', *Z. exp. angew. Psychol.*, 1960, **7**, 68–75.

KRISTOF, W. 'Über die Einordnung geometrische-optische Täuschungen in die Gemässigkeiten der visuellen Wahrnehmungen, teil 1', *Arch. ges. Psychol.*, 1961, **113**, 1–48.

KUNDT, A. 'Untersuchungen über Augenmass und optische Täuschungen', *Pogg. Ann.*, 1863, **120**, 118–58.

KÜNNAPAS, T. M. 'Influence of frame size on apparent length of a line', *J. exp. Psychol.*, 1955a, **50**, 168–70.

KÜNNAPAS, T. M. 'An analysis of the "vertical–horizontal illusion" ', *J. exp. Psychol.*, 1955b, **49**, 134–40.

KÜNNAPAS, T. M. 'Vertical–horizontal illusion and surrounding field', *Acta Psychol.*, 1957, **13**, 35–42.

KÜNNAPAS, T. M. 'Fixation and the vertical–horizontal illusion', *Acta Psychol.*, 1958, **14**, 131–6.

KÜNNAPAS, T. M. 'The vertical–horizontal illusion in artificial visual fields', *J. Psychol.*, 1959, **47**, 41–8.

LASHLEY, K. S., CHOW, K. L., and SEMMES, J. 'An examination of the electrical field theory of cerebral integration', *Psychol. Rev.*, 1951, **58**, 123–36.

LÁSKA, W. 'Über einige optische Urteilstäuschungen', *Arch. Physiol.*, 1890, 326–8.

LEIBOWITZ, H., and HEISEL, M. A. 'L'evolution de l'illusion de Ponzo en fonction de l'âge', *Arch. Psychol.*, 1958, **36**, 328–31.

LEIBOWITZ, H., and HARTMAN, T. 'Magnitude of the moon illusion as a function of the age of the observer', *Science*, 1959, **130**, 569.

LEIBOWITZ, H., and TOFFEY, S. 'The effects of rotation and tilt on the magnitude of the Poggendorf illusion', *Vision Res.*, 1966, **6**, 101–3.

LEIBOWITZ, H. W., and JUDISCH, J. A. 'The relation between age and the Ponzo illusion', *Amer. J. Psychol.*, 1967, **80**, 105–9.

LEIBOWITZ, H., BRISLIN, R., PERLMUTTER, L., and HENNESSY, R. 'Ponzo perspective illusion as a manifestation of space perception', *Science*, 1969, **166**, 1174–6.

LEWIS, E. O. 'The effect of practice on the perception of the Müller-Lyer illusion', *Brit. J. Psychol.*, 1908, **2**, 294–306.

LEWIS, E. O. 'Confluxion and contrast effects in the Müller-Lyer illusion', *Brit. J. Psychol.*, 1909, **3**, 21–41.

LEWIS, E. O. 'The illusion of filled and unfilled space', *Brit. J. Psychol.*, 1912, **5**, 36–50.

LIPPS, T. *Raumaesthetik und geometrisch-optische Täuschungen*, Leipzig, Barth, 1897.

LIT, A. 'The magnitude of the Pulfrich stereophenomenon as a function of binocular differences in intensity at various levels of illumination', *Amer. J. Psychol.*, 1949, **62**, 159–81.

LOEB, J. 'Über den Nachweiss von Kontrasterscheinungen im Gebiete der Raumempfindungen des Auges', *Pflüg. Arch. ges. Physiol.*, 1895, **60**, 509–18.

LOMBROSO, C. T., and CORAZZA, R. 'Central visual discharge time-locked with spontaneous eye movements in the cat', *Nature*, 1971, **230**, 464–7.

LUCHINS, A. 'The relation of size of light to autokinetic effect', *J. Psychol.*, 1954, **38**, 439–52.

LUCKIESH, M. *Visual illusions*, New York, Dover, 1922.

LUCKIESH, M., and MOSS, F. K. 'A demonstrational test of vision', *Amer. J. Psychol.*, 1933, **45**, 135–9.

LYTHGOE, R. J. 'Some observations on the rotating pendulum', *Nature*, 1938, **141**, 474 only.

MCCOLLOUGH, C. 'The variation in width and position of Mach bands as a function of luminance', *J. exp. Psychol.*, 1955, **49**, 141–52.

MCCOLLOUGH, C. 'Color adaptation of the edge-detectors in the human visual system', *Science*, 1965, **149**, 1115–16.

MCDOUGALL, W. 'Smoothly graded contrast', *Proc. physiol. Soc. Cambridge*, 1903, **1**, 19–20.

MCEWEN, P. 'Figural after-effects', *Brit. J. Psychol. Monogr. Suppl.*, 1958, **31**.

MCEWEN, P. 'Figural after-effects, retinal size and apparent size', *Brit. J. Psychol.*, 1959, **50**, 41–7.

MCFARLAND, J. H., WAPNER, S., and WERNER, H. 'Relation between perceived location of objects and perceived location of one's own body', *Percept. Mot. Skills*, 1962, **15**, 331–41.

MACH, E. 'Über die Wirkung der räumlichen Vertheilung des Lichtreizes auf die Netzhaut', *Sitzungsberichte der mathematisch-naturwissenschaftlichen Klasse der Kaiserlichen Akademie der Wissenschaften*, 1865, Vienna, 52/2, 303–22.

MACK, A. 'An investigation of the relationship between eye and retinal image movement in the perception of movement', *Percept. Psychophys.*, 1970, **8**, 291–8.

MACKAY, D. M. 'Moving images produced by regular stationary patterns', *Nature*, 1957, **180**, 849–50.

MACKAY, D. M. 'Perceptual stability of a stroboscopically lit visual field containing self-luminous objects', *Nature*, 1958, **181**, 507–8.

MACKAY, D. M. 'Interactive processes in visual perception' in Rosenblith, W. A. (Ed.). *Sensory Communication*, New York, Wiley, and M.I.T. Press, 1961*a*.

MACKAY, D. M. 'Visual effects of non-redundant stimulation', *Nature*, 1961b, **192**, 739–40.

MACKAY, D. M. 'Dynamic distortions of perceived form', *Nature*, 1964, **203**, 1097.

MACKAY, D. M. 'Visual noise as a tool of research', *J. gen. Psychol.*, 1965, **72**, 181–97.

MACKAY, D. M., and FIORENTINI, A. 'Evoked potentials correlated with a visual anomaly', *Nature*, 1966, **209**, 787–9.

MACKAY, A. L., and STROUD, R. M. 'An optical illusion', *Percept. Psychophys.*, 1968, **4**, 90.

MCLAUGHLIN, S. C., DESISTO, M. J., and KELLY, M. J. 'Comment on "Eye movement and decrement in the Müller-Lyer illusion" ', *Percept. Psychophys.*, 1969, **5**, 288 only.

MAFFEI, L., and CAMPBELL, F. W. 'Neurophysiological localisation of the vertical and horizontal visual components in man', *Science*, 1970, **167**, 386–7.

MAHEUX, M., TOWNSEND, J. C., and GRESOCK, C. J. 'Geometric factors in illusions of direction', *Amer. J. Psychol.*, 1960, **73**, 535–43.

MALHOTRA, M. K. 'Figural after-effects: an examination of Köhler's theory', *Acta Psychologica*, 1968, **14**, 161–99.

MARSHALL, W. M., and TALBOT, S. A. 'Recent evidence for neural mechanisms in vision leading to a general theory of sensory acuity' in Kluver, H. (Ed.). *Visual Mechanisms*, Biol. Symp., 1942, **7**, 117–64.

MATHEWS, M. L. 'Some temporal aspects of visual spatial interactions associated with illumination gradients', *Nature*, 1968, **218**, 1061–3.

MATIN, L., and MACKINNON, G. E. 'Autokinetic movement: Selective manipulation of directional components by image stabilization', *Science*, 1964, **143**, 147–8.

MEFFERD, R. B., Jr. 'Perception of depth on rotating objects: 4. Fluctuating stereokinetic perceptual variants', *Percept. Mot. Skills*, 1968a, **27**, 255–76.

MEFFERD, R. B., Jr. 'Fluctuations in perceptual organisation and orientation and perception of apparent movement', *Percept. Mot. Skills*, 1968b, **27**, 368–70.

MEFFERD, R. B., Jr. 'Perceptual fluctuations involving orientation and organisation', *Percept. Mot. Skills*, 1968c, **27**, 827–34.

MEFFERD, R. B., Jr. 'Perception of depth in rotating objects: 5. Phenomenal motion in stereokinesis', *Percept. Mot. Skills*, 1968d, **27**, 903–26.

MEFFERD, R. B., Jr. 'Perception of depth in rotating objects: 6. Effects of fixation and pursuit of the phenomenal motion of stereokinesis', *Percept. Mot. Skills*, 1968e, **27**, 1135–9.

MEFFERD, R. B., Jr. 'Perception of depth in rotating objects: 7. Influence of attributes of depth on stereokinetic percepts', *Percept. Mot. Skills*, 1968f, **27**, 1179–93.

MEFFERD, R. B., and WIELAND, B. A. 'Perception of depth in rotating objects: I. Stereokinesis and the vertical–horizontal illusion', *Percept. Mot. Skills*, 1967a, **25**, 93–100.

Mefferd, R. B., and Wieland, B. A. 'Perception of depth in rotating objects: II. Perspective as a determinant of stereokinesis', *Percept. Mot. Skills*, 1967b, **25**, 621–8.

Metzger, W. *Gesetze der Sehens*, Frankfurt, Waldemar Kramer, 1953.

Michaels, R. M. 'Anisotropy and interaction of fields of spatial induction', *J. exp. Psychol.*, 1960, **60**, 235–41.

Miles, W. R. 'Movement interpretations of the silhouette of a revolving fan', *Amer. J. Psychol.*, 1931, **43**, 392–405.

Millodot, M. 'Influence of accommodation on the viewing of an illusion', *Quart. J. exp. Psychol.*, 1968, **20**, 329–35.

Moed, G. 'Satiation-theory and the Müller-Lyer illusion', *Amer. J. Psychol.*, 1959, **72**, 609–11.

Morant, R. B., and Mikaelin, H. M. 'Interfield tilt after-effects', *Percept. Mot. Skills*, 1960, **10**, 95–8.

Morant, R. B., and Harris, J. R. 'Two different after-effects of exposure to visual tilts', *Amer. J. Psychol.*, 1965, **78**, 218–26.

Morgan, M. J. 'Estimates of length in a modified Müller-Lyer figure', *Amer. J. Psychol.*, 1969, **82**, 380–4.

Morinaga, S. 'Experimental study in Ebbinghaus illusion: II', *Jap. J. Psychol.*, 1932, **7**, 253–66.

Morinaga, S. 'Untersuchungen über die Zöllnersche Täuschung', *Jap. J. Psychol.*, 1933, **8**, 195–242, German summary 23–5.

Morinaga, S., and Ikeda, H. 'Paradox in displacement in geometrical illusion and the problem of dimensions: A contribution to the study of space perception', *Jap. J. Psychol.*, 1965, **36**, 231–8.

Motokawa, K. 'Field of retinal induction and optical illusion', *J. Neurophysiol.*, 1950, **13**, 413–26.

Motokawa, K., and Akita, M. 'Electrophysiological studies of the field of retinal induction', *Psychologia*, 1957, **1**, 10–16.

Motokawa, K., Nakagawa, D., and Kohata, T. 'Figural after-effect and retinal induction', *J. gen. Psychol.*, 1957, **57**, 121–35.

Mountjoy, P. T. 'Effects of self-instruction, information, and misinformation upon decrement to the Müller-Lyer figure', *Psychol. Record*, 1965, **15**, 7–14.

Mountjoy, P. T. 'New illusory effect of the Müller-Lyer figure', *J. exp. Psychol.*, 1966, **71**, 119–23.

Mulholland, T. 'The swinging disk illusion', *Amer. J. Psychol.*, 1958, **71**, 375–82.

Müller, G. E. 'Über das Aubertsche Phänomen', *Z. Sinnesphysiol.*, 1916, **49** 109–244.

Müller-Lyer, F. C. 'Optische Urteilstäuschungen', *Arch. Physiol.*, 1889, suppl. band, 263–70.

Müller-Lyer, F. C. 'Zur Lehre von den optischen Täuschungen. Über Kontrast und Konfluxion', *Z. Psychol.*, 1896, **9**, 1–16.

Münsterberg, H. 'Die verschobene Schachbrettfigur', *Z. Psychol.*, 1897, **15**, 184–8.

Musatti, C. L. 'Sui fenomeni stereocinetici', *Arch. Ital. Psicol.*, 1929, **3**, 105–20.

Myers, R. D. 'A new autokinetic illusion', *Amer. J. Psychol.*, 1959, **72**, 140–1.

Nakagawa, D. 'Müller-Lyer illusion and retinal induction', *Psychologia*, 1958, **1**, 167–74.

Neisser, U. *Cognitive Psychology*, New York, Appleton-Century-Crofts, 1967.

Novak, S., and Sperling, G. 'Visual thresholds near a continuously visible or a briefly presented light-dark boundary', *Optica Acta*, 1963, **10**, 187–91.

OBONAI, T. 'Contributions to the study of psychophysical induction: III. Experiments on the illusions of filled space', *Jap. J. Psychol.*, 1933, **8**, 699–720.

OBONAI, T. 'Induction effects in estimates of extent', *J. exp. Psychol.*, 1954, **47**, 57–60.

O'BRIEN, V. 'Contour perception, illusion and reality', *J. Opt. Soc. Amer.*, 1958, **48**, 112–19.

OGASAWARA, J. 'Motokawa's induction-field theory and form perception', *Psychologia*, 1958, **1**, 182–3.

OHWAKI, S. 'On the destruction of geometrical illusions in stereoscopic observation', *Tohoku Psychol. Folia*, 1960, **19**, 29–36.

OLSON, R., and ORBACH, J. 'Reversibility of the Necker Cube: VIII. Parts of the figure contributing to the perception of reversals', *Percept. Mot. Skills*, 1966, **22**, 623–9.

OPPEL, J. J. 'Über geometrisch-optische Täuschungen', *Jahresber. phys. ver. Frankfurt*, 1855, 37–47.

ORBACH, J., and SOLHKHAN, N. 'Size Judgments of disks presented against the zenith sky', *Percept. Mot. Skills*, 1968, **26**, 371–4.

ORBISON, W. D. 'Shape as a function of the vector field', *Amer. J. Psychol.*, 1939, **52**, 31–45.

OSGOOD, C. E. *Method and Theory in Experimental Psychology*, New York, Oxford University Press, 1953.

OSGOOD, C. E., and HEYER, A. W. 'A new interpretation of figural aftereffects', *Psychol. Rev.*, 1952, **59**, 98–118.

OSTER, G., and NISHIJIMA, Y. 'Moiré Patterns', *Sci. Amer.*, 1963, **208**, May, 50–63.

OVER, R. 'Explanations of geometric illusions', *Psychol. Bull.*, 1968, **70**, 545–62.

OVER, R. 'Comparison of normalization theory and neural enhancement explanation of negative aftereffects', *Psychol. Bull.*, 1971, **75**, 225–43.

OYAMA, T. 'Experimental studies of the figural after-effect: I. Temporal factors', *Jap. J. Psychol.*, 1953, **23**, 239–45.

OYAMA, T. 'Japanese studies on the so-called geometrical-optical illusions', *Psychologia*, 1960, **3**, 7–20.

OYAMA, T. 'The effect of hue and brightness on the size-illusion of concentric circles', *Amer. J. Psychol.*, 1962, **75**, 45–55.

PANTLE, A., and SEKULER, R. 'Size-detecting mechanisms in human vision', *Science*, 1968, **162**, 1145–8.

PAPERT, S. 'Centrally produced geometrical illusions', *Nature*, 1961, **191**, 733 only.

PAPERT, S. 'Regularities in the time courses of some visual processes', *Quart. Prog. Rep.*, no. 73, Res. Lab. in Electronics, M.I.T., April 1964, 244–7.

PARKER, N. I., and NEWBIGGING, P. L. 'Magnitude and decrement of the Müller-Lyer illusion as a function of pre-training', *Canad. J. Psychol.*, 1963, **17**, 134–40.

PARRISH, M., LUNDY, R. M., and LEIBOWITZ, H. W. 'Hypnotic age-regression and magnitudes of the Ponzo and Poggendorff illusions', *Science*, 1968, **159**, 1375–6.

PASTORE, N. 'Some remarks on the Ames oscillatory effect', *Psychol. Rev.*, 1952, **59**, 319–23.

PENROSE, L. S., and PENROSE, R. 'Impossible objects: A special type of illusion', *Brit. J. Psychol.*, 1958, **49**, 31–3.

PIAGET, J. 'Essai d'interpretation probabiliste de la loi de Weber et de celle des centrations relatives', *Arch. de Psychol.*, 1944, **30**, 95–138.

PIAGET, J. *Les Mechanismes Perceptifs*, Presses Universitaires de Gravee, 1961. (Translated by Seagrim, G. N., as *The Mechanisms of Perception*, London, Routledge & Kegan Paul, 1969.)

PIAGET, J., LAMBERCIER, M., BOESCH, E., and VON ALBERTINI, B. 'Recherches sur le développement des perceptions: I. Introduction à l'étude des perceptions chez l'enfant et analyse d'une illusion relative à la perception visuelle de cercles concentriques (Delbœuf)', *Arch. de Psychol.*, 1942, **29**, 1–107.

PIAGET, J. and VON ALBERTINI, B. 'Recherches sur le développement des perceptions: XI. L'illusion de Müller-Lyer', *Arch. de Psychol.*, 1950, **33**, 1–48.

PIAGET, J., and DENIS-PRINZHORN, M. 'Recherches sur le développement des perceptions: XVI. L'estimation perceptive des cotés du rectangle', *Arch. de Psychol.*, 1953, **34**, 109–32.

PIAGET, J., and LAMBERCIER, M. 'La perception d'un carré animé d'un mouvement de circumduction (effet Auersberg et Burmester)', *Arch. de Psychol.*, 1951, **33**, 131–95.

PIAGET, J., and OSTERRIETH, P. A. 'Recherches sur le développement des perceptions: XVII. L'evolution de l'illusion d'Oppel–Kundt en fonction de l'âge', *Arch. de Psychol.*, 1953, **34**, 1–38.

PIAGET, J., and PÉNE, F. 'Essai sur l'illusion de la médiane des angles en tant que mesure de l'illusion des angles', *Arch. de Psychol.*, 1955, **35**, 77–92.

PIAGET, J., and VURPILLOT, E. 'La surestimation de la courbure des arcs de cercle', *Arch. de Psychol.*, 1956, **35**, 215–32.

PIAGET, J., BANG, V., and MATALON, B. 'Note on the law of the temporal maximum of some optico-geometric illusions', *Amer. J. Psychol.*, 1958, **71**, 277–82.

PIAGET, J., FELLER, Y., and MCNEAR, E. 'Essai sur la perception des vitesses chez l'enfant et chez l'adulte', *Arch. de Psychol.*, 1958, **36**, 253–327.

PIAGET, J., and BANG, V. 'L'évolution de l'illusion des espaces divisés (Oppel–Kundt) en présentation tachistoscopique', *Arch. de Psychol.*, 1961a, **38**, 1–21.

PIAGET, J., and BANG, V. 'Comparaison des mouvements oculaires et des centrations du regard chez l'enfant et chez l'adulte', *Arch. de Psychol.*, 1961b, **38**, 167–200.

PIAGET, J., MATALON, B., and BANG, V. 'L'evolution de l'illusion dite "verticale–horizontale" de ses composantes (rectangle et équerre) et de l'illusion de Delbœuf en présentation tachistoscopique', *Arch. de Psychol.*, 1961, **38**, 23–68.

PIERCE, H. 'The illusion of the kindergarten patterns', *Psychol. Rev.*, 1898, **5**, 233–53.

PIKE, A. R., and STACEY, B. G. 'The perception of luminous Müller-Lyer figures and its implications for the misapplied constancy theory', *Life Sciences*, 1968, **7**, 355–62.

PLATEAU, J. 'Quatrimenote sur des nouvelles applications curieuses de la persistance des impressions de la retine', *Bull. Acad. Roy. Sci. B.A. Belg.*, 1849, **16**, 254–60.

PLATEAU, J. 'Vierte Notiz über eine sonderbare Anwendung des Verweilens der Eindrucke auf der Netzhaut', *Pogg. Ann.*, 1850, **80**, 287–92.

POLLACK, R. H. 'Figural after-effects: quantitative studies of displacement', *Aust. J. Psychol.*, 1958, **10**, 269–77.

POLLACK, R. H. 'Application of the sensory-tonic theory of perception to figural after-effect', *Acta Psychol.*, 1963, **21**, 1–16.

POLLACK, R. H. 'Some implications of ontogenetic changes in perception' in *Studies in Cognitive Development*, Elkind, D., and Flavell, S. H. (Eds.). New York, Oxford University Press, 1969.

POLLACK, R. H. 'Müller-Lyer illusion: effect of age, lightness, contrast and hue', *Science*, 1970, **170**, 93–5.

POLLACK, R. H., and CHAPLIN, M. R. 'Effects of prolonged stimulation by components of the Müller-Lyer figure upon the magnitude of the illusion', *Percept. Mot. Skills*, 1964, **18**, 377–82.

POLLACK, R. H., and SILVAR, S. D. 'Magnitude of the Müller-Lyer illusion in children as a function of pigmentation of the fundus oculi', *Psychonom. Sci.*, 1967, **8**, 83–4.

PONZO, M. 'Rapports de contraste angulaire et l'appréciation de grandeur des astres à l'horizon', *Arch. Ital. de Biol.*, 1912, **58**, 327–9.

PONZO, M. 'Urteilstäuschungen über Mengen', *Arch. ges. Psychol.*, 1928, **65**, 129–62.

POWER, R. P. 'Stimulus properties which reduce apparent reversal of rotating rectangular shapes', *J. exp. Psychol.*, 1967, **73**, 595–9.

PRENTICE, W. C. H., and BEARDSLEE, D. C. 'Visual "normalisation" near the vertical and horizontal', *J. exp. Psychol.*, 1950, **40**, 355–64.

PRESSEY, A. W. 'A theory of the Müller-Lyer illusion', *Percept. Mot. Skills*, 1967, **25**, 569–72.

PRESSEY, A. W. 'The assimilation theory applied to a modification of the Müller-Lyer illusion', *Percept. Psychophys.*, 1970, **8**, 411–12.

PRESSEY, A. W. 'An extension of assimilation theory to illusions of size, area and direction', *Percept. Psychophys.*, 1971, **9**, 172–6.

PRESSEY, A. W., and DEN HEYER, K. 'Observations on Chiang's "new" theory of geometrical illusions', *Percept. Psychophys.*, 1968, **4**, 313–14.

PRESSEY, A. W., and KOFFMAN, G. 'Figural after-effects, illusions and the dimensions of field dependence', *Psychonom. Sci.*, 1968, **10**, 279–80.

PRITCHARD, R. M. 'Visual illusions viewed as stabilised retinal images', *Quart. J. exp. Psychol.*, 1958, **10**, 77–82.

PULFRICH, C. 'Die Stereoskopie im Dienste der isochromen und heterochromen Photometrie', *Naturwissenschaften*, 1922, **10**, 553–64.

PURKINJE, J. E. *Beobachten und Versuche für Physiologie der Sinne. Beitrage zur Kenntnis des Sehens in subjektiver Hinsicht*, vol. I, Prague, 1823.

RAAB, D. H. 'Backward masking', *Psychol. Bull.*, 1963, **60**, 118–29.

RATLIFF, F. 'The role of physiological nystagmus in monocular acuity', *J. exp. Psych.*, 1952, **43**, 163–72.

RATLIFF, F. *Mach bands. Quantitative studies on neural networks in the retina*, San Francisco, Holden-Day, 1965.

RATLIFF, F., HARTLINE, H. K., and MILLER, W. H. 'Spatial and temporal aspects of retinal inhibitory interaction', *J. Opt. Soc. Amer.*, 1963, **53**, 110–20.

RECHTSCHAFFEN, A., and MEDNICK, S. 'The autokinetic word technique', *J. abnorm. soc. Psychol.*, 1955, **51**, 346.

RESTLE, F. 'Illusions of bent line', *Percept. Psychophys.*, 1969, **5**, 273–4.

RESTLE, F. 'Moon illusion explained on the basis of relative size', *Science*, 1970, **167**, 1092–6.

RESTLE, F., and MERRYMAN, C. 'Distance and an illusion of length of line', *J. exp. Psychol.*, 1969, **81**, 297–302.

RÉVÉSZ, G. 'Experiments on animal space perception', *Brit. J. Psychol.*, 1924, **14**, 386–414.

RÉVÉSZ, G. 'System der optischen und haptischen Raumtäuschungen', *Z. Psychol.*, 1934, **131**, 296–375.

RICHARDS, W. 'Apparent modifiability of receptive fields during accommodation and convergence and a model for size constancy', *Neuropsychologia*, 1967, **5**, 63–72.

RICHARDS, W. 'Illusory reversal of brightness contrast', *Percept. Mot. Skills*, 1968, **27**, 1169–70.

RICHARDS, W., and KAUFMAN, L. '"Centre-of-gravity" tendencies for fixations and flow patterns', *Percept. Psychophys.*, 1969, **5**, 81–4.

RICHARDS, W., and SMITH, R. A. 'Midbrain as a site for motion after-effect', *Nature*, 1969, **223**, 533–4.

RITTENHOUSE, D. 'Explanation of an optical deception', *Trans. Amer. phil. Soc.*, 1786, **2**, 37–42.

RIVERS, W. H. R. 'Observations on the senses of the Todas', *Brit. J. Psychol.*, 1905, **1**, 321–96.

ROBINSON, J. O. 'Retinal inhibition in visual distortion', *Brit. J. Psychol.*, 1968, **59**, 29–36.

ROCK, M. L., and FOX, B. H. 'Two aspects of the Pulfrich Phenomenon', *Amer. J. Psychol.*, 1949, **62**, 279–84.

ROCK, I., and EBENHOLTZ, S. 'The relational determination of perceived size', *Psychol. Rev.*, 1959, **66**, 387–401.

ROCK, I., and EBENHOLTZ, S. 'Stroboscopic movement based on change of phenomenal rather than retinal location', *Amer. J. Psychol.*, 1962, **75**, 193–207.

ROCK, I., and KAUFMAN, L. 'The moon illusion', Pt. II, *Science*, 1962, **136**, 1023–31.

ROGERS, B. J., and ANSTIS, S. M. 'Intensity versus adaptation and the Pulfrich stereophenomenon', *Vision Res.*, 1972, **12**, 909–28.

ROYCE, J. R., CARRAN, A. B., AFTANAS, M., LEHMAN, R. S., and BLUMENTHAL, A. 'Autokinetic phenomenon: A critical review', *Psychol. Bull.*, 1966, **65**, 243–60.

SANDER, F. 'Optische Taüschungen und Psychologie', *Neue Psych. Stud.*, 1926, **1**, 159–66.

SANFORD, E. C. *A course in experimental psychology. Part I: Sensation and perception*, Boston, Heath, 1903.

SAUCER, R. T. 'A further study of the perception of apparent motion by schizophrenics', *J. consult. Psychol.*, 1958, **22**, 256–8.

SAUCER, R., and COPPINGER, N. W. 'Standard stimulus conditions for thresholds of apparent movement', *Amer. J. Psychol.*, 1960, **73**, 435–9.

SCHILDER, P., and WECHSLER, D. 'The illusion of the oblique intercept', *J. exp. Psychol.*, 1936, **19**, 747–57.

SCHILLER, P., and WIENER, M. 'Binocular and stereoscopic viewing of geometric illusions', *Percept. Mot. Skills*, 1962, **15**, 739–47.

SCHNEIDER, C. W., and BARTLEY, S. H. 'A study of the effects of mechanically induced tension of the neck muscles on the perception of verticality', *J. Psychol.*, 1962, **54**, 245–8.

SCHRÖDER, H. 'Über eine optische Inversion bei Betrachtung verkehrter, durch optische Vorrichtung entworfener physischer Bilder', *Pogg. Ann.*, 1858, **105**, 298–311.

SCHUMANN, F. 'Beiträge zur Analyse der Gesichtswahrnehmungen', *Z. Psychol.*, 1900, **23**, 1–32; **24**, 1–33.

SCHUSTER, D. H. 'A new ambiguous figure: A three-stick clevis', *Amer. J. Psychol.*, 1964, **77**, 673 only.

SCHWEIZER, G. 'Über das Sternschwanken: I.', *Bull. de la société imperiale des naturalistes*, 1857, tome 30, no. IV, 440–57, Moscow.

SCOTT, T. R., JORDAN, A. E., and POWELL, D. A. 'Does the aftereffect of motion add algebraically to objective motion of the test stimulus?', *J. exp. Psychol.*, 1963, **66**, 500–5.

SEGALL, M. H., CAMPBELL, D. T., and HERSKOVITS, M. J. 'Cultural differences in the perception of geometrical illusions', *Science*, 1963, **139**, 769–71.

SEKULER, R. W., and PANTLE, A. 'A model for after-effects of seen movement', *Vision Res.*, 1967, **7**, 427–39.

SELTZER, W. J., and SHERIDAN, C. L. 'Effects of inspection figure persistence on a figural aftereffect', *Psychonom. Sci.*, 1965, **2**, 279–80.

SGRO, F. J. 'Beta motion thresholds', *J. exp. Psychol.*, 1963, **66**, 281–5.

SHERIF, M. 'A study of some social factors in perception', *Arch. of Psychol.*, 1935, no. 187, 60 pp.

SIMON, H. A. 'An information-processing explanation of some perceptual phenomena', *Brit. J. Psychol.*, 1967, **58**, 1–12.

SKINNER, B. F. 'A paradoxical color effect', *J. gen. Psychol.*, 1932, **7**, 481–2.

SKOLNICK, A. 'The role of eye movements in the autokinetic phenomenon', *J. exp. Psychol.*, 1940, **26**, 373–93.

SMITH, J. 'On the cause of color and the theory of light', *Amer. J. Sci. and Arts*, 1860, **29** (2nd ser.), 276–8.

SMITH, K. R. 'The satiational theory of figural after-effects', *Amer. J. Psychol.*, 1948, **61**, 282–5.

SMITH, K. R. 'The statistical theory of figural after-effects', *Psychol. Rev.*, 1952, **59**, 401–2.

SMITH, K. 'Attraction in figural after-effects', *Amer. J. Psychol.*, 1954, **67**, 174–6.

SMYTHIES, J. R. 'The stroboscopic patterns: I. The dark phase', *Brit. J. Psychol.*, 1959a, **50**, 106–16.

SMYTHIES, J. R. 'The stroboscopic patterns: II. The phenomenology of the bright phase and after-images', *Brit. J. Psychol.*, 1959b, **50**, 305–24.

SMYTHIES, J. R. 'The stroboscopic patterns: III. Further experiments and discussion', *Brit. J. Psychol.*, 1960, **51**, 247–55.

SPERLING, G. 'The information available in brief visual presentations', *Psychol. Monogr.*, 1960, **74** (whole no. 498), no. 11.

SPERLING, G. 'Negative afterimage without prior positive image', *Science*, 1960, **131**, 1613–14.

SPIGEL, I. M. 'Autokinetic movement of an intermittent luminance', *Psychol. Rec.*, 1963, **13**, 149–53.

SPITZ, H. H. 'Ganz's hypothesis on figural aftereffects', *Amer. J. Psychol.*, 1967, **80**, 462–464.

SPRINGBETT, B. M. 'Some stereoscopic phenomena and their implications', *Brit. J. Psychol.*, 1961, **52**, 105–9.

STACEY, B., and PIKE, R. 'Apparent size, apparent depth and the Müller-Lyer illusion', *Percept. Psychophys.*, 1970, **7**, 125–8.

STANDING, L. G., DODWELL, P. C., and LANG, D. 'Dark adaptation and the Pulfrich effect', *Percept. Psychophys.*, 1968, **4**, 118–20.

STEVENS, S. S. (Ed.). *Handbook of Experimental Psychology, New York, Wiley*, 1951.

STRATTON, G. M. 'Vision without inversion of the retinal image', *Psychol. Rev.*, 1897, **4**, 341–60 & 463–81.

SUMI, S. 'Paths of seen motion and motion aftereffect', *Percept. Mot. Skills*, 1966, **23**, 1003–8.

SUTHERLAND, N. S. 'Figural after-effects and apparent size', *Quart. J. exp. Psychol.*, 1961, **13**, 222–8.

SYLVESTER, J. 'Apparent movement and the Brown–Voth experiment', *Quart. J. exp. Psychol.*, 1960, **12**, 231–6.

TAUSCH, R. 'Optische Täuschungen als artifizielle Effekte der Gestaltungsprozesse von Grössen und Formenkonstanz in der natürlichen Raumwahrnehmung', *Psychol. Forsch.*, 1954, **24**, 299–348.

TAYLOR, M. M. 'Geometry of a visual illusion', *J. Opt. Soc. Amer.*, 1962a, **52**, 565–9.

TAYLOR, M. M. 'Figural after-effects: a psychophysical theory of the displacement effect', *Canad. J. Psychol.*, 1962b, **16**, 247–77.

THIÉRY, A. 'Über geometrisch-optische Taüschungen', *Phil. Stud.*, 1896, **12**, 67–126.

THOMPSON, S. P. 'Optical illusions of motion', *Brain*, 1882, **3**, 292.

TITCHENER, E. B. *Experimental Psychology: A Manual of Laboratory Practice*, New York, Macmillan, 1901.

TOCH, H. H. 'The effect of "meaning" on the autokinetic illusion', *Amer. J. Psychol.*, 1962, **75**, 605–11.

TOCH, H. H., and ITTELSON, W. H. 'The role of past experience in apparent movement: a revaluation', *Brit. J. Psychol.*, 1956, **47**, 195–207.

TOLANSKI, S. *Optical illusions*, London, Pergamon, 1964.

TRIMBLE, R., and ERIKSEN, C. W. ' "Subliminal cues" and the Müller-type illusion', *Percept. Psychophys.*, 1966, **1**, 401–4.

VIRSU, V. 'Tendencies to eye movement, and misperception of curvature, direction and length', *Percept. Psychophys.*, 1971a, **9**, 65–72.

VIRSU, V. 'Underestimation of curvature and task dependence in visual perception', *Percept. Psychophys.*, 1971b, **9**, 339–42.

VOGELSANG, C. J. 'The perception of a visual object during stimulation of the vestibular system', *Acta oto-laryngol.*, 1961, **53**, 461–9.

VOLKMAN, F. C. 'Vision during voluntary saccadic eye movements', *J. Opt. Soc. Amer.*, 1962, **52**, 571–8.

VURPILLOT, E. 'Piaget's law of relative centrations', *Acta psychol.*, 1959, **16**, 403–30.

WADE, N. J. 'Visual orientation during and after lateral head, body, and trunk tilt', *Percept. Psychophys.*, 1968, **3**, 215–19.

WADE, N. J. 'The interaction of postural systems in visual orientation', *Percept. Psychophys.*, 1969, **6**, 309–10.

WADE, N. J. 'Visual orientation during lateral head tilt when upright and supine', *Quart. J. exp. Psychol.*, 1970, **22**, 420–2.

WADE, N. J., and DAY, R. H. 'Development and dissipation of a visual spatial aftereffect from prolonged head tilt', *J. exp. Psychol.*, 1968a, **76**, 439–43.

WADE, N. J., and DAY, R. H. 'Apparent head position as a basis for a visual aftereffect of prolonged head tilt', *Percept. Psychophys.*, 1968b, **3**, 324–6.

WAGNER, H. L. 'The illusions and Ganz's theory of contour displacements', *Brit. J. Psychol.*, 1968, **58**, 361–8.

WAGNER, H. L. *Simultaneous and successive contour displacements*, Ph.D. Thesis, University of Wales, 1969.

WALLACE, G. K. 'Optical illusions', *Nature*, 1966, **209**, 327–8.

WALLACE, G. K. 'The critical distance of interaction in the Zöllner illusion', *Percept. Psychophys.*, 1969, **5**, 261–4.

WALLACE, G. K., and CRAMPIN, D. J. 'The effects of background density on the Zöllner illusion', *Vision Research*, 1969, **9**, 167–77.

WALLACH, H. 'The perception of motion', *Sci. Amer.*, 1959, **201**, no. 1, 56–60.

WALLACH, H., and O'Connell, D. N. 'The kinetic depth effect', *J. exp. Psychol.*, 1953, **45**, 205–17.

WALLACH, H., WEISZ, A., and ADAMS, P. A. 'Circles and derived figures in rotation', *Amer. J. Psychol.*, 1956, **69**, 48–59.

WALTERS, A. 'A genetic study of geometrical-optical illusions', *Genet. psychol. Monogr.*, 1942, **25**, 101–55.

WAPNER, S., and WERNER, H. *Perceptual development: An investigation within the framework of sensory-tonic field theory*', Worcester, Clark University Press, 1957.

WEBSTER, H. 'The distortion of straight and curved lines in geometrical fields', *Amer. J. Psychol.*, 1948, **61**, 573–5.

WEENE, P., and HELD, R. 'Changes in perceived size of angle as a function of orientation in the frontal plane', *J. exp. Psychol.*, 1966, **71**, 55–9.

WEINTRAUB, D. J., and VIRSU, V. 'The misperception of angles: estimating the vertex of converging line segments', *Percept. Psychophys.*, 1971, **9**, 5–8.

WEITZMAN, B. 'A figural aftereffect produced by a phenomenal dichotomy in a uniform contour', *J. exp. Psychol.*, 1963, **66**, 195–200.

WELFORD, A. T. (Ed.). *Ageing and human skill*, Oxford University Press, 1958.

WERTHEIMER, M. 'Experimentelle Studien über das Sehen von Bewegung', *Z. Psychol.*, 1912, **61**, 161–265. (Translation in Shipley, T. (Ed.). *Classics in Psychology*, Philosophical Library, New York, 1961.)

WESTHEIMER, G. 'Spatial interaction in human cone vision', *J. Physiol.*, 1967, **190**, 139–54.

WHEATSTONE, C. 'On a singular effect of the juxtaposition of certain colours under particular circumstances, with remarks by Sir D. Brewster', *Brit. Assoc. Rep.*, 1844 (Pt. 2), 10.

WHEELER, L., and LAFORCE, R. C. 'Sustained Bidwell afterimages: Effects of disc rotation speed, color-pulse chromaticity, and color-pulse luminance', *J. Opt. Soc. Amer.*, 1967, **57**, 386–93.

WHITE, J. F. 'A report on Myers' new autokinetic phenomenon', *Amer. J. Psychol.*, 1969, **82**, 124–6.

WHITESIDE, T. C. D., GRAYBIEL, A. and NIVEN, J. I. 'Visual illusions of movement', *Brain*, 1965, **88**, 193–210.

WICKELGREN, B. G. 'Brightness contrast and length perception in the Müller-Lyer illusion', *Vision Res.*, 1965, **5**, 141–50.

WILLEMS, E. P. 'Nonstimulus and nonretinal mechanisms in figural after-effects', *J. exp. Psychol.*, 1967, **74**, 452–4.

WILSON, J. 'Adaptation and repulsion in the figural after-effect', *Quart. J. exp. Psychol.*, 1965, **17**, 1–13.

WILSON, J. A. Personal communication, 1969.

WILSON, J. A. 'The computer and the psychology of perception' in Westby, G., and Apter, M. (Eds.). *The Computer in Psychology*, London, Wiley, 1972.

WILSON, J. A., and ANSTIS, S. M. 'Visual delay as a function of luminance', *Amer. J. Psychol.*, 1969, **82**, 350–8.

WINSLOW, C. N. 'Visual illusions in the dark', *Arch. of Psychol.*, 1933, no. 153, 83 pp.

WITKIN, H. A., DYK, R. B., FATERSON, H. F., GOODENOUGH, D. R., and KARP, S. A. *Psychological Differentiation*, London, Wiley, 1962.

WOBER, M. 'Confrontation of the H–V. illusion and a test of pictorial perception in Nigeria', *Percept. Mot. Skills*, 1970, **31**, 105–6.

WOHLGEMUTH, A. 'On the aftereffect of seen movement', *Brit. J. Psychol. Monogr.*, 1911, **1**, 1–117.

WOHLWILL, J. F. 'Developmental studies of perception', *Psychol. Bull.*, 1960, **57**, 249–88.

WOOD, R. J., ZINKUS, P. W., and MOUNTJOY, P. T. 'The vestibular hypothesis of the moon illusion', *Psychonom. Sci.*, 1968, **11**, 356 only.

WUNDT, W. *Grundzüge der physiologischen Psychologie*, Leipzig, Engelmann, 1893.

WUNDT, W. 'Die geometrisch-optischen Täuschungen', *Abhandl. mathphys. der sachs. Ges. Wiss.*, 1898, **24**, 53–178.

WÜRSTEN, H. 'Recherches sur le développement des perceptions: IX. L'évolution des comparaisons de longeurs de l'enfant à l'adulte avec variation d'angle entre la verticale et l'horizontale', *Arch. de Psychol.*, 1947, **32**, 1–144.

WURTZ, R. H. 'Response of striate cortex neurons to stimuli during rapid eye movements in the monkey', *J. Neurophysiol.*, 1969, **32**, 975–86.

YANAGISAWA, N. 'Reversed illusion in the Müller-Lyer illusion.', *Jap. J. Psychol.*, 1939, **14**, 321–6.

YARBUS, A. L. *Eye movements and vision*, New York, Plenum Press, 1967.

YOKOSE, Z., and KAWAMURA, H. 'A study of the direction of the field force in shape perception', *Jap. J. Psychol.*, 1952, **23**, 133–43.

ZANFORLIN, M. 'Some observations on Gregory's theory of perceptual illusions', *Quart. J. exp. Psychol.*, 1967, **19**, 193–7.

ZEGERS, R. T. 'The reversal illusion of the Ames trapezoid', *Trans. N.Y. Acad. Sci.*, 1965, **26**, 377–400.

ZENHAUSEN, R. 'The perception of rotation with an oscillating trapezoid', *Psychonom. Sci.*, 1968, **13**, 79–80.

ZIGLER, E. 'Size estimates of circles as a function of size of adjacent circles', *Percept. Mot. Skills*, 1960, **11**, 47–53.

ZÖLLNER, F. 'Über eine neue Art von Pseudoskopie und ihre Beziehungen zu den von Plateau und Oppel beschriebenen Bewegungsphänomenen', *Ann. Phys. Chem.*, 1860, **186**, 500–23.

ZÖLLNER, F. 'Über eine neue Art anorthoskopischer Zerrbilder', *Ann. Phys.*, 1862, **117**, 477–84.

ZUBER, B. L., and STARK, L. 'Saccadic suppression: Elevation of visual threshold associated with saccadic eye movements', *Experimental Neurology*, 1966, **16**, 65–79.

ZUSNE, L. 'Optical illusions: Output of publications', *Percept. Mot. Skills*, 1968, **27**, 175–7.

ANON. 'The artificial spectrum top', *Nature*, 1894, **51**, 113 only.

INDEX OF AUTHORS

(Page numbers in italics refer to illustrations)

INDEX OF SUBJECTS

(Page numbers in italics refer to illustrations)